HUMAN
DISEASES AND
CONDITIONS

HUMAN DISEASES AND CONDITIONS

Neil Izenberg, M.D.

Editor in Chief

Published in Association with the
Center for Children's Health Media,
The Nemours Foundation

Volume 1

Abscess–Dysrhythmia

Charles Scribner's Sons
An Imprint of The Gale Group
New York

The information in *Human Diseases and Conditions* is not intended to take the place of medical care by physicians and other health care professionals. This book does not contain diagnostic, treatment, or first aid recommendations. Readers should obtain professional advice in making all health care decisions.

Library of Congress Cataloging-in-Publication Data

Human diseases and conditions / Neil Izenberg, editor in chief.
    p. cm.
   "Published in association with the Center for Children's Health Media, the Nemours Foundation."
   Contents: V. 1. Abscess-Dysrhythmia.
   Includes bibliographical references and index.
   Summary: Present articles dealing with all kinds of diseases and disorders, from acne and brain tumor to tobacco-related diseases and yellow fever.
   ISBN 0-684-80543-X (set: alk. paper) —ISBN 0-684-80541-3 (v. 1 : alk. paper)
1. Medicine, Popular—Encyclopedias Juvenile. [1. Diseases—Encyclopedias. 2. Health—Encyclopedias.] I. Izenberg, Neil.

RC81.A2 H75 2000
616'.003 —dc21

                              99-051442

ISBN 0-684-80542-1 (vol. 2)
ISBN 0-684-80621-5 (vol. 3)

3 5 7 9 11 13 15 17 19 20 18 16 14 12 10 8 6 4 2

Printed in the United States of America

The paper used in this publication meets the minimum requirements of the American National Standard for Information Sciences—Permanence of Paper for Printed Library Materials, ANSI Z39.48-1992.

Editorial and Production Staff

Project Editor
Faye Zucker

Writers

Elizabeth Bass • Charles W. Carey, Jr. • Allan Cobb • Kristine Conner • John A. Cutter
Evelyn P. Kelly • Lynn M. L. Lauerman • Christopher Meehan • Sylvia K. Miller
Daphne Northrop • Ilene Raymond • Jordan P. Richman • Vita Richman • Eugenie Seifer
Linda Wasmer Smith • Giselle Weiss • Theodore Zinn • Faye Zucker

Editors, Researchers, Proofreaders

Tish Davidson • Lori De Milto • Alvin Fayman • Gretchen Gordon • Carol Holmes
Ronald Kaehler • Barry Katzen • Maxine Langweil • Lynn M. L. Lauerman • Linda J. Lotz
Brigitte Pelner • Judy Pokras • Samuel Schein • Andrew Schwartz • Sharon Sexton
Linda Wasmer Smith • Sherri Wynne Sussman

Editorial Assistants
Marshall H. Julie • Adrianne Wadewitz

Artist
Frank Forney

Photo Researcher
Martin Levick

Indexer
Julia Marshall, Marshall Indexing Services

Production Manager
Paul Wells

Compositor
V & M Graphics, Inc.

Designer
Lisa Chovnick

Senior Editor
Timothy J. DeWerff

Executive Editor
Sylvia K. Miller

Publisher
Karen Day

Contents

Contents

Preface

. . . .

Most of the time, for most people, the thousands of complex processes of the human body work just fine. But just about anything that can go wrong sometimes does go wrong, at least for some people. To know how to "fix" something that has gone wrong, one first has to know how it works. Because human beings do not come with a repair manual, the history of medicine is the history of doctors seeking to understand how to deal with injuries, illness, and disability—often by trial and error. When we seek to understand human diseases and conditions, we open the door to a better understanding of how our world works. We learn not just about others, but also about ourselves.

Today, the average life expectancy of the typical newborn in the United States is close to 80 years. One hundred years ago, a newborn baby could be expected, on average, to live about 47 years. Two thousand years ago, during the Roman Empire, the average life expectancy for a newborn Roman was only about 25 years. Why the vast improvement? Better genes? Not really.

The answer may be found in a combination of factors all working together. Perhaps most important is that many more babies now live beyond infancy. Until relatively recently, it was common—almost expected   for many newborns to die before their first birthday. Today, better nutrition, improved sanitation, safer water, the development of antibiotics, widespread immunization programs, and incredible improvements in surgical and medical treatments contribute to improved life spans. All these developments are direct results of better knowledge.

What will a typical American life span be like a hundred or a thousand years from now? Will new discoveries in medicine, gene therapy, or nutrition stretch average life spans beyond 100 years? Beyond 150 years or more? We cannot know for sure, but we can know that improved life spans will be the result of new knowledge and of new ways to apply what we learn.

That's where you, the readers of *Human Diseases and Conditions*, come in. Perhaps you will be the one responsible in the years to come for discovering an important new medical tool, helping to end cancer, discovering a cure for AIDS, expanding health care to those who do not have it in the United States and around the world. Perhaps your part will be more personal, as part of a health team caring for and comforting those who need you, or teaching and writing about health and science.

Should you use this book to diagnose or treat medical problems? No. This is a reference book. The human body is very complicated. Many medical problems have the same sorts of symptoms, and your doctor is trained to recognize the difference between those that seem alike but really are quite different. If you have medical concerns, do not try to diagnose and treat yourself (or your friends). Ask your doctor or a nurse.

Do doctors and scientists know everything there is to know about the human body, how it works, and its problems? Is this encyclopedia the "last word"? Not nearly. Every day, scientists and health care professionals all over the world improve their understanding of how the body works, and there is much more to say about health, disease, disabling conditions, and all that affects human functioning.

Preface

I hope *Human Diseases and Conditions* provides you with understandable, interesting reading. It has been an enjoyable experience for me.

Acknowledgments

Human Diseases and Conditions is remarkable for the quality and expertise of the editors who worked so hard to create it. Doctors Steven Dowshen, Harvey Cassidy, Howard Markel, and Joseph Masci are not only talented writers and editors but also exceptional physicians—experienced in the healing arts and highly regarded by the doctors who work with them. Their enthusiastic participation in the planning and in-depth review of this reference work resulted in content that is up-to-date and balanced. These good doctors have devoted hundreds and hundreds of hours to make *Human Diseases and Conditions* a very special book.

I feel particularly fortunate that Elizabeth Bass was a member of the core editorial team. As former science and health editor for the Long Island newspaper *Newsday*, Liz has an amazing breadth of knowledge and unparalleled talent for making difficult topics understandable. Contributing Editors Eugenie Seifer and Cathy Ginther also were deeply involved from the start in all editorial ways imaginable, including helping to shape the style and language. Given the complexity of the topics, that task was not an easy one.

The editors at Charles Scribner's Sons deserve thanks as well. Executive Editor Sylvia K. Miller conceived the project, found us, and guided us through much of its development. That task was completed by the able Timothy J. DeWerff, Senior Editor. Publisher Karen Day had the vision to imagine what the final result could be. Project Editor Faye Zucker deserves special words of praise for her devotion to this book. I appreciate her enthusiasm, patience, good judgment, and tireless efforts. The compositor, V&M Graphics, Inc., also merits a salute for completing the herculean task of typesetting the articles and creating the complex four-color page layouts.

My nieces Lia and Rebecca and my nephew Jake deserve thanks for reviewing several of the chapters prior to publication. They started reading them as an "assignment" from their uncle, but kept reading for the pleasure of learning. That was when I knew the editors were on the right path.

At The Nemours Foundation Center for Health Media, thanks go to Shirley Morrison, Jennifer Brooks, and Mara Gorman for their always dependable support, creativity, and guidance. The Nemours Foundation was the birthplace of *Human Diseases and Conditions*. Our effort to make the information in this encyclopedia accessible to students is in harmony with The Nemours Foundation's mission of improving the nation's health. We appreciate all the support The Nemours Foundation has provided to help create this reference work.

Neil Izenberg, M.D.
Editor in Chief

izenberg@KidsHealth.org

HUMAN DISEASES AND CONDITIONS

The Human Body: Systems Working Together

In recent years, stocks of high-fat fish have been declining in the waters off the west coast of the United States. This has caused the population of seals that eat the fish to decline as well. With fewer seals, the whales that normally feed on them have turned to eating sea otters. As the sea otters have diminished, the sea urchins they normally eat have shot up in numbers, and because sea urchins like kelp, the kelp beds are being decimated. There is more to this story. But the point is to illustrate what we call a system—in this case, an ecosystem.

What Is a System?

A system is a collection of parts that interact together for a common purpose. But a system is not just any old collection of parts. The parts are related in such a way that each depends on the others to do whatever job there is to be done. No single part can do the job alone, and any malfunction or delay is likely to affect the whole system.

A body system is a set of body parts that do a particular task. The human body itself is an example of a complex system—many sets of interacting parts that work to keep the human machine running. On any single day, we can estimate that your heart beats 103,689 times, your blood travels 168,000,000 miles, your digestive system processes 7.8 pounds of waste, and your lungs take in 438 cubic feet of air. These are only a few of the multitude of functions the human body performs. And while the least little mishap could cause a glitch in the system, amazingly, day in and day out over most of our lifetime, our bodies operate almost flawlessly.

Health and Wellness

The basic living unit of the body is the cell. There are about 200 different kinds of cells in our bodies, and about 5 trillion cells overall.

How One Cell Makes Five Trillion   Each human organism begins as a single cell—the fertilized egg, no bigger than the period at the end of this sentence. It becomes two cells, then four, then eight, and so on. As cells grow and multiply, they take on special roles that fit into four broad categories. For example, some cells develop force and movement. These are muscle cells, able to adapt flexibly to stress. Cells called neurons

Genes (DNA)

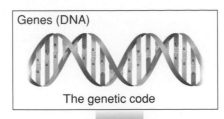

The genetic code

Proteins

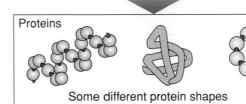

Some different protein shapes

Cells and tissues

  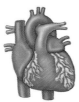

| Cells lining the stomach | Cardiac muscle cells of the heart | Neuron cell within the brain | Cells lining the lungs |

Organs

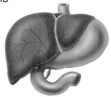  

| Liver and stomach | Heart | Brain | Lungs |

Systems

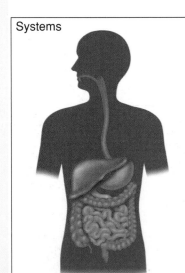 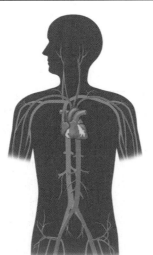 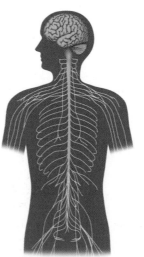 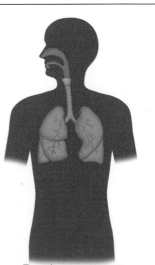

| Digestive system | Circulatory system | Nervous system | Respiratory system |

generate electrical signals and carry messages between our brains and our bodies. Epithelial cells are found wherever the body has a covering or lining, for example, the skin, or the wall of the stomach. Other cells called connective-tissue cells connect, anchor, and support the structures of the body.

All of this cellular activity is directed by our genes, instructions we inherit from our parents for how our bodies look and everything that they do. Genes do this by coding for the manufacturing of proteins, which are molecules that serve as the building blocks of life. Proteins are so important that everything we can imagine doing—even imagining!—is the result of some 20,000 different kinds of proteins working together.

From Cells to Organ Systems

Cells not only specialize, they also begin to migrate throughout the developing body. Small communities of like cells begin to stick together and to make multicellular structures we call tissues. Different kinds of tissues assemble into organs, such as the heart, liver, and brain. An organ is a part of a living thing that performs specific tasks. For example, the heart pumps blood, the liver (which has more than 500 functions) helps get rid of bodily poisons and stores vitamins, and the brain interprets electrical signals and makes decisions about what to do.

Different organs functioning together are termed systems (or sometimes, organ systems). For example, the respiratory system consists of the nose, pharynx, larynx, trachea, bronchi, and lungs. The parts of the respiratory system work together to take in the oxygen we need to survive, and to get rid of carbon dioxide (waste gas). The circulatory system consists of the heart, blood vessels, and blood. Its purpose is to transport blood containing oxygen and nutrients throughout the body's tissues. Because all of our organs require oxygen to function, the respiratory system depends on the circulatory system to transport the oxygen we breathe to all parts of our body.

Similarly, our muscular system together with our bones (called the musculoskeletal system) makes it possible for us to shake hands, to lift a bag of groceries, to smile or to speak, and to get up when we fall down. The energy to move our muscles comes from the food we eat, which is processed into usable fuel by yet another system, the digestive system.

To some extent, body systems overlap. By that we mean that some organs can be considered part of more than one system. The diaphragm, for example, is a muscle involved in breathing, and it is part of both the musculoskeletal system and the respiratory system. It takes nine months from start to finish to make a human infant. But even after we are born, our bones and brains continue to develop. Other major body changes will occur as we grow into teenagers and then adults, and later in our lives, too, as we experience the process we call aging.

The Body in Balance

Our bodies are complex, delicately calibrated biological machines. Like other machines, they work best at a certain temperature, a certain level of moistness, with a certain balance of chem-

Genes, which are inherited from parents, are made of DNA. Short for deoxyribonucleic (de-OK-se-ri-bo-noo-KLE-ik) acid, DNA is the primary material of the cell nucleus. It usually takes the shape of a double helix (a pair of spirals). Imagine it as a flexible ladder that has been twisted into a spiral. The two long edges of the ladder are made of chemical molecules called nucleotides. Each nucleotide includes a chemical called a base. There are four bases that occur in pairs, called base pairs. These are adenine and thymine (A–T) and cytosine and guanine (C–G). The base pairs form the rungs in the ladder, held together by chemical links called hydrogen bonds. If any of the base pairs are missing, out of place or repeated, the defective gene may cause a health problem. Or the defect may have such a minor effect that the person never notices it.

DNA sends genetic information through RNA (ribonucleic acid) to manufacture proteins that will build new cells. Proteins are often shaped like a single helix or ring. They are made up of amino acids containing nitrogen, hydrogen, oxygen, and sulfur. Proteins are the building blocks of cell protoplasm, which is the part of the cell that is outside the nucleus.

As cells grow and multiply, millions of them together form structures called tissues. Muscles, nerves, and bone are among the different kinds of tissue in the body. Tissue is grouped into organs, such as the heart, liver, and brain, which are masses of tissue that perform specific functions. Organs working together are termed systems: the digestive system, for instance, includes the mouth, esophagus, stomach, intestines, liver, and gall bladder. Systems working together make up the human body.

3,000 Years Ago: Ancient Egyptian Medicine

Scholars respect ancient Egyptian medicine, which made good use of herbs with medical benefits. The Greeks, the Romans, and Europeans of later eras used and respected several Egyptian prescriptions and tests.

This excellent reputation is one reason that the word "chemistry" may derive from "Keni," the ancient name of Egypt. The word "pharmacy" may come from the Egyptian "phrt," meaning "prescription." And the pharmaceutical symbol "Rx" may be derived from the Eye of Horus, the Egyptian god of health, whose parts were used in medical papyri (documents) to indicate drug quantities.

The papyrus that told ancient Egyptian doctors how to treat various ailments is similar to today's medical textbooks. Note the following description of a medical examination, diagnosis, and treatment, with additional parenthetical instructions from the scribe:

> *Instructions concerning a wound in the top of his eyebrow.*
> *If you examine a man having a wound in the top of his eyebrow,*
> *penetrating to the bone, you should palpate his wound (and)*
> *draw together for him his gash with stitching.*
> *You should say concerning him: "One having a wound in his*
> *eyebrow. An ailment which I will treat."*
> *Now after you have stitched it, you should bind fresh meat upon*
> *it the first day. If you find that the stitching of this wound is*
> *loose, you should draw it together for him with two strips of*
> *plaster, and you should treat it with grease and honey every day*
> *until he recovers. (As for "two strips of plaster," it means two*
> *bands of linen which one applies upon the two lips of the gap-*
> *ing wound, in order to cause that one lip to join to the other.)*

Here is an ancient Egyptian prescription for removing red inflammation from the eyes:

> *carob pods*
> *acacia leaves*
> *green eye paint*
> *milk from a woman who has given birth to a boy; to be made into a*
> *paste and applied to the outside of the two eyes.*

Perhaps the physician was treating conjunctivitis.

From *Civilizations of the Ancient Near East*, pp. 1794–1796. New York: Charles Scribner's Sons, 1996.

icals, and so on. Although conditions in the world around us are changing all the time, our bodies can adjust to these changes. For instance, when you are playing soccer on a hot summer day, your body heats up. Your brain registers the rise in your body temperature, and sends a message to your skin to release the excess heat by sweating. If not for your temperature-control system, the excess heat would cause havoc throughout your body.

A control system regulates something or keeps it in balance. The balancing act that those systems perform is called "homeostasis." In the same way that a thermostat acts to keep a house in temperature balance no matter what the weather is outside, so your body maintains physical and chemical settings to keep your cells, tissues, organs, and organ systems working smoothly.

Glucose (sugar), for example, is the major fuel that drives the engine of life. Glucose taken up by cells provides energy for the body's cells to perform their different tasks. But too much or too little sugar in the blood can make us ill or even kill us. We need calcium and iron, too, but too much is poisonous to our system. Homeostasis is a process of keeping the body in a state of balance. When the system fails, the result is abnormal functioning, which can result in disease or death. In carrying out our own vital activities, our bodies generate waste products. Our body's ability to get rid of these waste products is also part of its control system.

Aging Is Part of the Life Cycle   When we are young, we often are in a hurry to grow up because of the freedom to choose, which we like to think comes with being an adult. It may be hard to imagine that our bodies will ever be any different from what they are now. Yet just as the human organism grows from a single cell to a fully functioning person, over time it also begins to wear out or to malfunction—sometimes slowly, sometimes rapidly.

Health and Illness

One of the marvels of the human machinery is how rarely anything goes seriously wrong, and how good the body is at repairing and defending itself. But sometimes the magnitude of an injury or the cleverness or ferocity of a microbial invader is so great that the body is simply overwhelmed. In other cases, just as with nonliving machines, the body or a part of it breaks down because of age or malfunctions from other causes.

No System Is Perfect   The title of this encyclopedia is *Human Diseases and Conditions*. What do those words mean, and how did we decide which ones to include in the encyclopedia? There is no strict definition of what a disease is, but we can understand a disease as a process that interferes with a structure or function of the body, or as something that causes a change from good health.

The word "disease" sounds serious. In fact, most people reserve the term to mean a relatively serious process that may get worse or progress—for example, plague or lung cancer. For mild or temporary changes, such as a cold or flu, we generally use the term "illness." And when something is relatively serious but probably will not get worse, like

150 YEARS AGO: CHARLES DICKENS

Charles Dickens (1812–1870), one of England's greatest novelists, was fascinated by diseases. He studied them carefully, as a skilled physician would, in order to create unusual characters that were as realistic as possible.

Today, doctors can diagnose his characters' illnesses by reading his distinctive descriptions. For example, young Paul Dombey in *Dombey and Son* (1848) clearly has leukemia. The boy is always weak and tired; he says his bones ache. He is extremely susceptible to other illnesses and diseases. Finally, he has terrible headaches and fainting spells:

But Paul's head, which had been ailing more or less, and was sometimes heavy and painful, felt so uneasy that night, that he was obliged to support it on his hand. . . . But there seemed to be something the matter with the floor, for he couldn't stand upon it steadily; and with the walls, too, for they were inclined to turn round and round, and could only be stopped by being looked at very hard indeed.

Poor little Paul Dombey dies at six years of age in the novel, and his story is especially poignant because it is so vivid.

When Dickens himself died in 1870, a doctor wrote about him in the *British Medical Journal*: "What a gain it would have been to physic if one so keen to observe and so facile to describe had devoted his powers to the medical art."

Based on "Charles Dickens and the Art of Medicine" by Howard Markel, M.D., Ph.D., *Annals of Internal Medicine* (1984) 101:408–411.

a broken bone or cerebral palsy, we call it a "condition." As you can see, these terms and the disorders they represent can overlap.

A person changes through the days and years. When we think about human health, we can think about the dimension of time, too. Human diseases and conditions can be acute or chronic. Acute illness begins rapidly and lasts a short time, although in some cases it may leave a disability or long-term damage to the body. For instance, people who survived the infectious disease called smallpox were cured but often suffered disfiguring facial scars. Other examples of acute illnesses are pneumonia, measles, and poisonous snake bites. Chronic illnesses, on the other hand, usually begin slowly and go on for a long time, often for a lifetime. Diabetes mellitus, which results from the body's inability to handle sugar properly because of a lack of insulin, is an example of a chronic disease.

Because the body is a complex system, there are lots of ways in which things can go wrong—even though most of the time they do not. We can acquire conditions, such as alcoholic liver disease, or we can inherit them

100 YEARS AGO: MARK TWAIN

In Mark Twain's *The Adventures of Tom Sawyer*, Tom goes through a period of depression when his girlfriend Becky Thatcher becomes ill. Tom misses Becky at school and is afraid she might die.

During the 1800s, when the novel takes place, traveling salesmen and magazines and newspapers promoted all sorts of quack (fake) remedies, claiming they cured everything from warts to depression. Tom's aunt seems to have chosen a medication for him that would probably be available today only by prescription:

He no longer took an interest in war, nor even in piracy. The charm of life was gone; there was nothing but dreariness left. . . . His aunt was concerned. She began to try all manner of remedies on him. . . .

She had him out at daylight every morning, stood him up in the woodshed and drowned him with a deluge of cold water; then she scrubbed him down with a towel like a file, and so brought him to; then she rolled him up in a wet sheet and put him away under blankets till she sweated his soul clean and "the yellow stains of it came through his pores"—as Tom said.

Yet . . . the boy grew more and more melancholy and pale and dejected. She added hot baths, sitz baths, shower baths, and plunges. The boy remained dismal as a hearse. . . .

Tom had become indifferent to persecution by this time. This phase filled the old lady's heart with consternation. This indifference must be broken up at any cost. Now she heard of Pain-killer for the first time. She ordered a lot at once. She tasted it and was filled with gratitude. It was simply fire in liquid form. She dropped the water treatment and everything else, and pinned her faith to Pain-killer. She gave Tom a teaspoonful and watched with the deepest anxiety for the result. Her troubles were instantly at rest, her soul at peace again; for the "indifference" was broken up. The boy could not have shown a wilder, heartier interest if she had built a fire under him.

from our parents, such as hemophilia, a blood-clotting disorder. Malfunctions in any of our many body processes, like those caused by malnutrition or weakness in our body's defense systems, can leave us open to a variety of diseases and conditions, including diabetes and cancer.

Many diseases, including lethal diseases like smallpox, are infectious—that is, they can be spread from person to person. Conditions like Down syndrome and some forms of cerebral palsy are the result of something that goes wrong between the time of conception and the time of birth. Osteoarthritis and atherosclerosis are called degenerative diseases. Body parts just begin to wear out, malfunction, or fall apart, for reasons that are not always well understood. Sprains and broken bones, cuts, burns, stings, bites, and gunshot wounds are injuries to the body that can interfere with its structure or function.

Diagnostic Tests

Doctors use many different imaging and laboratory tests to diagnose diseases and injuries. Among the most common:

■ **X-rays** or radiographs are high-energy electromagnetic radiation waves that come from radioactive substances such as uranium and radium, used to create images on photographic film. The part of the body to be x-rayed is placed between the photographic film and the radioactive source. A protective shield is removed from around the radioactive source for a short period of time and the x-rays pass through the body to the film. When the photographic film is developed, the images of the body show up in shades of gray: skin and soft tissues are darkest because the rays pass through them to the film; denser tissues like bone are lightest because they absorb the rays and prevent them from reaching the film. Discovered in 1895 by the German physicist Wilhelm Konrad Röntgen (1845–1923), x-rays still are one of the most widely used radiologic tools.

■ **CT scans** are also called CAT scans, short for computerized axial tomography. CT scans show cross-sectional planes of the body or parts of the body such as the head, chest, or abdomen. A tube-shaped scanner takes multiple x-rays of the body while the patient lies on a platform. Dyes sometimes are administered to highlight different blood vessels, tissues, or organs. The cross-sectional x-rays are enhanced by a computer, which puts together all the scanning data to create composite, three-dimensional images that are printed or displayed on a screen as visual "slices" of the body.

Signs and Symptoms   Most of the time, what makes a person seek medical care are symptoms, which are problems resulting from an illness that trouble the person who experiences them. On the other hand, what physicians and other clinicians look for are signs, known as markers of disease. For example, in Wilson's disease, which is caused by an accumulation of copper in the tissues, a patient may seek medical care because of tremor (shaking) in the hands or arms. Now, many things can cause tremor. But a telltale sign of Wilson's disease is a golden-brown ring around the iris of the eye that a doctor would know to look for.

Symptoms usually are related to our ability to do things. They may reflect either acute or chronic problems. Bodily symptoms, such as a sore throat, swollen ankles, or aches, pains, and disabilities, may result from various kinds of problems in the body. Other symptoms, including common headaches or upset stomach, may be triggered by emotional, psychological, and interpersonal stresses.

Diagnosis   The name a clinician gives to a disease—the diagnosis—is important because it helps us understand how the disease is likely to affect the person and helps determine the kind of treatment the person should have.

In reaching a diagnosis, a clinician will take a medical history, that is, listen to the patient's account of the problem. He or she will also perform a physical examination to look for signs. Based on what the examination shows or what the clinician suspects, laboratory tests may be ordered. These are tests to examine bodily fluids such as blood and urine. Special procedures such as x-rays and magnetic resonance imaging (MRI) scans provide views of bodily structures that are not otherwise accessible. Special tests such as renal clearance tests (to test kidney function) and glucose tolerance tests can tell whether various body processes are working properly.

How Are Illnesses Treated?   There are a variety of ways to provide relief from the diseases and conditions we encounter. In the best case, treatment seeks to cure the problem. If a cure is not possible, then the purpose of treatment is to control the symptoms and, if possible, to prevent worsening of the disease or condition. An important goal is to allow a person to carry out the activities of daily living as well and as free from discomfort as possible.

The choice of treatment depends on the nature of the disease or condition. Surgery is a common form of treatment for removal of diseased organs and repair of malfunctioning ones, such as removing a diseased gallbladder or replacing a defective heart valve. Radiotherapy (the use of high-energy radio waves) is used to treat many forms of cancer. A change in diet is a feature of many treatment programs, depending on the disease; and other lifestyle changes may be required as well, for example, quitting smoking or increasing physical activity. Physical therapy is a staple of treatment for conditions that involve bones, muscles, and joints. Counseling and other psychological and psychiatric therapies may be recommended for emotional and mental disorders.

Commonly, when we think of treatment, we think about the use of medications (drugs) manufactured by pharmaceutical companies. Of course, herbal remedies have been around for thousands of years too, and many of today's medications are derived from them. Before 1900, very few standardized, manufactured drugs were available to cure, control, or prevent disease, among them morphine for pain, digitalis for heart ailments, and vaccines for diphtheria and smallpox. But following World War II, many new drugs and classes of drugs began to be developed. Today, available drug treatments include antibiotics, anti-inflammatory drugs, hormonal treatments, cardiovascular drugs, immunosuppressive drugs, antipsychotic and antidepressant medicines, pain relievers, and chemotherapeutic agents for the treatment of cancer, to name just a few. In addition, a variety of nonprescription, over-the-counter medicines are available to treat minor illnesses. These medications have helped save countless numbers of lives and eased the symptoms of millions.

The Health-Care System

How Does It Work? Before the beginning of the twentieth century, even in the United States, state-of-the-art health care was something only the rich could afford. The poor often were left untreated or were admitted to the hospital, often to die. But beginning in the 1940s, good health came to be looked on more as a right than a privilege. Health insurance, medical research, and the expansion of hospitals were all products of this change in perspective, which was in part a result of the need to organize medical care for large numbers of troops during World War II.

Another reason for the change in perspective was a shift in disease patterns. Until the beginning of the twentieth century, acute infectious diseases such as measles and smallpox were the prevailing afflictions of humankind. But beginning around 1900, improved sanitation, nutrition, and immunization made these diseases less common in the United States and the rest of the industrialized world. As a result, people began living longer—long enough for more of them to get the slowly developing diseases of age. In the industrialized world, chronic conditions came to dominate. And dealing with long-term continuous illness required a continuous system of care.

The United States differs from other industrialized countries in that the health-care system evolved piece by piece, reflecting the country's traditional emphasis on a market economy, the reluctance of the government to control people's lives, and the role of interest groups. As a result, the kind of medical care people receive depends on a number of factors: personal choice, what kind of care is available, how much knowledge and information people have, what (if any) insurance they have to cover the cost of care, and how wealthy they are.

Health Promotion Although "health care" and "medical care" are terms that deal with similar concerns, they differ in an important way. Health care is a more comprehensive term. It includes prevention—all the

Sonograms use sound waves to create pictures by bouncing the waves off tissues and converting the echoes into images. One of the most common types of sonography (ultrasound) is used to view a fetus during pregnancy.

MRIs are short for nuclear magnetic resonance images. MRIs use magnetic and radio waves instead of x-rays to scan the body, often producing even clearer images than do CT scans. When magnetic and radio waves are sent into a specific part of the body, different types of atoms in the cells vibrate and emit unique radio waves. These emitted radio waves are detected and converted by a computer into an image that can be displayed on screen or printed out. MRI is useful for identifying abnormalities in soft tissues such as the brain, spinal cord, kidneys, urinary tract, pancreas, and liver.

Laparoscopy is a procedure that uses a thin, lighted tube with a miniature camera to look inside the body. The patient remains awake but is given a local anesthetic to numb the part of the body being studied. The doctor inserts the laparoscope into the body through a very small incision and then views the camera images to guide the laparoscope. Other tools can be inserted through the same incision to take tissue samples for analysis in the laboratory or to remove tissue entirely. Usually, patients recover more quickly from laparoscopic surgery than from traditional surgery.

What's in a Name?

Tylenol® and acetaminophen (a-set-a-MI-no-fen) are pain medications that can be bought over the counter without a prescription. Which is better for mild muscle aches or headaches? The answer: they are the same drug.

Drugs often have three or more names: a brand name, a generic name, and a chemical name. The pharmaceutical company that applies for a drug patent often gives the drug its generic name (acetaminophen) and then patents a brand name, in this case Tylenol®.

When a company develops a new drug, it must spend a lot of money on research, development, and clinical trials to test the drug's safety and effectiveness on volunteers. If the drug proves to be safe and effective, then the U.S. Food and Drug Administration can approve it for sale. To protect its investment, the drug company files a patent to protect the drug from competition. During the patent period, usually seven years, the patent holder is the only company that can sell the drug. During this time, people who buy the drug are not paying just for the drug itself; they also are paying for the development, testing, and approval.

After the patent expires, competing companies may manufacture and market the same drug under its generic name, but they may not use its brand name. Generic drugs cost less because the companies that manufacture them do not need to spend nearly as much money on developing and testing the drug.

Drugs also have a third name, the chemical name. Chemical names usually are used only by chemists, because they are long and hard to pronounce. The chemical name for the active ingredient in Tylenol® and acetaminophen is N-(4-hydroxyphenyl) acetamide.

So which is better for mild muscle aches or headaches? In this case, both may do nicely. But be sure to check with a doctor. All drugs can be dangerous if not used correctly.

things someone can do to avoid disease—and health promotion—all the things someone can do to enhance fitness and well-being. Medical care, on the other hand, usually refers to the diagnosis and treatment of disease after it has developed. An effective health care system pays attention not only to curative medical services, but also to preventing disease and promoting health. By doing so, it may help large numbers of people who might not even realize the health care system has served them well.

What Purpose Does Medical Research Serve? Effective medications and therapies often come after years of careful research and investigation. The process can be expensive and difficult. In the United States, the National Institutes of Health (NIH), the Centers for Disease Control and Prevention (CDC), and the Food and Drug Administration (FDA) represent a spectrum of government agencies whose priorities range from basic research in the laboratory, to monitoring and control of disease, to approval and regulation of new drug treatments. In addition, many private companies also do research on new treatment.

An essential part of this process is what we call clinical trials—experimental tests of new drugs in patients. Because drugs can act so differently in people than in a test tube or in a lab mouse, medical research depends on clinical trials to move forward. Moreover, these trials are a required part of any application for Food and Drug Administration approval of new drugs.

To a great extent, the longer life spans of the past century are due not just to the development of new medications or surgical techniques, but to important public health measures such as improved sanitation, immunization programs, and the availability of bacteria-free drinking water. Toilets and drinkable water are something we tend to take for granted, but they have improved the health of more people than any "miracle" drug.

Health in the Developing World Unfortunately, such advances have not been universal. In many parts of the world—particularly in poor or developing nations of Africa and Asia—many people live crowded together without enough nutritious food to eat, clean water to drink, or sanitary systems to dispose safely of human waste. To make matters worse, the warm, moist climate in these areas makes it easy for many disease-causing parasites and bacteria to grow and spread. Nations and individuals may lack the money needed to prevent diseases and pay for medical care, especially up-to-date diagnostic equipment, antibiotics, and other drugs. As a result, acute infectious diseases that are rare in the United States still take a huge toll in death and illness, especially among children in impoverished parts of the world.

Living Healthy Lives

What Does It Mean to Be Healthy? We know the value of health by what is taken away from us when we do not have it. Health problems can affect our ability to move freely, to work, to create, to play, to enjoy food and life's other pleasures, to be able to remember things, and to have family and friends. To be denied any one of these capacities can lessen the quality of life.

Yet sickness is a part of life—something that happens to us—like being born, falling in love, or growing old. Our illnesses, or those of people we care about, are unavoidable elements of our day-to-day living. To the extent that we are healthy, we have an enhanced capacity for living. But having a disease or condition does not mean that we have to be miserable. It is not the perfection of individual body parts but what a person brings to a life that matters. It is possible to have a disease and to be happy and productive, or to have a condition and to be otherwise healthy. Apart from the care and treatment we receive from the medical establishment, how we respond to challenges to our physical well being depends most on our individual constitution and outlook, and on support from family, friends, and community.

We are fortunate to live in times when there are many things people can do to prevent or control certain kinds of illness and chronic conditions. We can help to keep ourselves and our children healthy by making sure we get vaccination shots, by shunning tobacco products and other substances of abuse, by getting enough physical exercise, and by eating nutritious foods in proper amounts. As we become adults, having screening tests for some of the more treatable forms of cancer, such as breast cancer and colorectal cancer, and tests for diabetes can help to catch diseases early, so that even if we do become ill, the disease will have less of a chance to damage or disable us.

Chronic diseases can be prevented and sometimes controlled by a variety of measures. For instance, a person with emphysema can keep the condition from getting worse by stopping smoking; patients with early alcoholic liver disease or pancreatitis can limit their illness if they stop drinking. Attention to safety can help to prevent many accidents, and injuries from certain kinds of accidents can be minimized, for example, by wearing seatbelts (in cars) and helmets (when riding bicycles or driving motorcycles or skating).

To an increasing extent, in fact, we are responsible for safeguarding our own health. But we depend on society to give us access to the educational and professional services we need. It also is important to remember that while our actions can make illness more or less likely, we cannot fully control whether we stay healthy or not. Sometimes people blame themselves for getting sick, as if they had somehow failed. Or they may feel guilty if their illness upsets their family or friends. But nobody wants to get sick, and nobody should be blamed for becoming ill.

A Supportive Community   Human beings are social animals. In sickness, as in health, we turn to others for advice, support, and companionship. At almost every level, we can find resources to help us cope:

  - states and communities

  - local public health and school health agencies

Complementary and Alternative Medicine

Vitamins, supplements, complementary treatments, and home remedies are promoted through advertisng and word of mouth. Before trying any alternative treatment or supplement, however, it is important to check with a doctor. Important questions to ask when evaluating complementary treatments:

  - What scientific evidence exists that the treatment is safe and effective?

  - How much does the treatment cost?

  - How many visits does the treatment require?

  - How long before the treatment results in improved health?

  - Could this treatment interfere with conventional medical care?

  - Could this supplement interfere with prescription medications?

  - Is the alternative practitioner willing to discuss the complementary treatment plan with the primary physician?

- health care providers

- health education centers

- books, websites, magazines, and other sources of information

- support groups for patients and caregivers.

In cases of severely debilitating illness, such as alcoholism or Alzheimer's disease or cerebral palsy, the family can be affected by the disease almost as much as the patient. No one should hesitate to ask for help. For example, a database called the Adaptive Device Locator System (ADLS-on-the-Web) is available on the Internet to help people find assistive technology—anything from motorized wheelchairs to specially crafted cups to make activities of daily living, such as eating and recreation, easier.

To make sure that the rights of those with disabilities are protected, in 1990, the U.S. Congress passed the Americans with Disabilities Act, which prohibits discrimination against people with disabilities (physical or mental impairment) in employment, housing, education, and access to public services.

Why We Wrote This Encyclopedia

There are said to be many thousands of human diseases and conditions. We editors who are physicians have seen quite a few of them, but certainly not all! We have chosen about 300 of them to include in these volumes for a variety of reasons. Some are very common. Others, while uncommon, have an important place in the history of humanity. Still others may be worrisome—so it is good to know the real facts about them. Some diseases and conditions are particularly interesting, or teach us something special. When we talk about health we also mean mental health, of course, and a number of the sections deal with this important area.

Most of the editors of this encyclopedia are doctors who particularly enjoy—and are experienced in—teaching and writing about health issues. Others of us are professional health writers and editors. We hope you enjoy using the encyclopedia as much as we enjoyed working on it.

Neil Izenberg, M.D.
Editor-in-Chief, *Human Diseases and Conditions*
Director, Nemours Center for Children's Health Media
The Nemours Foundation
KidsHealth.org
Pediatrician, Alfred I. duPont Hospital for Children
Wilmington, Delaware
izenberg@KidsHealth.org

Resources

KidsHealth.org. This website, supervised by the pediatric medical experts at the Alfred I. duPont Hospital for Children, offers articles, animations, and games about health.
http://www.KidsHealth.org

U.S. National Institutes of Health (NIH). This is the government agency that oversees most medical research in the United States. The search engine at its website can locate information about clinical trials and fact sheets about many of the diseases and conditions described in this encyclopedia.
http://www.nih.gov

U.S. Centers for Disease Control and Prevention (CDC). This is the government agency that tracks statistics about illnesses and deaths in the United States, posts notices about diseases for travelers, and assists local governments during medical emergencies.
http://www.cdc.gov

U.S. Food and Drug Administration (FDA). This is the government agency that monitors food and drug safety.
http://www.fda.gov

Americans with Disabilities Act (1990). Maintained by the U.S. Department of Justice (DOJ), the ADA home page has a search engine and an ADA information line.
Telephone 800-514-0301 (voice)
Telephone 800-514-0383 (TDD)
http://www.usdoj.gov/crt/ada/adahom1.htm

World Health Organization (WHO). This is the branch of the United Nations that tracks health and disease worldwide.
http://www.who.org

A

Abscess

An abscess is an accumulation of pus that can result from an infection in any part of the body. An abscess is often surrounded by red, swollen tissue.

An abscess is an accumulation or collection of pus* that can result from an infection in any part of the body. An abscess is often surrounded by red, swollen tissue. The pus is made up of a mixture of fluid and several kinds of cells: There are microorganisms that are causing the infection, there are immune-system cells that are fighting the infection, and there are millions of body cells that have died in the struggle. Although pus is not pleasant to look at, its presence means that the body is defending itself against disease-causing microbes*.

Some abscesses, like boils, are very common. They form just under the skin and usually go away on their own. Some abscesses can form in the gum near a tooth, and those often require treatment by a dentist. Still other abscesses form deep within the body, especially in the abdominal organs or the chest. These are rarer but can be very serious. They must be treated by a doctor and often require surgery.

What Causes Abscesses?

Abscesses may be caused by many different bacteria, fungi, or protozoans, which are kinds of disease-causing microbes. Abscesses result from infections that are or become localized or confined to one part of the body, as opposed to infections that spread throughout the body.

External abscesses Boils and carbuncles are common among teenagers, but virtually everyone gets them at some time. They are called external abscesses because they form on the surface of the body. They are quite similar to each other. The main difference is that carbuncles have a number of core areas where the pus forms, while boils have a single core at their center. Thus carbuncles may resemble a cluster of interconnected boils.

External abscesses commonly occur on the back of the neck or on the face. They also frequently form on moist parts of the body, such as the armpit or groin. Abscesses in hair follicles* may result in a condition called folliculitis (fo-lik-u-LY-tis). An abscess at the base of an eyelash, which is a special type of follicle, is called a sty.

KEYWORDS
for searching the Internet and other reference sources

Infection

Inflammation

* **pus** is a thick, creamy fluid, usually yellow or greenish in color, that forms at the site of an infection.

* **microbes** and **microorganisms** are small organisms that can cause disease and that can usually be seen only under a microscope. They include bacteria, viruses, protozoa, and fungi.

* **follicles** are tiny pits in the skin from which hair grows.

Dental abscesses A dental abscess or gumboil is an accumulation of pus in the gums or jaw tissues surrounding a tooth. It is usually formed as a result of infection by bacteria. A common contributing cause is dental decay, which is why regular dental checkups are important. Dental abscesses may also result from injuries such as a fracture in the tooth. If the cause is a dental cavity, the infection begins when the bacteria enter the pulp* portion inside the tooth. At this point, the condition is known as pulpitis (pul-PY-tis). An abscess on the gum is formed as the infection spreads from the pulp of the tooth.

Internal abscesses Abscesses may form in any organ or cavity of the body. There are many different kinds, and they may be caused by any of a variety of microorganisms. All abscesses occurring in the internal organs require medical attention.

- In the abdomen, abscesses may result from infections of the gall bladder, liver, kidney, intestine, or pelvic organs in women. They may also be a complication of abdominal surgery.
- An abscess that forms due to obstruction of the appendix is called appendicitis (a-pen-di-SY-tis), which usually causes severe pain in the lower right part of the abdomen. Doctors usually recommend surgery (appendectomy) to remove the appendix immediately. Otherwise the appendix may burst, causing the infection to spread through the abdominal cavity.
- In the lungs, abscesses may be a complication of pneumonia.
- In the throat, peritonsillar (per-i-TON-si-lar) abscess may result from the spread of tonsillitis, infection of the tonsils*. Peritonsillar abscess occurs frequently in young adults.
- Abscesses may also occur in the brain and in other organs of the body.

What Happens When People Get Abscesses?

External abscesses and dental abscesses most often are caused by *staphylococci*, which are bacteria in the staphylococcus (STAF-i-lo-KOK-us)

*__pulp__ is the sensitive area deep inside the central part of the tooth, where the nerves and blood vessels are located.

*__tonsils__ are paired clusters of lymph tissues in the throat. They help protect the body from bacteria or viruses that enter through a person's nose or mouth.

An external abscess is an accumulation of pus that results from bacterial infection. Abscesses that form under the skin may go away on their own. Some require drainage (removal of the pus).

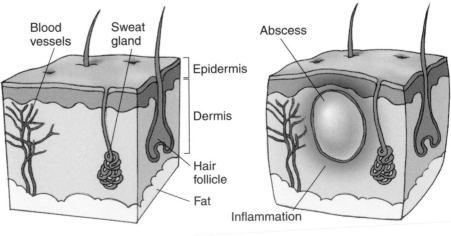

Blood vessels · Sweat gland · Epidermis · Dermis · Hair follicle · Fat

Healthy skin

Abscess · Inflammation

Abscess

group. The bacteria enter the body through the mouth, or through pores in the skin, or through minor cuts and abrasions, such as places where clothing chafes the body. An example of chafing is when a shirt or coat collar rubs the back of the neck. Often, the exact source of the infection is not known. The bacteria that usually cause boils are very common, and having boils does not mean a person is dirty or will spread infection to others.

Once the bacteria are under the skin, they are attacked by leukocytes*, which are white blood cells sent by the body's immune system to combat the bacteria. Pus forms as the white blood cells, bacteria, and destroyed cells accumulate, and the body creates a fibrous wall or lining to keep the infection sealed off from surrounding tissues. People who have conditions that may lower the body's immune response, such as diabetes, are more likely to get boils and carbuncles.

A person first notices a boil when it becomes a red, sore lump. As the pus builds up inside, the boil begins to swell. It also becomes more painful due to the increasing pressure on the nerve endings in the surrounding areas of the skin and to the inflammatory substances created by the body's response to the infection. Boils on the nose or ear are usually more painful than others. The pressure on the nerves is greater because the skin is tighter in these areas and cannot stretch as much.

Usually, a yellowish head, or point, forms on the boil as the pus forces its way toward the surface. Sometimes, however, the boil may subside and disappear on its own, if the immune system is able to overcome the infection early enough. If the boil does form a head, pressure may cause it to rupture, spilling the pus to the outside. Carbuncle infections, which have several closely adjoining points, usually are more severe than boils. They may be accompanied by headache, loss of appetite, chills, and fever. These signs and symptoms are easy to recognize, but if swelling is accompanied by fever, significant pain, or any unusual symptoms, then a visit to the doctor is advisable.

How Are Abscesses Treated?

External abscesses   Many simple abscesses are treated at home with warm moist compresses that help bring the infection to the skin surface so it can drain. While boils are draining, they are usually covered with dry, sterile dressings until they are completely healed. Healing may take several days or sometimes weeks.

Boils that are large, painful, or widespread should be treated by a doctor. This is particularly important if swelling is accompanied by fever, significant pain, or unusual symptoms, or if an abscess is firm with no tenderness. A doctor may prescribe an antibiotic to help fight the infection, or the doctor may lance the boil, which involves making a puncture or an incision with a sterile needle or a surgical knife to let the pus out. Lancing by a doctor only takes a couple of seconds and often results in remarkable pain relief and faster healing.

Dental abscesses   In a tooth where a dental abscess starts, the first symptom is often a painful twinge when eating hot or cold foods. As the

* **leukocytes** (LOO-ko-sites) are white blood cells sent by the body's immune system to fight infection.

"Furuncles"

Almost everyone gets a boil at some time in their life. Doctors call boils "furuncles" (FYOO-ryn-kulz). In the Bible (Job 2:7), the prophet Job was afflicted with boils from head to toe to test his faith in God.

17

infection spreads from the tooth to the gum, the pain becomes throbbing and continuous. A person with a dental abscess will have trouble chewing because pressing the teeth together can be extremely painful. If the abscess or gumboil bursts, the pain may be somewhat relieved. Sometimes people with dental abscesses also have a fever.

Dentists can diagnose dental abscesses by noting their patients' symptoms and by x-ray examination. Redness and swelling also may be directly observed in the gum around the tooth. The dentist might need to perform a root canal* procedure in order to save the tooth. If this treatment cannot stop the infection, the tooth may have to be removed. The dentist also may prescribe antibiotics and warm mouthwashes.

Internal abscesses   All abscesses occurring in the internal organs require medical attention. If possible, the source of the infection must be found and treated. Usually, treatment includes surgical drainage of the abscess and antibiotics.

*__root canal__ is a procedure in which a dentist cleans out the pulp of an infected tooth, removes the nerve, and then fills the cavity with a protective substance.

▶ See also
Acne
Appendicitis
Cavities
Cyst
Tonsillitis

Resources

Bark, Joseph P. *Your Skin: An Owner's Guide.* Upper Saddle River, NJ: Prentice Hall, 1995.

Turkington, Carol A., and Jeffrey S. Dover. *Skin Deep: An A–Z of Skin Disorders, Treatment, and Health.* New York: Facts On File, 1998.

Acne

Acne (AK-nee) is a condition in which there are pimples, black-heads, whiteheads, and sometimes deeper lumps on the skin.

KEYWORDS
for searching the Internet and other reference sources

Acne vulgaris

Comedones

Dermatology

Inflammation

Johnny's Story

Until he turned 13, Johnny's skin had always been clear. Soon after the start of eighth grade, though, Johnny noticed the first few pimples on his face. Before long, the problem had gotten much worse. Johnny's face was always broken out, and the pimples had spread to his neck, back, and chest.

Johnny was willing to try almost anything to get rid of the problem. He had heard that acne was caused by dirt or by eating certain foods, so he washed his face several times a day and gave up chocolate, nuts, and french fries. He also tried several acne medicines sold without a prescription. Nothing did the trick. Finally, Johnny went to see the doctor, who prescribed a medicine. Within a few weeks, the acne started to go away. Although Johnny had to keep using medicine and seeing the doctor for a while, he felt that his new and improved appearance was well worth the trouble.

What Is Acne?

Acne is the name for pimples or comedones*: blackheads, whiteheads, and sometimes deeper lumps that occur on the skin, especially on the face, neck, chest, back, shoulders, and upper arms and legs. Almost all teenagers have at least a little acne, and some adults have the problem as well. Although acne is not a serious health threat, it can affect how people look, which in turn can affect how they feel about themselves. When the acne is severe, it can leave permanent scars on the skin.

Acne occurs when hair follicles (FOL-li-culs) become plugged. A follicle is a tiny shaft in the skin through which a hair grows. The follicles are connected to sebaceous (se-BAY-shus) glands, which are small structures in the skin that make an oily substance called sebum (SEE-bum). This oil helps keep the skin and hair healthy. To reach the surface of the skin, the oil drains from the glands into the follicles, then leaves the follicles through tiny openings in the top. As it leaves the follicles, the oil carries away dead skin cells shed by the follicle linings.

> *comedo* (KOM-e-do) is an acne pimple. A blackhead is an open comedo. A whitehead is a closed comedo. Cosmetics that are labeled "non-comedogenic" (non-kom-e-do-JEN-ik) are less likely to cause pimples.

What Kinds of Acne Are There?

Sometimes the cells inside the follicles shed too fast and stick together, forming a white, cheesy plug at the surface of the skin. If the opening to the surface stays partly open, the top of the plug may darken, causing a blackhead. If the opening to the surface closes, the follicle may fill up and its wall may start to bulge, causing a whitehead. The mixture of oil and cells inside the follicle also aids the growth of bacteria. If the follicle wall bursts, the oil, cells, and bacteria spill into the skin. The result is redness, swelling, and pus, in other words, a pimple. Ordinary acne is made up of blackheads, whiteheads, and pimples.

At times, large, pus-filled lumps called cysts (pronounced SISTS) form deeper in the skin. This is a more severe form of acne. The lumps may be painful, and if they are not treated by a doctor, they may lead to permanent scars.

Who Gets Acne?

Nearly all teenagers have at least an occasional pimple. The problem usually starts between the ages of 10 and 13, and it typically lasts for 5 to 10 years. Acne usually goes away on its own by the early twenties. However, it can last into the twenties, thirties, and beyond. A few people get acne for the first time as adults. Acne strikes boys and girls about equally. However, boys are more likely than girls to have more severe, longer-lasting forms of the problem.

During the teen years, both boys and girls go through changes in their hormones*. One group of hormones, called androgens (AN-dro-jens), seem to play a role in acne. Among other things, androgens make the sebaceous glands work harder. The more oil the glands make, the greater the chance that the follicles will become clogged. Teenage boys

> *hormones* are chemicals that are produced by different glands in the body. Hormones are like the body's ambassadors: they are created in one place but are sent through the body to have specific regulatory effects in different places.

Healthy skin (left) has pores, hair folli-cles, and sebaceous glands that make an oily substance called "sebum." Sebum helps keep skin and hair healthy by carry-ing away dead skin cells that have been shed by the follicle linings. If the cells shed too fast and stick together, they may form a plug at the surface of the skin. If the opening to the surface stays partly open, the top of the plug may darken, causing a blackhead (center). If the open-ing to the surface closes, the follicle may fill up and its wall may start to bulge, causing a whitehead (right). If the follicle wall bursts, the oil, cells, and bacteria spill into the skin. The result is redness, swelling, and pus.

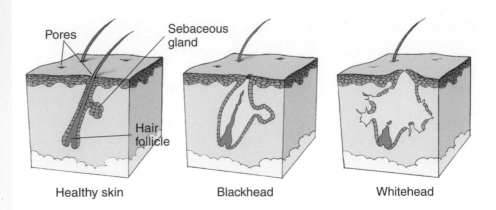

make ten times as much androgen as teenage girls, so it is not surprising that boys are more likely to get more severe cases of acne.

What Else Causes Acne?

Certain oily kinds of makeup and face cream can clog the openings of the skin and cause mild acne. That may mean that people who try to cover their pimples with makeup actually make the problem worse by causing new pimples. Oil-free products are labeled "non-comedogenic" (non-kom-ee-do-JEN-ik), meaning they should not cause blackheads or whiteheads, or "non-acnegenic" (non-ak-nee-JEN-ik), meaning they should not cause acne.

Several other things can cause acne or make it worse. These include certain medicines. People who work in fast food restaurants or garages may find that their acne is made worse by the constant contact with grease, motor oil, or chemical irritants. Many girls also find that their pimples get worse around the time of their periods.

What Does Acne Look Like?

Acne is typically found where the sebaceous glands are most numerous: on the face, neck, chest, back, and shoulders. Blackheads are spots with a dark top, whereas whiteheads are spots with a white center. Pimples look like small, red bumps. Some of them have a white center with a ring of redness around it. When pimples occur with no blackheads or white-heads, they may be a sign of another skin disease or a skin reaction to medication. Cysts are large, red bumps that are often painful. They may leave deep pits and scars after healing.

It is usually easy for a doctor to recognize acne by sight. It is smart to see a doctor whenever:

- acne interferes with a person's life

- acne spots are large, red, and painful

- acne causes dark patches to appear on a dark-skinned person

- acne scars remain when the acne spots heal

- treatment with nonprescription medication does not work

How Is Acne Treated?

Acne treatments work by stopping new pimples from forming. They do this by cutting back on the amount of oil the sebaceous glands make, the number of bacteria that are present in the skin, or the rate at which dead skin cells are shed. It is important to give an acne treatment enough time to do its job. It may take weeks for the skin to clear up, even if a treatment is working.

Over-the-counter medications   Milder cases of acne are often helped by lotions, creams, pads, and gels sold without a prescription. Many will dry out the skin if used too frequently, however, and it is important to follow label instructions carefully.

Prescription medications   A doctor may prescribe stronger medicines than those sold over the counter. When put on the skin in creams or lotions, such medicines may cause dryness and peeling. The doctor can offer advice on how to deal with these side effects.

Other treatments   The doctor may open pimples or remove blackheads and whiteheads in the office. A skilled doctor is the best one to do this. People who try to do it themselves may wind up making the acne worse and increasing the risk of scarring.

What *Doesn't* Cause Acne?

Acne is not caused by being dirty. Even the black in a blackhead is dried oil and dead skin cells, not dirt. Washing too often may actually irritate the skin and make the acne worse. In general, the following guidelines may help to prevent acne or to reduce its symptoms:

- not popping, squeezing, or picking at acne pimples, as this can just lead to more redness, swelling, and scars.

Retin-A and Accutane

Two drugs used to clear up severe cases of acne are Retin-A and Accutane. Both of these drugs are derivatives of vitamin A.

Retin-A (tretinoin) comes in a cream, gel, or liquid and is applied to the skin daily. Exactly how it works is unknown but it is thought to loosen and expel existing acne plugs in the skin glands and prevent new lesions from forming. Results are seen in about 2 or 3 weeks but treatment should be continued for at least 6 weeks. The most common side effect is skin irritation.

Accutane (isotretinoin) is taken orally. Accutane must be taken daily for 4 or 5 months, and results last for about one year. Accutane has some serious side effects such as chapped lips, dry, itchy skin, nosebleeds, irritation of the eyelids, joint and muscle pain, temporary hair loss, and rash. It is particularly important that Accutane not be taken by women who are pregnant or who may become pregnant during treatment as the drug can severely damage the developing fetus.

Dermatologists may prescribe lotions or creams to treat acne. © *Leonard Lessin/Peter Arnold, Inc.*

- Choosing oil-free makeup and face creams labeled "non-comedogenic" or "non-acnegenic."
- Avoiding things that can irritate the skin, such as grease, oil, and rubbing from clothes and sports equipment.
- Washing the face gently twice a day with a mild soap, then patting it dry.
- Shampooing hair regularly.
- For men who shave, shaving as lightly as possible to avoid nicking any pimples.

Acne also is not caused by the foods a person eats. Studies have shown that a strict diet alone will not clear up the skin. On the other hand, some people are still convinced that certain foods such as chocolate or french fries make their acne worse. It certainly could not hurt to cut back on junk food. A healthier diet is always a plus, whether or not it has an effect on acne.

Resources

Book

Silverstein, Alvin, Virginia Silverstein, and Robert Silverstein. *Overcoming Acne: The How and Why of Healthy Skin Care*. New York: William Morrow, 1990.

Organizations

The U.S. National Institute of Arthritis and Musculoskeletal and Skin Diseases posts a fact sheet about acne at its website.
http://www.nih.gov/niams/healthinfo/acne/acne.htm

American Academy of Dermatology, P.O. Box 681069, Schaumburg, IL 60168-1069. The AAD publishes a brochure called *Acne*.
Telephone 888-462-DERM
http://www.aad.org

AcneNet is the website created by Roche Laboratories, a drug company, and the American Academy of Dermatology.
http://www.derm-infonet.com/acnenet

▶ *See also*
Abscess
Skin Conditions

Acromegaly *See* Growth Disorders

Addiction and Dependency *See* Alcoholism; Substance Abuse

Addison's Disease

Addison's disease is a chronic condition that results when the adrenal glands are unable to produce enough of certain important hormones. This can lead to fatigue, low blood pressure, loss of appetite, and darkening of the skin.

KEYWORDS
for searching the Internet and other reference sources

Adrenocortical hormone deficiency

Aldosterone

Cortisol

Endocrine system

Hypotension

Metabolic system

*hormones are chemicals that are released by glands throughout the body to help regulate the body's function.

Many people know that U.S. President John F. Kennedy (1917–1963) suffered from back pain most of his life and that he was assassinated in 1963. But it was not until after his death that the public learned that President Kennedy also had Addison's disease. It is a rare condition that results when the body fails to produce enough of certain hormones* that help regulate important body functions.

What Is Addison's Disease?

Addison's disease develops because the adrenal glands do not produce enough of certain important hormones. The adrenal glands are thin triangular groups of cells about the size of an adult thumb. One adrenal gland is located above each of the two kidneys. Among other things, the glands release hormones known as cortisol and aldosterone. But the adrenal glands in people with Addison's disease are not functioning properly, which leaves the people without enough of the hormones they need to keep the body working normally.

Cortisol and aldosterone   Cortisol is needed to help the body respond to stresses such as diseases and infections. It also helps the body use sugars, proteins, carbohydrates, and other substances in food for energy. Aldosterone helps signal the kidneys to regulate the amount of salt and water retained in the body. This is important because without the proper amount of salt and water, blood pressure can drop.

Autoimmunity   Usually in Addison's disease, the adrenal glands do not work properly because the body's own immune system turns against the body and destroys part of the adrenal glands. The immune system releases antibodies to fight foreign substances in the body, like viruses. In Addison's disease, the antibodies and cells of the immune system destroy the outer part of the adrenal glands and cause them to release inadequate amounts of cortisol and aldosterone. No one is sure why this happens.

Other causes   The disease also can result from conditions that affect the functioning of the pituitary gland. People with tuberculosis may develop Addison's Disease if the infection involves and destroys the adrenal glands.

Thomas Addison   The nineteenth century British physician Thomas Addison (1793–1860) was the first to relate the symptoms of Addison's

The adrenal glands are located above each of the two kidneys. When people have Addison's disease, the adrenal glands do not produce enough of the hormones cortisol and aldosterone.

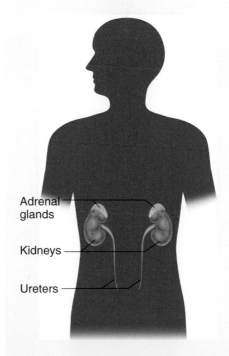

Adrenal glands

Kidneys

Ureters

Disease to problems with the adrenal glands. At that time, it was more common, because tuberculosis was widespread. Fortunately, Addison's disease is rare today. It strikes only about 1 of every 100,000 persons.

What Are Those Puzzling Feelings?

The first signs of Addison's disease can be puzzling to patients and their doctors. The lack of hormones in the body begin to leave the person feeling tired and their muscles seem weak. Patients also can feel dizzy, because of their low blood pressure. Appetite drops, and they start to lose weight from not eating as much. Because salt levels are out of balance in the body, people with Addison's might also hunger for salty foods, like potato chips.

Sometimes, people get sick to their stomachs and vomit, and they can develop dark areas on the skin, as if they are tanning. They also can seem unreasonably upset at things or become depressed.

Addison's usually develops slowly over many years. The symptoms might be noticed, but ignored as simply the result of working too hard or not exercising enough. About 25 percent of people with Addison's disease do not seek medical help until an accident or other illness triggers a sudden worsening of their symptoms. Without medical help, the sudden worsening can be fatal.

How Do Doctors Diagnose and Treat Addison's Disease?

Doctors have various tests to check for the proper levels of the hormones involved in Addison's disease. They also can use an x-ray or other diagnostic tests to get an image of the adrenal glands to see if they look damaged.

People with Addison's need to take prescription hormones to do the work of the missing cortisol and aldosterone. Most of the time, this allows people with Addison's to avoid the disease's symptoms.

They still might experience a return of severe symptoms, if they get ill with another condition. For this reason, doctors recommend that people with Addison's wear a medical identification bracelet that explains their condition. This is in case they become sick suddenly and are unable to communicate with those trying to help them.

With treatment, however, people with Addison's disease can live as long and typical a life as people without the disease do.

Resources

U.S. National Institute of Diabetes, Digestive, and Kidney Disease (NIDDK), Building 31,

President John F. Kennedy in his rocking chair in the White House Oval Office in May 1963. The public did not learn until after his death that President Kennedy had Addison's disease. © *1998 Fred Ward/Black Star.*

Room 9A-04, 9000 Rockville Pike, Bethesda, MD 28992. NIDDK posts a fact sheet about Addison's disease at its website. http://www.niddk.nih.gov/endo/pubs/addison/addison.htm

National Adrenal Diseases Foundation, 505 Northern Boulevard, Suite 200, Great Neck, NY 11021.
Telephone 516-487-4992

▶ *See also*
Hypertension
Immunodeficiency
Skin Conditions
Tuberculosis

AIDS and HIV

AIDS is the most severe form of disease caused by HIV (human immunodeficiency virus), a virus that damages the immune system, leaving a person open to many life-threatening infections.

KEYWORDS
for searching the Internet and other reference sources

Epidemic

HAART

Immunodeficiency

Infection

Protease Inhibitors

Retrovirus

Virology

How Did the AIDS Epidemic Begin?

In the early 1980s, doctors in New York and California began noticing a very unusual disease in a small number of young men. The men, who were mostly homosexual, were developing unusual infections and cancers, and some of them were dying. The infections were similar to those seen in children who are born with very weak immune systems. But these men had been healthy as children and should have had normal immune systems.

Government scientists searched for other cases of the disease, and found more and more of them. The disease also seemed to strike people who had received blood transfusions, and drug addicts who had shared needles with each other. Reports of the disease began to come in from other countries, including African and Caribbean countries, where it seemed to spread mainly by sexual contact between men and women. Some babies were born with it, too.

AIDS   Less than 20 years later, that mysterious disease had become one of the worst epidemics ever to strike humanity. AIDS (acquired immune deficiency syndrome) had killed almost 14 million people worldwide, including more than 3 million children, by the end of 1998. In the United States, AIDS had killed more than 400,000 people, including almost 5,000 children younger than age 15.

HIV   Even greater numbers of people are infected with the virus that causes AIDS, but have not yet developed the disease. In the United States, almost a million people are thought to be infected with HIV, the human immunodeficiency virus, and most do not know they are carrying the virus that causes AIDS. Within 10 years of becoming infected, about half of them will have developed AIDS. Worldwide, more than 33 million people are living with HIV infection, mostly in developing countries in Africa and Asia.

People at risk Like other sexually transmitted diseases, HIV infection is a particular risk among teenagers and young adults. In the United States, more than 110,000 people in their twenties have been diagnosed with AIDS, and it is likely that most of them became infected with HIV when they were teenagers. It is estimated that up to one quarter of all HIV infections in the United States—and half of all HIV infections worldwide—occur in teenagers and people in their early twenties.

Many billions of dollars have been spent to understand HIV/AIDS, to prevent it, and to treat it. Although there is still no cure and no proven vaccine, there has been progress. Because of new drugs, the number of deaths from AIDS fell sharply in the United States starting in 1996. Many Americans infected with HIV are living longer and better lives: they are going to school, working, raising their families, and enjoying life. There is hope that in the United States, HIV will soon be similar to other chronic* diseases, like diabetes or asthma: a serious disease, but one that is manageable with good medical care.

But in most other parts of the world, treatment is far too expensive for people with HIV and AIDS, and the epidemic is growing worse each year. Developing nations in Africa, Asia, the Caribbean, and South America have been hit hard. In some parts of Africa, the virus has infected a quarter of all adults and is reversing years of struggle to improve living conditions. Life expectancy is falling, and infant mortality (the infant death rate) is rising.

** **chronic** (KRON-ik) means continuing for a long period of time.*

AIDS, and the infections that occur in the disorder, can affect many parts of the body.

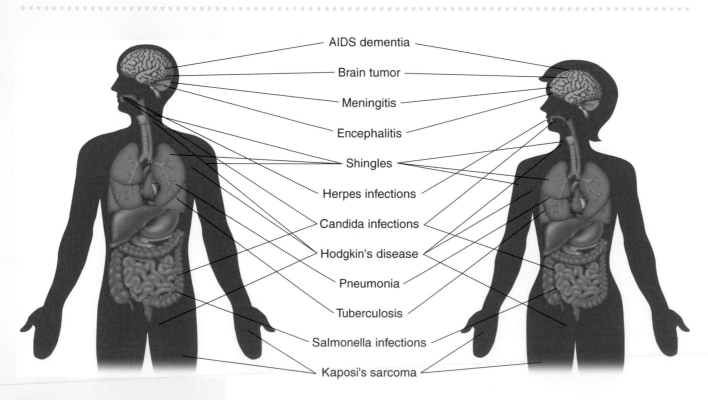

AIDS dementia

Brain tumor

Meningitis

Encephalitis

Shingles

Herpes infections

Candida infections

Hodgkin's disease

Pneumonia

Tuberculosis

Salmonella infections

Kaposi's sarcoma

Even in the United States, it is estimated that 40,000 people a year are still getting infected with HIV and, unless treatment improves, it still appears that almost all HIV-infected people will eventually die of AIDS.

Carl's Family: How Could This Happen?

When Carl's mother told him she had HIV, he could not believe it. After all, she worked full time, kept house, volunteered at church, and was raising two kids alone. She was the last person in the world he could imagine shooting up drugs. And in the eight years since Carl's father had died of a brain tumor, she had not been out on a date, let alone had relationships with men. How could she have caught HIV?

But Carl, now 15, found out that he had not been told the full story of his father's death. Yes, it had been cancer, but it was a kind of cancer—lymphoma of the brain—that is much more common in HIV-infected people. Carl's father had died of AIDS.

"I didn't know it until your father got sick," his mother said, "but when he was a teenager, your age, he got into drugs. He and his friends injected cocaine and heroin. After a couple of years, he stopped, he got his life together, and he even went to college. By the time he met me, he thought that other life was all behind him."

By the time Carl's father realized he had HIV in his body, he was already very sick. And he had already infected Carl's mother. Although a mother can pass HIV to her baby, neither Carl nor his sister was born infected. "It was just luck," his mother said. But Carl did not feel lucky.

How Does HIV Spread?

HIV infection can spread only when an infected person's body fluid (blood, semen, vaginal fluid, breast milk, or any body fluid containing blood) enters the bloodstream or contacts the mucous membrane* of another person.

Sexual intercourse, either homosexual (between men) or heterosexual (between men and women), is responsible for most cases of HIV infection. The virus also commonly spreads among people who share contaminated needles when they inject drugs. Infected mothers may pass it on to their babies during pregnancy, childbirth, or breast-feeding.

If blood is infected, transfusions can spread HIV. But in the United States, blood transfusions have been tested for HIV since 1985, and the risk of infection from a transfusion is extremely low.

Oral sex also can spread the virus, and at least one case has been reported in which the virus is thought to have spread through wet kissing (French kissing).

HIV does not spread through air, water, food, or objects like doorknobs or toilet seats. It is not spread by mosquitoes or by other insects. A person cannot "catch HIV" by playing with, going to school with, shaking hands with, hugging, or even living with an infected person. Fortunately, HIV is much less contagious than many other infections, including chickenpox, flu, or hepatitis B.

* **mucous membrane** is the kind of tissue that lines body openings, such as the mouth, vagina, and rectum, as well as the respiratory, intestinal, and genital tracts.

27

The U.S. and the World

The HIV/AIDS epidemic presents a very different picture in the United States and in the developing nations of the world, where 95 percent of all cases occur.

■ Worldwide, more than 75 percent of all infections in adults result from sex between men and women. In the United States, male-female sex accounts for less than 20 percent of infections, although this percentage has been increasing. Instead, most U.S. infections result from sex between men or from needle-sharing by drug users. The reason for this difference is not clear.

■ Worldwide, the death toll of 13.9 million continues to rise. An estimated 2.5 million people died of AIDS in 1998 alone, including more than 500,000 children, most of whom had been infected before or at birth. But in the United States, the death toll started falling in the late 1990s. From 1996 to 1997, for instance, it fell from 37,525 to 21,909.

■ Worldwide, about 1 in every 100 adults (ages 15 to 49) is infected. But in more than a dozen African nations, more than 10 in 100 people are infected. In some nations, including Botswana and Zimbabwe, more than 20 in 100 people have HIV. In the United States, the overall infection rate is about 1 in 200.

■ Worldwide, the epidemic has created more than 8 million "AIDS orphans," children younger than age 15 who have lost their mother or both parents to the disease. Ninety-five percent of them live in Africa. Less than half of 1 percent (about 45,000) live in the United States.

■ Worldwide, the number of children with AIDS continues to grow as more infected mothers pass on the virus to their babies. But in the United States, the number of children with AIDS fell in the late 1990s because treatment of mothers prevented the virus from spreading to their babies.

How Can HIV Infection Be Prevented?

Prevention of HIV infection is easy—and hard. People can completely protect themselves by never sharing needles, whether for drug use or such practices as tattooing or body piercing, and by avoiding all sexual contact. As people grow up and become sexually active, however, things become more difficult.

Safer sex The safest sexual relationship is between two uninfected people who have sex only with each other, sometimes called a monoga-mous (mo-NA-ga-mus), mutually faithful relationship. But there is no sure way to tell if a person is infected or not. People with HIV may seem completely healthy and often do not know they are infected. In the first few months after infection, they may even test negative on HIV tests.

So if people are sexually active, how can they reduce their chances of infection? One important step is not to have sexual contact with anyone who may be at risk of HIV infection. Who is at risk? Anyone who ever shared needles or engaged in promiscuous sex (had many sexual partners), as well as anyone who ever had a sexual partner who shared needles or engaged in promiscuous sex. Of course, often people are not truthful about past behavior. To judge whether a potential sexual partner is being honest, or is at risk, it may help to know the person well, over a long period of time. Unfortunately, however, that, too, is no guarantee.

Other safety measures Other steps to reduce the chances of infection include:

■ using latex condoms correctly and consistently during sexual activity

■ not engaging in anal sex or other sexual practices likely to cause breaks in the skin

■ not having sexual relations with multiple sexual partners

■ avoiding drugs and alcohol, since their use might prevent people from making good decisions about protecting themselves and others from HIV

■ getting prompt treatment for any sore or blister in the genital area, since these can act as an open door for HIV to enter the body.

What Does HIV Do in the Body?

Once HIV gets into the body, it attacks and enters white blood cells called CD4 helper lymphocytes (LIM-fo-sites). These cells are very important for the proper functioning of the immune system. When the virus begins to destroy CD4 cells more rapidly than the body can replace them, the immune system becomes so weak that severe infections and cancers can develop. The virus also can directly attack some organs, including the brain, the kidneys, and the heart.

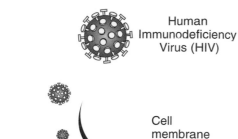

Human
Immunodeficiency
Virus (HIV)

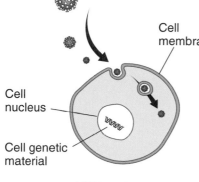

Cell
nucleus

Cell
membrane

Cell
nucleus

Cell
nucleus

Cell genetic
material

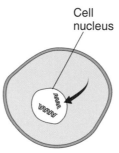

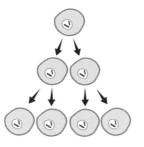

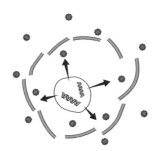

HIV invades
CD4 lymphocyte

HIV inserts its
genetic material
into the cell's nucleus

Dormant state:
1–10 years
HIV reproduces as
cell reproduces

HIV becomes active,
destroying the cell and
spreading widely

HIV is a special kind of virus called a retrovirus (see sidebar) and includes two species, or types. HIV-1, which is far more common and more severe, has caused the current epidemic. Different subtypes of it occur in different parts of the world. HIV-2, which is seen in some parts of West Africa, causes a milder version of AIDS.

One reason it has been impossible so far to find an HIV cure or vaccine is that the virus can mutate and change its genetic features with amazing speed. That means HIV can quickly grow resistant to a medicine, making the drug no longer effective. It also means that any drug or vaccine must be able to work against a wide range of different strains of HIV.

What Are the Symptoms?

HIV Infection Between two and four weeks after people get infected, most people develop a flu-like illness with fever, sore throat, muscle aches, and (often) a rash that looks a little like measles. After two weeks, this illness usually disappears. Others, however, get infected with no initial symptoms of illness. A person can transmit HIV to others without having had any symptoms.

Over the next few years, a person may suffer fevers, swollen glands, fatigue, weight loss, and diarrhea. These symptoms generally occur long before the serious complications that come with AIDS. Some people may have minor infections such as thrush (a yeast infection of the mouth) or shingles (a skin infection caused by the virus that causes chickenpox). Others do not have any symptoms until they develop AIDS itself.

Children, especially those who were infected before they were born, generally develop symptoms more quickly than adults. Often they are sick from birth or may fail to grow and develop at a normal rate.

▲

The retrovirus HIV invades a body cell called a CD4 helper lymphocyte. Once inside the lymphocyte, HIV combines its genetic material with the CD4 cell's genetic material. After that, whenever the CD4 cell reproduces itself, it also reproduces HIV. HIV can destroy CD4 lymphocytes and spread throughout the body during active AIDS infections.

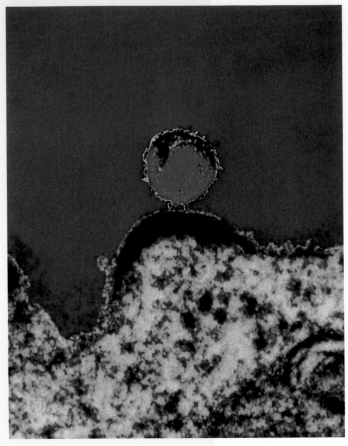

Under an electron microscope, a single virus (HIV) can be seen escaping from the body cell (CD4 lymphocyte) that it had invaded. *NIAID/NIH, Peter Arnold, Inc.*

AIDS AIDS is often heralded by infections or cancers that occur only in people whose immune systems have become very weak. Some of the most common are:

▪ Pneumocystis carinii (nu-mo-SIS-tis ka-RIN-ee) pneumonia (PCP), the most common complication of AIDS in the United States since the epidemic began. It causes fever, cough, and shortness of breath.

▪ Cerebral toxoplasmosis (tok-so-plaz-MO-sis), which can destroy parts of the brain. It usually begins with a headache and often paralyzes one side of the body.

▪ Cryptococcal meningitis (krip-to-KOK-al men-in-JI-tis), an infection of the brain and of the meninges, which is the membrane lining the central nervous system. It begins with fever and headache, and it can cause coma.

▪ Intestinal infections caused by parasites such as cryptosporidiosis (krip-to-spo-rid-e-O-sis) or isosporiasis (i-sos-po-RY-a-sis).

▪ Eye infections caused by cytomegalovirus, which can cause blindness.

▪ Infections caused by bacteria called *Mycobacterium avium*, which resemble tuberculosis.

▪ Cancers, including Kaposi's sarcoma (which causes purplish skin nodules), lymphoma (which may affect any organ, especially the brain and intestinal tract), and invasive cervical cancer (a genital-tract cancer in women).

▪ AIDS dementia, in which people have difficulty thinking, remembering, and concentrating.

▪ In addition, many common infections (such as syphilis and ordinary pneumonia) are more common or more severe in people with AIDS. The most striking example is tuberculosis, which is 100 times more likely to cause illness in a person who has HIV than in an uninfected person.

The illnesses described above often are treatable, and some can be prevented with medication. But they keep recurring. People who are said to "die of AIDS" usually die from one of these illnesses. Worldwide, for instance, it is estimated that tuberculosis kills as many as 1 in 3 people with AIDS.

How Is HIV/AIDS Diagnosed?

Doctors may suspect HIV infection from the symptoms, especially if a person has one of the rare infections mentioned above. But HIV infection can only be diagnosed by blood tests.

Testing for HIV Doctors recommend testing for all people who think they may have been exposed. Testing is also recommended for all pregnant women and for newborns whose mothers either tested positive for HIV or were not tested during pregnancy. Such testing should lead to treatment that cuts the baby's risk of getting HIV from the mother. Treating an infected woman with the drug AZT (zidovudine) during pregnancy and delivery, and treating her newborn with the same drug after birth, reduces the baby's risk of getting HIV from about 25 percent to about 6 percent.

The most common HIV test detects antibodies, which are substances the body makes to fight the virus. This test may not show infection until several months after it has occurred. For that reason, a person who was recently infected may test negative. So people who think they may have been exposed to the virus should be tested immediately and again six months later.

In addition, for the first year or so of life, a baby born to an infected mother may test positive for HIV even if the baby is not infected.

WHERE DID HIV COME FROM?

Since the identification of AIDS in 1981, and the discovery of HIV (the human immunodeficiency virus that causes AIDS) in 1983, scientists have tried to discover the origin of the virus. They came to suspect that it had developed in Africa from a monkey virus known as SIV (simian immunodeficiency virus) and that it might have spread to humans from chimpanzees.

But it was not until 1999 that an international team of researchers found what could be the missing link: a virus that seems to be a genetic blend of HIV and SIV. It was found in one subspecies of chimpanzee, *Pan troglodytes troglodytes*, but it seems to cause them no illness. Researchers suspect that humans first became infected with SIV about 50 years ago when they were exposed to the chimps' blood while hunting the animals for food. Once in humans, it appears, the virus changed into the deadlier HIV we know today.

Researchers were elated at the discovery of the microbe they called SIVcpz (cpz stands for chimpanzee). Because it does not make infected chimps sick, studying what it does in their bodies may help scientists learn how to prevent HIV from making people sick. And it may help them prevent the spread of other viruses to humans in the future.

But the scientists got a harsh surprise. The type of chimp involved, they learned, soon may be extinct in the wild. Logging is driving the animals out of their rainforest homes in West and Central Africa, and they are being butchered as game meat. Now scientists are trying to save the chimps, as well as study them.

"We cannot afford to lose these animals," said Dr. Beatrice Hahn of the University of Alabama, one of the lead researchers involved. "Chimpanzees may represent both cause and solution to the AIDS problem."

What Is a Retrovirus?

One reason HIV is so dangerous is that it is a special kind of virus—a retrovirus. This means that it reproduces itself in a backward or "retro" manner. To understand what that means, it helps to know some basic information about viruses.

Viruses are tiny microbes—much smaller than bacteria—that are made largely of nucleic acid, the substance that makes up genes. They work by invading a cell and using the cell's energy and machinery to make copies of themselves.

The virus's nucleic acid may be either DNA (deoxyribonucleic acid) or RNA (ribonucleic acid). DNA viruses make direct copies of their DNA, and most RNA viruses make copies of their RNA. This copying process is called transcription. Retroviruses contain RNA but copy it into DNA in a process called reverse transcription. Then the viral DNA—called a provirus—is inserted directly into the genetic core of the cell. That means that whenever the cell reproduces itself, by making copies of its own DNA, it also makes copies of the retrovirus's DNA.

In the case of HIV, the virus invades CD4 helper lymphocytes, which are white blood cells important to the immune system.

Testing for CD4 lymphocytes   Once a person is known to be infected, a different blood test is done periodically to see how well the person's immune system is working. The test measures the level of CD4 lymphocytes, the type of white blood cell targeted by HIV. If the number of these cells falls below a certain level—or if the person has certain severe infections like those described earlier—then the person is said to have AIDS.

How Is HIV/AIDS Treated?

Drugs to fight the virus directly are generally prescribed as soon after infection as possible. These drugs block protease and reverse transcriptase, which are important enzymes* that the virus makes in order to reproduce itself. The drugs are used in combinations of three to five medications, which is a form of treatment called HAART (highly active antiretroviral therapy).

The most powerful of these drugs are also the newest, so no one knows how effective they may be in the long run. But it is clear that they postpone the development of AIDS and often make other symptoms less frequent and less severe. Unfortunately, HIV may become resistant to one or more of the drugs. In addition, all the anti-HIV drugs have side effects that make them difficult for many patients to take. It is not yet known whether these drugs reduce the chance that an infected person will pass HIV to someone else.

Besides the antiviral drugs that attack HIV directly, other medications can help prevent or treat some of the serious infections that come with AIDS.

Bob's Story: Hanging on for Something Better

Bob became infected with HIV as a teenager, when he began to realize he was gay and had sex with a series of strangers without using condoms. At the time, he was feeling confused, lonely, and reckless. But he also thought his sexual partners were too young to be infected.

Now Bob is 25 and has AIDS, but his doctor says he is doing well. To keep things that way, Bob takes five different medicines—19 pills—every day. Two of them are easy: he takes one pill each to prevent pneumonia and to control a yeast infection that he always seems to have in his mouth and throat. The pneumonia pill is big and hard to swallow, but the other one is not as bad. The other three medicines attack HIV directly. They include AZT, the oldest anti-HIV drug; epivir, a newer but similar drug, and nelfinavir, a type of drug called a protease inhibitor. Bob is supposed to take six pills in the morning, five at lunchtime, and six at suppertime.

Bob drives a cab. When he gets busy at work, it is hard for him to remember to take the pills at just the right time and to be sure he has water with him. Plus, the nelfinavir gives him diarrhea. He has also noticed that he is beginning to develop a large pot belly. His doctor warned him that the nelfinavir might cause this.

* **enzymes** are natural substances that speed up specific chemical reactions in the body.

Histoplasmosis and HIV

In some areas of the United States, especially southern and southwestern areas, almost 80 percent of the population tests positive for the fungal infection histoplasmosis (his-to-plaz-MO-sis).

In the past, only people with severe cases of histoplasmosis required treatment, but HIV and AIDS have caused an increase in those numbers.

People with HIV, AIDS, and other immune system diseases should avoid activities that increase their chance of exposure to histoplasmosis. Such activities include cleaning chicken coops, disturbing soil beneath bird-roosting sites, and exploring caves. Once infected, people with histoplasmosis and HIV require ongoing treatment.

Some days he feels encouraged thinking how the drugs are helping him. Other days he gets so depressed about all the pills and the side effects that he feels like giving up. But for now, he has decided to do what the doctor said and try never to miss a single dose. He just hopes he can keep hanging on and that better medicines come out soon.

Living with HIV/AIDS

In the early days of the epidemic, parents picketed outside schools to keep HIV-infected children out, and workers feared sitting next to someone with AIDS. Today, most Americans realize that HIV cannot be caught just by being around someone who has it. But people infected with HIV still can face stigma and discrimination. For many people, telling family and friends they are infected also means revealing something they have been keeping secret about themselves—that they are gay, or that they have used illegal drugs, or that they have had sex with many people. This can be very difficult, especially for young people who are gay and may fear rejection by their families. Often, however, people with HIV find that family and friends are very supportive.

To help stay healthy with HIV, good health habits become even more important. These include:

- for everyone: eating ample amounts of nutritious food, exercising, and getting adequate rest

- for drug addicts: stopping drug use

- for smokers: quitting smoking

- for people who have no symptoms: getting regular check-ups, preferably by doctors who have a lot of experience treating HIV/AIDS

- for people who are taking medications: taking them properly and consistently, because taking these medicines on and off can cause a person's virus to become resistant to them.

Many people with HIV live normal lives for many years. Even those who struggle with bouts of illness often carry on with great fortitude and continue to enjoy their lives, just like people with any other chronic, life-threatening illness.

Resources

Books

Brodman, Michael, M.D., John Thacker, and Rachel Kranz. *Straight Talk About Sexually Transmitted Diseases*. New York: Facts on File, 1994. This book focuses on prevention for young people and includes explicit discussion of more and less risky sexual activity.

Protease Inhibitors

Protease (PRO-tee-ace) inhibitors slow down the spread of HIV. Protease is an enzyme that HIV uses to cut long protein chains and other enzymes into small pieces. HIV then uses the small pieces to make copies of itself. Protease inhibitors are drugs that are similar to the protein chains that the protease enzyme normally cuts. The inhibitors work by interfering with the cutting action.

Protease inhibitors do not stop HIV from making copies of itself, but with use of the inhibitors, many of the HIV copies are defective containing improperly cut pieces.

Because the copies are defective, they cannot infect other cells. Protease inhibitors do not kill the virus, but they greatly reduce the number of infectious virus copies made, which slows down the spread of HIV through the body.

Ervin Magic Johnson retired from the Los Angeles Lakers basketball team after he learned he was infected with HIV. *Reuters/Lee Celanos, Archive Photos.*

Monette, Paul. *Borrowed Time: An AIDS Memoir*. New York: Harcourt, 1998. This is the story of a gay couple living with AIDS during the early days of the epidemic.

Organizations

Aegis.com. This is an online AIDS bulletin board service run by a non-profit foundation. Its database is particularly strong on treatment options, news articles from around the world, history, and legal rulings. It offers a package called *The Basics* for people who have just learned they have HIV. http://www.aegis.com

National AIDS Hotline/HIV Hotline. This 24-hour service is run under the auspices of the U.S. Centers for Disease Control and Prevention (CDC).
Telephone 800-342-AIDS

The National Institutes of Health offer information on their website. http://ww.niaid.nih.gov/publications/hivaids.htm

The U.S. Centers for Disease Control and Prevention (CDC) has a Division of HIV/AIDS Prevention website that offers information and links to other federal websites.
http://www.cdc.gov/aids
http://www.cdc.gov/hiv
http://www.cdc.gov/nchstp/hiv_aids/dhap.htm

The World Health Organization's WHO Initiative on HIV/AIDS and Sexually Transmitted Infections (HIS) posts country-specific information and fact sheets about AIDS at its website.
http://www.who.int/asd/

▶ See also
Cancer
Cyclosporiasis and Cryptosporidiosis
Cytomegalovirus
Immunodeficiency
Lymphoma/Hodgkin's Disease
Meningitis
Parasitic Diseases
Pneumonia
Pregnancy, Complications of
Sexually Transmitted Diseases
Shingles
Substance Abuse
Syphilis
Thrush
Toxoplasmosis
Tuberculosis
Uterine/Cervical Cancer
Viral Infections

KEYWORDS
for searching the Internet
and other reference sources

Amelanosis

Hypomelanosis

Hypopigmentation

Melanocytes

Vision

* **genes** are chemicals in the body that help determine a person's characteristics, such as hair or eye color. They are inherited from a person's parents and are contained in the chromosomes found in the cells of the body.

Albinism

Albinism is an inherited condition in which a person lacks the usual amount of the pigment melanin, which is the substance that gives color to skin, hair, and eyes.

What Is Albinism?

Albinism (AL-bi-niz-im) is a disorder that occurs when a person inherits various genes* that are defective in their ability to make the pigment melanin (MEL-a-nin). Melanin is the main substance that determines a person's skin, hair, and eye color. In the United States, albinism affects approximately 1 in 17,000 people.

The outward signs of albinism vary depending on the amount of pigment a person has, and many people with albinism have skin much lighter than that of their family members. People with albinism also may have white or pale yellow hair, and light-colored eyes. Sometimes the eyes look pink because they contain no pigment to mask the red of the blood vessels in the retina*.

Albinism always affects vision to some degree. The genes that cause albinism also cause abnormal development of the nerve connections between the eyes and the brain. The retina and the iris (the colored portion of the eye) are also affected by albinism.

What Causes Albinism?

Albinism is an inherited condition that can be caused by a number of different genes.

- **Type 1 albinism:** This form of albinism is characterized by almost no pigmentation and is caused by a defect in a gene for an enzyme* that makes pigment.

- **Type 2 albinism:** People with Type 2 albinism usually have some pigmentation; this type is caused by a defect in a gene called the "P" gene.

- **Hermansky-Pudlak syndrome (HPS):** A different defective gene causes Hermansky-Pudlak syndrome, which is a form of albinism characterized by easy bruising and bleeding and a susceptibility to lung and bowel disease. Skin, hair, and eye color vary from person to person with HPS.

- **Ocular (eye) albinism:** This form of albinism affects mainly the eyes; hair and skin may not look unusual.

Most people with albinism are born to parents without the condition, but both parents must carry a copy of the defective gene and both must pass on that copy to their child. Albinism is a recessive trait,

* **retina** is the back inner surface of the eyeball that plays a key role in vision. This surface contains millions of light-sensitive cells that change light into nerve signals that the brain can interpret.

* **enzymes** (EN-zymz) are natural substances that speed up specific chemical reactions in the body.

Many people with albinism have skin and eyes much lighter than that of their family members. People with albinism often have vision problems and must take care to protect their skin from sunburn. © *Joe McDonald/Visuals Unlimited.*

* **chromosomes** (KRO-mo-somz) are threadlike structures inside cells on which the genes are located.

Albinism and the Eyes

Vision is always affected by albinism. Vision problems that can affect people with albinism include:

- sensitivity to bright light
- crossed eyes or "lazy" eyes
- back-and-forth movement of the eyes
- farsightedness
- nearsightedness
- blurry vision

▶ *See also*
Genetic Diseases
Farsightedness
Nearsightedness
Strabismus

meaning that if a person inherits even one good copy of the gene, he or she will not have the condition. Each time parents who both carry the trait have a child, there is a 25 percent chance that the child will have albinism regardless of whether it is a boy or a girl. Ocular albinism is the exception; most cases are caused by a sex-linked genetic defect. This means that the defective gene is carried by the X chromosome*, which is one of two chromosomes that determine a person's sex. Sex-linked diseases occur most often in males.

Living with Albinism

Vision problems and protecting the skin are the biggest health problems for people with albinism. The lack of pigment makes eyes and skin very sensitive to sunlight and the skin prone to burning. Vision problems vary from person to person. Some people simply need glasses to correct their vision, but others need surgery. Some people can see well enough to drive a car, whereas others are legally blind. All people with albinism need consistent and continuing eye care.

People with albinism also face social and emotional hurdles as they learn to live with being different. Emotional support from family and friends is essential to building self-esteem in a child with albinism.

Resources

National Organization for Albinism and Hypopigmentation (NOAH), 1530 Locust Street, Number 29, Philadelphia, PA 19102-4415.
Telephone 800-473-2310
http://www.albinism.org

The Hermansky-Pudlak Network, One South Road, Oyster Bay, NY 11771-1905.
Telephone 800-789-9477
http://www.medhelp.org/web/hpsn.htm

Alcoholism

Alcoholism is a disease in which people keep craving and drinking excessive amounts of beer, wine, or other alcoholic beverages, even when the drinking harms their health and causes problems at home, school, or work.

When friends told Roberta she was drinking too much, Roberta kept saying it was not as if she were smoking marijuana or taking cocaine. It was just beer, she told all her friends, something that many people in her school had tried. And besides, she said, her parents drank every night.

A Heavy Drinking Toll

Heavy drinking places a heavy burden on the body. It has been estimated that 25 to 40 percent of the patients in general hospital beds in the United States are there because of illnesses caused by alcohol. These include cirrhosis (scarring) of the liver, hepatitis (inflammation of the liver), and cancer of the liver. But the liver

Roberta's best friend, Mia, sipped a beer with her one Friday before a football game. But Mia decided that drinking beer was not something she wanted to do, even though Roberta kept pressuring her to try it again.

Mia became worried when she saw that Roberta did not seem able to control her drinking. Drinking was all that Roberta talked about during the week: How she would get her older friends to buy the beer; how she and her boyfriend would hide it in her purse and sneak it into the game; and how her parents did not even know she had taken one of their beers last night.

When Mia tried to make a joke about how much Roberta had drunk last week, and asked if that was why Roberta missed their volleyball game the next day, Roberta got mad.

"What are you talking about?" Roberta said. "I only had two beers. And who cares about some dumb game?"

Mia knew that Roberta was lying, because she had seen Roberta take four beers and sip from a bottle of peppermint schnapps. Mia knew that before Roberta had gotten into the habit of drinking, volleyball used to be her favorite sport.

Mia wondered: What was happening to her friend?

What Is Alcoholism?

Among adults in many social circles, a drink or two of an alcoholic beverage is a common part of many social events in everyday life. People have a glass of wine with dinner or toast the bride and groom with champagne at weddings. Fans at sporting events and people at picnics have a beer. There is even some research that suggests that moderate drinking by adults can lower the risk of heart disease and stroke.

"Moderate" drinking is no more than two drinks a day for adult men and no more than one drink a day for adult women and people who are age 65 or older. But millions of Americans drink too much, leading to problems with their health and affecting their families, friends, schoolwork, and jobs. About 14 million people in the United States either abuse alcohol or have the disease alcoholism, according to the U.S. National Institute of Alcohol Abuse and Alcoholism. Other surveys put the number as high as 20 million people. It is a widespread problem, with some experts estimating that more than half of all Americans say they have a close relative with an alcohol problem.

Alcoholism is a disease that can affect anyone, from young people like Roberta to the elderly. The numbers are increasing, especially for boys and girls who are younger than the legal drinking age. More boys and men are affected than girls and women.

People with alcoholism are addicted to alcohol, so they feel a physical and mental urge to drink. As time passes, the person's urge to drink becomes an uncontrollable craving, like a starving person's hunger for food. This craving for alcohol leads people to behave recklessly, and as a result they wind up failing in school, missing work deadlines, or driving drunk. Yet even when their drinking begins to result in bad grades, family fights at home, legal problems, or job loss, people with alcoholism continue to drink unless they seek help.

is not the only organ affected. Excessive drinking also has these effects:

- It raises the risk of cancers of the lip, mouth, neck, esophagus, stomach, pancreas, and breast. People with alcoholism are 10 times as likely to get cancer as the overall population.

- It can raise blood pressure, disturb heart rhythms, and cause heart failure and stroke.

- It impairs memory and thinking ability, ranging from one-time "blackouts," in which the person cannot remember a night of hard drinking, to permanent brain damage and dementia (confusion and memory loss).

- It can cause numbness or tingling hands and feet; painful, swollen muscles; increased risk of broken bones; and infections.

- In men, it can cause impotence (inability to have an erection).

- In women, it can cause infertility (inability to have a baby).

- If continued during pregnancy, it can cause the baby to be born with fetal alcohol syndrome, which may include heart problems and mental retardation.

- It can cause uncontrollable bleeding from the esophagus and stomach so severe that a person bleeds to death.

In the mid 1990s, about 20,000 people a year in the U.S. died as a result of alcoholism. Another 45,000 died of illnesses that are considered alcohol related.

Then there are the injuries that drinking makes more likely: falls, fires, drowning, homicides, suicides, and, of course, traffic accidents. Up to half of all adults injured in accidents, crimes, and suicide attempts are thought to have been drinking beforehand.

The U.S. and the World

- The World Health Organization reports that misuse of alcohol is "a major burden to nearly all countries in the world," resulting in disability, domestic violence, child abuse, and death. WHO says there are about 750,000 alcohol-related deaths annually and that "alcohol-related diseases and injuries account for between three to four per cent of the annual global burden of disease and injury."

- Alcoholics Anonymous has almost 2 million members worldwide in almost 100,000 groups. There are more than 30,000 Al-Anon and Alateen groups meeting in 112 countries.

- Almost 82 percent of Americans 12 and older say they have used alcohol sometime in their lives, according to a 1997 survey. About 40 percent between ages 12 and 17 said they had tried alcohol at some point and 20.5 percent of this age group said they used it in the last month.

- Total per capita alcohol consumption in the U.S. has dropped since its all-time peak of 2.76 gallons per person (14 and older) in 1980 and 1981. By 1996, it was 2.19 gallons per capita.

- The top American state for per capita alcohol consumption in 1996 was New Hampshire (4.16 gallons per person 14 and older). The lowest state was Utah (1.29).

*genes are chemicals in the body that help determine a person's characteristics, such as hair or eye color or the risk of getting diseases like alcoholism. They are inherited from a person's parents and are contained in the chromosomes found in the cells of the body.

People who are addicted to alcohol start to need alcohol more often and in greater amounts in order to get the same physical and emotional feelings they used to get when they drank less. Their drinking continues even as their health problems and personal problems increase. If they stop drinking, they may shake, sweat, and feel anxious or sick to their stomach. These are symptoms of withdrawal, their body's adjustment to being denied alcohol.

Not everyone who drinks excessively meets the medical definition of alcoholism. When drinking leads to problems but not all the symptoms are physically dependent on alcohol, the disorder is called alcohol abuse. Alcoholism can almost never be overcome unless the person stops drinking completely. People who drink too much, but who do not have alcoholism (are not dependent on alcohol), sometimes can cut their drinking to moderate amounts. But often they, too, need to stop drinking completely. Fortunately, programs can help people stay sober and help families cope.

"If My Mother Drinks Too Much, Will I?"

Alcoholism runs in families, and many people with alcoholism say they have a close relative with alcoholism, too. But just because a parent or grandparent has it does not mean that the child or grandchild will develop alcoholism. There are many complex circumstances that appear to contribute to whether someone develops alcoholism.

Genes   Scientists know that alcohol is processed differently in the bodies of people with alcoholism, but no direct link between a gene* or set of genes and how alcohol is processed has been proven. It may be that inheriting certain genes results in personality or emotional characteristics that increase the chances that children would abuse alcohol.

Friends and family   The attitudes of family and friends toward drinking alcohol may affect whether people develop alcoholism. Those who abuse alcohol often have family or friends who make it easier or more acceptable to drink excessively.

Stress   The stress of meeting deadlines for school assignments or coping with personal problems is a normal part of life, but some people use alcohol in an attempt to escape stressful situations. People coping with such conditions as depression and post-traumatic stress disorder also sometimes drink excessively. It is important to remember that it is not a weakness that keeps people drinking when they are under the powerful grip of alcoholism. Rather, alcoholism is a disease, much the same as other physical and mental conditions, and its treatment requires support from professionals, family, and friends.

"Is Roberta an Alcoholic?"

Mia told her mother about Roberta's drinking, and about how concerned she was. But it was hard for Mia to believe that her friend really

200 YEARS AGO

Alcoholism first began to be considered a medical problem, rather than a moral one, in the late eighteenth century. In 1788, Thomas Trotter, M.D. (1760–1832) published his *Essay Medical, Philosophical, and Chemical on Drunkenness*, which defined alcoholism as "a disease produced by a remote cause . . . that disorders the function of health."

The temperance movement continued to espouse abstinence from alcohol. In 1846, the American artist Nathaniel Currier (1813–1888) published his lithograph *The Drunkard's Progress:*

From the First Glass to the Grave. Currier depicted a man whose downfall began with "a glass with a friend" (step 1) but ended with "desperation and crime" (step 8) and "death by suicide" (step 9), leaving a widow and orphaned child behind.

Nathaniel Currier's lithograph *The Drunkard's Progress: From the First Glass to the Grave* was published in 1846. *The Library of Congress/Photo Researchers, Inc.*

Drunk Driving

- Almost 40 percent of U.S. traffic deaths involve alcohol. In 1998, the number of people who died in alcohol-related crashes was 15,935. High as that was—one death every 33 minutes—it was the lowest level in 17 years.

- One reason for the decline may have been nationwide efforts to reduce drunk driving. The campaign, focused largely on young people, includes work by such groups as MADD (Mothers Against Drunk Driving) and SADD (Students Against Drunk Driving). Besides seeking tighter enforcement of drunk driving laws, advocates have tried to discourage underage drinking and have promoted alternatives to drunk driving, such as the designated driver. That works this way: if a group of people drink alcohol at a party, bar, or ball game, at least one person (called the designated driver) sticks to soft drinks so that he or she can drive the others safely home.

*blood alcohol level is the amount of alcohol in a person's blood. It can be measured with a device that tests for a small amount of alcohol in the breath. In the United States, most states now consider people impaired if their blood alcohol level is 0.07 to 0.10 or higher.

*binge drinking is having five or more drinks in a row within a few hours.

was a person with a disease, because Roberta had started drinking only a few months earlier. Mia could see that Roberta was showing some of the signs of alcoholism, but she did not understand how it could develop so quickly.

Alcoholism often develops over many years, but it can develop quickly, especially in teenagers. Alcohol is the most widely used and abused drug among young people. Although the legal drinking age in the United States is 21, more than 50 percent of high school seniors and about 25 percent of eighth graders report having used alcohol.

Roberta liked to say that drinking beer was not like using illegal drugs like marijuana and cocaine. But the fact is, the dependency and unfortunate consequences that can result from people drinking alcohol are similar to those that result from taking drugs that are less socially acceptable.

Alcoholism is often considered a hidden disease. People who abuse alcohol become skilled at hiding their drinking. Families sometimes help, because they feel embarrassed by their loved one's actions. Also, as the disease progresses, the alcoholic's tolerance for drinking increases. This means they may appear sober even after many drinks or even with an elevated blood alcohol level*.

There are many signs that indicate people are developing alcoholism. These signs include:

- Drinking despite bad consequences to health or problems at home, at school, or at work.

- Displaying behavior that, if they were sober, would embarrass drinkers or their families.

- Denying there is a problem even when it becomes obvious to others.

- Becoming annoyed at those who criticize their drinking.

- Drinking alone rather than with others, especially to avoid people or situations that had been important in the past.

- Having mood swings or anger when drinking.

- Having blackouts in which they forget what happened when they were drunk.

- Feeling nauseated, anxious, sweaty, and shaky when they stop drinking.

The amount or frequency of a person's drinking is not a factor in determining whether that person has alcoholism. Some people drink excessively every day, whereas others drink in binges* every month or so. Some people drink amounts that would not be a problem for other people, but that are a problem for them. The important thing is whether the amount people drink causes the physical and emotional symptoms of alcoholism and harms their personal lives.

A highway patrol officer uses a Breathalizer field test to screen a driver for evidence of alcohol consumption. © *Custom Medical Stock Photo*.

Blood Alcohol Levels

When people drink alcohol, it passes through their stomachs and intestines and is absorbed into the bloodstream, just like any other food or beverage.

The alcohol gets into the body's cells, especially those in the part of the brain that control behavior. Like a tranquilizer, the alcohol dulls the central nervous system, resulting at first in a relaxed feeling.

The liver eventually converts most of the alcohol into waste products like carbon dioxide and water. But the liver can handle only about one drink per hour. More than that amount begins to make a person drunk, resulting in poor judgment, emotional changes, and problems with walking, movement, and talking. Drinking too much alcohol will kill a person.

The effect of alcohol is complex. A full stomach can slow the absorption of alcohol into the bloodstream. Many men and people who weigh more than average usually do not feel the effects of alcohol as quickly as women and people whose weight is average or less. Alcohol also makes the effects of medications more extreme, especially cold medicines that cause drowsiness. If a person is in poor health, sleepy, or tired, alcohol's effects will increase in that person.

In the United States, most states now consider people impaired if their blood alcohol level is 0.07 to 0.10 or higher. A 100-pound person can approach or exceed that level after drinking only two drinks in one hour. Someone who weighs 140 to 160 pounds could be legally drunk after three to four drinks in two to three hours. And even at lower levels, judgment and driving skills are likely to be impaired.

---

* **impotence** (IM-po-tens) is failure of a man to achieve or to maintain an erection.

How Do Doctors Diagnose Alcoholism?

There are several ways for doctors to determine if a person has the disease of alcoholism. Doctors or other health professionals can use standard screening tests to see if patients have alcohol problems. These tests can include such questions as "Have you ever awakened the morning after drinking the night before and found that you could not remember part of the evening before?" and "Do you ever try to limit your drinking to certain times of the day or to certain places?"

Doctors also can look for physical signs, like liver problems, although these usually indicate that the person has had alcoholism for a long time. The liver is the organ that processes alcohol in the body. Too much alcohol damages the liver over time, causing it to become fat. In some cases, alcoholics develop cirrhosis (si-RO-sis) of the liver (scarring) or hepatitis (inflammation of the liver). Chronic alcohol use also can damage the pancreas.

Alcohol abuse also can cause sleep disorders and malnutrition. It also appears to increase the risk for some forms of cancer and heart disease. People who drink too much are more likely to be injured in car accidents and to become victims of homicides or rapes. Men who drink too much are at risk for impotence*, and women who drink when they are pregnant endanger their unborn babies.

How Do People Recover from Alcoholism?

Treatment for alcoholism can succeed if the person stops drinking now and forever. Doctors do not say the disease is "cured," because patients always are at risk of developing the disease again if they drink. Patients cannot simply cut down on their drinking. They must stop.

Alcoholics often deny they have a problem, which makes it difficult to get them to seek professional help. Family members, friends, school

Alcoholism affects many different parts of the body. ▶

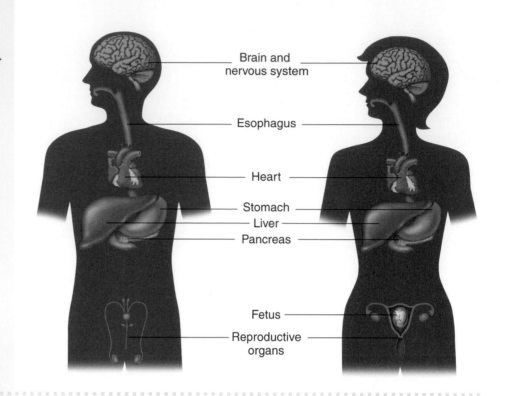

Brain and nervous system

Esophagus

Heart

Stomach
Liver
Pancreas

Fetus

Reproductive organs

counselors, employers, and health professionals usually must take the lead by discussing the alcohol abuse and its consequences.

Experts say it must become clear to the person with alcoholism that there will be no more "rescue missions" if the drinking continues. The person with alcoholism needs to know that if the drinking causes divorce, job loss, or poor performance in school, no one will be there to help, unless the person seeks treatment. It can be a good idea for family members to seek the aid of someone trained in dealing with alcoholism.

If the disease is in its earlier stages, support groups like Alcoholics Anonymous are a first step to recovery. Family members often seek help at Alanon or similar support groups for the emotional troubles they face.

Advanced alcoholism often is treated with a week-long stay in a residential treatment center or hospital detoxification* unit. Doctors help patients cope with the withdrawal symptoms, which in advanced cases can include delirium tremens*. Doctors may prescribe medications that help reduce the craving for alcohol or that cause people to feel sick if they try to resume drinking alcohol.

The recovery from alcoholism's physical and emotional effects can be a long process. Self-help groups like Alcoholics Anonymous, individual counseling with a therapist, and visits with health professionals often are needed.

With treatment, many people with alcoholism recover to resume the parts of their lives that were disrupted when they drank. But sometimes they go back to drinking for a period and once again have problems with their health and personal life. People who are recovering from alcoholism often say they must take life "one day at a time," because they must maintain constant watchfulness so that they do not resume their drinking.

* **detoxification** (de-tox-i-fi-KAY-shun) is the process of breaking dependence on an addictive substance.

* **delirium tremens** are also called "the DTs" or Alcohol Withdrawal Delirium. The DTs may occur two to three days after a person with long-term alcoholism stops drinking. Symptoms include rapid heartbeat, sweating, abnormally high blood pressure, an irregular tremor, delusions, hallucinations, and agitated or wild behavior. The delirium and other withdrawal symptoms usually subside in three or four days.

Resources

Books

Chiu, Christina. *Teen Guide to Staying Sober*. Minneapolis: Hazelden Information Education, 1988. This is a good basic overview on alcohol for people who drink and for those who want to learn ways to say no.

Rodowsky, Colby. *Hannah in Between*. New York: Troll Associates, 1996. This is the story of a woman with alcoholism and how it affects her life and her teenage daughter.

Langsen, Richard C., and Nicole Rubel. *When Someone in the Family Drinks Too Much*. New York: Dial Books for Young Readers, 1996.

Organizations

U.S. National Institute of Alcohol Abuse and Alcoholism, 6000 Executive Boulevard, Willco Building, Bethesda, MD 20892-7003.
This government agency offers lots of good information at its website, including an easy-to-follow list of "frequently asked questions." Some material is available in Spanish.
http://www.niaaa.nih.gov/

Alanon-Alateen offers local support groups and meetings that are free, anonymous, and confidential. Their publications include *Courage to Be Me: Living with Alcoholism* and *Alateen: A Day at a Time*.
Telephone 888-4AL-ANON or 888-425-2666
http://www.al-anon-alateen.org/

Alcoholics Anonymous offers local support groups and meetings that are free, anonymous, and confidential. Their basic program involves "12 Steps" to recovery. Their publications include *A Message to Teenagers: How to Tell When Drinking Is Becoming a Problem*.
http://www.alcoholics-anonymous-anonymous.org/

▶ See also
Cancer
Cirrhosis of the Liver
Depressive Disorders
Fetal Alcohol Syndrome
Genetic Diseases
Heart Disease
Hepatitis
Sleep Disorders
Stress-Related Illness
Stroke
Post-Traumatic Stress Disorder
Substance Abuse

Allergies

Allergies are abnormally sensitive reactions to usually harmless substances in the air people breathe, the things they touch, or the foods they eat.

KEYWORDS
for searching the Internet and other reference sources

Antibodies

Antigens

Immunotherapy

The Immune System

The human body is filled with special cells and organs that stand ready to fight invaders. Together they are called the immune system.

Antibodies   One line of defense in the immune system is a protein called an antibody. These antibodies are like the hall monitors of the bloodstream, constantly looking around for troublemakers. When they spot a troublemaker, the antibody grabs it to make sure it does not cause problems and then removes it. Antibodies are an important way the body fights infections, colds, viruses, and diseases. Antibodies roam through the bloodstream and look for foreign substances that are not supposed to be there.

Antigens Foreign substances in the body are called antigens. Usually, antigens are things we want removed, like a virus. Sometimes, however, the antibodies attack a usually harmless substance that in most people would not cause the immune system to swing into action. There are hundreds of substances in the air people breathe, the food they eat, and the things they touch that may cause this reaction. When it occurs, people are said to have allergies. It is a disorder than affects more than 50 million Americans.

What Are Allergies?

When Latrell plays outside during some months of the year, he sneezes and his throat feels itchy. When Melinda visits an apartment where there is a cat, she finds her eyes start to water. When Mrs. Gonzalez feeds her baby formula with a milk product, the baby cries and seems to have a stomach ache. And when Bobby touches anything with metals like chrome, his skin develops hives.

All of these are examples of allergic reactions. Most people can play outside, pet animals, drink milk, and touch metals without any problems. But for millions of people with allergies, these things and hundreds more can cause their bodies' immune systems to jump into action. Their reactions can be as mild as a stuffy nose or as severe as death.

People can be allergic to many things, but most allergies fall into four main categories:

- Things that are inhaled, such as pollen, dust, mold spores, and pet dander*.

- Things that are eaten, such as milk and items made with milk; eggs; shellfish like shrimp; and peanuts and other nuts.

- Things that are injected, such as penicillin and some other medications, or the venom from an insect sting.

- Things that are touched, such as nickel in costume jewelry, dyes in nail polish and shampoos, and latex*.

How Do Antibodies Cause Allergy Symptoms?

The first time the body's immune system is confronted with a foreign substance like a virus, it remembers the substance. This allows the body's

* **pet dander** refers to microscopic parts of the pet's skin that flake off and get into the air people breathe.

* **latex** (LAY-tex) is a substance made from a rubber tree and is used in such things as medical equipment (especially gloves), toys, and other household products.

immune system to disarm the foreign substance with antibodies the next time it is encountered.

The body can produce millions of different antibodies. Their job is to capture the foreign substance by binding onto it, like two puzzle pieces fitting together. These antibodies are also called immunoglobulins (im-mune-o-GLOB-u-linz).

IgE An antibody known as immunoglobulin gamma E (IgE) causes allergic reactions by attacking substances that are foreign, but which usually are harmless to most people, like pollen, food, and metals. When IgE attacks, it causes special cells known as mast cells to release chemicals that irritate people with allergies.

Mast cells Mast cells are found in large quantities in places like the nose, eyes, lungs, stomach, and intestines. As mast cells release irritating chemicals, the tissues swell and produce the other symptoms of inflammation and allergies.

But why do everyday substances like food cause allergic reactions in some people and not others? Scientists believe the tendency may be something inherited from parents. Other possible reasons range from lifestyle to changes in the environment.

What Kinds of Allergies Do People Have?

Many people have more than one thing that causes their allergies.

Allergic rhinitis The most common allergy is allergic rhinitis (ry-NITE-is), which is commonly known as hay fever. It affects about 35 million people in the United States, many of whom are allergic to pollen and mold spores from plants and trees. Allergic rhinitis causes a runny nose, sneezing, and itchy nose and throat.

Skin allergy Another common problem is skin allergy, whose medical name is allergic dermatitis. Hundreds of substances in metals, cosmetics, shampoos, some medications, and other chemicals can cause an allergic reaction when some people come into contact with them. It causes the skin to itch and develop a rash. About 10 percent of children have allergic dermatitis.

Latex allergy Recently, there has been a lot of interest in allergic reactions to natural latex rubber, which is used in many medical devices, toys, and other things around the house. A latex allergy can cause symptoms like allergic dermatitis, but it also can cause anaphylaxis, the most dangerous allergic reaction, which can cause death unless people are treated quickly.

Insect stings Insect stings can trigger an allergic reaction, including anaphylaxis. The stings can cause minor reactions in most people, like

Allergy Rates and Lifestyles

In the 1960s, about 3 percent of American children had allergic dermatitis, or allergic reactions to things they touched. By the late 1990s, that number had increased to 10 percent. The numbers are similar or even higher for asthma and other allergic disorders. Why the increase?

The American Academy of Allergy, Asthma and Immunology suggests several reasons, ranging from differences in how bodies are functioning, to changes in lifestyle and the environment, to better reporting and diagnoses of allergies.

Lifestyle factors that may influence allergy rates:

- People are living in houses and working in offices that are better insulated than in the past, and they are spending more time in them. This puts them in contact more often with dust mites and other pollutants that cause allergies.

- Poverty also appears to be a factor. Increasing numbers of poor people have asthma, and often cannot get the medical care they need.

Anaphylaxis and Epinephrine

Anaphylaxis is the most dangerous allergic reaction, and it can cause death unless people are treated quickly.

Unlike other allergic reactions that usually affect just the nose, skin, or stomach, anaphylaxis affects many parts of the body. Anaphylactic shock is a medical emergency: the throat and airways to the lungs may swell, causing trouble with breathing. Blood pressure may drop, and people may feel nauseated and have diarrhea and stomach cramps. Without immediate medical treatment, people with anaphylactic shock may lose consciousness and die.

Like all allergies, anaphylaxis results from an abnormal reaction to something that does not cause trouble for most people. People cannot know they are at risk of anaphylaxis until they are exposed more than once to an insect sting, food, or other substance. Common triggers include:

- **Insect stings**, with as many people as 5 percent of the population at risk of anaphylaxis from stings from bees, wasps, or fire ants. About 40 deaths a year result from such stings in the U.S.

- **Medications**, especially penicillin.

- **Foods**, especially peanuts, shellfish, and some food additives.

- **Latex**.

The best prevention is avoiding situations and substances that can cause the reaction.

The most common treatment is epinephrine (ep-i-NEF-rin), also known as adrenaline. People who have had anaphylactic shock often carry epinephrine, which can be injected with a needle.

* **dust mites** are tiny insects that live in dust and in materials like carpets, pillows, mattresses and furniture.

pain, swelling, and itching around the sting. But for some, the sting causes an allergic reaction throughout the body.

Food allergies Reactions to certain specific foods also are common. When some people eat foods like eggs, milk, shellfish, or peanuts, they experience an allergic reaction. It can manifest as itching in the mouth and throat, hives, stomach cramps, nausea, vomiting, or diarrhea.

Asthma Certain foods as well as allergens that are inhaled also contribute to asthma, a chronic lung disease that affects up to 17 million Americans.

How Do Doctors Diagnose Allergies?

The symptoms of allergies are varied and similar to the symptoms of other disorders. For example, a runny nose could signal allergic rhinitis, a cold, or influenza. Diarrhea could mean a food allergy or food poisoning from bacteria in contaminated food.

This can make it difficult for doctors to diagnose allergies. The first thing doctors usually do is take the medical history of both the person with the possible allergy and the history of family members. Doctors are looking for the situations where the allergic reactions occur and whether other family members have a history of allergies, since they tend to run in families. They also want to rule out other possible causes of the reaction.

Doctors may use an allergy skin test. This involves placing a small amount of various substances on the skin to see if any of them cause an allergic reaction. Or the doctors may test the blood for the presence of IgE, the antibody that exists in higher levels in people with allergies than in people without them.

If doctors suspect the allergy is to a particular food or material (like dairy products or latex), they usually try to have patients avoid them and see if the symptoms get better.

How Do Doctors Treat Allergies?

Avoiding allergens Once doctors determine that patients have an allergy, the first line of defense is avoiding the substance as much as possible. In some cases, that can be relatively easy, such as if people are allergic to a particular food, like nuts, milk, or shrimp, or to a substance, like nickel or chrome. Allergies to pet dander can be limited by not having animals in the home and by avoiding them in other places.

It gets more difficult to avoid substances like pollen, mold spores, and dust mites*. But even these things can be avoided to some extent. For example, people can stay indoors more or close their windows during times when pollen and mold spores are high in their areas. And dust mites can be controlled by removing rugs, or by vacuuming rugs often, by covering pillows and mattresses with protective material, by washing sheets regularly in hot water, and by using special filters on heaters and air conditioners.

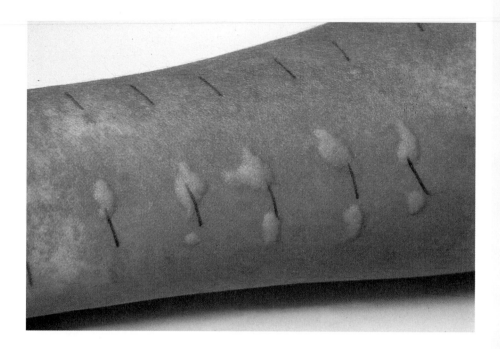

Medic Alert Tags

Medic Alert tags and bracelets are useful for people with drug allergies. Wearing the tag or bracelet can alert medical personnel to the allergy in the event of an accident or loss of consciousness.

Some companies offer medical alert tags that have an identification number that is unique for the individual. In the event of an accident, a doctor anywhere could retrieve the patient's medical history.

"Peanut-Free" Zones

Some schools have discussed the need for a "peanut-free" zone, which would be an area where no peanut or peanut products could be served or eaten. It sounds odd, but the schools are reacting to increasing reports of a dangerous allergy to a lunchroom staple, peanut butter, as well as to other foods made with peanuts.

Peanuts and other nuts are among the most common foods that cause allergic reactions, and the reaction can be particularly dangerous if it causes anaphylaxis. Experts estimate that more people die each year from allergic reactions to peanuts than from bee stings.

People with peanut allergy can react to very small amounts; some may react just from smelling peanuts. Because such small amounts of peanuts can trigger an allergic reaction, some schools have removed peanut butter and similar foods from their menus.

As children grow, they sometimes find that their allergies get better. Until then, it is important to avoid things that cause allergic reactions and, for food allergies, always to read food labels carefully. Food manufacturers sometimes change ingredients, so even familiar foods and familiar brand names may not remain peanut free.

Antihistamines and decongestants　There are many over-the-counter and prescription medications for allergy. Some people take them only when symptoms occur. Others use them daily to prevent allergy symptoms or at least to make them less severe. Histamine is one of the chemicals released in mast cells when people have allergic reactions. Antihistamine medications help neutralize the chemical. Often antihistamines are taken with a decongestant, which helps open nasal passages. Some antihistamines cause drowsiness, although newer versions do not cause as much sleepiness as older ones.

Another alternative for people with allergic rhinitis are sprays that are used in the nose. Some of these help reduce swelling in the nose, and others work to prevent mast cells from releasing their chemicals. Some of these are available without a prescription and others require a prescription.

Immunotherapy　For some patients, doctors suggest immunotherapy, which commonly involves allergy shots. By injecting a small amount of an allergen into patients, immunotherapy aims to help the body become less sensitive by regularly exposing it to the substances that cause the allergic reaction. Immunotherapy is used for people who are allergic to substances like pollen, dust mites, and animal dander, but not for people allergic to foods. The shots are given as often as several times a week at first and then reduced to about once a month for three to five years afterward.

Living with Allergies

Allergies can be anything from an annoyance to a life-threatening illness. Most people, however, can find ways to live with their allergies by avoiding those things that cause them, and by seeking treatment when necessary.

Resources

Books

The American Lung Association Asthma Advisory Group, with Norman H. Edelman, M.D. *Family Guide to Asthma and Allergies: How You and Your Children Can Breathe Easier.* Boston: Little Brown, 1998.

Pressman, Alan, Herbert D. Goodman, and Rachelle Bernadette Nones. *Treating Asthma, Allergies and Food Sensitivities (Physicians' Guide to Healing).* New York: Berkley, 1997.

Organizations

U.S. National Institute of Allergy and Infectious Diseases, Office of Communications and Public Liaison, Building 31, Room 7A-50, 31 Center Drive MSC 2520, Bethesda, MD 20892-2520. http://www.niaid.nih.gov/

American Academy of Allergy, Asthma and Immunology, 611 East Wells Street, Milwaukee, WI 53202. http://www.aaaai.org/

ALS *See* Amytrophic Lateral Sclerosis

Altitude Sickness

Altitude sickness is an illness caused by the lack of oxygen in the air at high altitudes. It is sometimes called "high-altitude sickness."

What Is Altitude Sickness?

Altitude sickness is caused by a lack of oxygen. Altitude sickness can affect anyone at high altitude. The symptoms begin to appear at different elevations above sea level in different people. Altitude sickness usually is seen in mountain climbers, trekkers, skiers, and travelers to high-altitude areas. Factors that contribute to altitude sickness are the person's physical condition and fitness and the rate of ascent to a higher altitude. Altitude sickness usually starts to affect people at an elevation of 7,000 feet to 9,000 feet above sea level. However, some people experience the effects as low as 5,000 feet.

What Are the Symptoms of Altitude Sickness?

Altitude sickness usually appears within hours of reaching high altitude. Symptoms may include:

- headache
- irritability

▶ *See also*
Asthma
Bites and Stings
Hives
Immunodeficiency
Skin Conditions

KEYWORDS
for searching the Internet and other reference sources

Anoxia

Hypoxia

Pulmonary system

Did You Know?

During the 1968 Summer Olympics in Mexico City, athletes arrived up to two weeks early to help them become accustomed to the altitude. Mexico City is at an altitude of over 7,000 feet above sea level, and many of the athletes live at much lower elevations. The athletes who had trained at a high altitude prior to the Olympics had a distinct advantage.

- dizziness
- muscle aches
- fatigue or insomnia (difficulty sleeping)
- loss of appetite
- nausea or vomiting
- swelling of the face, hands, and feet.

More severe altitude sickness may cause swelling of the brain, which can lead to hallucinations, confusion, difficulty in walking, severe headaches, and extreme fatigue. Severe altitude sickness also may cause accumulation of fluid in the lungs, resulting in shortness of breath even while resting. Severe altitude sickness can be life threatening and must be treated immediately.

How Is Altitude Sickness Treated?

Diagnosis and treatment of mild altitude sickness generally is not necessary because the symptoms tend to subside within a day or two. Doctors sometimes recommend that people with altitude sickness take aspirin or ibuprofen to relieve the muscle aches. Mountain climbers sometimes take medication that prevents or treats many of the symptoms.

Severe altitude sickness is a serious and life-threatening medical condition that must be treated by a doctor with oxygen therapy and medicine to reduce brain swelling and fluid in the lungs. People with severe altitude sickness should be moved to a lower altitude to help lessen the symptoms.

Can Altitude Sickness Be Prevented?

The simplest way to avoid the symptoms of altitude sickness is to ascend to high altitude slowly. This allows the body a chance to become accustomed to the lower oxygen content of the air at high altitude. When people are planning to drive or to fly to a high-altitude location, it is important that they take it easy for the first few days and that they limit physical activity while the body is still getting used to the higher altitude.

▶ See also
Bends
Jet Lag

Alzheimer's Disease

Alzheimer's disease is an incurable disease that strikes mostly elderly people, gradually destroying nerve cells in their brains and little by little erasing their ability to remember, think, and take care of themselves.

KEYWORDS
for searching the Internet and other reference sources

Dementia

Geriatrics

Neurology

Joe's Story

Joe's grandmother seems to do the strangest things. She repeats stories she told him in almost the exact words she used during his last visit. She forgets the words for common objects, like the television or her cane. She puts her purse in the oven and sometimes comes to dinner with her dress inside out.

At times, his grandmother does not recognize him or his mom. That scares Joe the most.

At first, the family simply thought she was getting old. Joe's grandmother is in her eighties, and his mother told him that sometimes at her age people have trouble remembering things.

But over the past year, Joe's grandmother's forgetfulness and odd behavior have gotten worse. She gets angry and is suspicious of everyone. The family now knows her problem involves more than just a touch of forgetfulness, which happens to everyone once in a while.

Joe's grandmother has a disease called Alzheimer's (ALTS-hy-merz).

A Disease That Is Like a "Long Goodbye"

Just as Joe's mother said, as people get older sometimes they have trouble remembering. Alzheimer's disease often seems at first like normal, everyday forgetfulness. But it progresses until the memory problems cause the person to forget, for example, how to tie his shoes or what year it is. As time passes, the person with Alzheimer's fails to recognize loved ones or even remember who he is. Eventually, the disease makes it impossible for a person to live without help.

The disease is sometimes called "the Long Goodbye," because family members feel as if they are saying goodbye to the person they once knew so well as the disease affects their loved one's mental abilities more year after year.

Alzheimer's disease is a dementia* that affects more than 4 million Americans. There are more than 70 types of dementia that can be caused by strokes, Parkinson's disease, alcoholism, and other diseases and conditions.

Alzheimer's disease is the most common cause of dementia. Alzheimer's is very rare in people younger than 65, gets more common with age and is especially common in people over the age of 85.

The brain of a person with Alzheimer's disease contains abnormal plaques, or dense clumps, of a protein called amyloid and abnormal tangles of another protein called tau. The plaques form between neurons, or brain cells. The tangles form within the cells. These deposits prevent the brain from working properly. In addition, the production of a brain chemical called acetylcholine decreases. This chemical is a neurotransmitter, which means that it helps signals move from one nerve cell to another in the brain. So the drop in this chemical hinders communication between brain cells.

The brain in harmed in another way, too. The cells no longer get all the energy they need to work properly because the cell's glucose metabolism (the chemical process that provides the cells with energy) is reduced. Eventually, large numbers of brain cells die, and connections between the cells are broken. Although the German doctor Alois Alzheimer first described the disease in 1906, it was not until the 1980s that scientific and public awareness about this disease became widespread.

* **dementia** (dee-MEN-sha) is a term that describes any condition that causes a person to lose the ability to think, remember, and act.

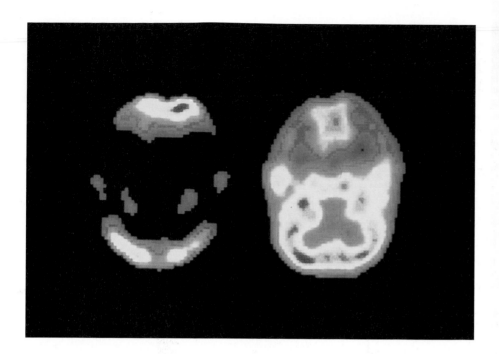

What Causes Alzheimer's Disease?

Alzheimer's disease does not result from any single factor, but rather from a number of factors that combine in different ways for different people.

Researchers have identified at least three genes* that appear to cause some of the cases of the rare familial form of the disease. Almost everyone who has one of those genes, called APP, presenilin-1, and presenilin-2, gets the disease. But taken together, these three genes account for only a small share of all Alzheimer's cases. In addition, scientists have identified at least one gene that seems to play a role in many cases of the more common sporadic Alzheimer's disease. This gene is called APOE, and it comes in three different forms (APOE2, APOE3, and APOE4). The APOE4 version increases the risk of Alzheimer's, especially in people of European or Japanese descent. But unlike the familial Alzheimer's genes, APOE4 does not always cause Alzheimer's. Many people who have the gene do not have the disease, and many people who have the disease do not have the gene. This kind of gene is called a risk or susceptibility gene because it increases risk but does not cause a disease by itself. Scientists think that other factors must interact with APOE4 for the disease to occur and that other genes probably are involved in Alzheimer's as well.

Researchers have suggested that Alzheimer's disease results when the natural processes of aging do not occur normally. The fibers and plaques in the brain of a patient with Alzheimer's disease also are found in the brains of people who do not show signs of the disease. It appears that as a person ages, something causes brain cells to die and clumps of fibers and plaques to develop. But in persons with Alzheimer's disease, this natural process moves more quickly, causing a larger buildup of damaging material in the brain.

Researchers are trying to understand why these changes happen so fast in people with Alzheimer's. There are various possibilities:

* **genes** are chemicals in the body that help determine a person's characteristics, such as hair or eye color. They are inherited from a person's parents and are contained in the chromosomes found in the cells of the body.

*stroke A stroke occurs when a blood vessel bringing oxygen and nutrients to the brain bursts or becomes clogged by a blood clot or other particle. As a result, nerve cells in the affected area and the specific body parts they control do not properly function.

- Minor, undetected strokes* cut off blood supply to parts of the brain. This causes cells to die, and as a result fibers and tangles of dead nerve cells and abnormal proteins develop.

- Infection from a virus might cause damaging processes in the brain.

- An injury to the head, perhaps from a bad fall or car accident, might trigger damaging reactions over time in people with certain genes linked to Alzheimer's disease.

- Lifestyle factors, such as smoking and poor nutrition, might accelerate the aging process.

What researchers do know is that Alzheimer's disease is not a natural part of aging. Alzheimer's is a disease that we are slowly learning about as research continues.

"Who Are You? Get Out of My House!"

The first sign of Alzheimer's disease usually is memory loss. Grandmother cannot remember where she put her car keys. Grandfather forgets to let out the cat. It happens to everyone, they say.

But slowly, a pattern develops. The person forgets the way to the local grocery store, where he has gone for years. Simple tasks, such as making change or using a common device like a phone, start to seem as complex as designing a spaceship.

People with Alzheimer's disease feel anxious in this early stage. But they often become adept at overcoming the problems. If Grandfather forgets names, he might start calling everyone "Sport" or "Pal." If Grandmother forgets how to get to church or a friend's house, she might start asking family or neighbors to take her.

But Alzheimer's disease is like a fog that slowly covers the landscape. Skills continue to erode. At first, perhaps a boiling pot of water was forgotten on the stove, but now the person with Alzheimer's might insist he never put that pot there in the first place, or even forgets that boiling water can burn.

The disease begins to affect the person's ability to perform activities of daily living. She forgets how to use the shower or cook or drive. She may get lost in the neighborhood or drive miles in the wrong direction without realizing it. She often starts to show strange behavior or poor judgment, such as putting jewelry in the freezer or wearing a nightgown to the store.

Sometimes things seem clear. At other times, they are confusing or impossible to understand. As the disease moves through this middle stage, family members become sure something is wrong, especially as their loved one fails to recognize them. Even if clear moments return, the family knows the problem is not just "old age."

By the final stage, things become even more difficult. Memory is so poor that the person might not recognize her own children and grandchildren during any visit. She might have clear memories of her childhood and imagine she is a schoolgirl, but does not remember what grade

Drs. Alzheimer and Kraepelin

Alzheimer's disease was named after Alois Alzheimer (1864–1915), a German physician who studied the cells and tissues of the central nervous system.

Several different doctors had been studying and writing about this disease, but it did not get its now familiar name until 1911. That was the year when the German psychiatrist Emil Kraepelin (1856–1926) referred to it as "Alzheimer's disease" in a published article.

her grandchild is in. Many Alzheimer's patients start wandering, as if looking for something familiar. Others become fearful or angry and yell at loved ones. They often accuse the people who take care of them of wanting to harm them or steal their things. Most people with Alzheimer's disease are cared for at home, which is a challenging task for the family that is compared to a "36-hour day" because the job is difficult both physically and emotionally.

In the end, almost everyone with Alzheimer's disease needs the kind of advanced care a family cannot provide easily at home. They lose control of bodily functions, such as the ability to go to the toilet themselves. They cannot walk or feed themselves and eventually lose almost all ability to speak, think, and act. Many must move into a nursing home with a full-time staff of aides, doctors, and nurses.

Death usually comes from complications related to age, such as pneumonia, heart disease, or malnutrition, rather than Alzheimer's disease itself.

"How Do We Know Grandfather Has Alzheimer's Disease?"

Alzheimer's is a difficult disease to distinguish from other kinds of mental problems. Doctors usually begin by taking a medical history and doing a physical examination to make sure some other condition or other type of dementia is not the real cause of the memory and behavior problems. Many diseases and conditions can cause symptoms similar to those of Alzheimer's. Some, such as vitamin deficiencies, can be corrected easily; others can be treated with prescription drugs.

Doctors also will administer a variety of verbal and written tests to assess how well the person's brain is functioning. They will interview the person and his family about recent events, looking for examples of the symptoms we mentioned earlier. If a person is younger than 60 years old, a genetic test might be ordered, because most cases of Alzheimer's disease in people who are between 40 and 59 years old are linked to the presence of certain genes that can be identified. Sometimes, doctors look for signs of a stroke or abnormal areas in the brain using X-rays or other high-technology equipment that allows a look inside the body, such as a magnetic resonance imaging (MRI) machine. With all this sophisticated equipment and testing, accuracy of diagnosis is 85 to 90 percent.

Once other possible causes of the symptoms have been ruled out, doctors begin to suspect strongly that a person has Alzheimer's disease. If the symptoms continue to worsen with time and no other explanation can be found, doctors say someone has Alzheimer's disease. But at this point, the diagnosis is not confirmed completely without a direct examination of brain tissue at autopsy after the person has died. Doctors look for the presence of plaques and fibers, which look like small, tangled spiral staircases.

"Is Alzheimer's Disease a Slow Death Sentence?"

Research into how Alzheimer's disease affects the brain has led to the development of two drugs that help relieve some of the symptoms in

Did You Know?

- Alzheimer's disease can occur in people in their thirties, but it is most common in people over age 65. Almost 90 percent of cases occur in the elderly, and as many as 50 percent of people over age 85 might have the disease.

- Four million people in America have Alzheimer's. One of the most famous is former U.S. President Ronald Reagan.

- Studies suggest that as many as 19 million adults and children have a relative with the disease. As many as 37 million Americans know someone with it.

- As more Americans live to advanced ages in the 21st century, the number of people with Alzheimer's could reach 14 million.

- The disease costs American businesses more than $33 billion a year. Most of that, $26 billion, comes from employees who must miss work to care for relatives with Alzheimer's disease. The rest is money spent on health insurance, research, and taxes for government programs like Medicare.

- Patients with Alzheimer's disease can live as long as 20 years with the disease. The average person lives eight years after diagnosis of the condition.

some people. The drugs do not cure the disease or slow its progression. These drugs may work by improving how nerve cells communicate in the brain, which can lessen some of the symptoms in people with mild to moderate forms of Alzheimer's. The relief, however, is not permanent, and the drugs do not work for everyone.

Many drugs that offer hope of slowing the disease's relentless march and perhaps reversing some of its effects are under development and could become available in coming years. Currently, doctors may prescribe drugs that can help a patient with Alzheimer's disease with problems associated with the disease, such as depression, sleeplessness, and agitation.

At present, there is no known way to prevent the disease. There are, however, some promising studies. One such study suggests antioxidants like vitamin E might prevent damage to cells, including those in the brain. Antioxidants (an-tee-OX-i-dents) are substances that appear to block the effects of free radicals, which are harmful substances that are created when food is turned into energy in the body's cells. Researchers are investigating whether these free radicals play a role in many diseases, from glaucoma to some cancers, and whether increased intake of antioxidants like vitamin E can prevent or slow these diseases. But they are far from proving this theory.

Scientists have seen apparent benefits in people who take anti-inflammatory drugs like ibuprofen (i-bu-PRO-fen), a pain reliever. Researchers studied sets of twins in which one twin got Alzheimer's and the other didn't. They discovered that often the twin who did not get Alzheimer's disease was taking anti-inflammatory drugs for arthritis. Like antioxidants, the drug might work by blocking cell damage from free radicals.

Another promising area of research involves the benefits of estrogen, a female reproductive hormone. Estrogen levels drop in women in their late forties and fifties as they enter menopause*. Often they take estrogen as a prescription drug, because it controls undesirable side effects of menopause, including the weakening of their bones. Some studies suggest that women who take estrogen have sharper mental skills and face less risk of Alzheimer's disease than those who do not.

A project to test estrogen's benefits for Alzheimer's disease is under way. But doctors warn that estrogen might have harmful side effects for some women, such as some with a family history of breast cancer.

Some people promote the benefits of an over-the-counter nutritional herbal supplement called ginkgo biloba. They say it helps improve memory. One American study in 1997 did show some improvement in patients with Alzheimer's disease who took the extract. But more research is needed to confirm the study. Doctors urge caution because ginkgo biloba can cause problems for people with blood disorders or for those who are on aspirin therapy. Also, like other over-the-counter nutritional supplements, ginkgo biloba does lnot have to meet rigid scientific and government standards and so may vary in strength and levels of impurities.

*menopause (MEN-o-pawz) is the time of life when women stop menstruating (having their monthly period) and can no longer become pregnant.

Living with Alzheimer's Disease

Alzheimer's disease tears apart a person's life as it slowly marches along its course. For the loved ones, like grandchildren, it can be difficult to watch as the disease progresses.

It is important to understand that not all cases of forgetfulness are signs that a beloved grandmother or parent is developing Alzheimer's disease. In most cases, the disease does not appear to run in families, so a grandchild will not get Alzheimer's just because a grandparent has it.

And even if the disease is confirmed, many people live for years when they find ways, with the help of family and doctors, to stay involved with life.

Resources

Alzheimer's Association, 919 North Michigan Avenue, Suite 1100, Chicago, IL 60611-1676, (800) 272-3900. The leading support organization for people with Alzheimer's and their families, with chapters in many communities. The association maintains an extensive library, including many books written for younger readers and available for borrowing. Its website offers detailed information.
http://www.alz.org

Alzheimer's Disease Education and Referral Center, P.O. Box 8250, Silver Spring, MD 20907-8250, (800) 438-4380. Known as the ADEAR Center, it is a resource center on Alzheimer's sponsored by the National Institute on Aging (NIA). It is a place to get the NIA's annual progress report on the disease, as well as other information. The Center's website provides a wealth of informative material.
http://www.alzheimers.org

Mace, Nancy, Peter Rabins, and Paul R. McHugh. *The 36-Hour Day: A Family Guide to Caring for People with Alzheimer Disease, Related Dementing Illnesses, and Memory Loss in Later Life, Third Edition.* Baltimore: Johns Hopkins University Press, 1999. A classic guide for people caring for loved ones with Alzheimer's disease. The title refers to how long the day seems to busy caregivers.

The National Institutes of Health posts information about Alzheimer's disease on its website.
http://www.alzheimers.org/pubs/adfact/html

When Is Forgetting Just Forgetting?

Many older people worry when they seem to forget things, like where they placed a favorite book or the name of the neighbor's grandson. But this does not mean they have Alzheimer's.

Researchers know that as a person ages, they often start to have problems with their memory and retaining new information. "There is probably a direct relationship between the number of reminder notes that you write (or the frequency with which you forget things) and your age," writes Leonard Hayflick, Ph.D., in *How and Why We Age* (Ballantine Books, 1996). "It is firmly established that older people do not perform as well on memory tests as do younger people."

But if it is not Alzheimer's disease, what causes these changes in memory? Part of it involves a slowing of reaction time as we age. That means an elderly person might need more time to respond when they are trying to remember something.

Sometimes, poor eyesight or hearing might make it appear an older person is forgetful. Other conditions, such as fatigue, depression, and even anxiety over looking foolish, can cause an elderly person to forget information.

Amebiasis

Amebiasis (am-e-BY-a-sis) is an infection of the large intestine by the single-cell parasite Entamoeba histolytica *(ent-a-ME-ba his-to-LIT-i-ka). It frequently causes diarrhea or dysentery.*

*parasites are creatures that live in and feed on the bodies of other organisms. The animal or plant harboring the parasite is called its host.

Amebiasis is a disease caused by an ameba, or microscopic parasite*, called *Entamoeba histolytica*. At one stage in the ameba's life cycle, it is enclosed in a protective wall called a cyst. Infection begins when a person swallows cysts in contaminated food or water. Amebiasis is found worldwide, including the United States, but it is most common in tropical areas where sanitation is poor.

When swallowed, the cysts resist destruction by stomach acids and travel to the intestine. In the intestine, the amebae (plural) emerge from their cysts and multiply, usually without causing any symptoms. In some people, however, for unknown reasons, the amebae invade the walls of the large intestine, where they cause abdominal pain, bloody diarrhea (dysentery), and sometimes fever. At this stage, there is a danger that the amebae will invade other body organs.

During the infection, the amebae produce cysts that pass out of the intestines in the stools. Outside the body, the cysts can survive for days or weeks. In areas with poor sanitation, drinking water contaminated with human waste can quickly spread amebiasis and the cycle begins again.

What Are the Signs and Symptoms of Amebiasis?

Most ameba infections are asymptomatic, which means there are no symptoms. Even without symptoms, however, cysts are still produced, and the person is considered a carrier or cyst passer.

Amebic colitis Symptoms occur primarily when the amebae attack the wall of the large intestine. This is known as amebic colitis. The most common symptom is abdominal pain that begins gradually. Additional symptoms may include diarrhea that contains blood or mucus, frequent bowel movements, and a constant nagging feeling of needing to move the bowels. In about one third of cases, fever is present.

Amebic dysentery In rare cases, the symptoms of amebic colitis worsen to fever, chills, and severe diarrhea with blood and mucus. This

▶

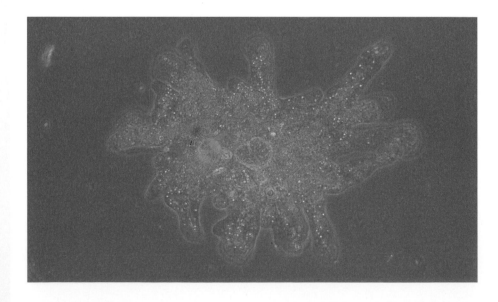

Entamoeba histolytica ameba under an electron microscope. The ameba's extensions are called "pseudopodia" (soo-do-PO-de-a). It uses them to move about and also to surround its food before ingesting it. © 1992 Alex Raksosy, Custom Medical Stock Photo.

condition is known as amebic dysentery (DIS-en-ter-y) and often leads to severe dehydration (excessive loss of body water).

Hepatic amebiasis   If the amebae move through the bloodstream to other parts of the body, pockets of infection and pus can form in other organs. In about 1 percent of cases, the amebae infect the liver and cause a condition known as hepatic (he-PAT-ik) amebiasis. The symptoms of hepatic amebiasis include fever, a distended (swollen) abdomen, and pain and tenderness in the area of the liver just below the right ribs.

How Is Amebiasis Diagnosed and Treated?

The most common method for diagnosing amebiasis is examining stained stool smears under a microscope. *Entamoeba histolytica* also can be identified from samples of tissue obtained during visual examination of the colon with a flexible instrument called a colonoscope (ko-LON-o-scope) or during surgery.

If doctors find *Entamoeba histolytica*, they will prescribe medication for asymptomatic carriers (who can spread amebiasis if the amebae are not killed) and for people with active infections. Treatment usually lasts for about three weeks.

How Is Amebiasis Prevented?

There is no vaccine or prophylactic (disease-preventing) drug for amebiasis. Prevention of amebiasis depends on maintaining clean drinking water supplies, disposing of human waste properly, and using appropriate hygiene measures, such as thoroughly washing hands after going to the bathroom and before eating.

Municipal water supplies approved by local health departments in the United States are usually considered safe. When camping or traveling in other countries, however, it is important to use water only from safe sources and to avoid sources such as mountain streams.

Resources

The U.S. Food and Drug Administration's Center for Food Safety and Applied Nutrition posts a *Bad Bug Book* at its website that includes a fact sheet about *Entamoeba histolytica*.
http://vm.cfsan.fda.gov/~mow/chap23.html

The U.S. Centers for Disease Control and Prevention (CDC) has a Division of Parasitic Diseases that posts a fact sheet about amebiasis infection at its website.
http://www.cdc.gov/ncidod/dpd/amebias.htm

The U.S. and the World

- Nearly 500 million people worldwide may be carrying the *Entamoeba histolytica* parasite, but only about 50 million people develop symptoms of amebiasis.

- Although the *Entamoeba histolytica* parasite is found in the United States, the disease is a much larger problem in developing nations in the tropical areas of Africa, Latin America, and Asia. Poor sanitation, inadequate water treatment, and the use of human waste as fertilizer contribute to the problem.

- Worldwide, amebiasis causes up to 110,000 deaths each year, but fewer than a handful of those deaths occur in the United States.

▶ *See also*
Diarrhea
Giardiasis

KEYWORDS
*for searching the Internet
and other reference sources*

Brain injury

Memory

Mental disorders

Neurologic disorders

*concussion is an injury to the brain that results from a blow to the head. It may or may not cause a loss of consciousness.

Amnesia

Amnesia (am-NE-zhah) is the loss of memory about one or more past experiences that is more than normal forgetfulness.

"Where am I? Who am I? Who are you?"

Many movies and television programs show people losing their memory after a whack on the head. They awake mumbling about their identity. Sometimes the memory even returns after another whack. In reality, physical trauma such as a concussion* can cause temporary or permanent amnesia, but it seldom happens as simply as shown in movies and on television. The idea of fixing a memory problem such as amnesia with another blow is pure fiction.

What Is Amnesia?

Amnesia is a disorder that can have complex physical and psychological causes. It can last from a few hours to a lifetime. The common symptom is an inability to remember the past. The person with amnesia might forget a particular event or one or more periods of time. The amnesia might involve a total loss of memory about the event or period, or it might leave a person with fuzzy memories of the past. In some cases, amnesia might keep the person only from retrieving old memories of events that happened before an illness or injury. In other cases, it might keep the person from storing new memories of events that happened afterward.

Amnesia is not normal forgetfulness. If a student can not recall where a notebook was left, that is normal. If, however, the student can not remember where the school is, the problem might be amnesia. Everyone forgets once in a while, but it is a special concern for older men and women, who often find themselves forgetting names and details. This, too, can be perfectly normal, because the ability to retrieve memories often slows with age. There are, however, specific diseases and conditions that can cause older people to have trouble with memory, such as Alzheimer's disease*.

*Alzheimer's disease is a condition that leads to a gradually worsening loss of mental abilities, including memory, judgment, and abstract thinking, as well as changes in personality.

What Causes Amnesia?

Amnesia can result from a medical disorder or injury, such as Alzheimer's disease, a stroke*, or a car accident. Abuse of drugs and alcohol, lack of certain vitamins, exposure to toxins such as carbon monoxide, and certain prescription medications also can cause amnesia. Psychological trauma can cause people to repress memories. This means that they block unacceptable ideas and impulses out of consciousness. For example, a person who sees a loved one being murdered might find it hard to recall any details of the event.

*stroke is an event that occurs when a blood vessel bringing oxygen and nutrients to the brain bursts or becomes clogged by a blood clot or other particle. As a result, nerve cells in the affected area of the brain cannot function.

How Is Amnesia Diagnosed and Treated?

The first sign of amnesia often is confusion and disorientation. People might try to fill in the blanks in memory or even deny that they have forgotten an event or period of time. If the cause is physical, the reason for the amnesia might be obvious, such as a brain injury or stroke. If it is psychological, amnesia might be harder to diagnose, which means doctors often rely on interviews with family members as well as their own observations.

Treatment for amnesia varies, depending on what caused it. If the cause is physical, the condition causing the amnesia is treated. In some cases, this will reverse the amnesia. In other cases, however, the damage can be permanent, such as from a stroke or drug and alcohol abuse. Amnesia that involves a psychological cause usually is treated with counseling.

Resources

Book

Noll, Richard, and Carol A. Turkington. *The Encyclopedia of Memory and Memory Disorders*. New York: Facts on File, 1994. A reference book about memory problems.

Organizations

American Psychiatric Association, 1400 K Street Northwest, Washington, DC 20005. An organization of physicians. Its website has information about amnesia caused by psychological trauma, Alzheimer's disease, and abuse of drugs and alcohol.
http://www.psych.org

▶ See also
Alzheimer's Disease
Alcoholism
Concussion
Stroke
Substance Abuse

Brain Injury Association, 105 North Alfred Street, Alexandria, VA 22314. A national support organization. Its website has information about amnesia caused by a brain injury.
http://www.biausa.org

Amyotrophic Lateral Sclerosis

Amyotrophic lateral sclerosis (ALS) is a rare disease that affects the motor neurons of the body. These cells make up the nerves that control movement of the voluntary, or skeletal, muscles. The cause of ALS is unknown in most cases, but it is known that some cases are hereditary, or run in families. People cannot catch ALS from each other.

KEYWORDS
for searching the Internet and other reference sources

Motor neurons

Neuromuscular system

Amyotrophic lateral sclerosis (a-my-o-TROF-ik LAT-er-al skle-RO-sis) (ALS) is also called Lou Gehrig's disease after the famous baseball player who died after developing the condition. ALS is uncommon. In the United States, only one or two cases are diagnosed in every 100,000 people in a year. According to the Amyotrophic Lateral Sclerosis Association, about 30,000 Americans have ALS. ALS is rarely diagnosed in people younger than age 40. It occurs more often in men than in women. Fewer than 10 percent of cases run in families. The Pacific island Guam has been reported to have an unusually high number of people with ALS.

What Happens to People with ALS?

ALS affects the motor neurons* of the body. Typically, it produces weakness and paralysis in the muscles it affects, and it causes these muscles to waste away. About 40 percent of people with ALS first notice clumsiness in their hands when they try to perform such routine tasks as buttoning a shirt. Others may become aware of weakness in their legs, or that their speech has become slower.

As time goes on and ALS causes the muscles to waste away, the person's arms and legs become weaker. There may be muscle spasms, weight loss, and difficulty in breathing, eating, and swallowing. ALS does not affect the mind, however, and people with ALS are able to think as clearly as before. There is no loss of sensation, or sense of touch.

People usually die within a few years after they develop ALS. In a very few cases, symptoms may stabilize at some point, remaining the same for years without getting any worse.

How Is ALS Diagnosed and Treated?

Physicians can distinguish ALS from other diseases of the nervous system by its usually late onset in life, and by the progressive nature (worsening of symptoms) of the illness. The fact that the sense of touch is not affected also helps in diagnosis. Multiple sclerosis (MS), a more common disease affecting the nervous system, is similar to ALS, but MS attacks the nervous system in a number of different ways rather than involving only the motor nerves.

Physicians perform different kinds of medical tests to diagnose ALS. Tests may include:

■ EMG (electromyogram), which measures the electrical activity of the muscles

■ CT (computerized tomography), which uses computers and x-rays to record internal body images

■ MRI (magnetic resonance imaging), which uses magnetism to create internal body images

■ muscle or nerve biopsy, in which a small sample of tissue is removed from the body and studied under a microscope

■ blood and urine studies.

* **neurons** are nerve cells. Most neurons have extensions called dendrites through which they send and receive signals from other neurons.

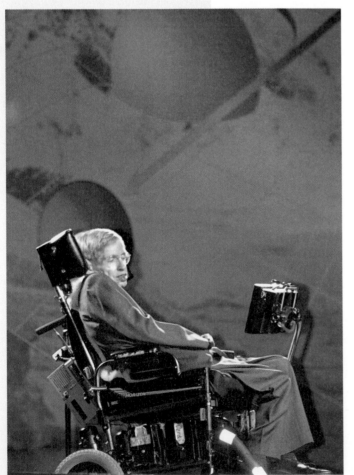

British scientist Stephen Hawking has ALS. ALS causes the muscles to waste away and may be accompanied by muscle spasms, weight loss, and difficulty in breathing, eating, and swallowing. But ALS does not affect the mind, and people with ALS continue to think clearly. Hawking, whose specialty is theoretical physics, is known as a visionary thinker; he has given many popular lectures on astronomy by using a computerized speech synthesizer. *Reuters/Claudia Daut/Archive Photos.*

How ALS Got Its Medical Name

ALS was first described and given its name by the great French neurologist Jean-Martin Charcot (1825–1893). Charcot noted in detail the wasting of muscles (amyotrophy) and the hardening (sclerosis) of motor nerves along the sides (laterally) of the spinal cord. In France, ALS is known as "la maladie de Charcot," and in Great Britain it is called "motor neurone disease."

Is There a Cure for ALS?

There is no known cure for ALS, but there are a few medications that can ease the muscle spasms and possibly even slow the rate at which symptoms get worse. People who have ALS need to be able to maintain an independent lifestyle as much as possible. Physical therapy, such as massage and regulated exercises, can reduce disability somewhat by helping the muscles to work better. Such aids as canes, walkers, and wheelchairs can help people with ALS move about and take care of themselves. Mechanical ventilation (machine-assisted breathing support) is often needed in the later stages of the disease.

Resources

Books

Robinson, Ian, and Maggie Hunter. *Motor Neurone Disease: Experience of Illness*. London and New York: Routledge, 1998. An adult but mostly nontechnical book about ALS.

Robinson, Ray. *Iron Horse: Lou Gehrig in His Time*. New York: Harper Collins, 1991. A biography of Lou Gehrig, containing information about his struggle with ALS.

Organization

Amyotrophic Lateral Sclerosis Association, 27001 Agoura Road, Suite 150, Calabasas Hills, CA 91301-5104. The Amyotrophic Lateral Sclerosis Association website has information about ALS patients, families, caregivers, support groups, health care providers, and ongoing research.
http://www.alsa.org

Lou Gehrig's Disease

Lou Gehrig, who played first base for the New York Yankees from 1923 to 1939, was one of the greatest players in the history of baseball. His lifetime batting average was .340, and he hit .361 in six World Series. He twice led the American League in home runs, and he tied for home runs with Babe Ruth once.

Gehrig, whose nickname was the Iron Horse, also set a major league record in 1939 for playing 2,130 consecutive games. His career ended in that year, however, when he developed ALS. Because of his fame, attention was drawn to this condition. In the United States, it has commonly been referred to as Lou Gehrig's disease ever since.

Lou Gehrig was elected to the Baseball Hall of Fame in 1939. He showed his well-known winning spirit during the recognition day held in his honor at Yankee Stadium on July 4, 1939, when he said: "Today I consider myself the luckiest man on the face of the earth. . . . I may have had a tough break, but I have an awful lot to live for."

Gehrig died of ALS just two years later at the age of 37. His story was the subject of several books as well as the 1942 film *Pride of the Yankees*.

▶ *See also*
Multiple Sclerosis
Paralysis

Anemia

Anemia is a condition that occurs when there are too few properly functioning red bloods cells to carry enough oxygen to the body. Anemia may have different underlying causes. Treatment of anemia depends on its cause and may involve dietary changes, medication, and blood transfusions.

KEYWORDS
for searching the Internet
and other reference sources

Erythrocytes

Hematology

Hemoglobin

Hemolysis

Carrie's Story

When Carrie turned thirteen, she was determined to finally lose all of what she called her "baby fat." She longed to look like the skinny models who graced the covers of the fashion magazines. Carrie stopped eating the well-balanced meals her mother made. Instead, she grabbed rice cakes or low-fat chips to stop the hunger pangs. At about the same time, Carrie got her period for the first time.

It was not long before Carrie started to feel lightheaded whenever she stood up, and in gym class she had to stop and rest every five minutes. Her gym teacher noticed Carrie's behavior and how pale she looked and suspected that Carrie had iron deficiency anemia. This type of anemia is very common in teenage girls because of poor eating habits and iron loss due to menstruation.* At the coach's suggestion, Carrie visited her doctor. Together Carrie and her doctor came up with a healthy diet and exercise plan to help Carrie reach an appropriate weight and keep her iron level normal.

*menstruation (men-stroo-A-shun) is the discharge of bood and tissue through the vagina that occurs periodically to women of child-bearing age. Because it usually occurs at about four-week intervals, it is often called the "monthly period."

What Is Anemia?

Anemia (a-NEE-me-a) is not a disease in itself. Instead, it is a sign that the body has a problem with its red blood cells. The blood of a person with anemia does not contain enough red blood cells or enough of the protein hemoglobin (he-mo-GLOW-bin). Anemia can develop because of poor nutrition, excessive blood loss, destruction of red blood cells, abnormal hemoglobin, or from a number of other causes. But no matter what causes anemia, the result is always the same: the blood does not carry enough oxygen to the cells throughout the body, so the body cannot function normally.

How Is Blood Made in a Healthy Person?

Blood consists of red blood cells, white blood cells, platelets, and plasma. Red blood cells, or erythrocytes (e-RITH-ro-sites), are the most numerous cells in the blood and give blood its red color. The tissues and cells in the body require oxygen to function properly, and erythrocytes are specialized to carry and distribute oxygen because they contain hemoglobin. Hemoglobin has the unique property of being able to absorb oxygen in the lungs, where it is plentiful, and release oxygen to the cells of the body, where it is needed. Hemoglobin consists of four protein molecules, called globins, and up to four heme molecules. The heme molecules are red-pigmented, nonprotein, iron-binding compounds, and they are responsible for binding to and transporting oxygen and carbon dioxide.

In a healthy person, erythrocytes are produced by a process called hematopoiesis (he-ma-tow-po-EE-sis). Hematopoiesis takes place in the bone marrow, which is the tissue that fills the center of most bones. All blood cells originate from one type of cell in the marrow called a stem cell. As red blood cells are produced from stem cells and mature in the marrow, they begin to fill with hemoglobin. A healthy red blood cell contains about 300 hemoglobin molecules, and these take up most of its volume.

When erythrocytes mature, they also get rid of most of the normal components of cells (such as DNA, the nucleus, the endoplasmic reticulum, and the mitochondria). Without these components, erythrocytes cannot grow and divide, so they have a short life. Each cell survives for only about 120 days. The spleen, which is an oval organ located between the stomach and the diaphragm on the left side of the body, contains cells called macrophages (MAK-ro-fayj-ez). The macrophages engulf and break down the old, dying erythrocytes and recycle the iron from the hemoglobin molecules so that it can be used to make more hemoglobin. Every second, about 2 million erythrocytes die, and they must be replaced by hematopoiesis at exactly the same rate.

If the body detects a shortage of red blood cells, the kidneys make a hormone called erythropoietin (ee-rith-ro-po-EE-tin). This protein is secreted into the blood, which then signals the bone marrow to make more red blood cells.

The U.S. and the World

- UNICEF estimates that 2 billion of the world's 6 billion people are iron deficient, which is one of the leading causes of anemia worldwide.

- More than 50 percent of children under age 4 in developing nations are anemic, according to the World Health Organization.

- An estimated 110,000 people worldwide died of anemia in 1998. About 95,000 of them lived in low- and middle-income nations.

- In 1997, 4,471 people died of anemia in the United States. About 65 percent of them were 75 years or older.

- A 1995 estimate put the number of Americans with anemia at 4.1 million, including 2.5 million under age 45.

- The death rate from anemia is about 42 percent higher for women than for men.

- The death rate from anemia is almost 70 percent higher for people of African ancestry than for people of European ancestry.

GRANNY HEATH AND LIVER THERAPY

Before and during the early twentieth century, the ingestion of great amounts of liver served as an effective means for preventing and treating most types of anemia.

In *My Second Life* (1944), author and physician Thomas Hall Shastid recalls his school teacher "Granny Heath," who advocated that, cooked or raw, the liver of just about any farm animal was the perfect remedy for what she called the "littleness of blood."

Medical history records that Dr. George R. Minot (1885–1950), Dr. William Parry Murphy (b. 1892), and Dr. George Hoyt Whipple (1878–1976) were the actual creators of the first effective treatment for pernicious anemia using liver. They were awarded the Nobel Prize in 1934 for their research on blood chemistry and histology, which established the scientific basis for successful use of liver therapy.

What Is Different in a Person with Anemia?

Blood production is a complex process that requires communication between many parts of the body, including the bone marrow, the kidneys, and the spleen. There are many places in the process where something can go wrong. Problems with stem cells, replication and maturation of erythrocytes, the manufacture of hemoglobin, improper signaling between the kidney and bone marrow (erythropoietin), and problems with spleen function (destruction of cells by macrophages) can result in anemia. A person can have anemia because of an inherited blood disorder, because of a blood condition he or she acquired somehow, and even because of diseases not directly related to the blood.

There are several dozen types of anemia that are categorized by their underlying cause. When doctors test blood for anemia, they often describe the blood by the hemoglobin content of red blood cells (color) and by the size and shape of red blood cells. These descriptions can point a doctor toward the underlying disorder. Treatment is specific for each type of anemia and is based on treating the underlying disease.

What Are the Different Types of Anemia?

There are three broad categories of causes of anemia. First, when someone is injured and loses a great deal of blood, anemia can develop because the body's total blood volume is lost faster than it can be replaced. In the second category, the process of making red blood cells in the body is not working normally: bone marrow does not make enough erythrocytes, the erythrocytes do not contain enough hemoglobin, or the hemoglobin does not function correctly. In the third category, red blood cells are destroyed faster than the marrow can replenish them. Some of the most common types of anemia in each category are described below.

First Category: Anemia from Blood Loss

People who lose a lot of blood very quickly, like those who have been injured in an accident, had a blood vessel burst, or have lost blood during surgery, can become anemic because the body cannot make blood as fast as it is being lost. In cases where blood loss is life threatening, a person can have the lost blood replaced through a blood transfusion*. In less severe cases, the body will slowly bring the blood volume and hemoglobin content back to normal by itself. In fact, a person can lose two-thirds of his or her blood volume over a 24-hour period without dying. Other people have a place in their body that is constantly bleeding a little bit, such as a wound in the skin or mucous membranes inside the body (ulcer). In these cases, the source of bleeding needs to be found and treated, and dietary supplements of iron often are needed to help boost hemoglobin production.

Second Category: Decreased Production of Red Blood Cells

Anemias caused by a decreased production of red blood cells are also called hypoplastic anemias, and many different conditions and disorders can cause this kind of anemia.

* **blood transfusion** is the process of giving blood (or certain cells or chemicals found in the blood) to a person who needs it.

Nutritional causes   Certain important vitamins and minerals, such as iron, vitamin B12, and folic acid, are necessary for the bone marrow to make hemoglobin and erythrocytes. If these elements are missing from the diet or are not absorbed from the diet, anemia can develop. Adding food rich in these elements or adding supplements to the diet helps replenish the blood supply.

Iron deficiency anemia occurs when a person does not eat enough foods containing iron or when the body has problems absorbing iron. A low iron level in the body means that there is not enough iron available to make hemoglobin, which results in decreased production of red blood cells. This is a very common type of anemia, especially in infants and teenagers, who need lots of iron to fuel growing bodies. Also, 30–50% of American women are at risk for anemia because of blood loss during menstruation and inadequate amounts of iron in their diets to offset these monthly losses. Iron deficiency anemia is characterized by small red blood cells.

Pernicious anemia occurs when a person does not eat enough foods containing vitamin B12 or is unable to absorb B12 properly. To absorb vitamin B12, the lining of the stomach must produce hydrochloric acid and make a chemical that scientists call "intrinsic factor." If acid production is decreased or intrinsic factor is missing, the vitamin cannot be absorbed. This type of anemia usually affects adults between the ages of 50 and 60, but it is rare in African American and Asian people. People with a poor diet, bulimia, anorexia nervosa, diabetes, or thyroid disease, or who have had stomach surgery, stomach cancer, or a family history of pernicious anemia are prone to this problem. It usually develops gradually, so the symptoms are hard to detect.

Genetic causes   Sometimes people are born with diseases that diminish the body's ability to produce red blood cells. Thalassemia (thal-a-SEE-me-a) and sideroblastic (sid-er-o-BLAS-tik) anemia both occur because the bone marrow cannot produce hemoglobin normally.

Thalassemia is an inherited disorder in which the rate of hemoglobin production is too low. In this condition, the globin portion of hemoglobin is defective. This disorder is most common in people of Mediterranean, African, and Asian ancestry. Thalassemia is divided into two categories: major and minor. People born with thalassemia major have severe anemia during the first year of life that results in slow growth, abnormal bone development, and an enlarged liver and spleen. People with thalassemia minor often do not have any symptoms.

In **sideroblastic anemia**, the heme molecule of hemoglobin is not made correctly. This problem can be a genetic disorder, but it also can occur in people suffering from alcoholism, people exposed to toxins such as lead, or people who have acquired bone marrow disorders.

Aplastic anemia and bone marrow disorders   Aplastic anemia describes a category of anemias in which the hematopoietic (blood-forming) cells of the bone marrow are destroyed. In many cases, doctors do not know why these cells have been destroyed. In other cases, the blood-forming cells are destroyed by cancer of the bone marrow or by exposure to toxic chemicals, radiation, certain antibiotics, or other medications. A bone marrow transplant from an identical twin or from a relative with compatible cell types can be used to treat aplastic anemia, but it is often difficult to find a donor with the right cell type. Finding treatment for aplastic anemia is an active field of research.

Infection and other disorders   People who frequently are ill with infections are prone to anemia because the infection causes the production of red blood cells to slow down. Anemia is very common in people with AIDS because their immune systems* do not function normally and they are prone to infections. People who have diseases of their kidneys often develop anemia because the kidneys no longer respond to decreases in red blood cells by producing enough erythropoietin.

Third Category: Hemolytic Anemias

Hemolytic anemias are caused by the premature destruction of red blood cells. Erythrocytes can be destroyed too quickly or too early because of infection, because the hemoglobin produced is abnormal, because the spleen does not function properly, or because a person has been exposed to certain drugs or toxic chemicals. Red blood cells can have defects in the membrane that surrounds them, which leads to their destruction by macrophages. Hemolytic anemia also can be caused by problems with the immune system.

Sickle cell anemia and genetic causes   Sickle cell anemia is the most well-known type of hemolytic anemia. It is a genetic disease, meaning that a person inherits the genes* for the condition from his or her parents. If the person received only one copy of the affected gene (from one parent), he or she is said to have the sickle cell trait. A person who received the gene from both parents will have sickle cell disease. This type of anemia occurs most frequently in people of African ancestry. In the United States, 0.3% of the African-American population (over 50,000 people) has this disorder. People with sickle cell disease frequently have severe anemia, episodes of pain, delayed growth, and increased infections. People with sickle cell trait usually have no symptoms of anemia and grow and develop normally.

In a person with sickle cell anemia, the hemoglobin is different from that in healthy erythrocytes and it causes the red blood cells to be shaped like crescents. Because of this shape, they cannot easily flow through the bloodstream and they are destroyed faster than the body can replace them.

Autoimmune diseases   People with autoimmune diseases, such as rheumatoid arthritis, can develop hemolytic anemia. In autoimmune diseases, the body's immune system does not work correctly. In addition to destroying foreign cells, such as bacteria that cause infection, the abnormal immune system attacks and destroys its own cells, including

* **immune system** fights germs and other foreign substances that enter the body.

* **genes** are the material in the body that helps determine physical and mental characteristics, such as whether a person has brown hair or blue eyes.

erythrocytes. In some people, drugs that reduce the immune system's activity (immunosuppressives) are used to treat anemia.

How Do People Know If They Are Anemic?

People who have mild anemia often have no symptoms. For people with more severe anemia, how they feel depends on how old they are, how fast the anemia developed, and what other illnesses they might have. If the anemia develops rapidly, a person is more likely to be aware of symptoms. If it develops over a long period of time, even people with moderate anemia may have few obvious symptoms.

Like Carrie, people with moderate to severe anemia may feel tired, weak, dizzy, and short of breath, all because the cells of the body are not getting enough oxygen. This lack of oxygen can cause them to be irritable and lose interest in what is going on around them. Sometimes people with moderate to severe anemia look pale and waxy, and some people develop a yellow color to the skin (jaundice) because of excess destruction of their red blood cells. They can also experience headaches, loss of appetite, indigestion, a sore tongue, bleeding gums, insomnia (difficulty sleeping), a rapid heartbeat, fatigue, and poor concentration. Some women experience menstrual period irregularities.

Doctors as Detectives: Diagnosing Anemia

Dealing with anemia can be a complex process. Determining if a patient is anemic is easy, but finding the underlying cause can be more difficult.

To test for anemia, a doctor usually orders a complete blood count (CBC). A technician or nurse takes a small sample of blood. The blood is tested for the amount of hemoglobin it contains and the numbers and volume of the different types of blood cells. Some of the blood also is smeared onto a slide so that the size of the cells can be measured and the color and shape of the blood can be gauged.

Once anemia has been confirmed, the doctor has to become a detective. The doctor finds clues by examining the patient and by asking the patient and his or her family about their medical history. Here are some of the questions the doctor may ask:

- What are your symptoms, when did they start, and how long have they lasted?

- Do other people in your family have anemia?

- What illnesses have you had recently?

- What do you eat in your diet?

- Have you recently bled a lot?

- What drugs/medications have you taken recently?

Almost all cases of anemia can be identified by laboratory tests along with the patient's history and a physical examination.

What Do Babies and Teenage Girls Have in Common?

Infants and teenage girls are at risk of developing iron-deficiency anemia. Teenage girls are at risk because they lose blood when they begin to menstruate and because they are undergoing growth spurts. These factors combined with an iron-poor diet (many teenage girls are concerned about their weight and how they look, so they go on diets that do not provide enough iron) often result in anemia.

Babies need lots of iron to fuel their rapid growth; their blood volume is expanding as quickly as the rest of their body is growing. Many doctors test 6- to 12-month-old babies for anemia, even if they seem to be happy and healthy, because historically, many babies developed iron-deficiency anemia between these ages. Today, only 2 to 3 percent of middle class infants develop anemia, and this is largely due to the iron added to baby formula and baby cereals. For breastfed babies, the iron in cereal or in supplements is especially important, because breast milk cannot provide enough iron. For older children and adults, adding a food with vitamin C, such as oranges, cantaloupe, or broccoli, helps the body to absorb the iron. Unfortunately, the rates of anemia are higher in poor communities because of poor nutrition.

Eating Right to Prevent Anemia

Good nutrition plays a big part in preventing or treating many types of anemia. A healthy diet should include eating foods every day that contain:

- **Vitamin B12:** meat, fish, and dairy (this vitamin is only found in animal products).

- **Folic acid:** dark green leafy vegetables, meat, eggs, orange juice, and whole-grain cereals.

- **Iron:** beef; molasses; carob; collards, kale, and turnip greens; dried fruit; dried peas and beans; egg yolks; liver; oysters; potatoes in their skin; pumpkin; sardines; soy flour; spinach; wheat germ; whole grains; iron-fortified cereals.

Because the marrow is where blood cells are made, and it is here that many problems can occur, in a few cases a bone marrow sample may be needed in order to find the cause of the anemia. In this procedure, a needle is inserted into the hip bone to obtain a sample of bone marrow. It is then analyzed for the types and activities of the cells.

Anemia is the body's way of saying that something is wrong, and it should never be ignored. The doctor should always search for the underlying cause of anemia.

Scientific Research

Treatment of anemia depends entirely on the cause. Anemia gets a lot of scientific attention because it is a sign of so many different diseases and disorders. Research is focused both on better ways to diagnose anemia and on developing new ways to treat it. In some cases, anemia is difficult or impossible to treat.

For anemias caused by excessive or chronic bleeding, stopping blood loss is the first step. In some cases, a blood transfusion is used to replenish the volume of blood in the body. For people with dietary causes of anemia, eating a diet rich in the deficient nutrient or taking supplements such as iron or vitamins often fixes the problem.

Treatment for other anemias is more complex. For people with hemolytic anemias, finding out why the red blood cells are being destroyed prematurely is essential. In some people, the spleen must be removed to stop the premature destruction of erythrocytes.

One method of treating certain anemias caused by decreased production of red blood cells is to supply the body with erythropoietin (EPO). Different research groups have manufactured EPO to treat anemias caused by rheumatoid arthritis, HIV, kidney disease, and cancer. Other drugs are aimed at stimulating red cell production in people with sickle cell disease and some types of thalassemia.

Resources

Books

Bloom, Miriam. *Understanding Sickle-Cell Disease.* University Press of Mississippi, 1995.

Davies, Jill. *Anemia: A Guide to Causes, Treatment and Prevention.* Thorsons Publishers, 1994.

Davies, Jill. *Recipes for Health: Anemia.* Thorsons Publishers, 1995.

Uthman, Ed. *Understanding Anemia.* University Press of Mississippi, 1998.

Walker, Dava Jo, Van Wright, Cornelius and Hu, Ying-Hwa. *Puzzles.* Lollipop Press, 1996. (This is a children's book about a 9-year-old girl with sickle-cell anemia.)

Organizations

Aplastic Anemia Foundation of America (AAFA, Inc.), P.O. Box 613, Annapolis, MD 21404. The AAFA provides emotional support, patient assistance, funds for research, and educational material about anemia.
Telephone 800-747-2820
http://medic.med.uth.tmc.edu/ptnt/00001045.htm

Sickle Cell Association, Texas Gulf Coast, 2626 South Loop West, Suite 245, Houston, TX 77054.
Telephone 713-666-0300
http://www.sicklecell-texas.org

Aneurysm

An aneurysm (AN-you-rizm) is an abnormal widening of a blood vessel that may cause massive bleeding, shock, or death if it ruptures (breaks open).

Why Are Aneurysms Called "Silent Killers"?

Aneurysms are sometimes called "silent killers" because they may go undetected for years until they break open. The wall of a section of an artery*, vein*, or other blood vessel may become weak and begin to bulge, like an underinflated balloon whose air is squeezed from the ends to the middle. The bulge may grow slowly for years until one day the blood vessel wall gives way. When this happens, it becomes a medical emergency that may lead to death.

Aneurysms occur most often in the aorta, the large artery that runs from the heart down through the abdomen. More than 15,000 people a year die when an aneurysm in this area breaks. Aneurysms can occur in other parts of the chest and body. When they occur in the brain, they may lead to stroke*.

How Do Aneurysms Happen?

Aneurysms result when the normal structure of blood vessels becomes weak in one area. This can occur when fatty deposits of cholesterol accumulate on the walls of the blood vessels but also may result from infection or from trauma or be congenital*. An increased incidence of aneurysm may be seen with certain conditions, such as syphilis or Marfan syndrome. Many times, however, an aneurysm develops without any known cause.

The condition affects many more men than women. It also occurs more often in people who are older than age 55, who are smokers, or who have high blood pressure. People with other family members who have had aneurysms are more likely to develop aneurysms themselves.

Did You Know?

Cooking acidic foods like tomatoes in cast iron skillets or pans can add significant amounts of iron to the diet.

▶ *See also*
Fainting (Syncope)
Hemorrhage
Sickle Cell Anemia

KEYWORDS
for searching the Internet and other reference sources

Cardiovascular system

Cerebrovascular system

Circulatory system

* **artery** An artery is a vessel that carries blood from the heart to tissues in the body.

* **vein** A vein is a vessel that carries blood to the heart. Veins have greater capacity and thinner walls than arteries and contain valves that prevent blood from flowing backward and away from the heart.

* **stroke** A stroke occurs when a blood vessel bringing oxygen and nutrients to the brain bursts or becomes clogged by a blood clot or other particle. As a result, nerve cells in the affected area of the brain, and in the specific body parts they control, do not function properly.

* **congenital** means present at birth.

Monster of a Headache

R.E.M. was rocking their way through Europe during their 1995 "Monster" Tour when drummer Bill Berry got a sudden, terrible headache and could not see. Berry had a brain aneurysm, which was operated on immediately. The surgery was a complete success, and the band was able to finish touring with their excellent drummer.

*ultrasound exams or sonograms use inaudible sound waves that can be projected by special equipment to produce an image or picture of an organ or tissue. This can help doctors to diagnose an illness and determine how best to treat the patient.

People with aneurysms develop bulges in the walls of an artery, vein, or other blood vessel. A: A healthy artery. B: Artery with an aneurysm.

▼

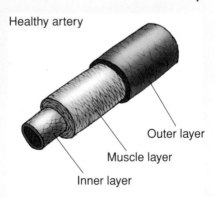

Healthy artery

Outer layer
Muscle layer
Inner layer

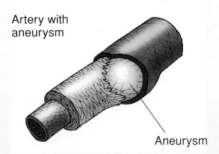

Artery with aneurysm

Aneurysm

There usually are no signs of a growing aneurysm. Sometimes, people feel pain in their abdomen, if that is where the aneurysm is. A large aneurysm in the abdomen may press against the spine and cause back pain. A burst aneurysm in an artery can kill a person quickly. One in the brain can cause symptoms of a stroke, like shock, numbness, paralysis, and vision loss.

How Do Doctors Diagnose and Treat Aneurysms?

Fortunately, many aneurysms can be detected before they burst. Doctors often are able to feel the pulsating sensation of abdominal aneurysms through the skin. Also, aneurysms often cause subtle changes in how the heart sounds, and doctors might notice these changes when listening to the heart. The most reliable methods of checking for aneurysms are x-rays, ultrasound* exams, and other scans that give more detailed images of the body.

Wait and see   If an aneurysm is discovered, sometimes a doctor will adopt a "wait-and-see" strategy, but often this depends on the aneurysm's location, size, and the person's overall health. Small aneurysms might be checked every six months or so to be sure they are not growing. Aneurysms usually grow slowly, especially if the person adopts healthy lifestyle habits, which include not smoking, controlling blood pressure, exercising, reducing weight if necessary, not drinking alcoholic beverages, and eating an appropriate diet.

Surgery   Sometimes surgery is required. One method involves removing the section that is bulging and replacing it with an artificial blood vessel. Newer techniques involve snaking a thin, flexible wire up from an artery in the leg to the aneurysm, where a tube or coils are attached to the artery's walls on either side of the aneurysm.

How Are Aneuryms Prevented?

It is most important to catch aneurysms before they break open. More than 60 percent of people whose aneurysms burst die before they reach the hospital, and a large percentage may die during or after emergency surgery. Regular medical care, surgery, and changing lifestyles allow the vast majority of people with aneurysms to recover.

Resources

The U.S. National Institute of Neurological Disorders and Stroke posts a fact sheet about cerebral aneurysm at its website. http://ninds.nih.gov/healinfo/DISORDER/Aneurysm/aneurysm.htm

American Heart Association, 7272 Greenville Avenue, Dallas, TX 75231. The American Heart Association posts information about aortic aneurysms and many other heart conditions at its website. Telephone 800-242-8721 http://www.amhrt.org

National Stroke Association, 96 Inverness Drive East, Suite I, Englewood, CO 80112-5112. The National Stroke Association website contains information about aneurysms and new surgical techniques. Telephone 800-787-6537
http://www.stroke.org

The Heart and Stroke Foundation of Canada posts a fact sheet about aneurysm at its website.
http://www.hsf.ca/az/atoz-a.htm

▶ See also
Hemorrhage
Marfan Syndrome
Stroke

Angina *See* Heart Disease

Animal Bites

Animal bites are wounds caused by the teeth of a wild or domestic animal or human.

Are Animal Bites Dangerous?

Animal bites can range from mild to serious. When the skin is not broken, bites usually are not dangerous. When skin, muscles, or tendons are torn, bones are crushed, a deep hole is made (a puncture), or the wound becomes infected by germs in the saliva, then animal bites can be very serious. In these cases, a doctor should examine the wound.

Rabies Rabies is a viral disease that affects the nervous system. A rabid animal, whose saliva contains the rabies virus, can infect another animal or a person by biting them. Any mammal* can get rabies, but it is extremely rare among pets or domestic animals in the United States because they are vaccinated against it. Nine out of ten cases of rabies occur

KEYWORDS
for searching the Internet and other reference sources

Infection

Injury

Trauma

Wounds

*****mammals** are warm-blooded animals with backbones, who usually have fur or hair. Female mammals secrete milk from mammary glands to feed their young. Humans are mammals.

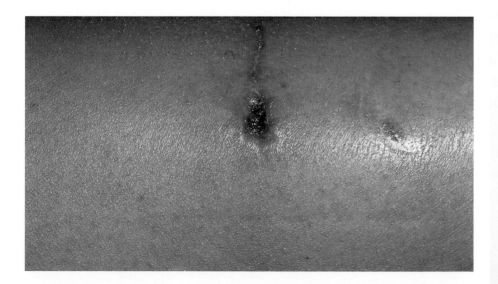

Dog bites usually occur on the hands, face, or legs. This bite is on the leg of an adult. Most dogs do not bite unless they are provoked or teased or protecting their puppies. Children should be taught always to ask permission before petting a dog and never to pet unknown dogs. Dog bites should be examined by a doctor. Infections are rare, but if they do occur, they usually cause redness, swelling, and tenderness around the wound site. *© 1995 Dr. P. Marazzi/Science Photo Library, Custom Medical Stock Photo.*

in wild animals, particularly skunks, raccoons, bats, foxes, groundhogs, and rodents. Rarely is rabies transmitted to people, but people who have been bitten by rabid animals need to get immediate treatment before the infection begins, or they may die. Deaths are rare, however: between 1990 and 1995, only 18 people died of rabies in the United States.

Who Bites and Why?

Household pets, such as dogs and cats, cause the majority of animal bites in the United States, and most bites are from animals known to the person bitten.

Dogs   Dog bites usually occur on the hands, face, or legs. About a million people a year seek medical care for dog bites in the United States, and millions more bites are unreported. Sixty percent of those bitten are children, so dog bites are a major health problem of children. Dog bites rarely become infected, and rabies in dogs is rare. On average, 12 people, mostly young children, die each year from dog bites.

Most dogs do not bite unless provoked or teased, so most dog bites can be prevented by following simple guidelines that include:

- Asking permission from a dog's owner before petting the dog

- Not petting unknown dogs

- Not teasing dogs or pulling their ears or tails

- Not bothering dogs when they are eating or sleeping

- Not bothering a dog who is protecting puppies

- Not running away from a growling dog, but instead backing away very slowly or waiting calmly for the dog to leave.

Cats   Cat bites and scratches also are very common, and they are more likely than dog bites to become infected. Cat bites most often involve the hands, followed by the legs, face, and torso. Rabies is rare in cats, but it is more common in cats than in dogs. One infection caused by cat bites or cat scratches is called Cat Scratch Disease. It causes enlargement of the lymph nodes* but usually goes away by itself after about three weeks.

Humans   Human bites are dangerous because the human mouth contains bacteria that can cause serious infection. The most common human bite wound is a "fight bite," one that occurs when one person punches another person and cuts his knuckles on his opponent's teeth. Children sometimes bite other children or adults, and these wounds result from skin being caught between the teeth. The situation can be made worse when people are embarrassed about the bite and do not see a doctor right away, because delay in treatment can allow an infection to develop.

Other Animals   Mice, rats, guinea pigs, and hamsters sometimes bite, as do exotic pets such as ferrets, snakes, and birds. Horses, mules, sheep,

*** lymph node** is a round mass of tissue that contains immune cells that fight harmful microorganisms. Lymph nodes may become enlarged during infections.

pigs, and goats also can bite. Wild animals like skunks, raccoons, and bats bite thousands of people each year, and these bites can be very dangerous because the animals might have rabies.

Wild or wounded animals should never be approached. If a wild animal that usually avoids people instead starts to approach or to seem friendly, it may be sick. An adult should be notified about a sick animal right away. They should call police or park rangers or animal control officers who have been trained to handle sick and injured animals.

How Are Animal Bites Treated?

All bites should be cleaned as soon as possible. If the skin is broken but not torn or bleeding, the wound should be washed with soap and water and treated with antibiotic cream to prevent infection. If the bite is a puncture wound or is bleeding, pressure should be applied to stop the bleeding. In all cases, the wound should be examined by a doctor, who may recommend antibiotics, as well as a tetanus shot if the person has not had one in the last 10 years.

A person with a bite wound should watch for signs of infection, such as redness, swelling, and tenderness around the wound site. If any of these symptoms appear, they should see a doctor immediately.

Resources

American College of Emergency Physicians (ACEP), 1111 19th Street NW, Suite 650, Washington, DC 20036.
Telephone 800-320-0610
http://www.acep.org

American Veterinary Medical Association (AVMA), 1931 North Meacham Road, Suite 100, Schaumburg, IL 60173.
Telephone 847-925-8070
http://www.avma.org

▶ *See also*
Bites and Stings
Cat Scratch Disease
Rabies
Zoonoses

Anorexia Nervosa *See* Eating Disorders

Anxiety Disorders

Anxiety disorders are a group of conditions that cause people to feel extreme fear or worry, sometimes accompanied by such symptoms as dizziness, chest pain, or difficulty sleeping or concentrating.

What Are Anxiety Disorders?

Everyone worries now and then about things such as passing an upcoming math test or being chosen for a team. However, people who worry

KEYWORDS
for searching the Internet
and other reference sources

Behavior

Mental disorders

Phobias

Psychology

Post-traumatic stress disorder

Separation anxiety disorder

excessively may be experiencing an anxiety (ang-ZY-eh-tee) disorder. One type of anxiety disorder, known as generalized anxiety disorder, involves excessive or unrealistic worry about two or more life issues (such as school, work or money) for at least six months. According to the U.S. National Institute of Mental Health, anxiety disorders as a group are the most common mental disorder in the United States.

What Causes Anxiety Disorders?

It is not clear why anxiety disorders occur. The causes may well vary with the condition and involve a number of factors. Some anxiety disorders tend to run in families, for instance. Other factors may include traumatic experiences or psychological conflicts in a person's past. In recent years, attention has focused on biological factors, chiefly chemical imbalances in the brain.

Neurons*, or nerve cells, are at the center of all mental activity and, therefore, all mental disorders. The brain contains billions of neurons that communicate with each other.

Within each neuron are chemicals known as neurotransmitters*. When a message is sent from one neuron to another, the receiving neuron binds the released neurotransmitter by means of cell structures known as receptors*. Each receptor has a different effect. Receptors have been linked to a number of chemical and cellular effects that are turned on or off, depending on the message. Chemical abnormalities within the neuron can affect this on and off mechanism and contribute to mental disorders.

Researchers have found that people who have an imbalance of a neurotransmitter called serotonin often show persistent anxiety. Serotonin is a chemical that sparks the "fight or flight" response, the brain's normal response to a threat. Faced with pressure from a tough French test or danger from a rattlesnake, the amygdala, an almond-shaped part of the brain, may signal a state of arousal. This, in turn, will trigger the "fight or flight" response. Symptoms include a rapid heartbeat, a jump in blood pressure, sweating, nausea, trembling, and hyperventilation.

In a healthy person, this burst of energy is useful and helpful in responding to a real situation, such as a tough test or a hissing snake. In those with generalized anxiety disorder, however, these symptoms arrive without good cause. Many people continue to have symptoms of "fight or flight" even when there is no real threat. The result is a life so clouded by worry and anxiety at that people cannot function normally at school, at work, or at home.

How Do People Know They Have an Anxiety Disorder?

Generalized anxiety disorder   Although it can develop in adulthood, generalized anxiety disorder often strikes children and adolescents. When people have this disorder, unrealistic worries nag at them most days for at least six months. In addition, they have at least three of these symptoms: restlessness, irritability, a tendency to tire easily, difficulty concentrating, muscle tension, and disturbed sleep. In order to

*****neurons** are nerve cells. A typical neuron has a cell body, several short extensions called dendrites, and one long extension called an axon. The dendrites carry nerve impulses from other neurons toward the cell body. The axon carries nerve impulses away from the cell body to other neurons.

*****neurotransmitters** are brain chemicals that let brain cells communicate with each other and therefore allow the brain to function normally.

*****receptors** are cell structures that form a chemical bond with specific substances, such as neurotransmitters. This leads to a specific effect.

be diagnosed as a disorder, the worry must cause significant distress or get in the way of normal functioning.

Separation anxiety disorder Separation anxiety disorder affects only children under age 18. Children worry excessively for at least four weeks about leaving their home, their parent, or their caregiver. They may fear that something will happen to them if they are separated from the parent or that the parent will never return if permitted to leave. Often these children refuse to go to school, claiming stomachaches or headaches. They may refuse to sleep alone or be alone in the house. They often have nightmares and physical symptoms, such as upset stomachs. Of course, many young children do not like to be away from their parents. For separation anxiety to be diagnosed as a disorder, it must be extreme.

Panic disorder People with panic disorder have panic attacks. During a panic attack, the heart pounds, the hands shake, and people can grow weak and dizzy as pain grips their chest and a sense of unreality—is this really happening?—grips their mind. They may feel as if they are smothering, or going crazy, or about to die. People with severe panic attacks may go to hospital emergency rooms because they are certain that they are having a heart attack.

Panic attacks come on suddenly, without warning or apparent reason, and are over in minutes. Many people have an occasional bout of panic, but only a relatively small number go on to have panic disorder. People with panic disorder have repeated panic attacks and suffer crippling anxiety about when and where their next attack will occur. In extreme cases, they may be afraid to go out of their house for fear they will suffer a panic attack when they are in a place where escape is difficult, such as a crowded bus. This fear is called agoraphobia. Like other anxiety disorders, panic disorder usually starts when people are teenagers or young adults. It is more common in women than men.

How Are Anxiety Disorders Treated?

Treatment for anxiety disorders often involves behavioral therapies that teach people how to deal with worry in a more constructive manner. People with phobias or obsessive-compulsive disorder often are helped by therapy that, in a controlled way, exposes them to the thing they fear until they become accustomed to it and their fear lessens.

Cognitive therapy* can teach people to respond to difficult situations with thoughts that help prevent panic or worry. Relaxation techniques* can help people relieve muscle tension and breathe slowly and deeply so they do not hyperventilate (breathe too quickly and shallowly) and become dizzy. Biofeedback* can help them learn to monitor and control their own brain wave activity.

In addition to these therapies, various medications may help, particularly those that work by balancing out serotonin levels. Medications can be used alone or along with behavioral therapies. Although not a cure, the right drug often can relieve anxiety symptoms. If one drug does not work in a matter of weeks, there usually are others that can be tried.

Other Anxiety Disorders

- **Separation anxiety disorder,** in which children have an extreme fear of being separated from their parent or caregiver.

- **Panic disorder,** which causes sudden bouts of overwhelming terror.

- **Phobias,** which are irrational fears about specific things, such as snakes or flying in planes.

- **Post-traumatic stress disorder,** in which people relive a crisis, such as wartime combat, in nightmares and waking flashbacks.

- **Obsessive-compulsive disorder,** in which people are plagued by unwanted thoughts and may endlessly repeat a ritual, such as washing their hands.

* **cognitive therapy** is a form of counseling that helps people work to change distorted attitudes and ways of thinking.

* **relaxation techniques** are exercises such as meditation that help people reduce the physical symptoms of stress.

* **biofeedback** is a technique that helps people gain some voluntary control over normally involuntary body functions.

Behavioral therapy for separation anxiety disorder may involve both individual and family therapy. Therapists try to teach the parents how to encourage healthier behaviors in the child, and they try to teach the child ways to reduce anxious feelings. Medications also may be helpful for children.

Living with an Anxiety Disorder

One of the hardest parts of living with an anxiety disorder is overcoming the stigma attached to any mental illness. People need to recognize that people with these disorders, like people with any other illness, cannot easily "just stop worrying." The symptoms are real and have a biological basis.

Resources

Books

Lee, Jordan, and Carolyn Simpson. *Coping with Anxiety and Panic Attacks*. New York: Rosen Publishing Group, 1997. A book that offers advice for young people on dealing with anxiety disorders.

Organizations

American Psychiatric Association, 1400 K Street Northwest, Washington, DC 20005. An organization of physicians that provides information about anxiety disorders on its website. http://www.psych.org

Anxiety Disorders Association of America, 11900 Parklawn Drive, Suite 100, Rockville, MD 20852. A national nonprofit organization that promotes public awareness of anxiety disorders. http://www.adaa.org

U.S. National Institute of Mental Health, 6001 Executive Boulevard, Room 8184, MSC 9663, Bethesda, MD 20892-9663. A government institute that provides information about anxiety disorders. Telephone 888-8-ANXIETY http://www.nimh.nih.gov

▶ *See also*

Mental Disorders

Obsessive-Compulsive Disorder

Phobias

Post-Traumatic Stress Disorder

Apnea *See* Sleep Apnea; Sleep Disorders; Sudden Infant Death Syndrome (SIDS)

Appendicitis

Appendicitis (ap-pen-di-SY-tis) is the inflammation of the appendix (ap-PEN-dix), which is a small organ that branches off the large intestine. The inflammation usually begins abruptly, causes a characteristic right-sided abdominal pain, and may lead to rupture or bursting of the appendix and to severe illness.

KEYWORDS
for searching the Internet and other reference sources

Inflammation

Vermiform appendix

What Is Appendicitis?

Acute* appendicitis occurs when the vermiform (VER-mi-form) appendix becomes infected with bacteria. Vermiform means shaped like a worm. The appendix is a narrow, finger-shaped tube, usually 3 to 6 inches long, that branches off the large intestine into the lower right side of the abdomen. Inflammation is the body's response to this infection. Once the appendix becomes inflamed, it must be removed so that it does not break, or rupture, and spread the infection to the rest of the abdomen, a condition known as peritonitis*. The appendix has no known function, and its removal has no adverse effect on the body.

Who Gets Appendicitis?

Each year, appendicitis affects 1 in 500 people. Anyone can develop appendicitis, but it is most common in young people between 15 and 24 years old, and it affects boys more often than girls. Appendicitis is not preventable. Surgical removal of the appendix, appendectomy (ap-pen-DEK-to-mee), is a common reason for abdominal surgery in children. People can die from appendicitis if it is left untreated, but this is rare.

What Happens to People with Appendicitis?

David's appendicitis happened suddenly, when he awoke at 1:00 am with a terrible bellyache. He blamed it on the chips and ice cream he had eaten after dinner and tried to go back to sleep. By 7:00 am, his belly-ache was worse, he was not hungry, and he felt very hot. He told his parents about the intense pain in his right side, and they took him to see the doctor immediately. A series of events followed rapidly.

*acute means rapid in onset, and short-lasting. Conditions that continue for a long period of time are called "chronic."

*peritonitis (per-i-to-NI-tis) is inflammation of the peritoneum (per-i-to-NE-um), which is the membrane that lines the abdominal cavity.

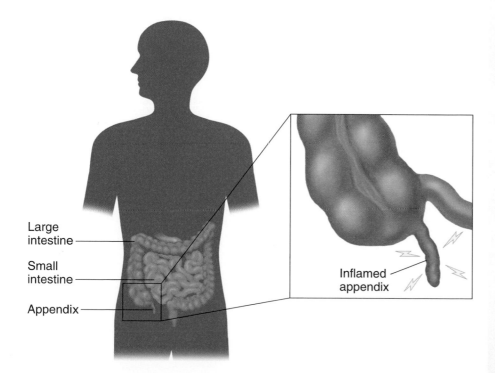

Large intestine
Small intestine
Appendix
Inflamed appendix

Appendicitis occurs when the appendix, located at the large intestine, becomes infected with bacteria and inflamed.

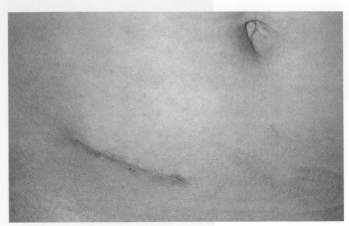

This is an appendectomy scar on the lower right side of the abdomen one week after surgery. New surgical techniques can make scars less noticeable. *Dr. P. Marazzi/ Science Photo Library. Photo Researchers, Inc.*

* **general anesthesia** (an-es-THE-zha) means using drugs or inhaled gases to create a state of unconsciousness and muscle relaxation throughout the body to block pain during surgery. Local anesthesia blocks or numbs pain in one part of the body while patients remain awake.

► See also

Abscess

March 2, 10:00 am   The doctor asked David lots of questions about the pain: Was it constant? Did the right side hurt the most? Was the pain worse when he moved, coughed, or took a deep breath? Was he nauseated? He said yes to all of them. David's abdomen felt hard when the doctor touched it, and when the doctor pushed on the right lower part, David yelled. A nurse took David's temperature and a blood sample.

March 2, 12:00 pm   The doctor returned and reported that David's blood test showed more white blood cells than usual, which is one of the signs of inflammation. David's other symptoms of fever and abdominal pain led the doctor to diagnose appendicitis and to advise David's parents to check him into the hospital.

March 2, 8:00 pm

David had been at the hospital for several hours. The nurses kept checking on him, asking him about the pain, and pushing on his abdomen. The pain did not go away and started to get worse. David's doctor decided that David should be taken to the operating room right away to have an appendectomy (surgical removal of the appendix). To prepare David for the surgery, the doctor explained about general anesthesia* and showed David where he would receive a small cut in the abdomen through which the surgeon would remove the diseased appendix. The doctor and nurses kept reassuring David and his parents that he would be fine as they do this kind of surgery all the time.

March 2, 10:00 pm   David awoke in the hospital recovery room, groggy, tired, and a little sore. His appendix, which had not yet ruptured, had been removed at 8:00 am.

March 4, 8:00 am   David went home from the hospital, minus his appendix, but otherwise healthy. He was still aware of a slight soreness at the site of his appendectomy scar.

Within a couple of weeks, David was back to doing just about everything he had done before his appendicitis. His appendectomy surgery had been a complete success.

Resource

The U.S. National Digestive Diseases Information Clearinghouse posts a fact sheet about appendicitis at its website.
http://www.niddk.nih.gov/health/digest/summary/append/index.htm

Arrhythmia *See* Dysrhythmia; Heart Disease

Arteriosclerosis *See* Heart Disease

Arthritis

Arthritis refers to inflammation of the joints, often accompanied by pain, stiffness, or swelling. Arthritis may occur in many different diseases and medical conditions.

KEYWORDS
*for searching the Internet
and other reference sources*

Autoimmune diseases

Inflammation

Joints

Osteoarthritis

Rheumatoid arthritis

Jenny's Story

For many years, Jenny's father was a dedicated runner. He got up early each morning for a 3-mile jog, and on weekends he sometimes ran as far as 10 miles or competed in road races. He even talked about training for a marathon, which would mean running more than 26 miles in one race. Gradually, however, Jenny began to hear her father mention that his knees were hurting when he ran, and that they remained painful for a few hours after he stopped. Jenny noticed that his knees looked swollen, and that he sometimes had trouble sleeping because the pain annoyed him so much.

Jenny's father assumed the pain was simply a running injury that would get better with rest. But when the pain did not go away, Jenny's father visited a doctor. He was told he had a type of arthritis known as osteoarthritis (os-te-o-ar-THRY-tis). This surprised Jenny, because her father was only in his forties. She thought that arthritis was only a problem for older people like her grandparents.

What Is Arthritis?

Arthritis is a common problem for many older people, but it can affect anyone, from toddlers to centenarians*. Although people use the term as if it were only one disease, arthritis actually refers to a condition found in a large group of disorders. The major symptoms of arthritis affect the areas in and around joints, making them stiff, swollen, and often painful. In addition to the joints, certain types of arthritic diseases may affect other parts of the body, including the heart and lungs.

* **centenarians** are people who are at least 100 years old.

As a group, the various forms of arthritis are among the most common medical conditions. About 1 of every 6 people, or more than 40 million Americans, have it. Arthritis usually is chronic, which means the problem can last to some degree for months, years, or the rest of people's lives.

Arthritis affects millions of people. Although there are many types, the most common are:

- Osteoarthritis

- Rheumatoid arthritis*

- Juvenile rheumatoid arthritis

* **rheumatoid arthritis** (ROO-ma-toid ar-THRY-tis) is a chronic autoimmune disease characterized by pain, swelling, stiffness, and deformation of the joints.

*gout occurs when deposits of uric acid in the joints cause inflammation and pain.

*fibromyalgia (fi-bro-my-AL-ja) is a group of disorders that are characterized by achy, tender, and stiff muscles.

*contagious means transmitted from one person to another.

- Gout*
- Fibromyalgia*
- Lupus
- Lyme disease

These conditions develop for a variety of reasons, but they are not contagious*. Some forms of arthritis, however, can develop from contagious infections, like sexually transmitted diseases or viruses that cause mumps and rubella (German measles). One form of arthritis, Lyme disease, develops from the bite of an infected tick. Sometimes arthritis occurs as one of the symptoms seen in conditions that primarily affect other organs. For example, inflammatory bowel disease may have arthritis as one of its symptoms.

What Is Osteoarthritis?

Jenny's father has osteoarthritis, the most common type of arthritis in adults. About 21 million Americans, almost half of those with arthritis, have this kind. Osteoarthritis is sometimes called "wear-and-tear" arthritis.

Arthritis may affect many different parts of the body, including shoulders, elbows, hands, hips, and knees (left). In healthy joints (top right), a flexible cushion of cartilage allows bones to slide past each other smoothly. But in arthritis (bottom right), cartilage loss forces the bones to touch without their usual cushioning, which creates pain and inflammation.

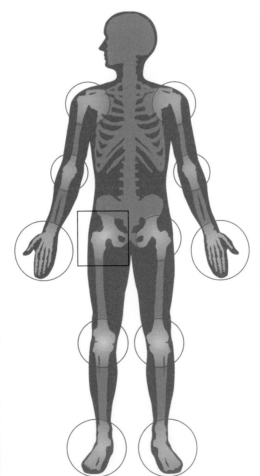

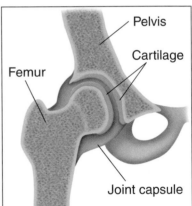

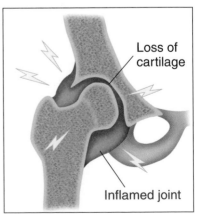

That is because the pain, stiffness, and swelling often result from the wearing down of the protective tissues within and around joints.

More than 150 possible trouble spots The human body contains more than 150 joints that connect more than 200 bones. There are small joints in toes and fingers; larger ones in the spine, elbows, and knees; and even bigger ones like the hips and shoulders. The bones do not touch directly. Instead, a tough, smooth, rubbery layer of tissue called cartilage covers the ends of the bones. When a knee, elbow, or other joint moves, the cartilage allows the bones to slide past each other smoothly. Cartilage also is flexible and absorbs some of the weight placed upon certain joints, such as the knee.

People with osteoarthritis, however, have lost some of the smooth cartilage in their joints. Eventually, the cartilage can wear away so much that the ends of the bones touch without any cushioning. The bones also can grow small spurs or bumps, which is why some people with osteoarthritis have lumps in their joints. These lumps often are most noticeable in the hands.

Those odd pains Osteoarthritis usually is felt first in the knees, hips, feet, spine, or fingers. These are joints that bear much of the body's weight or are used often for everyday activities. The pain increases as the cartilage between the bones is worn down. People often start to avoid using the joint. For example, people might exercise less if pain is in the knees. This only makes the problem worse. It leads to increased stiffness, because muscles around the joints begin to weaken from disuse.

Stress No one is exactly sure why osteoarthritis happens, but often it results from stresses placed on the joint. In the example of Jenny's father, his years of running on hard surfaces caused damage to his knee cartilage. The pounding on pavement was too much stress for the cartilage to absorb.

Other types of stress or injury also can lead to osteoarthritis. People whose jobs involve hard physical labor (like construction workers) or repetitive tasks (like assembly line workers) can develop osteoarthritis. An injury to a knee or elbow also can increase the risk of osteoarthritis. Certain activities like football or ballet can put a person at greater risk for developing osteoarthritis.

Even the stress of too much body weight contributes to the disease. People who are significantly overweight are more prone to osteoarthritis because their weight places extra stress on joints, especially knees and hips.

Age Many older people also develop osteoarthritis, even if they never put extra stress on their joints. That is because as people age, the rubbery cartilage tissue loses some of its ability to stretch and can become thinner. This places people at greater risk for osteoarthritis as they age.

Heredity Not all older people develop osteoarthritis, just as not all runners or laborers do. This is one reason doctors believe heredity may play a role in determining who is at greatest risk for this type of arthritis.

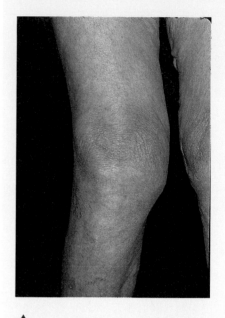

▲

Osteoarthritis is sometimes called "wear and tear arthritis" and often affects the knee joints, making them stiff, swollen, and painful. *Dr. P. Marazzi/Science Photo Library. Photo Researchers, Inc.*

Diagnosis It is important to understand what type of arthritis people have, because treatments vary. Doctors diagnose osteoarthritis based on the symptoms they see. They might look for loss of cartilage and bone spurs with x-rays. Doctors also look for other causes of the pain. For example, blood tests can show if the problem is rheumatoid arthritis instead.

If it hurts, why do doctors want patients to exercise? Once doctors have determined the problem is osteoarthritis, they tell patients something that might seem to make little sense. They want them to exercise the joint. This does not mean Jenny's father should return to running. It does mean he and others with the disease need to work with their doctors to find the best way to exercise.

Appropriate exercise can strengthen the muscles around the joint and help lessen the stiffness. Often, the exercises are different from those done in the past. Some give up running for swimming or water aerobics. Others walk or ride stationary bikes. If the pain is severe, a physical therapist who specializes in helping patients learn appropriate exercises might get involved. If people are overweight, doctors advise them to take off the pounds.

The pain of arthritis is often treated with aspirin or other over-the-counter drugs that reduce swelling. There also are prescription drugs that are stronger and can help if the pain is extreme.

Often the pain of osteoarthritis decreases with treatment. For some people, however, surgery is performed to remove stray pieces of damaged cartilage, to smooth bone spurs, or in severe cases to replace damaged joints with mechanical ones. Hips and knees are the most likely candidates for replacement.

What Is Rheumatoid Arthritis?

The ancient Greeks believed the body was filled with various substances they called "humors." Sometimes they said the humors got out of balance and caused illnesses, such as the aches and pains of swollen joints. The humors, they believed, could get back in balance, and the pain would subside. But the problems also could return. One disease the Greeks observed is what we now call rheumatoid (ROO-ma-toid) arthritis. "Rheuma" derives from a Greek word that means "flux" or "discharge." The Greeks believed the humors were fluxing, or flowing, through the body to cause the bouts of pain.

When the body turns on itself In a way, rheumatoid arthritis is a disease in which substances in the body are out of balance. The body fights infections with chemicals known as antibodies. But in rheumatoid arthritis, the antibodies turn against healthy areas of the body and cause the thin covering around joints to become inflamed.

The pain usually starts in the hands or feet, but rheumatoid arthritis can affect many different joints as well as other parts of the body, like the heart and lungs. The disease's cause is unknown. Some researchers believe that the immune system's attack on healthy tissues may be caused by the body's overreaction to viral infection.

More than 2 million Americans have rheumatoid arthritis, and most of them are women. Although it can start at any age, including a juvenile form that children get, the disease usually strikes women between the ages of 35 and 50.

It is known as the most disabling of the various diseases that cause arthritis. Rheumatoid arthritis can lead to deformed joints, extreme pain, and loss of the ability to do common tasks like walking.

Stiffness in the morning The symptoms of the disease can develop in a few days, months or years. For most people, a joint in the hands, feet, arms, or legs feels stiff, as it does in osteoarthritis and other forms of arthritis. Rheumatoid arthritis, however, has a few distinctive features. People tend to feel worse in the morning after awakening. They also can get a fever, and their joints can seem warm to the touch.

At first, the antibodies damage only the thin covering around joints. This covering contains cells that produce fluid that keeps joints lubricated and working properly. As the covering is damaged, it becomes thicker. Soon, damaging cells appear and eat away cartilage, bone, and other tissue. Swelling and pain result, and the joints become deformed. People with rheumatoid arthritis also can develop small bumps around joints, especially hands and elbows. Often, the disease flares up and then subsides on its own. Some people, however, receive no relief without treatment.

Diagnosis Doctors diagnose rheumatoid arthritis with special blood tests. They also look for other causes of the joint problems and use x-rays to look at the spaces between bones to see if they are narrowing.

Treatment Over-the-counter medications like aspirin can ease the pain. Stronger prescription pain relievers and anti-inflammatory drugs also are available. Weight loss is urged for people who are too heavy. Some people need surgery to replace badly damaged joints in the arms, legs, or hips.

Many people, however, learn to live with the disease through a combination of rest and exercise. When the symptoms are at their worst, patients with rheumatoid arthritis try to avoid putting stress on the joint to help reduce damage to the joint. But when the symptoms are less severe, doctors want the patients to exercise to maintain flexibility in the joints and strength in the muscles around them.

Patients with rheumatoid arthritis often learn relaxation techniques, because the disease is known to flare up in times of emotional stress.

What Is Juvenile Rheumatoid Arthritis?

Juvenile rheumatoid arthritis is one of several common forms of juvenile arthritis that cause swelling and pain in the joints. There are a great variety

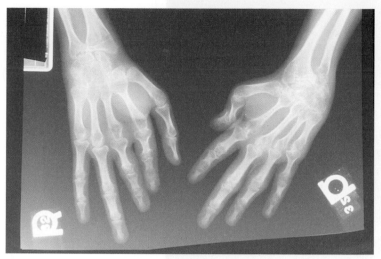

Doctors use x-rays to diagnose rheumatoid arthritis, which often affects the hands. People with rheumatoid arthritis may feel stiffness when they wake up in the morning, and their joints may feel warm to the touch. © *1998 Michael English, M.D., Custom Medical Stock Photo.*

The U.S. and the World

■ About 355 million people worldwide have arthritis, according to the Arthritis Foundation. Some forms, like rheumatoid arthritis, appear to be increasing in the developing nations of Africa, while their incidence appears to be decreasing in the United States and Western Europe.

■ About 40 million people in the United States (15 percent of the population) were reported to have arthritis in the late 1990s. But as baby boomers age, those numbers are expected to rise. By 2020, close to 60 million people in the United States are expected to have arthritis.

■ Florida has the highest percentage (almost 20 percent) of residents with arthritis. By 2020, it is still expected to lead the nation, with almost 25 percent of its residents having arthritis.

■ Alaska, with about 10 percent of residents having arthritis, has the lowest percentage now. It also is expected to be the lowest in 2020.

■ Arthritis affects all age groups, including more than 275,000 children under age 17.

■ Almost two thirds of people with arthritis are females. Among older women, it is the most common chronic condition.

■ In the United States, the estimated cost of arthritis to society is about $65 billion per year. About 25 percent is due to medical costs, and the remainder is from lost wages and productivity.

■ When the new arthritis medication Celebrex was released for sale in the United States in 1999, it sold more than $600 million in new prescriptions during its first six months on the market.

of symptoms among children with arthritis. The causes are unknown, although heredity is believed to play a role.

Juvenile rheumatoid arthritis affects children under age 16. Although very similar to the adult form of rheumatoid arthritis, 50 to 75 percent of young patients will "outgrow" the disease. Children are treated the same way that adults are: with pain medication, exercise, and careful treatment to prevent joints from becoming deformed.

What Are the Other Forms of Arthritis?

Osteoarthritis is the most common form of arthritis, and rheumatoid arthritis is the most disabling. But there are more than 100 diseases that are accompanied by the symptoms of arthritis. Here are a few of the other major ones, as well as a couple of unusual types:

Gout   Gout causes extreme pain that develops suddenly, often in the big toe. The pain, swelling, and redness develop because uric acid crystals build up in the joint. Uric acid is a natural substance found in the body that usually is passed out through the kidneys and urine. When uric acid is not removed from the body, crystals form and settle in the joints. Gout often is associated in people's minds with excessive eating and drinking. Although those activities, as well as obesity, increase the risk for gout, it can develop for no apparent reason. About 2.1 million Americans have gout, and about 90 percent of them are men.

Fibromyalgia   Fibromyalgia causes pain in the muscles and in the ligaments and tendons that are attached to bones around joints. Often, people with fibromyalgia are excessively tired and have trouble sleeping. The causes are unknown, although people with the disease often experience psychological stress. This does not mean the disease or its pain are not real. Unlike other forms of arthritis, fibromyalgia affects muscles and tissues around joints, not the joints themselves. It also does not lead to permanent damage. More than 3.5 million Americans have fibromyalgia, and most of them are women.

Lupus   Lupus is a disease that affects joints as well as other body parts, like the kidneys, nervous system, heart and skin. There are many symptoms of lupus, including fatigue, rashes, chest pain, fever, and sensitivity to sunlight. Like rheumatoid arthritis, lupus is an autoimmune disease with no known cause. In autoimmune diseases, the cells in the body that usually fight infections attack healthy cells and tissue instead. The disease mostly strikes women in their childbearing years. Women of African ancestry are almost three times as likely to develop lupus as women of European ancestry are. Overall, it affects as many as 500,000 people in the United States.

Lyme disease   Lyme disease is a bacterial infection spread by the bite of an infected insect known as a deer tick. The first signs are usually fever and a red rash on the skin where the bite occurred. Joint problems may follow, but the disease usually can be overcome with medication. It is a special concern for people who spend time outdoors in certain regions of the United States.

Living with Arthritis

Severe arthritis can limit the ability to walk, dress, or bathe easily. There are a growing number of devices that are sold to help people with arthritis have an easier time with simple tasks. Such things as easy-to-open bottles, handles on poles to reach high objects, and electric scooters can help people with severe arthritis to live independently.

Although doctors do not yet know how to prevent arthritis, there are many things people can do to reduce its impact, including:

- maintaining a healthy weight
- exercising to maintain joint flexibility and muscle strength
- exercising carefully, especially in contact sports like football
- wearing well-cushioned sneakers when walking or running on hard surfaces
- getting adequate rest
- following the doctor's instructions about pain medications
- learning relaxation techniques to reduce flare-ups in times of stress

With a fuller understanding of arthritis, its limitations, and its treatments, people with arthritis can lead full and happy lives.

Resources

Books

Moyer, Ellen. *Arthritis: Questions You Have-Answers You Need*. Allentown, PA: People's Medical Society, 1997. An easy-to-follow book that answers dozens of questions about many forms of arthritis.

Schwarz, Shelley Peterman. *250 Tips for Making Life with Arthritis Easier*. Atlanta: Longstreet Press, 1997. Published in conjunction with the Arthritis Foundation, this book focuses on living with arthritis and describes ways to make homes friendlier to people with arthritis.

Organizations

The Arthritis Foundation, 1330 West Peachtree Street, Atlanta, GA 30309. A national support organization with many local chapters. It publishes books, brochures, and fact sheets about all aspects of arthritis. Many are posted on its website.
Telephone 800-283-7800
http://www.arthritis.org

"Rheumatism"

Rheumatism is a non-medical word that many people use to refer to many different forms of arthritis, including rheumatoid arthritis. Older men and women sometimes talk about "having a touch of rheumatism" when their joints ache, especially on cold, rainy days.

KEYWORDS
*for searching the Internet
and other reference sources*

Foodborne illnesses

Infestation

Parasites

* **parasites** are creatures that live
in and feed on the bodies of other
organisms. The animal or plant
harboring the parasite is called its
host.

The roundworm *Ascaris lumbricoides* is
the largest of the human intestinal parasites. *Sinclair Stammers/Science Photo
Library, Photo Researchers, Inc.*

▶

The American Academy of Orthopaedic Surgeons, 6300 North River
Road, Rosemont, IL 60018-4262. An organization of physicians. Its
website offers detailed information about arthritis and joint replacement.
Telephone 800-346-2267
http://www.aaos.org

Asbestosis *See* **Pneumoconiosis**

Ascariasis

*Ascariasis (as-kah-RI-ah-sis) is an infection of the intestines by para-
sitic roundworms that usually causes no symptoms but is sometimes
serious.*

The world is full of roundworms. Hundreds of thousands of different kinds
inhabit the Earth, and a few types inhabit the bodies of humans, as well.
The most common of these is a worm called Ascaris (full name *Ascaris
lumbricoides*), which is estimated to infect 1 billion people worldwide.

Ascariasis, which is what the infection or infestation is called, usually
occurs in tropical and subtropical areas where sanitation is poor and where
raw or improperly treated human sewage is used to irrigate or fertilize crops.
Most cases occur in Africa and Asia, but it has been estimated that 4 million people in the United States carry *Ascaris* (AS-ka-ris), most of them
in rural southeastern areas.

Ascaris is a parasite*. Like many other parasites, it usually leads a live-
and-let-live existence, doing little damage to its host. But unlike many

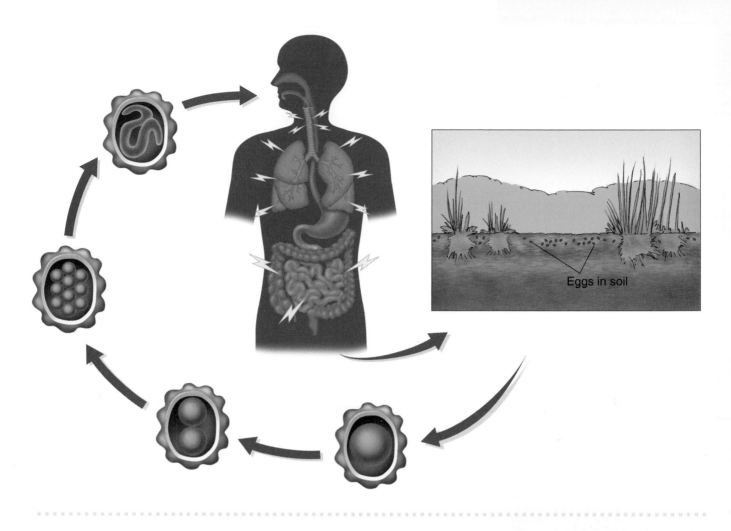

Eggs in soil

parasites, it infects only humans. Although *Ascaris* worms are found in people of all ages, children are most likely to be heavily infected.

What Is the Life Cycle of the *Ascaris* Worm?

Adult *Ascaris* worms live in the upper portion of the small intestine. They are 20 to 40 cm (8 to 15 inches) long, 3 to 6 mm (1/8 to 1/4 inch) in diameter, and live for about 1 year. Fertilized females produce up to 240,000 microscopic eggs a day, which pass out of an infected person's body in the stool. Fertilized eggs must remain in the soil for 2 to 3 weeks before they can infect another person. The eggs, however, can remain alive and viable* in soil for years.

Infection usually begins when soil containing eggs gets on people's hands. If they eat or touch their mouths before washing their hands, the eggs can get into their mouths and be swallowed. The eggs may also get into the body in food that has been contaminated with human waste.

The eggs hatch in the small intestine and release free-swimming larvae. The larvae penetrate the wall of the small intestine and enter the bloodstream. Next comes the pulmonary* stage of the infection, when the larvae enter the lungs and move up the bronchial tubes, which are the passages that carry air to and from the lungs. They finally reach the pharynx

▲

Ascariasis infections begin when people swallow worm eggs that they have picked up from infected food or from soil. When the eggs hatch in the small intestine, they become larvae and swim through the bloodstream to the lungs, and then on to the throat, where they are swallowed. Back in the stomach and small intestine, the larvae become adults, mate, and produce new eggs. The entire cycle, from eggs being swallowed to new eggs being produced, takes about 2 to 3 months.

* **viable** means an organism can survive, grow, develop, and function.

* **pulmonary** is the adjective that refers to the lungs.

Did You Know?

- About 1 billion people worldwide are infected with *Ascaris* worms.

- An adult *Ascaris* worm is 20 to 40 cm long.

- A female *Ascaris* worm can produce 240,000 eggs a day.

(FAR-inks), the back of the throat, where they are swallowed. Then they move through the stomach and back to the small intestine where they were hatched. In the small intestine, they become adults and mate, and the females begin producing eggs. The entire cycle, from eggs being swallowed to new eggs being produced, takes 2 to 3 months.

What Are the Symptoms of Ascariasis?

Ascariais usually causes no symptoms. In heavy infections, however, abdominal cramps occur, and occasionally a mass of worms can block the intestines, causing pain, vomiting, and bloating. Adult worms also can block other parts of the digestive tract, such as the appendix, bile duct, or pancreatic duct, causing similar symptoms. When the larvae are migrating through the lungs, they may cause a fever, dry cough, wheezing, and sometimes asthma.

How Is Ascariasis Diagnosed and Treated?

Since *Ascaris* produces such an abundance of eggs, they often can be seen when stool samples are examined under a microscope. Less commonly, an adult worm may be passed in the stool or may crawl up the throat and try to exit through the mouth or nose. *Ascaris* larvae may be identified in sputum or phlegm coughed up during the pulmonary stage.

Doctors may prescribe several different oral medications to treat ascariasis. If the intestine is blocked, surgery may be necessary. If the pulmonary stage is severe, corticosteroids may be prescribed to lessen the symptoms.

How Can Ascariasis Be Prevented?

Thoroughly washing fruits and vegetables in clean water, washing hands before eating or preparing food, and washing hands after using the bathroom are advised. Improved sanitation and hygiene in developing countries would cut the risk of infection in those areas. Coupled with such improvements, routine or preventive treatment with deworming drugs, called anthelmintic (ant-hel-MIN-tik) medications, could reduce the prevalence of ascariasis worldwide.

Resources

The U.S. Food and Drug Administration's Center for Food Safety and Applied Nutrition posts a Bad Bug Book on its website with information about *Ascaris lumbricoides* and other parasitic worms. http://vm.cfsan.fda.gov/~mow/

The U.S. National Center for Infectious Diseases (NCID) has a Division of Parasitic Diseases (DPD) website that offers information about ascariasis and its geographic distribution. http://www.cdc.gov/ncidod/dpd/dpd.htm

▶ *See also*
Asthma
Parasitic Diseases

Asthma

Asthma (AZ-ma) is a condition in which the airflow in and out of the lungs may be partially blocked by swelling, muscle squeezing, and mucus in the lower airways. These episodes of partial blockage, called asthma "flares" or "attacks," can be triggered by dust, pollutants, smoke, allergies, cold air, or infections.

KEYWORDS
for searching the Internet and other reference sources

Breathing

Lungs

Pulmonary system

Respiratory system

A Breathless Story

When Stacy was young, her parents noticed that she seemed to get tired more quickly than her friends while playing. She also had repeated coughing spells, and her breathing was sometimes noisy. After examining Stacy, asking lots of questions, and having her use a little machine to measure her breathing, the doctor diagnosed her problem as asthma. As part of the way Stacy took care of herself, she sometimes had to take asthma medicine at school. This made her teachers and friends interested in learning more about asthma. When Stacy was 12, she began a schoolwide project with the help of her teacher and the nurse. The goal was to make her school more asthma-friendly. No smoking was allowed, even during after-school events. Extra steps were taken to keep the school as free as possible of things that can trigger asthma flares, such as dust, mold, cockroaches, and strong fumes from paint and chemicals. A plan was set up to let students with asthma take their own medicines at school. Special lessons were offered to all students and teachers about what asthma is and how to help a classmate who has it. The result was a school that was a healthier place not just for Stacy but for everyone.

What Is Asthma?

Several changes happen inside the airways in the lungs of people who have asthma. First, there is inflammation, or swelling, of the lining of the airways. Second, the swollen tissues make a thick, slippery substance called mucus (MYOO-kus). Third, the muscles around the airways may squeeze tight, causing the airways to narrow. These three processes—inflammation, mucus production, and muscle constriction—combine to reduce the size (the diameter) of the airways. That makes it harder to breathe, like trying to blow air through a narrow straw.

During an asthma attack, these changes get worse. The airways swell on the inside while they are being squeezed on the outside. At the same time, thick mucus plugs the smaller airways. The person may start to make whistling or hissing sounds with each breath. The person's chest may also feel tight. In addition, the person may cough to try to clear the lungs.

What Triggers Asthma?

People with asthma have what are sometimes called "sensitized" airways. Everyday things that cause little or no trouble for most people can sometimes cause people with asthma to have a flare or attack. These things are

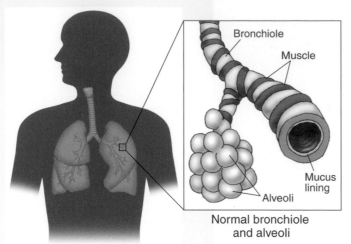
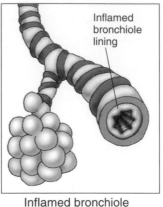
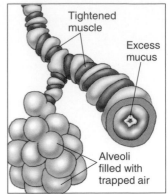

Bronchiole

Muscle

Mucus lining

Alveoli

Normal bronchiole and alveoli

Inflamed bronchiole lining

Inflamed bronchiole and alveoli

Tightened muscle

Excess mucus

Alveoli filled with trapped air

Bronchospasm during asthma attack

▲

Asthma attack: **1.** Location of bronchial tubes/alveoli. **2.** Normal. **3.** Inflamed. **4.** Bronchospasm with trapped air.

known as asthma triggers. There are two main kinds of triggers. The first are allergens (AL-er-jens), or substances that trigger an allergy. Examples of allergens that may trigger asthma are pollens, molds, animal dander (small scales from fur or feathers), dust mites, cockroaches, and certain foods and medicines. Most of these allergy-causing substances enter the body through the air people breathe, but some are swallowed.

The second kind of asthma trigger has nothing to do with an allergy but causes the same kind of reaction in the airways. Asthma can be triggered or made worse by irritating substances in the air, such as tobacco smoke, wood smoke, fresh paint, cleaning products, perfumes, workplace chemicals, and air pollution. Some other triggers include cold air, sudden changes in air temperature, exercise, heartburn, and infections of the airways, such as a cold or the flu. Exactly which of these might trigger a reaction varies from person to person.

Who Gets Asthma?

Asthma is one of the most common health problems in the United States. The number of people with the condition has grown rapidly in recent years. The reason for this increase is not yet known. About a third of these people are children under age eighteen. Asthma is more common in African American children than in white children, although the reason for this is not clear. It may have to do with environmental conditions.

What Are the Symptoms?

Following are the most common symptoms of asthma. A person may have all, some, or just one of these symptoms:

- **Shortness of breath**
- **Coughing**, particularly if it lasts longer than a week
- **Wheezing** (whistling or hissing sounds made primarily when breathing out)
- A feeling of **tightness or discomfort in the chest**

The degree to which asthma interferes with a person's daily life varies significantly. Some people have ongoing problems. They may have attacks anywhere from a couple of times a week to almost constantly. Their ability to take part in physical activities may be limited until, with treatment, they are able to get their asthma under control. Those with milder problems are usually able to do whatever they want to do, so long as they reduce their environmental triggers, take their medicine as directed, and follow any other advice from their doctors.

Childhood asthma   Babies often wheeze when they have a cold or other infection of the airways, blockage of the airways, or other problems. This symptom may go away on its own with no ill effects. However, if the problem is severe, lasts a long time, or comes back, treatment may be needed. In older children, normal breathing should be quiet. Wheezing may be a sign of asthma, but it can also signal an infection, lung disease, heartburn, heart disease, a blood vessel blocking the airways, or even a piece of food or other object (such as part of a toy) lodged in the airway. In addition to noisy breathing, asthma in children can cause rapid breathing and frequent coughing spells. Parents may also notice that the child tires quickly during active play.

Nighttime asthma   Asthma tends to get worse at night. Nocturnal (or nighttime) asthma occurs while a person is sleeping. For some people, nocturnal asthma is one of many symptoms; other people seem to have coughing or wheezing only at night.

Exercise-related asthma   Up to four out of five people with asthma have trouble with noisy breathing during or after exercise. This

FOUR CENTURIES OF MEDICAL RESEARCH

The word "asthma" comes from the Greek word for "panting," which is a symptom that occurs in several different pulmonary (lung) disorders.

Asthma was first depicted as a disease rather than a symptom by the English chemist Thomas Willis (1621–1675).

In 1698, Sir John Floyer first gave the first formal account of an asthma attack or "fit." However, an accurate diagnosis of asthma was not possible until the early nineteenth century when the celebrated French physician René Laënnec (1781–1826) invented the stethoscope.

During the early nineteenth century, asthma was treated in a variety of ways including whiffs of chloroform and even the smoking of ordinary tobacco.

is known as exercise-induced asthma. Other symptoms include coughing, a rapid heartbeat, and a feeling of tightness in the chest five to ten minutes after exercise. Cold or dry air, high pollen counts, air pollution, a stuffed-up nose, and an infection of the airways are all things that tend to make the problem worse. Types of exercise that may lead to wheezing include running, using a treadmill, and playing basketball—in short, exercises that are aerobic (designed to increase oxygen consumption).

Job-related asthma   Occupational asthma is caused by breathing in fumes, gases, or dust while on the job. Asthma can start for the first time in a worker who was previously healthy, or it can get worse in a worker who already had the condition. Symptoms include wheezing, chest tightness, and coughing. Other symptoms that may go along with the asthma include a runny or stuffed-up nose and red, sore, itchy eyes. The asthma may last for a long time, even after the worker is no longer around the substance that caused it.

Severe attacks   Status asthmaticus (STA-tus az-MAT-i-kus) is a severe asthma attack that does not get better when the person takes his or her medicine as usual. This kind of attack is an emergency that must be treated right away in a hospital or doctor's office, where other medicines may be used.

How Is Asthma Diagnosed?

The doctor will do a physical checkup and ask questions about symptoms and when they occur. In addition, the doctor may do various tests to help identify asthma and its causes. These are some of the tests that may be done:

Allergy tests   Allergy tests help identify which things a person is allergic to. Skin tests are most common. Tiny amounts of possible allergens are put on the skin, and the skin is checked to see which substances, if any, cause a reaction. In another type of allergy test, a blood sample is checked for certain antibodies, which are substances made in the blood to fight foreign or harmful things. People with allergies may have high levels of immunoglobulin E (IgE) antibodies. However, the blood test is generally not considered as sensitive as the skin test, and it cannot check for as many allergens.

Chest x-ray.   An x-ray is an invisible wave that goes through most solid matter and produces an image on film. In this case, a special picture is made to show how the lungs look.

Lung-function tests.   These tests show how well the lungs are working. In one test, the person blows into a device called a spirometer (spi-ROM-i-ter), which measures the amount of air going in and out of the lungs. Another test uses a peak flow meter to measure how fast the person can breathe air out of the lungs. A peak flow meter is a simple, hand-held device that can be used at home. Many people with asthma use peak flow meters regularly to check for early warning signs of an upcoming asthma attack. This gives them time to take certain medicines that can often stop the attack.

Why Is Treatment Needed?

Asthma that is not under control can cause many problems. People miss school or work, must go to the hospital, and can even die (rarely) because of asthma. With a doctor's help, though, it is possible to control asthma. People with well-controlled asthma have few, if any, symptoms during the day and can sleep well at night. They can also take part in their usual activities, including sports and exercise. However, the asthma does not go away just because the symptoms do. A person needs to keep taking care of the condition as part of life: avoiding triggers, not smoking, and living in a healthful, clean environment. This is true even if the asthma is mild.

How Is Asthma Treated?

Besides avoiding exposure to asthma triggers, the chief way that asthma is treated is with various medicines. One key to good control is taking the right medicine at the right time. There are two main kinds of asthma medicines: those that help with long-term control of the disease, and those that give short-term relief when a person is having an asthma attack.

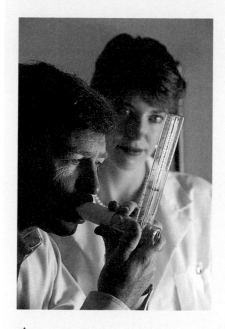

▲

A man with asthma uses peak-flow meter. © *Will and Deni McIntyre, Photo Researchers, Inc.*

Long-term control medicines   Long-term control medicines are taken every day to help prevent symptoms before they start. It may take several weeks for these medicines to produce their best results, though. The most effective ones work by reducing swelling in the airways. Many are inhaled, or breathed into the lungs. Not everyone needs such medicines. However, they may be very helpful for people who have daytime asthma symptoms three or more times a week or nighttime symptoms three or more times a month. These are some medicines for long-term control of asthma:

- **Inhaled corticosteroids** (kor-ti-ko-STER-oids). These strong drugs prevent and reduce swelling in the airways. They also make the airways less sensitive to triggers. However, they work only if they are used regularly. These drugs are taken every day by people with long-lasting asthma. They are not the same as the unsafe steroids some athletes use to build muscles.

- **Other inhaled drugs**. These medications also help prevent and reduce swelling in the airways and make the airways less sensitive. However, it can take four to six weeks of regular use before they start to work. These drugs are taken every day by people with long-term asthma, but they can also be used before exercise or contact with a trigger.

- **Oral corticosteroids**. These drugs are taken by mouth in pill or liquid form. Unlike inhaled corticosteroids, they sometimes cause serious side effects when used for a long time. However, they can

Breathtaking Facts

- More than 17 million people in the United States have asthma. Of these, almost 5 million are children.

- About one in every ten children has asthma-like symptoms.

- About three out of four children with asthma continue to have symptoms as adults.

- Asthma results in about 3 million lost days of work each year among American adults.

- According to the Centers for Disease Control and Prevention (CDC), between 1980 and 1994, the number of Americans who reported having asthma rose 75 percent.

Winning Ways

Jackie Joyner-Kersee (b. 1962) has often been called the world's greatest female athlete. What many fans never suspect is that she is also an asthma patient. Joyner-Kersee became active in sports at age nine. As a teenager, she was an all-state player in basketball and a Junior Olympics champion in pentathlon, an athletic contest in which each person takes part in five different events. While still in high school, Joyner-Kersee began having trouble breathing. When she first found out that she had asthma, she did not take it seriously. She often skipped her medicine. After a serious asthma attack, though, she realized that she had to work to control the condition just as she worked to win at sports. After college, Joyner-Kersee went on to win six Olympic medals as well as to break the world and Olympic records in the heptathlon, an athletic contest with seven different events: 100-meter hurdles, high jump, shot put, 200-meter dash, long jump, javelin, and 800-meter race. Today she serves as a spokesperson for groups that educate the public about asthma.

often be used safely for a short time to treat severe asthma attacks and to quickly bring asthma under control. They are sometimes taken every day or every other day by people with the most severe asthma.

- **Long-acting bronchodilators** (brong-ko-DY-lay-tors). These drugs relax the muscles around the airways, making it easier to breathe. They can prevent or reduce narrowing of the airways. However, they keep working only if they are used regularly. These drugs are inhaled or taken by mouth in a pill. Some are especially useful for preventing nighttime or exercise-related asthma.

- **Antileukotrienes** (an-ti-loo-ko-TRY-eens). This is a new class of asthma drugs. These drugs prevent and reduce swelling in the airways and make the airways less sensitive to triggers. They also prevent squeezing of the muscles around the airways. These drugs are taken regularly by mouth in a pill. So far, they have been used mainly for mild asthma in patients of age twelve and older.

- **Allergy vaccines.** In some cases, a person's asthma symptoms can be prevented or lessened by giving a course of special allergy injections over months or years. These shots contain small amounts of the allergens that are triggering the person's asthma. The course of injections causes the person to become less sensitive to the allergen when exposed to it.

Short-term relief medicines   Short-term relief medicines are taken only when needed to relax and open the airways quickly. They can be used to relieve symptoms or to prevent them if a person's peak flow meter readings begin to drop, signaling an upcoming asthma attack. However, the effects last for only a few hours. They cannot keep the symptoms from coming back the way long-term control medicines can. These drugs are inhaled and are taken at the first sign of trouble or before contact with a trigger.

Medicines that provide short-term relief of asthma are called short-acting bronchodilators. These drugs relax the muscles around the airways, making it easier to breathe. They begin to work within five minutes, and their effects last for four to six hours. Such drugs are taken right after symptoms start or just before exercise.

How Are Inhaled Medicines Taken?

Many asthma medicines are made to be breathed into the lungs. Such inhaled drugs go straight to the place where they are needed. The most popular device for taking inhaled medicines is a metered dose inhaler, which gets the drug to the lungs in exact amounts. The inhaler is a small, hand-held canister with a button that the person pushes to make the medicine spray out. Often a tube, called a spacer, is attached to the canister to make it easier to use.

Another type of device that is sometimes used to take inhaled medicines is a nebulizer (NEB-you-lyz-er), which turns liquid medicine into a very fine mist. These devices are helpful for babies, young children, and elderly or very sick adults who would have trouble handling a metered dose inhaler.

Breathing Easier

People with asthma should try to figure out what makes their symptoms worse and take steps to avoid or control those things. Here are a few ways that many people control some common asthma triggers. Not all of them will work for everyone.

Pollens and outdoor molds   To control pollens and outdoor molds, people with asthma often:

- keep windows and doors closed when pollen or mold spore counts are high.

- avoid walking in gardens and fields when they are in bloom and when pollen and mold spore counts are highest.

- ride with the car windows shut and the air conditioner on during pollen season.

- ask their doctors about starting or increasing a long-term control medicine before peak pollen season begins.

Indoor molds   To control indoor molds, people with asthma often:

- fix leaky faucets, pipes, and other sources of water.

- clean moldy surfaces with a product that contains bleach.

- remove wallpaper, which can have mold growing on it.

- get rid of houseplants, which can gather mold and dust.

Animal dander   Dander is small scales from the hair of animals, like cats, and from bird feathers. Some people are allergic to it, and people with asthma often:

- keep pets with fur or feathers out of their homes, if possible.

- have pets stay out of bedrooms, in particular, and keep bedroom doors closed.

- remove carpets and cloth-covered furniture, or keep pets away from these things.

- use polyester-fill rather than feather pillows, and avoid down quilts.

Jackie Joyner-Kersee uses an asthma inhaler after winning the 800-meter race (part of the women's heptathlon) at the World Athletics Championships in Stuttgart, Germany, July 17, 1993. *Corbis/Reuters*

Dust mites   People with asthma often find that they are allergic to dust because of the tiny animals that live in the dust, called mites. Many people with asthma find that it helps to keep their homes especially clear of dust. For example, they:

- wash their bedding each week in hot water (it must be hotter than 130 degrees F to kill mites).
- enclose mattresses and pillows in special dust-proof covers, or wash pillows each week in hot water.
- try not to sleep or lie on cloth-covered furniture or cushions.
- remove carpets in bedrooms and those laid on concrete.
- keep stuffed toys out of beds, and wash the toys each week in hot water.
- wear a dust mask while vacuuming, or have someone else do the vacuuming.

Cockroaches   Many people with asthma are sensitive to cockroach droppings and make a special effort to get rid of these stubborn creatures by:

- keeping all food out of bedrooms.
- storing food and garbage in closed containers and never leaving food or crumbs sitting around.
- using poison bait, powder, gel, paste, or traps (following label instructions) to kill cockroaches.
- staying out of the room until the odor goes away if a spray is used to kill roaches.

Certain foods and medicines   It is important to:

- avoid foods that have caused problems in the past.
- tell the doctor about any past reactions to medicines.

Smoke and strong odors   Smoking is not good for anyone, the person smoking or people who are in the same room with tobacco smoke. People with asthma are especially endangered by tobacco smoke and find it is best not to smoke, to ask other family members to quit smoking, and to ask visitors not to smoke.
   People with asthma also:

- avoid using a wood-burning stove, kerosene heater, or fireplace, if possible.
- try to stay away from strong odors and fumes, such as perfume, hairspray, and fresh paint.

Exercise   It is healthy for just about everyone to exercise, and people with asthma are no exception. To make their exercise and sports more enjoyable, people with asthma usually:

- warm up for six to ten minutes before exercising.

- avoid exercising outside when air pollution or pollen counts are high or when the air is cold.

- pick activities that do not cause symptoms; running sports are the most likely to trigger problems.

- ask a doctor about taking medicine before exercise to prevent symptoms.

Resources

Books

American Lung Association and Norman H. Edelman. *The American Lung Association Family Guide to Asthma and Allergies: How You and Your Children Can Breathe Easier.* New York: Back Bay Books, 1997.

Weiss, Jonathan H. *Breathe Easy: Young People's Guide to Asthma.* Washington, DC: Magination Press, 1994.

Organizations

Allergy and Asthma Network/Mothers of Asthmatics, 2751 Prosperity Avenue, Suite 150, Fairfax, VA 22031.
Telephone 800-878-4403
http://www.aanma.org

American Academy of Allergy, Asthma and Immunology, 611 East Wells Street, Milwaukee, WI 53202.
Telephone 414-272-6071
http://www.aaaai.org

American College of Allergy, Asthma and Immunology, 85 West Algonquin Road, Suite 550, Arlington Heights, IL 60005.
Telephone 847-427-1200
http://allergy.mcg.edu

American Lung Association, 1740 Broadway, New York, NY 10019.
Telephone 800-LUNG-USA
http://www.lungusa.org

Asthma and Allergy Foundation of America, 1125 Fifteenth Street N.W., Suite 502, Washington, DC 20005.
Telephone 800-7-ASTHMA
http://www.aafa.org

Asthma Information Center. This website is run by the *Journal of the American Medical Association.*
http://www.ama-assn.org/special/asthma/asthma.htm

U.S. National Heart, Lung, and Blood Institute, NHLBI Information Center, P.O. Box 30105, Bethesda, MD 20824-0105. NHLBI has an

Asthma Management Model System and runs a National Asthma Education and Prevention Program.
Telephone 301-592-8573
http://www.nhlbisupport.com/asthma
http://www.nhlbi.nih.gov

The U.S. Centers for Disease Control, located in Atlanta, Georgia, posts information on asthma at
http://www.cdc.gov/nceh/programs/asthma/default.htm

▶ *See also*
Allergies
Emphysema
Heartburn (Dyspepsia)

KEYWORDS
for searching the Internet and other reference sources

Ophthalmology

Optometry

Vision

Astigmatism

Astigmatism (a-STIG-ma-tiz-um) is an eye condition that causes objects to appear blurry because the front part of the eye is misshapen.

The eyeball usually is round and nearly the same size as a ping-pong ball. The front part contains a clear layer of tissue called the cornea and the lens that help to focus the light that enters the eye. When people have astigmatism, the cornea and/or the lens is misshapen and their curved surfaces are unequal. If the curve is only slightly off shape, then only objects at a distance might appear blurry. People with more serious astigmatism, however, may see the world as if they were looking in a funhouse mirror that distorts all images.

Who Gets Astigmatism?

Astigmatism is a common problem. Many people may have slight variations in the shape of their cornea or lens that do not cause problems with their eyesight. In others, however, these structures are shaped in ways that distort the light that enters the eye. The cornea usually is smooth and rounded, like the surface of a ping-pong ball that is cut in half. A person with astigmatism, however, might have a cornea that is curved more like the top of a football, as if the ping-pong ball were pulled out from its edges. Or the cornea may have peaks and valleys on its surface, instead of a smooth, rounded covering, and that too will distort vision.

No one is sure what causes astigmatism. It usually is present at birth and often is found in several members of the same family. This means that in some cases the trait is inherited, like hair color and eye color.

What Happens to Vision When People Have Astigmatism?

These variations in the shape of the cornea or lens cause the images a person with astigmatism sees to be out of focus when they reach the retina. The retina is made of layers of light-sensitive cells at the back of the eyeball that act like the film in a camera. The distorted image is projected onto the retina and transmitted to the brain for processing through the optic nerve.

The first signs of astigmatism depend on how severely the cornea or lens is misshapen. If it is only a mild problem, people with astigmatism may find that they have headaches or tired eyes at times, or distorted vision at certain distances. Those with more severe astigmatism may find they have blurry vision that makes reading, playing sports, and other activities difficult. Often, the problem is found during an eye exam in school, at the doctor's office during a check-up, or when a parent notices that a child is having trouble seeing well.

What Is the Treatment for Astigmatism?

Astigmatism is managed with prescription eyeglasses or contact lenses. These help change the way that images are focused as they pass through the cornea and the lens. With eyeglasses, images can appear clear and undistorted when they reach the retina. Usually, astigmatism does not get worse as people get older.

Resources

Book

Cassel, Gary H., M.D., Michael D. Billig, O.D., and Harry G. Randall, M.D. *The Eye Book: A Complete Guide to Eye Disorders and Health*. Baltimore: Johns Hopkins University Press, 1998. A good general reference on eye problems.

Organization

The U.S. National Eye Institute posts a resource list of eye health-related publications and organizations at its website. http://www.nei.nih.gov/publications/sel-org.htm

▶ See also
Farsightedness
Nearsightedness

Atherosclerosis *See* Heart Disease

Athlete's Foot

Athlete's foot is a skin infection caused by a fungus. It affects the soles of the feet and the spaces between the toes.

KEYWORDS
for searching the Internet
and other reference sources

Dermatophytes

Tinea pedis

What Is Athlete's Foot?

The human body is home to many different kinds of fungi. Most never cause a problem. Athlete's foot is caused by one group of fungi called

*microorganisms are living organisms that can only be seen using a microscope. Examples of microorganisms are fungi, bacteria, and viruses.

*contagious means transmittable from one person to another.

*synthetic means produced artificially or chemically rather than grown naturally.

dermatophytes (der-MA-to-fites), which are microorganisms* that live on the skin, hair, and nails. Dermatophytes need a warm, moist environment to survive and to reproduce, like the feet of athletes, for example. But, in fact, anyone with wet or sweaty feet may be prone to getting athlete's foot. Athlete's foot is also called tinea pedis (TIN-e-a PED-is), or ringworm of the foot.

How Do People Get Athlete's Foot?

Athlete's foot is somewhat contagious*, and the most common places where people catch it are also the dampest ones: public showers, pool areas, wet towels, and bath mats. People who wear the same shoes or sneakers all the time are more likely to develop athlete's foot, as are people who wear shoes or socks made from certain synthetic* materials such as rubber, vinyl, or nylon. Anything that keeps the feet warm, wet, and sweaty gives the fungus an opportunity to grow and survive.

What Are the Signs and Symptoms of Athlete's Foot?

Athlete's foot is a condition with very specific symptoms, and these symptoms can be mild or intense, depending on the case and the person. A person with athlete's foot may feel burning and stinging on the soles of the feet and in between the toes. The skin can feel very itchy as well. The fungus causes the skin to become red, flaky, or soggy. Sometimes, the skin can become cracked.

How Do Doctors Diagnose and Treat Athlete's Foot?

Diagnosis   When examining a patient with athlete's foot, a doctor will usually have an easy time making a diagnosis, because the fungi that cause skin problems are usually easy to recognize. Just to be sure, the doctor may take a small scraping of skin to gather some of the fungus. The fungus can then be cultured, or grown, in a small dish in a laboratory. This gives the doctor an opportunity to identify the fungus, if present.

Treatment   Most cases of athlete's foot can be cured with antifungal creams or sprays, which are put directly on the skin to kill the fungus. Many of these creams and sprays are available without a prescription at drugstores. If athlete's foot persists, doctors may prescribe stronger antifungal creams than those available over the counter or possibly an antifungal medication to be taken orally. If a bacterial infection has developed along with the fungal infection, then the doctor may also prescribe an antibiotic to kill the bacteria.

How Do People Prevent Athlete's Foot?

People who tend to get athlete's foot can do some simple things to help prevent it. The most important step is to keep the feet as dry as possible, because the fungi that cause athlete's foot do not like dry places. Taking a few extra minutes to dry feet thoroughly after showering, bathing, and swimming can help a lot. Other methods of prevention include:

- Wearing sandals and avoiding bare feet around a pool area or a public shower
- Wearing shoes that are well ventilated, such as sneakers with small holes on their tops or sides to let air in and out
- Wearing shoes and sneakers made of leather rather than of synthetic materials such as vinyl and nylon
- Wearing cotton or wool socks rather than polyester socks
- If possible, not wearing the same pair of shoes or sneakers every day, as switching between pairs gives shoes a chance to dry out after being worn.

Those people who are particularly prone to athlete's foot may find they can keep the fungi away by using antifungal powders on their feet every day.

Resource

American Podiatric Medical Association, 9312 Old Georgetown Road, Bethesda, MD 20814. The American Podiatric Medical Association has a foot care information center and publishes *Your Feet: An Owner's Manual* and other public education materials. Telephone 800-366-8227 or 800-foot-care

▶ See also
Fungal Infections
Ringworm

Attention Deficit Hyperactivity Disorder (ADHD)

Attention deficit hyperactivity disorder (ADHD) is a condition that makes it hard to pay attention, sit still, or think before acting.

KEY WORDS
for searching the Internet and other reference sources

Attention deficit disorder (ADD)

Hyperactivity

Impulsivity

Psychology

Psychostimulant drugs

Ritalin

A Tale of Two Students

Justin and Katie are both seventh-grade students with ADHD. They act quite differently at school, however. Justin has a very hard time sitting still and staying in his seat. His classmates and teachers think of him as "hyper." Justin gets bored easily, so he tends to talk too much and get into trouble. He also bothers the other students around him, which leads them to get angry at him.

Katie does not wiggle and fidget the way Justin does. She has lots of trouble keeping her mind on her work and paying attention to the teacher, however. Katie also forgets which assignments she is supposed to do. She finds it tougher than most to keep up with her backpack, books, and school supplies. Sometimes she loses her homework, and sometimes she just forgets to turn it in.

* **hyperactivity** (hi-per-ak-TIV-it-tee) is overly active behavior, which makes it hard to sit still.

What Is ADHD?

ADHD (also called ADD by many people) is a condition that can show itself as trouble with a poor attention span, easy distractability, hyperactivity*, and/or impulsiveness. People with ADHD may have only one or two of these problems, or they may have all three. Those with an attention problem have a hard time keeping their mind on any one thing for long. They may get bored with a task after only a few minutes. People who are hyperactive seem to be in constant motion. They may feel restless and squirm or fidget a lot. People who are overly impulsive seem not to think before they say or do things. They may take dangerous risks or blurt out embarrassing comments without thinking.

Of course, everyone has trouble paying attention or sitting still now and then. However, such problems occur more often and are more severe in people with ADHD. They begin before age seven, although they may not be recognized as signs of ADHD until later. The problems show up both at home and away, and they can lead to trouble with school, work, or relationships with family, friends, and teachers.

What Causes ADHD?

Scientists do not know for sure what causes ADHD. However, they believe that certain parts of the brain do not work the same way in people with ADHD as in people without it. Such people may have an altered balance of key brain chemicals, called neurotransmitters*, that affect how the brain works. Some research also suggests that in some cases use of alcohol or drugs by the mother during pregnancy can harm development of the baby's brain cells. This may be one cause of ADHD, although it is likely there are many causes.

* **neurotransmitters** (noo-ro-TRANS-mit-ers) are brain chemicals that let brain cells communicate with each other and therefore allow the brain to function normally.

A person's genetic makeup may be involved. ADHD seems to run in families. Children with ADHD usually have at least one parent, brother, sister, or other close relative with the disorder. Scientific studies have also found that, if one identical twin has ADHD, the other twin is likely to have it as well.

What Does *Not* Cause ADHD?

Experts used to think that attention problems were caused by slight brain damage or minor head injuries. However, we now know that most people with ADHD have no sign of brain damage or history of head injury. Another theory was that overactive behavior was caused by refined sugar and food additives. However, scientists found that eating a special diet seemed to help only about 5 percent of children with ADHD, mostly very young children or those with food allergies. It is true, however, that too much caffeine (found in coffee, tea, and some sodas) or some red/yellow dyes can add to hyperactive behaviors.

These things usually do not cause ADHD:

- ■ Too much sugar

- ■ Food allergies

■ Too much television

■ Poor teachers or schools

■ Poor parents or home life

Who Gets ADHD?

ADHD is one of the most common of all conditions in childhood. It affects 3 to 5 percent of school-age children. This means that, on average, at least one child in every classroom in the United States needs help for the disorder. Two to three times more boys than girls have ADHD.

Many parents first notice overactive behavior when their child starts to walk as a toddler. However, such behavior usually is not labeled as ADHD until the child reaches elementary school. Without treatment, the disorder usually stays about the same through childhood and the early teen years. Problems caused by ADHD often improve during the late teen years and adulthood. Many adults are left with only a few signs of ADHD, but a few still have the full disorder.

What Are the Signs of ADHD?

Inattention (in-a-TEN-shun) means a poor attention span. These are some signs of inattention:

■ Not paying close attention to details

■ Making careless mistakes

■ Having trouble keeping the mind on tasks

■ Seeming not to listen when spoken to

■ Not following instructions

■ Not finishing schoolwork or chores

■ Having trouble getting organized

■ Avoiding or disliking schoolwork

■ Being easily distracted

■ Losing things

■ Being forgetful

Hyperactivity (hy-per-ack-TIV-i-tee) means overly active behavior. These are some signs of hyperactivity:

■ Fidgeting with the hands or feet

■ Squirming when seated

■ Not staying seated when expected to

■ Running or climbing around too much

■ Feeling restless a lot

Stigmatizing ADHD

ADHD got its current name during the 1980s. It has been referred to by other names throughout the years. Many of those names created a negative stereotype for children with ADHD, including:

■ "morbid defects in moral control" (1900s)

■ "restlessness syndrome" (1920s)

■ "brain injured syndrome" (even though evidence of brain damage could not be demonstrated) (1940s)

■ "minimal brain dysfunction" (1950s and 1960s).

■ Having trouble doing quiet activities

■ Seeming to be on the go all the time

■ Talking too much

Impulsivity (im-pul-SIV-i-tee) means having less control over behavior. These are some signs of impulsivity:

■ Blurting out answers before questions are finished

■ Having trouble waiting for a turn

■ Butting into other people's conversations or games

How Is ADHD Diagnosed?

Many things besides ADHD can cause similar kinds of problems. For example, depression can lead to trouble paying attention, while anxiety can make it hard to sit still. A learning disability can lead to poor school performance, while small seizures can cause mental lapses. Even an ear infection that leads to on-again-off-again hearing loss can look like ADHD. In addition, everyone has trouble staying focused and getting organized at times. This is why it is so important that ADHD be diagnosed by a trained medical or mental health professional.

A doctor or counselor usually watches the child or young adult's behavior and asks the patient to answer several questions, some of which deal with current signs of ADHD. Other questions deal with early child-hood, medical problems, and family history. Parents and teachers may also be asked for examples of their experiences with the patient. Although there is no sure test for ADHD, the patient may be asked to take a number of tests, possibly including a computer test that measures the ability to pay attention. Instructions to press a key when a certain letter or shape appears on the screen can measure ability to pay attention. A medical doctor may do further tests to rule out other disorders, such as hearing loss because of ear infections, mild seizures, anxiety, or depression.

How Is ADHD Treated?

ADHD is usually treated with both medication and counseling, although sometimes only one or the other is needed. Medication helps people with ADHD focus and pay attention. Counseling helps them cope with problems related to ADHD. For example, the aim of counseling might be to improve study skills, boost self-esteem, or learn how to get along better with others.

Benefits of medication The medications most often used to treat ADHD fall into a class of drugs known as stimulants (STIM-yoo-lants). Such drugs may have an arousing effect when taken at higher doses by adults. When taken by children with ADHD, however, they have the opposite effect. The drugs can help such children calm down and improve their ability to focus and learn. No one knows exactly how these drugs work to control ADHD. However, they may work by increasing the amount and activity of some of the brain chemicals known as neurotransmitters. Nine out of ten typical children with ADHD get better on one of these drugs. If one stimulant medicine does not help, another can be tried.

If stimulant medicines do not work, or if there are problems such as depression along with ADHD, other kinds of medicine may be used.

Risks of medication   When taken as directed by a doctor, stimulant medicines are considered safe. They usually do not make the patients "high" or jittery. They may cause other unwanted side effects*, however. Some patients may lose weight, feel less hungry, or temporarily grow more slowly. Others may have trouble falling asleep. If such side effects occur, they can often be handled by changing the dose or drug. A doctor needs to keep close tabs on the growth of any patient taking these medicines.

> * **side effects** are symptoms like headache, dizziness, or stomachache that may be caused by prescription medications.

Stimulant medications sometimes are abused by teenagers, who take them at higher doses and in other ways than prescribed. This can be very dangerous, especially when the medicine is abused along with other drugs.

In recent years, there has been much debate about whether stimulant medicines are prescribed too often. Critics argue that some children who do not have true ADHD may be given the drugs as a way to control their difficult behavior. However, a study by the American Medical Association, published in 1998, found that this problem is not widespread.

Benefits of counseling   Counseling involves talking to a trained mental health professional about problems. Children with ADHD often do not feel very good about themselves. They may struggle with their schoolwork, or they may find it hard to make and keep friends. They may get into a lot of trouble with parents and teachers. Talking to a counselor can help them work out such problems. A counselor can offer ideas on making better grades, dealing with teasing, and getting along at school and home.

One form of counseling that is often used for ADHD is cognitive behavioral therapy (COG-i-tiv bee-HAYV-yoor-al THER-a-pee). This type of counseling lets people work directly to change their current behavior. Cognitive behavioral therapy might involve practical help, such as helping a person learn to think through tasks and keep a schedule. It might also involve teaching new behaviors, by giving praise or rewards each time the person acts in a desired way.

How Can Schools Help?

ADHD is considered a disability under federal law if it seriously interferes with a student's ability to learn. As a result, students with ADHD may be eligible for special school services. In order to get this help, a student usually has to take special tests. These may include an IQ test, which measures the student's ability to learn, and an achievement test, which measures what the student has actually learned about different subjects. Once testing is completed, school officials meet with the student's parents to go over the results and decide whether special services are needed. They discuss the student's problem areas as well as steps the school will take to help.

Children with ADHD are often as "smart" as other children, but their problems in school can stem from having a hard time paying attention and sitting still. Some make very good grades, but others struggle to do well. These children may need to be evaluated for learning differences, even after medicine or counseling are begun. Teachers can help such students by setting goals and giving rewards for reaching them. Students with ADHD may also need more one-on-one teaching and shorter work periods.

What About Self-Help?

People with ADHD can do things to make their lives easier. There is a good side to having this disorder. People with ADHD are often full of energy and ideas. The trick is to channel this energy in a positive way.

Coping at School   Some students with ADHD find that it is helpful to:

- Let their teachers know about ADHD, and ask for their help.
- Ask the teacher to repeat instructions, if needed, rather than guessing.
- Write down homework assignments in a notebook, and mark them off as they are done.
- Put homework in a backpack as soon as it is finished.
- Break large assignments down into small, simple tasks.
- Do homework in a quiet place, and take regular, short breaks.
- Sit at the front of the class, where it is easier to pay attention
- Take notes, which makes it easier to stay focused on the material.
- Tape reminder notes to a school locker.

Coping at Home   Many people with ADHD find it helpful to:

- talk to friends and family about ADHD, and ask for their help
- have a routine for doing regular chores, such as getting ready for school
- make a daily list of things to do, then plan the best order for doing them
- use a chart to stay on track, marking off tasks as they are finished
- store similar items, such as all video games, together in one place

■ find physical activities, such as sports, to burn off excess energy

■ tape reminder notes to the bathroom mirror.

What About the Future?

There is no "cure" for ADHD. Half of all children with ADHD will still show signs of the disorder as adults. However, these signs may lessen over time, and such adults can be helped by the same medicines and counseling that help children. In addition, as children with ADHD grow up, they often learn how to direct their enormous energy into useful activities, such as sports or work.

Resources

Books

Nadeau, Kathleen G. *Help4ADD@HighSchool.* Silver Spring, MD: Advantage Books, 1998.

Nadeau, Kathleen G., and Ellen B. Dixon. *Learning to Slow Down and Pay Attention: A Book for Kids About ADD,* 2nd edition. Washington, DC: Magination Press, 1997.

Quinn, Patricia O. *Adolescents and ADD: Gaining the Advantage.* Washington, DC: Magination Press: 1995.

Quinn, Patricia O., and Judith M. Stern. *Putting on the Brakes: Young People's Guide to Understanding Attention Deficit Hyperactivity Disorder.* Washington, DC: Magination Press, 1991.

Magazine

ADDvance. 1001 Spring Street, Suite 118, Silver Spring, MD 20910, 888-238-8588. A magazine for women and girls with ADHD, published by Advantage Books.
http://www.addvance.com

Organizations

Children and Adults with Attention Deficit Disorders, 8181 Professional Place, Suite 201, Landover, MD 20785. The nation's largest group for people with ADHD.
Telephone 800-233-4050
http://www.chadd.org

National Attention Deficit Disorder Association, 9930 Johnnycake Ridge Road, Suite 3E, Mentor, OH 44060. Another national group for young people and adults with ADHD.
Telephone 440-350-9595
http://www.add.org

KEYWORDS
for searching the Internet
and other reference sources

Behavior

Brain disorders

Pervasive Development Disorder

Psychology

A.D.D. Warehouse, 200 N.W. 70th Avenue, Suite 102, Plantation, FL 33317. An excellent selection of books and other products that deal with ADHD.
Telephone 800-233-9273
http://www.addwarehouse.com

Autism

Autism (AW-tiz-um) is a brain disorder that affects a person's ability to communicate with and relate to other people and limits the person's interests and activities.

A World of His Own

Like many children with autism, Jamie was concerned with order. Even as a young child, he kept his toys in the exact same spot on his shelves and would become very angry if anything was moved. He might throw toys, break dishes, or even kick his mother. Most of the time, though, Jamie ignored other people. He seemed to live inside his own head. When things became noisy or confusing in the real world, Jamie would bite himself until he bled. When Jamie started school, he was put in a special class where things were calm and his activities were carefully planned. By the time he was 14, Jamie seemed more relaxed. He would talk to others if they talked to him first. He was also taking medicines that helped him control his anger. However, he still liked everything to be orderly.

What Is Autism?

Autism is a brain disorder that seems to isolate people in worlds of their own. It can lead to a wide range of unusual behavior. People with autism have trouble communicating with and relating to others. They are

Three autistic children in school in Pittsburgh, Pennsylvania. Two are interacting with an adult who is outside the photograph. © *Andy Levin, Photo Researchers, Inc.*

unable to understand other people's thoughts, feelings, and needs. In many cases, language and intelligence are affected, and people with autism may have a limited number of interests and activities.

Many people with autism repeat the same actions, such as rocking or twirling their hair, over and over. Some hurt themselves by banging their heads or biting their arms. Others seem painfully sensitive to touch, sound, taste, or smell. They may strongly dislike any form of physical contact. Children with autism may refer to themselves by name instead of "I" or "me." Some speak in a singsong voice.

What Causes Autism?

Studies suggest that autism may result from problems before birth that keep the brain from developing normally. The brain of an unborn baby starts out with just a few cells that grow and divide until the brain contains billions of special nerve cells, called neurons (NOOR-ons). Each neuron sends out long fibers that connect with other neurons to pass signals from one part of the brain to another or from the brain to the rest of the body. When a neuron receives a signal, it releases chemicals called neurotransmitters, which send the signal to the next neuron. Studies of people with autism have found that some of their neurons are smaller than normal. They also have short nerve fibers, which may affect signaling. In addition, studies suggest that people with autism may have an unusually high amount of the neurotransmitter called serotonin (ser-o-TO-nin). Scientists are studying the effect of such differences.

Who Gets Autism?

Autism occurs in people all over the world of every race and background. Estimates are that two to ten out of every 10,000 people have autism. If the milder forms of autism (see PDD sidebar) are included, this number can go as high as twenty in 10,000. Males are three to four times more likely than females to have the disorder. However, girls with autism tend to have more severe symptoms and lower intelligence.

Genes* may play a role in autism. Families who already have one child with autism have a greater risk of having a second child with the disorder. However, autism does not seem to be caused by one particular gene. Some scientists think that autism may be due to a cluster of faulty genes. In most cases, these genes cause only mild symptoms, such as reading problems, but under certain conditions, full-blown autism may result.

What Other Disorders May Occur?

Other disorders often go along with autism:

- **Mental retardation.** Many people with autism are mentally retarded to some degree, which means that their intelligence is well below average.

- **Seizures.** A seizure is a sudden burst of uncontrolled electrical activity in the brain that can result in brief blackouts to convulsions (intense, uncontrolled muscle spasms throughout the body).

Pervasive Development Disorder (PDD)

Recently, it has been recognized that there is a range for autism—from severe to relatively mild. The term "pervasive developmental" refers to milder cases that do not have all the signs of autism. People with PDD all have some degree of delayed or abnormal language, difficulty with social interaction, and some unusual behaviors or perseverations (overfocus) on ideas or actions.

* **genes** are chemicals in the body that help determine a person's characteristics, such as hair or eye color. They are inherited from a person's parents and are contained in the chromosomes found in the cells of the body.

***X chromosome** (X KRO-mo-som). A chromosome is a structure inside the body's cells containing DNA, the genetic material that helps determine characteristics, such as whether a person has brown hair or blue eyes. The X chromosome carries many different genes. Females have two X chromosomes, while males have only one.

About one third of children with autism have seizures, which can be controlled with medicine.

■ **Fragile X syndrome.** This disorder is associated with a faulty X chromosome*. About one out of ten people with autism, mostly males, have fragile X syndrome, which causes mental retardation.

■ **Asperger's syndrome.** Children with Asperger's syndrome, considered a mild form of autism, have a consuming interest in, or obsession with, one subject—often something unusual for their age. They generally have average or above-average intelligence and impressive verbal skills but lack nonverbal and social skills.

What Are the Symptoms of Autism?

The symptoms of autism can range from mild to severe. In some children, hints of future problems are apparent at birth and become more noticeable as the child's development lags behind that of other children. In others, everything seems fine at first, but between eighteen months and three years of age, the child starts to reject others and may seem to slip backward in development.

Communication   Healthy babies look at other people's faces and react to sounds. Babies with autism avoid eye contact and seem unable to hear. They may start making speech sounds, then suddenly stop. About half of people with autism are never able to speak; others may start talking as late as age five to eight years.

Those who do speak often use language in unusual ways. For example, they may say the same thing over and over or speak only in single words. Some children with autism have echolalia (ek-o-LA-lee-a) and only parrot back what they hear. Some speak in a singsong or robot-like voice.

People with autism also have trouble communicating with body language. Most people smile when talking about things they like or shrug when they cannot answer a question. People with autism often do not use their faces and bodies in this way, and their tone of voice may not indicate their true feelings.

Relationships   Usually, babies smile at familiar faces, and past the age of 7 to 9 months they show signs of fear around strangers. Babies with autism act as if they are unaware of the comings and goings of other people. They may seem impossible to reach. Some resist hugs and cuddling. Others accept physical contact but do not hug back. Older children with autism rarely seem to seek love and comfort from others.

Children with autism also have trouble understanding what other people are thinking or feeling, and they are unable to see things from someone else's point of view.

Interests   Babies are fascinated by the world around them. They reach for objects and play with toys, constantly moving from one thing to another. Babies with autism often seem stuck on one activity. They may repeat one movement, such as rocking back and forth or flicking their fingers. Children with autism may also become obsessed with certain objects. For example, a child who is obsessed with watches might grab strangers' arms to look at their wrists.

Senses   Many people with autism seem painfully sensitive to touch, sound, taste, or smell. They might cover their ears and scream at the sound of a vacuum cleaner. Other senses may be extremely dull. Some children with autism do not seem to notice extreme cold or pain, to the point where they might break an arm and never cry.

Talents   Some people with autism have remarkable talents. For example, at an early age, when other children are drawing lines and scribbles, some children with autism can draw detailed, realistic pictures. Other children learn to read before they even start to speak. Still others can play a song on the piano after hearing it once. A few people with autism can even memorize whole television programs or pages of the phone book.

How Is Autism Diagnosed?

Since the symptoms of autism vary so widely, it can be hard to diagnose. Parents are usually the first ones to notice that something is wrong. A doctor can rule out problems such as hearing loss, speech problems, mental retardation, and other brain disorders. If autism is suspected, the child can see a specialist.

There is no single test for autism. The doctor will closely note the child's language and actions around other people and ask the parents about the child's symptoms and development.

How Is Autism Treated?

There is no cure for autism, but there is reason for hope.

Thinking in Pictures

Temple Grandin is a gifted animal scientist who has earned a Ph.D. Today she invents equipment for handling livestock, writes books, and gives lectures. Yet as a child, Grandin had many of the signs of full-blown autism. As a baby, she would stiffen when picked up and struggle to be put down. By age two, she was sometimes overpowered by her ultra-sharp senses. She screamed, flew into rages, and threw things. At other times, she found that focusing intently on one thing, such as an apple or her hand, made her feel calmer and safer. Grandin's mother put her in a special class with strict routines designed for children with speech problems. By age four, Grandin had started to speak, and by age five, she could go to regular school. As an adult, she recalled her experiences in a book called *Thinking in Pictures*. The book begins: "I think in pictures. Words are like a second language to me." Today Grandin uses the way her brain works to imagine how the parts of the complicated equipment she invents will fit together.

AUTISM IS NOT SCHIZOPHRENIA

The term "autism" was introduced by the psychiatrist Eugen Bleuler in 1911 to refer to a group of symptoms observed in people with schizophrenia. Bleuler described the symptoms as "detachment from reality," with a "predominance of inner life" withdrawn from the external world.

The Johns Hopkins psychiatrist Leo Kanner (1894–1981), founder of child psychiatry as a medical specialty, first identified autism as a disorder distinct from schizophrenia. Kanner believed that people with autism had not withdrawn from participation in the external world, but that autism was a fundamental inability to relate, from the beginning of life. In 1944 he designated the condition as "early infantile autism."

The Real "Rain Man"

In the movie *Rain Man,* actor Dustin Hoffman portrays a man with autism who is a savant, or a person with mental deficiencies who is exceptionally gifted in one area. To prepare for the role, Hoffman studied real-life "rain man" Joe Sullivan. Like Sullivan, Hoffman's character insists on eating cheese puffs with toothpicks and mutters the same things over and over to himself. Also like Sullivan, the character can do complicated math in his head and name the day of the week for any date past or future. When the movie came out in 1988, Sullivan was a high school graduate who held a job shelving books at a library.

Behavioral treatments   Some treatments focus on using rewards to teach new skills, then using the new skills to replace problem behaviors. Others build on the special interests, skills, and needs of the particular child. Studies have shown that such treatments are most likely to work if they involve a regular routine and planned activities and teach tasks as a series of simple steps. It also helps if the parents are involved, and with training, parents can continue the treatment at home.

Medicines   No medicine can fix the brain problems that seem to cause autism. However, doctors may prescribe medications to reduce symptoms such as head banging or violent outbursts. Some medications also decrease seizures and lessen problems related to paying attention. Most such drugs affect the amount of signaling chemicals, such as serotonin in the brain.

Special education   Special education classes can help a child with autism learn as much as possible. For some, this means mastering simple skills such as dressing and handling money. For others, this means learning to read, write, and do math. Many people with autism finish high school, and a few even earn college degrees. The sooner a child gets help, the greater the chance for learning.

Can Autism Be Outgrown?

People do not outgrow autism. In general, those with milder forms (PDD) do better in their day-to-day lives. Over time and with help, however, the symptoms of autism may get better. Although most adults with autism need lifelong training and help taking care of themselves, some go on to lead nearly normal lives.

Resources

Book

Grandin, Temple. *Thinking in Pictures, and Other Reports from My Life with Autism.* New York: Vintage Books, 1995.

Organizations

Autism Research Institute, 4182 Adams Avenue, San Diego, CA 92116. A group that studies autism.
Telephone 619-281-7165
http://www.autism.com/ari

Autism Society of America, 7910 Woodmont Avenue, Suite 300, Bethesda, MD 20814-3015. A group for people with autism and their families.
Telephone 800-3AUTISM
http://www.autism-society.org

The National Institutes of Health posts information about autism on its website at:
http://www.nimh.nih.gov/publicat/autism.htm

U.S. National Institute of Mental Health (NIMH), NIMH Public Inquiries, 5600 Fishers Lane, Room 7C-02, MSC 8030, Bethesda, MD 20892-8030. NIMH publishes a pamphlet called *Autism*.
Telephone 301-443-4513
http://www.nimh.nih.gov

The U.S. Centers for Disease Control, located in Atlanta, Georgia, posts information about autism on its website at:
http://www.cdc.gov/nceh/programs/CDDH/

B

Babesiosis

Babesiosis is a rare disease carried by ticks infected with the Babesia parasite. It most often affects cows, horses, sheep, dogs, and cats, but it can be transmitted to people through tick bites.

KEYWORDS
for searching the Internet
or other reference sources

Piroplasmosis

Tickborne diseases

Watch out for that tick! Ticks carry many different diseases, including babesiosis (ba-bee-ze-O-sis), Lyme disease, and Rocky Mountain spotted fever.

What Are *Babesia*?

Babesia (ba-BEE-ze-a) are protozoa, or one-celled organisms, that often live as parasites* infecting cows, horses, sheep, goats, dogs, cats, and other animals. Ticks pick up *Babesia* when they feed on infected animals. The protozoa then multiply in the tick, and when the tick bites a person or another animal, the protozoa travel from the tick into the new host, where they begin multiplying again.

* **parasites** are creatures that live in and feed on the bodies of other organisms. The animal or plant harboring the parasite is called its host.

What Happens When People Get Babesiosis?

The *Babesia* parasite invades the body's red blood cells and can destroy them. If left untreated, babesiosis may destroy red blood cells faster than the body can replace them.

Symptoms   Doctors believe that many cases of babesiosis do not cause any symptoms. But in some cases, symptoms may start one to four weeks after the tick bite occurs, and symptoms may last for several weeks or months. People with babesiosis may experience fever, chills, sweating, fatigue, and anemia. Its symptoms are similar to those of malaria.

Diagnosis and treatment   Doctors diagnose babesiosis by examining blood under a microscope. If they detect the parasite, they will prescribe medications to fight the infection and to rid the body of the parasite. Babesiosis is usually curable, although repeated courses of treatment may be necessary.

Most patients recover with few, if any, lasting effects. The most serious and sometimes fatal cases are found in elderly people, in pregnant women, in people who have had their spleens* removed, or in people with immune deficiencies.

* **spleen** is an organ near the stomach that helps the body fight infections.

115

How Do People Prevent Babesiosis?

The best methods of prevention are the use of insect repellant and proper clothing. People in tick-infested areas should wear long-sleeve shirts and long pants tucked into socks or boots. That can help to keep ticks from reaching the skin. If ticks do attach to the skin of people or pets, the ticks should be removed with tweezers.

Resource

The U.S. National Institute of Allergy and Infectious Diseases has information about babesiosis and other tickborne diseases at its website. http://www.niaid.nih.gov/factsheets/tickborn.htm

▶ *See also*
Lyme Disease
Malaria
Rocky Mountain Spotted Fever
Zoonoses

KEYWORDS
for searching the Internet and other reference sources

Antibiotics

Antibiotic resistance

Bacteriology

Drug resistance

Infection

*microorganisms are living organisms that can only be seen using a microscope. Examples of microorganisms are bacteria, fungi, and viruses.

Bacterial Infections

Bacterial infections are illnesses that occur when harmful forms of bacteria multiply inside the body. They range from mild to severe. Although they include such deadly diseases as plague, tuberculosis, and cholera, these and many other bacterial infections can be prevented by good sanitation or cured by antibiotics.

Bacteria are everywhere: in soil, in water, in air, and in the bodies of every person and animal. These microorganisms* are among the most numerous forms of life on Earth.

Most bacteria are either harmless, or helpful, or even essential to life. Bacteria break down (decompose) dead plants and animals. This allows chemical elements like carbon to return to the earth to be used again. In addition, some bacteria help plants get nitrogen. Without them, plants could not grow. In the human body, bacteria help keep the digestive tract working properly.

Like viruses, however, bacteria can cause hundreds of illnesses. Some bacterial infections are common in childhood, such as strep throat and ear infections. Others cause major diseases, such as tuberculosis, plague, syphilis, and cholera. The infection may be localized (limited to a small area), as when a surgical wound gets infected with a bacterium called *Staphylococcus* (staf-i-lo-KOK-us). It may involve an internal organ, as in bacterial pneumonia (infection of the lungs) or bacterial meningitis (infection of the membrane covering the brain and spinal cord).

Some bacteria, such as pneumococcus (noo-mo-KOK-us), which is also called *Streptococcus pneumoniae*, almost always cause illness if they get into the body. Others, such as *Escherichia coli*, usually called by the short form *E. coli*, often are present without doing harm. If the immune system is weakened, however, these bacteria can grow out of control and start doing damage. Such illnesses are called "opportunistic infections." They have become more common in recent years, in part because AIDS, organ transplants, and other medical treatments have left more people living with weakened immune systems.

How Are Bacteria Different?

Unlike other living cells, bacteria do not have a membrane enclosing their nucleus, the part of the cell containing DNA, or genetic matter. Unlike viruses, most bacteria are complete cells that can reproduce on their own without having to invade a plant or animal cell. Some bacteria, however, do need to live inside another cell just as viruses do.

How do bacterial infections spread?   Different bacteria spread in different ways. Examples include:

- through contaminated water (cholera and typhoid fever)
- through contaminated food (botulism, *E. coli* food poisoning, salmonella food poisoning)
- through sexual contact (syphilis, gonorrhea, chlamydia)
- through the air, when infected people sneeze or cough (tuberculosis)
- through contact with animals (anthrax, cat scratch disease)
- through touching infected people (strep throat)
- from one part of the body, where they are harmless, to another part, where they cause illness (as when *E. coli* spread from the intestines to the urinary tract).

How do bacteria cause illness?   Bacteria can cause illness in several ways. Some destroy tissue directly. Some become so numerous that the body cannot work normally. And some produce toxins (poisons) that kill cells. Exotoxins are poisons released by live bacteria. Endotoxins are poisons released when the bacteria die.

How Are Bacterial Infections Diagnosed and Treated?

Symptoms of bacterial infections vary widely but often include fever.

Diagnosis   Doctors may test the blood, sputum, or urine for evidence of harmful bacteria. If a lung infection is suspected, the doctor may take a chest x-ray or do a biopsy, taking cells from an infected area to be examined. If meningitis is suspected, the doctor may do a spinal tap, using a needle to extract a sample of the spinal fluid surrounding the spinal cord for testing.

Treatment   Most bacterial infections can be cured by antibiotic drugs, which were one of the great medical success stories of the twentieth century. These drugs either kill the bacteria or prevent them from reproducing. Penicillin, the first antibiotic, is still used to treat some infections.

Food Poisoning

Food poisoning is often the result of bacterial contamination. Important precautions for preventing food poisoning include:

- Avoiding raw or undercooked meat, poultry, seafood, and eggs.
- Avoiding non-pasteurized dairy products.
- Throwing out food items that are old or have an "off" smell.
- Keeping foods cold until ready to serve.
- Storing and cooking foods properly.
- Washing knives, cutting boards, cooking utensils, and food preparation areas after every use.
- Washing hands before preparing food, before eating, and after using the bathroom.

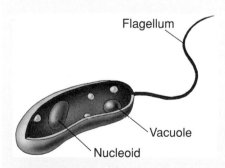

Anatomy of an individual bacterium. Its DNA (genetic material) is in the nucleoid area, but it is not enclosed within a membrane. This bacterium uses its flagellum (tail) to move around.

117

Flesh-Eating Bacteria

A virulent strain of *Streptococcus A* bacteria caused illness in 117 people in Texas between December 1997 and March 1998. Of those 117 infections, 26 (17 adults and 9 children) resulted in deaths. Described in media coverage as "flesh-eating bacteria," these pathogens caused their damage through a process called hemolysis (he-MOL-y-sis), which causes red blood cells to disintegrate. The Texas outbreak was short lived, and experts still do not know how it started.

Seen under an electron microscope are *Staphylococcus aureus* bacteria from a group that is resistant to antibiotics. Some of them are dividing to reproduce. *Dr. Kari Lounatmaa/Science Photo Library, Photo Researchers, Inc.*

▼

Other widely used antibiotics include amoxicillin, bacitracin, erythromycin, cephalosporins, fluroquinolones, and tetracycline. Sometimes antitoxins are also given to counter the effects of bacterial toxins, as in the case of tetanus or botulism.

How Are Bacterial Infections Prevented?

Young children commonly get shots of vaccine to prevent diphtheria, whooping cough, tetanus, and *Hemophilus influenza B*, all bacterial infections. In addition, vaccines are available to help prevent cholera, meningococcal and pneumococcal infections, plague, and typhoid fever.

For many bacterial infections, good living conditions are the best prevention. That means clean water supplies, sanitary disposal of human waste, well-ventilated housing that is not overcrowded, and prompt medical treatment for people who do get sick.

Other steps include:

- Washing hands (before handling food; after using the toilet; after touching animals; after having contact with infected people).

- Washing fruits and vegetables before eating.

- Cooking meat thoroughly.

- Abstaining from sexual contact, or using condoms during sexual activity.

How Do Bacteria Become Drug Resistant?

Each kind of bacteria can be killed by certain antibiotics and each kind is naturally resistant to others. But in recent years, some bacteria have developed resistance to antibiotics that used to kill them. This is one of the big problems in controlling infectious diseases.

How does resistance occur? In some cases, it occurs by chance. As bacteria reproduce, mutations (variations) in their genes occur all the time. One of these mutations may happen, by chance, to make one bacterium in a person's body less vulnerable to a drug. This bacterium multiples along with other bacteria. While other bacteria are killed off by the drug, the mutated—or resistant—bacterium thrives, and eventually spreads from person to person.

Why does resistance occur more often now? Humans can make drug resistance far more likely to develop than it would simply by chance. They do this when they use antibiotics that are not needed or when they do need antibiotics but stop taking them too soon.

Here is how those practices can increase resistance: Let us say that a man has a bacterial infection. He takes an antibiotic, feels better, and stops taking the drug in five days, even though the doctor said to take it for 10 days. Inside the man's body, the drug may have killed, say, 80 percent of the bacteria. That was enough to make the man feel better. But the bacteria still alive are the 20 percent that were toughest, the ones best able to survive the drug. If the man had kept taking the antibiotic, the toughest bacteria might have been killed on Day 8, 9, or 10. But now, left alone, they start to multiply. Soon the person feels sick again. But this time, all the bacteria in his body are the tougher kind. A scientist would say the person's behavior "selected" the most resistant bacteria for survival.

A similar process occurs when doctors prescribe antibiotics that are not needed. Let us say that a girl has a cough and fever. The doctor prescribes antibiotics on the chance that the girl has a bacterial infection. But she actually has a virus, and viruses cannot be treated with antibiotics. The girl's immune system, her natural defense system, fights off the virus as it would have without the drug. Meanwhile, the antibiotic kills off some bacteria that usually live harmlessly in the girl's throat. The bacteria in her throat that survive are those that are better at resisting the antibiotic. Later, if those bacteria get into her ears, her lungs, or some other part of her body where they can cause illness, the antibiotic may not work as well against them.

If events like these happen countless times, in countless people, eventually strains of bacteria may arise that partially or completely resist a drug that used to kill them.

Resources

U.S. Centers for Disease Control and Prevention (CDC). CDC posts a fact sheet called *Bacterial Diseases* at its website.
http://www.cdc.gov/health/diseases.htm

U.S. Food and Drug Administration (FDA). The FDA posts a *Bad Bug Book* at its website that offers fact sheets about many different pathogenic bacteria.
http://vm.cfsan.fda.gov/~mow/intro.html

Bad Breath *See* Halitosis

Baldness (Alopecia) *See* Hair Loss

Bedsores (Pressure Sores)

Bedsores, also called pressure sores or decubitus (de-KU-bi-tus) ulcers, are skin sores caused by prolonged pressure on the skin, usually in people who are paralyzed, bedridden, or too weak to move around much.

► *See also*
Botulism
Campylobacteriosis
Cat Scratch Disease
Cholera
Chlamydial Infections
Diphtheria
Ear Infections
Endocarditis
Food Poisoning
Gonorrhea
Legionnaire's Disease
Leprosy
Lyme Disease
Meningitis
Osteomyelitis
Peptic Ulcer
Plague
Pneumonia
Rheumatic Fever
Rocky Mountain Spotted Fever
Salmonellosis
Strep Throat
Syphilis
Tetanus
Toxic Shock Syndrome
Typhoid Fever
Tuberculosis
Typhus
Whooping Cough
Zoonoses

KEYWORDS
for searching the Internet and other reference sources

Decubitus ulcers

Dermatology

*septicemia (sep-ti-SE-me-a) means a bacterial infection in the blood that spreads throughout the body, with potentially fatal results.

*coma is an unconscious state, like a very deep sleep. A person in a coma cannot be awakened, and cannot move, see, speak, or hear.

*contagious means transmitted from one person to another.

What Are Bedsores?

Bedsores develop when the skin is compressed between a protruding bone, like a hipbone or elbow, and an external surface, like a wheelchair or mattress, over a long period of time. This compression limits the flow of blood in blood vessels that bring nutrients and oxygen to the skin and remove wastes. Without oxygen or nourishment, the underlying tissue may deteriorate, and a hole may open in the skin. If left untreated, bacteria can infect the skin opening, and lead to septicemia* or infection of muscle or bone.

Because protein and fluids help keep skin healthy and supple, elderly people with a poor diet often are at risk for skin-damaging bedsores. Other people at risk include those who cannot move much or shift their positions, perhaps because they have had a paralyzing stroke, or a long illness, or are in a coma*. People in wheelchairs or with spinal cord injuries, particularly those who cannot sense pain well, also are vulnerable to skin sores because they may not feel the ulcer forming. Bedsores are not contagious*.

What Are the Symptoms of Bedsores?

A typical bedsore starts as a red area on the skin that may feel hard or warm to the touch. In people with darker skin, the sore may show as a shiny spot on the skin. If pressure is removed at this point, complications can be prevented. If the pressure is not removed, a blister, pimple, or scab may form over this area, which is a sign that the tissue beneath is dying. Eventually, a hole, or ulcer, will form in the skin. The dead tissue may appear small on the skin surface, but it may be larger in deeper tissues. The damage may extend all the way to the bones.

To diagnose bedsores, health care providers examine the skin for redness, blisters, openings, rashes, or warm spots, paying particular attention to bony areas. Any spots previously broken or healed over also are checked, as scar tissue can break open.

How Are Bedsores Treated and Prevented?

Bedsores can be prevented and treated in their early stages by relieving pressure on the body. This means changing a person's position in bed at least every two hours and in a wheelchair every 10 to 15 minutes. People at risk for bedsores should check themselves carefully at least twice daily or ask their caregivers to do so. Doctors recommend using long-handled mirrors to help with these exams.

Other helpful methods to prevent bedsores include:

- using soft pillows to cushion the legs, back, and arms from pressure

- using special mattresses or egg-crate foam mattresses to reduce pressure

- keeping bedclothes unwrinkled and free of crumbs

- keeping skin clean and dry, free of sweat, urine, and stool
- eating a balanced diet and drinking lots of fluids to help skin stay healthy.

If a bedsore does develop, treatment may include antibiotics to treat infections and special gels or dressings to promote healing. In more serious cases, doctors may need to remove the dead tissue and use surgery to close the open sore. If the bedsore reaches the bone, then the affected bone tissue may have to be removed as well.

Resource

The U.S. National Institutes of Health (NIH) has a search engine at its website that locates information for doctors, nurses, and caregivers about pressure ulcers and bedsores.
http://www.nih.gov

▶ *See also*
Paralysis
Skin Conditions

Bedwetting (Enuresis)

Bedwetting (known as enuresis) is the involuntary release of urine past an age when control usually is expected.

KEY WORDS
for searching the Internet and other reference sources

Enuresis

Incontinence

Urinary tract

Bobby's Story

Bobby felt ashamed when he woke up and discovered his underwear and bed sheets were wet again. He had urinated while sleeping. It bothered Bobby because at age 10 he thought he was too old for such things to happen.

What Is Bedwetting?

Bobby's reaction is understandable, because wetting the bed can be connected in people's minds with being a baby. But bedwetting is a common condition, even for 10-year-olds like Bobby, and people should not feel shame over it. It is estimated that 30 percent of children at age 4, 10 percent at age 6, 3 percent at age 12, and 1 percent at age 18 experience bedwetting. It is not a sign of personal weakness to wet the bed. Instead it can be the result of deep sleep, stress, or other conditions.

The condition is called nocturnal enuresis (nok-TER-nal en-yu-REE-sis). Nocturnal means occurring at night, and enuresis comes from the Greek word that means "to urinate in." It is estimated that each night from 5 to 7 million children in the United States wet their beds while sleeping.

Bedwetting occurs in both boys and girls, although it is more common in boys. Adults, too, experience the condition, although in much smaller

*incontinence (in-KONT-e-nans) is the failure to control urination or bowel movement.

What If I Get Invited to a Sleepover?

Many children who wet their beds fear sleeping anywhere but at home. They are worried they will urinate during a sleepover or at camp. It can cause them to withdraw from important social activities like these.

However, studies show that many children who wet their beds at home do not do it while sleeping somewhere else. Doctors say this might happen because children are not sleeping as soundly as they do at home. Deep sleep is a common reason children do not wake up when they need to urinate.

The parents of children who wet their bed sometimes can ease the situation by talking things over with the parents of the friend before the sleepover. Alerting the friend's parents might help overcome any uneasiness if bedwetting occurs.

Also, it can help to follow the advice about not drinking before bedtime and setting an alarm to get up at night for a bathroom break.

numbers. About 1 percent of adults wet their beds. Some older men and women, as they age, develop incontinence* during the day and at night, often because of medical conditions or medications they take.

Most children are toilet trained by age 3, although some continue to use diapers or training pants while sleeping. Past that age, many children might wet their beds once in a while, especially if they are sick or particularly tired. After the age of 6, if bedwetting continues to occur, doctors often will recommend treatment.

A common condition that runs in families   No one is sure exactly what causes some children to wet their beds more often than others.

Children who have a parent who wet the bed as a child are more likely to wet the bed themselves. The chances range from 40 to 75 percent, depending upon whether one or both parents experienced bedwetting.

What Causes Bedwetting?

Many children with enuresis appear to be exceptionally deep sleepers. They are not awakened easily by the urge to urinate.

Other children have bladders that develop more slowly than most. The bladder is the sac in which urine is stored until it is released.

Infections of the urinary tract (kidneys, bladder) and diabetes also can lead to bedwetting.

It also is a common reaction to stress. For example, some younger children who are toilet trained resume wetting their beds after a new baby is born or parents separate. Starting a new school or moving to a new town also can trigger the condition or make it worse.

How Is Bedwetting Treated?

Bedwetting often frustrates parents and embarrasses children. Most people stop bedwetting without any treatment by the time they are 6 years old. It is important to remember that with family support and medical advice, almost all children overcome the condition.

There are several techniques that often help. Limiting drinking liquids near bedtime can be helpful, as can avoiding caffeinated beverages, such as colas. Sometimes parents also wake their children after a few hours of sleep to encourage them to go to the bathroom. This can help children to start to wake up when they experience the urge to urinate. Some children use a bedwetting alarm, which awakens them if the bed becomes wet. In some cases, a doctor can prescribe a medicated nasal spray that temporarily reduces urine production during the night.

Doctors say it is important for parents to offer encouragement to children and help them understand it is a common condition. Children also should realize they probably know people who have similar experiences, but it is not something many children discuss with their friends or classmates.

Sometimes bedwetting is not overcome with these techniques. Some children might need special counseling about stress in their lives. Other might need medication that controls the bedwetting.

Resources

Maizels, Max, Diane Rosenbaum, and Barbara Keating. *Getting to Dry: How to Help Your Child Overcome Bedwetting.* Harvard Common Press, 1999.

KidsHealth.org posts numerous articles about childhood conditions, including enuresis, at its website. http://KidsHealth.org

► *See also*
Incontinence

Bell's Palsy

Bell's Palsy is a sudden weakness or loss of function of certain facial muscles, usually on one side of the face, caused by swelling of a facial nerve.

KEYWORDS
for searching the Internet and other reference sources

Neurology

Otolaryngology

Half a Face

Fifteen-year-old Shelly woke up one morning feeling like she had just received a shot of Novocain from the dentist. When she looked in the mirror, she saw that her face seemed limp on one side. She could not smile, and only one side of her face seemed to work. Shelly screamed for her parents and they came running. When they saw her face, they became worried that she had had a stroke* or had developed a brain tumor. They rushed her to the hospital emergency room.

At the hospital, the doctor examined Shelly and asked her and her parents about Shelly's medical history. Then the doctor performed several diagnostic tests to find out whether she had high blood pressure or Lyme Disease. At that point, the doctor was able to explain that the symptoms indicated Bell's Palsy, a fairly common and harmless condition.

It took three weeks for Shelly's condition to go away, and those three weeks felt more like three years to Shelly, but she was grateful that it was not something more serious.

What Is Bell's Palsy?

Bell's Palsy is a condition that occurs when the facial nerve becomes irritated. The facial nerve runs from the brain through a small hole in the skull. Sometimes the facial nerve becomes irritated or swollen. The irritated nerve does not send normal signals to the muscles on one side of the face. The result is partial or complete loss of muscle function (called "palsy").

The symptoms of Bell's Palsy begin suddenly and usually worsen over two to five days. The sudden numbness or weakness characteristic of Bell's Palsy gets worse during the day, and the face feels stiff and pulls to one side. People with Bell's Palsy typically have problems closing one

** **stroke** may occur when a blood vessel bringing oxygen and nutrients to the brain bursts or becomes clogged by a blood clot or other particle. As a result, nerve cells in the affected area and the specific body parts they control cannot function.*

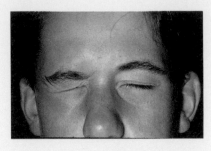

▲

Bell's Palsy causes muscle weakness or loss of muscle function on one side of the face, which can result in a lopsided appearance. In this case, the weakness is on the left side of the face, which appears more relaxed. © *1992 Science Photo Library, Custom Medical Stock Photo.*

eye and cannot wrinkle their forehead. They may feel pain behind the ear, they may experience involuntary facial movements called "tics," and hearing in the ear on the affected side may be very sensitive. They also may drool and have trouble eating and talking.

People with a stroke can look like they have Bell's Palsy, so it is important to visit a doctor to find out what is causing facial paralysis. People with Bell's Palsy often fear a brain tumor, but the symptoms of a brain tumor usually occur more gradually than the sudden start of Bell's Palsy.

What Causes Bell's Palsy?

Bell's Palsy is an idiopathic (id-e-o-PATH-ik) disease, which means that its cause is unknown or uncertain. One possible cause of Bell's Palsy is irritation of the facial nerve after a viral infection, such as herpes zoster (which causes shingles) or herpes simplex (the cold sore virus). It also may be related to a blow to the face that damages the nerve or to conditions such as Lyme disease, diabetes, and high blood pressure.

Bell's Palsy may happen to men and women of all ages but is most common between the ages of 30 and 60. Pregnant women and people with diabetes, a cold, or the flu are more susceptible than the average person. One person in 60 to 70 develops Bell's Palsy during his or her lifetime, which translates to about 40,000 people per year in the United States.

How Is Bell's Palsy Treated?

Eighty percent of people with Bell's Palsy begin to recover several weeks after their symptoms begin, and they recover completely within several months without treatment. A few people never recover completely and some of their symptoms continue permanently.

During recovery, the biggest concern is protecting the exposed eye from dryness and injury. Doctors will sometimes prescribe antiviral medications during the first 5 to 6 days of the onset of Bell's Palsy, and anti-inflammatory drugs sometimes help reduce swelling of the nerve.

BELL AND THE BRAIN

Sir Charles Bell (1774–1842) was a Scottish scientist who studied anatomy (the structure of organisms). His investigations of the brain have been called the "*Magna Carta* of Neurology." The *Magna Carta* or "great charter," was a famous document in English history, so this is quite a compliment to Sir Charles Bell. He received the first medal awarded by the Royal Society of Great Britain for his book, *New Idea of Anatomy of the Brain*. Bell was the first to describe how sensory neurons (nerve cells) carry messages to the brain and how motor neurons carry messages to muscles and glands. Because of his work with nerve anatomy, Bell's Palsy was named after him.

Resources

Book

Dambach, J.P. *Surviving Bell's Palsy: A Patient's Guide to Facial Paralysis Management.* Homosassa, FL: J.P. Dambach, 1997. This book describes the emotional effects of Bell's Palsy. It is not a medical guide but a tool for discussion by patients and doctors.

Organizations

The U.S. National Institute of Neurological Disorders and Stroke posts a fact sheet about Bell's Palsy at its website.
http://www.ninds.nih.gov/patients/Disorder/bells/bells.htm

National Centers for Facial Paralysis, Inc. This organization has offices in eight cities.
Telephone 888-30BELLS
http://www.bellspalsy.com

Bell's Palsy Research Foundation, 9121 East Tanque Verde, Suite 105-286, Tucson, AZ 85749.
Telephone 520-749-4614

American Academy of Otolaryngology, Head and Neck Surgery, Inc., 1 Prince Street, Alexandria, VA 22314.
Telephone 703-836-4444

▶ *See also*
Diabetes
Herpes
Hypertension
Lyme Disease
Paralysis
Shingles

Bends

The bends is a painful condition that occurs in scuba divers who ascend too quickly or in aviators flying at high altitudes. Also called decompression sickness, the bends results when bubbles from dissolved gases form in the blood or in tissues because of rapidly decreasing pressure.

KEYWORDS
for searching the Internet and other reference sources

Decompression sickness

Hyperbaric chamber

Scuba diving

*caisson (KAY-son) means a watertight container that divers or construction workers use under water.

The bends is also called decompression sickness or caisson* sickness. When a person is scuba diving, the water pressure increases with depth. As depth increases, the pressure of the air breathed also must increase. This causes more of the air to dissolve in the bloodstream.

How Is the Body Affected?

The main components of air are oxygen and nitrogen gases. Oxygen is continuously used by the body, but nitrogen is not used. When a diver ascends, the pressure decreases and the blood can no longer hold all the nitrogen dissolved in it.

If a diver ascends slowly, the nitrogen escapes into the lungs and is breathed out harmlessly. But if the diver ascends rapidly, the nitrogen forms bubbles in the blood that can lodge at joints such as the elbow or knee and cause pain. In severe cases, extreme pain causes the sufferer to double over, hence the common name "the bends."

Symptoms of the bends usually show up within 90 minutes of diving but may take as long as two days. Minor cases cause itching, rash, joint pain, or skin discoloration. Severe cases cause symptoms such as extreme pain at the joints, headache, seizures, hearing problems, nausea and vomiting, back or abdominal pain, vision disturbances, or chest pain.

How Do Doctors Treat the Bends?

Minor cases of the bends usually require no treatment, although a doctor should be consulted. Treatment of severe cases, however, requires a hyperbaric (hy-per-BARE-ik) chamber, a device that creates pressure to redissolve the gas bubbles. The patient is placed under high-pressure conditions, and then the pressure is slowly decreased. Prompt treatment increases the chances for a complete recovery.

What Do Scuba Divers Need to Know?

There are about 5 million people who scuba dive. Scuba divers must be certified and must take training classes, where they learn how to dive safely to avoid decompression sickness. The bends is a preventable condition when safety rules are followed strictly.

Resource

Marine Medical Systems, 84 North Main Street, South Norwalk, CT 06854. Marine Medical Systems posts a fact sheet about diving injuries and decompression sickness at its website.
Telephone 800-272-3008
http://www.marinemedical.com/diving.htm

▶ *See also*
Altitude Sickness

Bilharzia *See* **Schistosomiasis**

Bipolar Disorder *See* Depressive Disorders

Birth Defects

KEYWORDS
*for searching the Internet
and other reference sources*

Genetics

Pregnancy

Amniocentesis

Infant mortality

A birth defect is an abnormality in the body structure or chemistry of a newborn child. It may be caused by hereditary factors (that is, by genetic causes), by environmental influences that affect the embryo or fetus in the mother's womb, or by a combination of factors. Often, the cause of a birth defect is unknown.

Birth defects sometimes are called congenital anomalies (kon-JEN-i-tal a-NAM-a-leez). Congenital means present at birth, and anomalies are abnormalities or irregularities. An abnormality present at birth usually is not considered a birth defect unless it results in a disease or in a physical or mental disability. For example, birthmarks are seldom considered birth defects because they usually do not cause health problems.

The March of Dimes estimates that 3 to 5 percent of babies born in the United States have some type of birth defect. Some birth defects, such as cleft palate, occur infrequently. Others, such as some congenital heart defects, are more common. Some hereditary defects are more common in certain populations than in others. For example, sickle-cell anemia, an inherited blood disease, occurs mainly in people of African ancestry, whereas Tay-Sachs disease, a fatal disorder of body chemistry, primarily affects people of eastern European Jewish ancestry.

How Do Hereditary Factors Cause Birth Defects?

Each of us has genes* that are inherited from our parents. The genes occur in pairs along threadlike bodies called chromosomes*, which are located in the nucleus* of each cell in the body. Genes determine our inborn characteristics, or traits. These traits include how we look and how the chemical substances in our bodies function. In the case of birth defects, the genes also may determine abnormalities if they are faulty in some way.

Mendelian inheritance patterns   The simplest patterns of birth defect inheritance are called Mendelian, named for the Austrian monk Gregor Mendel who observed them in the nineteenth century. In Mendelian inheritance, traits (including defects) can be transmitted by way of dominant or recessive genes.

It works this way: A child inherits two copies of each gene, one from the mother and one from the father. If a defective gene is dominant, a child who inherits even one copy of it will have the defect. That is because the defective copy "dominates," or overwhelms, the normal copy inherited from the other parent. But if a defective gene is recessive, the child would have to inherit two defective copies—one from the mother and one from the father—in order to have the defect. A person who inherited only one defective copy would be healthy but could pass the defective copy on to his or her own children. These kinds of inheritance patterns cause what researchers call autosomal (aw-to-SO-mal) birth defects.

Examples of autosomal dominant birth defects are Huntington's disease, a nervous system disorder, and Marfan syndrome, which is characterized by tallness, elongated bones, and heart problems. Some birth defects, such as Huntington's disease, may not show symptoms for many years.

Other birth defects are determined by genes located on the X chromosome (the X and Y chromosomes determine the sex of an infant). Such abnormalities are said to be X-linked. Hemophilia, a blood disorder, and color blindness are examples of X-linked birth defects.

Many hereditary birth defects, however, are not simply dominant, recessive, or X-linked. They may be produced instead by multiple faulty genes.

*__genes__ are chemicals in the body that help determine a person's characteristics, such as hair or eye color. They are inherited from a person's parents and are contained in the chromosomes found in the cells of the body.

*__chromosomes__ are thread-like structures inside cells on which the genes are located.

*__nucleus__ is the part of the cell that contains its genetic information.

The U.S. and the World

■ An estimated 515,000 people worldwide died of birth defects in 1998. Almost 93 percent of those deaths were in low- and middle-income nations.

■ More than 28 million people worldwide live with birth defects, and about 93 percent live in countries with low or middle income.

■ Birth defects are the leading cause of infant mortality in the United States. In 1997, 6,178 children died before their first birthdays because they had one or more birth defects. That number is 22 percent of all children who died under age 1.

■ The most common birth defects involve the heart. About 28 percent of the children under age 1 who died of birth defects in 1997 had problems with their hearts. The second most common category comprised defects of the respiratory system, accounting for about 16 percent of the deaths that year.

■ The death rate from birth defects in the United States dropped 37.7 percent between 1979 and 1997. One reason for the decrease is improved medical care for infants with birth defects.

■ Children with birth defects who survive their first year still may die of complications from the defects later in life. In 1997, 11,912 people of all ages died of birth defects, with only about half under age 1.

■ About 150,000 babies a year are born with a birth defect in the United States. The rate in the mid-1990s put the United States twenty-fifth in the world, with twice as many birth defects per 1,000 live births as the nation with the lowest rate, Japan.

Chromosome abnormalities   Some birth defects are caused by extra, missing, incomplete, or misshapen chromosomes. Down syndrome, one of the most common birth defects, usually is caused by the presence of an extra chromosome in the cells. Down syndrome produces mental retardation, short stature, and distinctive facial features. Defects involving the sex chromosomes can produce problems in sexual development, including sterility, which is an inability to have children.

How Do Environmental Factors Cause Birth Defects?

Birth defects also can be caused by environmental factors, either alone or together with faulty genes. "Environmental" here refers to the environment in the mother's uterus, or womb, rather than to the earth's environment. However, scientists are studying the possible influence on birth defects of poisons in the earth's environment.

Pregnant women who consume excessive amounts of alcohol during the early stages of pregnancy risk having babies with fetal alcohol syndrome. Children with this disorder may have various defects in growth, facial appearance, and mental ability. Scientists are studying whether even moderate use of alcohol can damage a fetus. Smoking during pregnancy increases the likelihood that the baby will have lower than normal weight at birth, increasing the risk of defects.

Some illnesses in a pregnant woman can cause damage to the fetus. For example, German measles (rubella) can cause deafness, blindness, and heart defects in the newborn. Sexually transmitted diseases also can be transmitted to the fetus or to the newborn at birth.

Certain medications have been linked to birth defects. The most famous is the drug thalidomide (tha-LID-o-mide), a sedative that in the early 1960s was found to cause greatly shortened arms and legs in many newborn infants. Many other medications, including tranquilizers and antibacterial and anticancer drugs, can cause congenital abnormalities.

Other environmental factors believed to increase the risk of birth defects include poor nutrition and the age of the mother. For example, the older a pregnant woman is, the more likely she is to give birth to a child with Down syndrome. If the expectant mother is 35 or older, experts recommend that the fetus be tested.

How Do Doctors Diagnose Birth Defects?

Some birth defects can be diagnosed while the child is still in its mother's womb. A procedure called ultrasound, which uses sound waves to produce an image of a fetus on a screen, can detect some malformations. For example, a defect called spina bifida, in which a part of the spinal cord is exposed, can be discovered by ultrasound.

In a procedure called amniocentesis (am-nee-o-sen-TEE-sis), a small sample of fluid surrounding the fetus is removed through a needle and examined. This test is useful in detecting inborn metabolic (body chemistry) defects and abnormalities in the chromosomes.

Many birth defects can be diagnosed by a doctor's physical examination of a newborn baby. Other tests, including x-rays, may be ordered if doctors suspect a birth defect; blood tests can detect certain disorders of the blood or body chemistry. Many infants with defects can develop normally if they receive prompt treatment.

How Do Doctors Treat Birth Defects?

Not every birth defect affects the quality of life of the person who has it. Some birth defects have little effect, except perhaps on appearance.

Several birth defects can be treated to prevent or reduce their harmful effects. Surgeons can perform operations to correct such malformations as clubfoot, cleft palate, cleft lip, and structural defects in the heart and digestive tract. Treatment can lessen the symptoms of cystic fibrosis, an inherited disease that interferes with breathing. In some cases, disorders such as hydrocephalus (hy-dro-SEF-a-lus), a damaging buildup of fluid in the head, can be remedied even before birth.

Doctors can sometimes treat inborn disorders of body chemistry with medications and special diets. For example, prompt treatment can prevent brain damage in phenylketonuria (fen-il-kee-to-NOOR-ee-a), or PKU, a metabolic defect that can produce severe mental retardation. Special education, rehabilitation, and the use of special devices and machines can help to offset some mental and physical handicaps, such as blindness and deafness.

How Do Doctors and Parents-to-Be Prevent Birth Defects?

No one can guarantee that a baby will be born "perfect" and healthy. However, there are ways to minimize the likelihood of having a child with a

Thalidomide and Phocomelia

Thalidomide is a sedative, a medication prescribed to calm the nerves. If taken in the early months of pregnancy it can cause a birth defect called phocomelia (fo-ko-MEE-lee-a), in which the arms, legs, or both are very short and underdeveloped.

Thalidomide was prescribed for pregnant women in Europe in the late 1950s and early 1960s until it was linked to phocomelia in thousands of newborn babies. Fortunately for Americans, thalidomide never was sold in the United States because the U.S. Food and Drug Administration refused to approve it. An employee of this federal agency, Dr. Frances Kelsey, insisted that thalidomide's safety had not been proven. Many people think Dr. Kelsey saved hundreds or even thousands of children from severe birth defects.

The thalidomide tragedy led to an increase in government control over the marketing of drugs throughout the world, and the use of thalidomide is now banned or strictly controlled in most countries.

Thalidomide may prove helpful in the treatment of such serious diseases as AIDS and leprosy, and researchers are continuing to study its therapeutic uses.

◀

Professional tennis instructor Butch Lumpkin was born with the short arms and deformed fingers characteristic of phocomelia, which resulted from the use of Thalidomide during pregnancy. *UPI/Corbis-Bettmann.*

preventable birth defect. Some of the most important ways involve lifestyle. A prospective mother should understand that many things she does may have an effect on the new life growing inside her:

- Pregnant women should not smoke or drink alcoholic beverages, nor should they use drugs of any kind unless prescribed by a doctor.

- Certain vitamins, if taken in proper amounts by the mother-to-be, can help prevent some birth defects. For example, folate (folic acid) taken during pregnancy can help prevent certain defects of the spinal column and central nervous system, including spina bifida.

- Vaccination well before pregnancy can prevent birth defects that might occur if the mother were to develop German measles while pregnant.

Couples should seek genetic counseling before planning to have a child if the mother, father, or relatives have hereditary abnormalities.

Resources

Books

Kidd, J. S., and R. A. Kidd. *Life Lines: The Story of the New Genetics*. New York: Facts on File, 1999. This survey for young adults discusses the evolution of the study of genetics.

Marshall, Elizabeth L. *The Human Genome Project: Cracking the Code Within Us*. New York: Franklin Watts, 1997. A look at this international project and the scientists doing the research.

Organizations

U.S. Centers for Disease Control and Prevention (CDC). CDC posts several fact sheets about birth defects at its website.
http://www.cdc.gov/health/diseases.htm
http://www.cdc.gov/nceh/programs/infants/brthdfct/prevent/bd_rev.htm

The March of Dimes Birth Defects Foundation, 1275 Mamaroneck Avenue, White Plains, NY 10605. The mission of this national organization is to improve the health of babies by preventing birth defects and infant mortality. Its website offers information on the cause and prevention of birth defects.
Telephone 888-663-4637
http://www.modimes.org

▶ *See also*

Cleft Palate

Clubfoot

Color Blindness

Cystic Fibrosis

Deafness and Hearing Loss

Down Syndrome

Fetal Alcohol Syndrome

Genetic Diseases

German Measles (Rubella)

Hemophilia

Huntington's Disease

Hydrocephalus

Marfan Syndrome

Phenylketonuria

Sexually Transmitted Diseases

Sickle-cell Anemia

Spina Bifida

Tay-Sachs Disease

Birth Marks *See* Skin Conditions

Bites and Stings

Many insects, spiders, reptiles, and other animals can bite or sting humans. A person's reaction to bites and stings depends on the type and amount of venom (if any) injected into the bite, whether the person is allergic to the venom, and whether the biting animal was carrying a disease-causing agent.

KEYWORDS
*for searching the Internet
and other reference sources*

Infection

Vectors

Venom

Wounds

What Kinds of Animals Bite or Sting?

In addition to bites by mammals such as dogs, cats, and humans, many other animals can bite or sting people. Some animals inject venom, which is a poisonous substance, into the skin when they bite. Depending on the type of venom, a person can experience pain, itching, red bumps, nerve damage, or, rarely, death. Bites from mosquitoes and ticks also can be dangerous in places where those biters are vectors* (carriers) for diseases caused by bacteria, viruses, or parasites.

* **vectors** are animals or insects that carry diseases and transfer them from one host to another.

Some of the animals that sting or bite are described in the following sections. For most of these animals, the best way to prevent being bitten or stung is to avoid areas where they live or to wear protective clothing when there is the possibility of encountering them.

Insects

Mosquitoes   In many parts of the United States, mosquitoes are a summertime annoyance. Only the females among these small flying insects bite. When they bite, they inject saliva into the skin. The red itchy bump that appears at the site of the bite is an allergic reaction to the saliva. Mosquito bites go away on their own after several days. Mosquito repellent sprays help deter mosquitoes from biting, and calamine lotion or hydrocortisone cream may help ease the itching caused by bites.

In some parts of the world, certain types of mosquito can transmit diseases. For example, parasites carried by mosquitoes cause malaria and filariasis (fil-a-RY-a-sis). Mosquitoes also spread the viruses that cause dengue fever, yellow fever, and some types of encephalitis.

Chiggers   Chiggers, also called redbugs, are the larvae (immature stages) of red mites. They live in woods, pastures, and areas with high grass and weeds. Chiggers attach to a person's clothing and then move to bare skin around the tops of socks, armpits, or waistbands. There they bite the skin, inject a fluid that dissolves cells, and suck up the liquefied tissue. Chiggers cause extremely itchy bumps that can keep itching for days after the larvae are removed. Bathing and scrubbing after exposure to chiggers will kill or dislodge them, and rubbing alcohol followed by calamine lotion is said to help relieve the itching.

Anaphylactic Shock

For most people, insect bites cause pain or itching. For some people, however, insect bites can cause anaphylactic (an-a-fa-LAK-tik) shock. This is a severe allergic reaction that can be caused by insect bites or certain foods and drugs. The severity of the allergic reaction varies from person to person, but in general, this is what happens:

The reaction usually begins within minutes of being bitten or stung. To neutralize the insect's venom, a person's body releases huge amounts of chemicals called histamines, which cause the blood vessels to expand. A little bit of histamine helps to heal infected tissue and fight germs in the bloodstream, but too much lowers blood pressure and keeps the lungs from working properly.

At first, a person might begin sneezing, itching, and feeling weak, nauseated, and panicky. The chest and stomach muscles then begin to tighten. The lungs start working abnormally, making it very difficult to breathe, and the heart loses its normal rhythm, making it hard for blood to circulate as it should.

Anaphylactic shock must be treated quickly or it may cause death. A shot of a chemical called epinephrine usually is given to stimulate the heart and improve airflow through the lungs. Antihistamines and other drugs are given to counteract the allergic reaction, raise blood pressure, and increase the flow of blood.

People who know they are allergic to insect venom often learn how to use an anaphylaxis kit, which contains epinephrine and antihistamine, and they keep the kit nearby at all times.

Fire Ants   In the United States, fire ants come in a variety of types: imported (from South America) or native, red or black. Different types live in different geographic regions, but they are most common in the southeastern states. Fire ants usually build mounds in soft soil, but sometimes they nest in the walls of buildings.

Fire ants are very aggressive and territorial. When a person or animal disturbs their nest, they swarm. Thus, many ants can sting people at once. The venom causes a painful burning sensation, hence the name "fire" ant, followed by tiny itchy white blisters. Fire ant stings can be fatal, but only to the small number of people who are allergic to their venom.

Ticks   Ticks live in woods and fields all over the United States. Their flat dark bodies are about the size of a match head. Ticks bite humans and other animals because they need blood to survive. Usually, a tick bite causes only minor itching or irritation, but ticks also spread a number of diseases with their bites, including Rocky Mountain spotted fever and Lyme disease, both of which can be very serious illnesses. If a tick is seen on the skin, tweezers should be used to pull the tick up and out of the skin. The bite should be washed with soap and water and watched for signs of infection.

Spiders   Almost all spiders have glands that contain venom, but only 20 to 30 of the 30,000 species of spider in the world are potentially dangerous to humans. Spider bites can cause pain, nausea, fever, and cramps, but the majority of bites are minor and cause only swelling, a blister, and temporary pain. The brown recluse spider and the black widow spiders are the most dangerous spiders found in the United States. Tarantulas also bite, but the bite usually is no worse than a bee sting.

The brown recluse spider is mostly found in the south central United States, in dark places like woodpiles, sheds, and barns. With legs extended, this spider can be as large as a half-dollar. Males and females look alike and vary in color from orange to brown. They are covered with short hairs and have a violin-shaped marking on their back. Brown recluse bites usually are not fatal, but the spider's venom can cause serious illness, especially for children and the elderly.

Following a bite by a brown recluse spider, the skin around the bite may quickly become warm and swollen. Within about 15 minutes the bitten person may become dizzy and sick to the stomach. Other symptoms include fever, chills, weakness, convulsions, and joint pain. After about four days, the bite area gets hard to the touch, and it takes about six to eight weeks for the body to recover. There is no known antidote for brown recluse venom, so treatment involves several medications, usually antibiotics, antihistamines, and steroids.

Black widow spiders live in all parts of the United States but are most common in the warmer parts. They live in the same types of places as brown recluse spiders. Black widows are about a half inch long (not including the legs), and they can be identified by the reddish-orange hourglass shape on the belly of their black bodies.

Black widow spiders do not bite unless they are disturbed. Among black widows, only adult females bite. The juveniles and adult males are harmless. Most people who are bitten by black widows experience some swelling and redness at the bite site, followed by increasing pain for up to 48 hours. Black widow venom affects the nervous system, and it may cause cramps in the legs, arms, and chest. Other symptoms include sweating, chills, convulsions, fever, nausea, headache, and breathing difficulty. Treatment involves cleaning the bite and receiving antivenin* medicine and antibiotics. In 99 percent of the cases, complete recovery takes place within a few hours. Complications do occur occasionally in children, the elderly, or people with allergies, and in the most serious cases they may result in death.

* **antivenin** is an antibody (protein) capable of neutralizing a specific venom.

Scorpions Scorpions are about as long as an index finger. They have eight legs and a curled tail with a stinger on the end. There are 30 different kinds of scorpions in the United States, and they can be found all over the country. The stings of two species, both of which live in the southwestern states, can be fatal.

A scorpion's venom causes a burning feeling in the skin, followed by swelling and discoloration of the skin. About a day later, the face, mouth, and jaw muscles become hard to control. Other symptoms include nausea, vomiting, drooling, convulsions, and difficulty breathing. Scorpion bites are treated with antivenins and other medications to control muscle spasms and convulsions. In 99 percent of cases, complete recovery occurs after three days. However, if a person is particularly sensitive to the venom, and if muscle spasms begin right after the sting, then the person may die.

Bee and stinger. People who are allergic to bee stings may be taught to carry an anaphylaxis kit with them in case of a severe allergic reaction. © *David M. Phillips, Visuals Unlimited.*

▼

Bees, Wasps, and Yellow Jackets Honeybees and bumblebees are fat and round, and when they sting they leave their stinger in the skin. Wasps and yellow jackets are long and thin, and when they sting they keep their stinger and they can sting again. All of these insects inject venom into the skin, which causes pain, itching, swelling, and redness. For most people, bee stings are painful but not dangerous. However, some people are allergic to bee venom; for these people, bee stings can be fatal unless they are given medication right away. "Africanized" bees, also often called "killer" bees, are dangerous because they swarm and many bees can sting a person at once. Even nonallergic people can be killed by killer bees, but this is very rare.

After a sting, the stinger should be scraped off the skin, as pulling it out may squeeze more venom into the bite. Ice or cold compresses may help reduce pain and swelling.

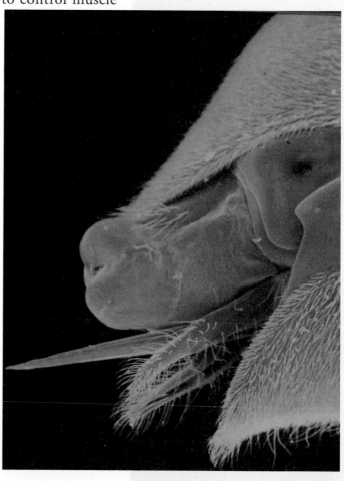

Snakes

Twenty species of poisonous snake live in the United States, and at least one type can be found in every state except Maine, Alaska, and Hawaii. Pit vipers, which include the rattlesnakes, copperheads, and cottonmouths, cause 99 percent of poisonous snake bites in the United States. Coral snakes cause the other 1 percent.

Venoms of different snake species range in toxicity, and a poisonous snake does not always release venom when it bites. The poisons in some species are mild, whereas others are neurotoxins (noor-o-TOK-sins) that may cause damage to the brain or spinal cord or cause people to stop breathing.

Any snake bite should be treated as an emergency because many people do not know what kind of snake bit them, and even nonpoisonous snakes can cause infection or an allergic reaction. Each year, up to 15 people die out of about 8,000 people bitten by poisonous snakes.

How to treat snakebites is a controversial* topic, but most doctors agree that ice packs, tourniquets*, and incisions should not be used. Bites should be washed with soap and water, the bitten area should be kept still and lower than the heart, and a doctor should be seen as soon as possible. Most bites do not occur in remote areas, so medical care is usually close by. Suction devices from snakebite kits or a bandage wrapped snugly 2 to 4 inches above the bite might slow the spread of venom until a hospital can be reached. Bites of poisonous snakes often are treated with antivenin.

Jellyfish

The oceans are home to many types of animal that bite or sting. The most familiar culprit is the jellyfish. All types of jellyfish have stinging tentacles that can cause a burning welt on a person's skin. In Australia, the sting of the box jellyfish can be fatal, but most jellyfish stings are just painful. Jellyfish such as the Portuguese man-of-war and sea nettles are common in coastal waters in the United States near the Atlantic Ocean. Avoiding contact with jellyfish while swimming can sometimes be difficult, especially when there are many of them in the water. Vinegar, calamine lotion, and antihistamines are said to help relieve the pain of stings.

Resources

Books

Aaseng, Nathan. *Poisonous Creatures (Scientific American Sourcebooks)*. New York: Twenty First Century Books, 1997.

Foster, Steven, Roger Caras, Norman Arlott, and Amy Eisenberg. *A Field Guide to Venomous Animals and Poisonous Plants*. New York: Houghton Mifflin, 1998.

Nichol, John. *Bites and Stings: The World of Venomous Animals*. New York: Facts on File, 1990.

* **controversy** means discussions with many different and opposing points of view.

* **tourniquet** is a device, often a bandage twisted tight around an arm or a leg, used to stop blood flow or hemorrhage.

134

Organization

The U.S. Centers for Disease Control and Prevention, Division of Vector-Borne Infectious Diseases, 1300 Rampart Road, Colorado State University Foothills Research Campus, P.O. Box 2087, Fort Collins, CO 80522.
Telephone 970-221-6400
http://www.cdc.gov/ncidod/dvbid/dvbid.htm

Black Lung Disease *See* **Pneumoconiosis**

Bladder Cancer

Bladder cancer occurs when cells in the bladder, the muscular sac that stores urine, divide without control or order. Bladder cancer sometimes spreads to other parts of the body.

Smoking and Bladder Cancer?

Cigarette smoking is most commonly associated with lung cancer, but smokers also are two to three times more likely than nonsmokers to develop bladder cancer. Cigarette smoke contains harmful cancer-causing chemicals called carcinogens (kar-SIN-o-jenz). People can greatly reduce their risk for bladder cancer by quitting smoking or not starting in the first place.

Some factories and industrial plants release chemical carcinogens, which may explain why bladder cancer is more common in urban areas than rural. Exposure to certain kinds of chemicals at work also appears to increase risk. This includes people who work in the rubber, chemical, and leather industries, as well as hairdressers, machinists, metal workers, printers, painters, dry cleaners, textile workers, and truck drivers. That does not mean that most of these workers will develop cancer. In fact, most will not. However, they should be aware of their risk and take precautions to decrease their exposure to chemical carcinogens.

In many cases, though, bladder cancer seems to develop without an apparent specific cause.

What Is Bladder Cancer?

The bladder is the hollow muscular sac in the lower abdomen that stores urine, the waste produced when the kidneys filter the blood. Cancer usually begins when cells on the surface of the bladder wall begin dividing without control or order, forming a growth called a tumor. Over time, this tumor can grow through the bladder wall and spread to nearby organs.

Each year, nearly 55,000 Americans learn that they have bladder cancer. It is one of the ten most common forms of cancer, affecting men twice as often as women and usually occurring between ages 50 and 70.

▶ *See also*

Animal Bites

Dengue Fever

Elephantiasis

Lyme Disease

Malaria

Rocky Mountain Spotted Fever

Yellow Fever

Zoonoses

KEYWORD
for searching the Internet and other reference sources

Oncology

The bladder is the hollow muscular sac in the lower abdomen that stores urine, which is the waste produced when the kidneys filter the blood.

▶

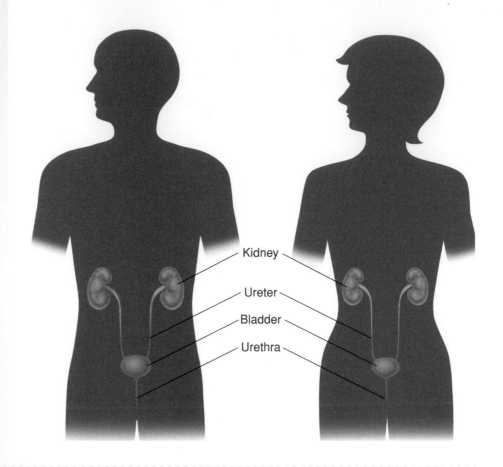

Kidney
Ureter
Bladder
Urethra

* **urethra** is the tube through which urine is discharged from the bladder to the outside of the body.

Early symptoms typically include blood in the urine and frequent or painful urination. However, these symptoms also may be caused by other conditions, so it is important to have them checked by a doctor.

How Is Bladder Cancer Diagnosed and Treated?

Diagnosis When doctors want to evaluate someone for bladder cancer, they usually perform a physical exam and test a urine sample to check for blood and cancer cells. They also can insert a thin, lighted tube called a cystoscope (SIS-to-skope) through the urethra* to examine the lining of the bladder. If they suspect cancer, they perform a biopsy by removing a tissue sample through the tube and sending the sample to be examined under a microscope. The appearance of the cells indicates whether or not cancer is present.

If cancer is found, doctors often will want to know whether the cancer has spread outside the bladder. To determine this, they may perform tests that create images of the inside of the body, including:

- **Intravenous pyelogram (IVP):** This is a series of x-rays of the kidneys and bladder taken after a dye is injected into a vein.

- **CT scans:** Also called computerized tomography scans, these are series of detailed pictures of areas inside the body created by a computer linked to an x-ray machine.

- **MRIs:** Magnetic resonance images are created through a procedure that uses a large magnet linked to a computer to create detailed pictures of areas inside the body.

- **Ultrasound:** These images are created by bouncing sound waves off tissues inside the body and converting the echoes into pictures.

- Bone scans.

- Chest x-rays.

Treatment The usual treatments for bladder cancer are surgery, radiation therapy, chemotherapy, biological therapy, or a combination of them. This usually depends upon how much of the bladder is involved and whether or not the cancer has spread to other parts of the body. In almost all cases, a surgeon will remove tumors and any surrounding tissue that is affected.

If the tumors are only on the surface of the bladder wall, the doctor can insert a tool with a small wire loop on the end through the urethra and burn them away with an electric current, a process called fulguration (ful-gu-RAY-shun).

If the cancer has grown into or through the muscular wall, part or all of the organ is removed in a procedure called cystectomy (sis-TEK-to-mee). Sometimes, nearby reproductive organs need to be removed as well.

Radiation therapy is another common treatment for bladder cancer. Internal radiation involves placing a small container of radioactive material, called a radiation implant, directly into the bladder to destroy the cancer cells. Radiation also can come from a machine outside the body that focuses high-energy rays on the affected area to kill cancer cells. Sometimes radiation is given before or after surgery, or along with anti-cancer drugs called chemotherapy.

Biological therapy, also known as immunotherapy, is a form of treatment that attempts to trigger the body's own disease-fighting immune system against the cancer.

Living with Bladder Cancer

People who have part or all of the bladder removed often have to make some adjustments in their activities of daily living. When people lose just part of the bladder, they may find that they need to go to the bathroom more frequently. When the entire bladder is taken out, they have to learn a new way of emptying the urine from their bodies.

Urostomy Upon removing the bladder, surgeons construct a new passageway to take over the bladder's function in a procedure called a urostomy. They might use a piece of the small intestine to create a tube that carries the urine to an opening in the stomach area, called a stoma, where it is collected in an attached bag. The patient must empty the bag periodically. A newer method uses part of the small intestine to make a new storage pouch inside the body, collecting the urine there instead of emptying it into a bag. Patients learn to use a tube called a catheter to drain the urine through either a stoma or the urethra.

Special therapists work with bladder cancer patients to teach them to care for themselves and their stomas after surgery. They can answer questions, address emotional and physical concerns, and suggest sources of additional information about urostomy. People who have a urostomy usually can resume all the activities they enjoyed before the operation.

Resources

U.S. National Cancer Institute (NCI). NCI is one of the National Institutes of Health. It posts a fact sheet called *What You Need to Know about Bladder Cancer* at its website.
Telephone 800-4-CANCER
http://cancernet.nci.nih.gov/wyntk_pubs/bladder.htm

American Cancer Society Cancer Resource Center. Information is available from ACS by telephone or online.
Telephone 800-ACS-2345
http://www3.cancer.org/cancerinfo/specific.asp.

American Foundation for Urologic Disease, 1126 North Charles Street, Baltimore, MD 21201. The American Foundation for Urologic Disease publishes *Family Urology Magazine*.
Telephone 410-468-1800
http://www.afud.org

▶ *See also*
Cancer
Tumor

Bladder Infection *See* Urinary Tract Infection

Blindness

Blindness is the absence of all or most vision.

KEYWORDS
for searching the Internet and other reference sources

Amaurosis

Amblyopia

Ophthalmology

Retinopathy

Vision

Corrine tried to imagine how she would describe a bird to her sister Amy, who might never be able to see one. She could say that it is small, that it has feathers, and that it sings. At least those are the things her sister can feel and hear. But how could she describe the red of a male cardinal and distinguish it from the reddish-brown of a female cardinal, when Amy might never see anything at all? And what about all the other things Corrine's sister might not see: the television shows and the movies, the picture books Corrine saved to give her, the blue sky, the faces of their mom and dad.

Corrine's sister Amy was born prematurely. The doctors told Amy's family that she had retinopathy (ret-i-NOP-a-thee) of prematurity. This condition results when the blood vessels in the eyes of a premature baby grow abnormally and cause bleeding and scarring. It may result in total or partial blindness.

More than 1 million people in the United States are blind, which means they cannot see at all or their vision is very poor. Another 14 million people have severe visual impairments that cannot be corrected with eyeglasses, according to the group Research to Prevent Blindness, Inc. Many diseases and injuries can cause blindness. There are treatments that can restore partial or complete eyesight for some people with blindness. Others, however, will remain blind for the rest of their lives.

Is There Hope in the Darkness?

Corrine's sister Amy might not lose her vision. Doctors now can use a probe to "freeze" parts of the eye and prevent permanent damage from retinopathy of prematurity. Thousands of other people with potentially vision-threatening conditions, such as strabismus*, glaucoma*, and cataracts*, also can benefit from treatments, especially if the disorders are detected early. Others whose conditions cannot be reversed or improved may benefit from special devices like voice-recognition software for computers and from programs that train guide dogs to assist with daily tasks like walking, going to school, and working.

What Causes Blindness?

Many conditions may cause blindness. The most common cause of vision loss in infants and young children is amblyopia (am-ble-O-pe-a).

Amblyopia Amblyopia is the loss of vision in one eye that results when the eyes are misaligned or not working together correctly in a condition known as strabismus (stra-BIZ-mus). About 3 to 5 percent of children have strabismus, which usually is present from birth or develops during infancy. In most cases, there is no known cause for the condition, which often makes a person look cross-eyed. With early diagnosis and treatment,

* **strabismus** is a condition that causes the eyes to cross or not work together correctly, which may lead to permanent loss of vision in one eye.

* **glaucoma** is a group of disorders that cause pressure to build in the eye, which may result in vision loss.

* **cataracts** result from cloudiness of the lenses in the eyes that usually develops as a person ages. They often impair vision.

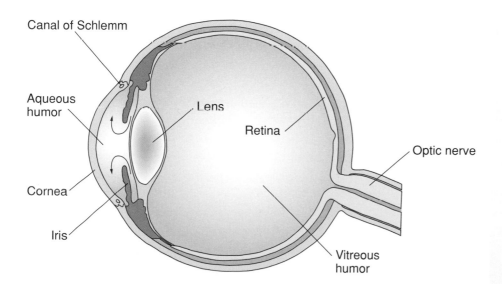

Canal of Schlemm

Aqueous humor

Lens

Retina

Cornea

Iris

Optic nerve

Vitreous humor

Anatomy of the eye. The optic nerve (also referred to as the second cranial nerve) sends messages from the eyes to the brain, making it possible to see.

Trachoma

Trachoma is a chronic infection of the eye by *Chlamydia trachomatis* bacteria. The bacteria infect the linings of the eyelid, causing them to become thick and rough. If the condition is untreated or if the infection returns, the eyelashes can turn inward and cause small scars on the eyes' surfaces. Eventually, blindness results. Trachoma is the leading cause of preventable blindness in the world.

Trachoma is spread through contact with the discharge from the eyes of infected persons. For example, if infected people rub their eyes and then shake another person's hands, the bacteria that cause trachoma can be spread. Also, using the handkerchief or towel of an infected person can spread the bacteria.

Today, about 10 percent of the world's population live in areas where trachoma is a problem, including Africa, Asia, Australia, Latin America, and some poorer areas of the United States.

Treatment can stop trachoma before it blinds people. Antibiotic ointments or oral antibiotics are used to treat the disease. The World Health Organization (WHO) has established a WHO Alliance for the Global Elimination of Trachoma. WHO hopes to achieve its goal by the year 2020 through prevention, antibiotics, and surgery to repair eyelids.

---

* **retina** is the area at the inside rear of the eyeball that acts like film in a camera to capture the image a person sees.

* **optic nerve** is the nerve that sends messages, or conducts impulses, from the eyes to the brain, making it possible to see. The optic nerve is also referred to as the second cranial nerve.

the eye that is not pointing straight can be trained to develop normal vision. For some people, surgery is needed to align the eye correctly.

Cataracts Some children are born with cataracts, which cloud the lens in the eye and prevent images from being seen clearly or at all. People also develop cataracts as they age, which makes it one of the most common causes of reduced vision. More than 400,000 new cases of cataracts develop each year in the United States. Surgery to remove cataracts is common for adults and for those few children with them. This restores vision in more than 90 percent of cases.

Diabetes Diabetes may lead to vision loss if diabetic retinopathy develops. Diabetic retinopathy, one of the leading causes of blindness in adults, results in vision loss if blood vessels supplying the eye's retina* are damaged by the disease. The blood vessels sometimes leak or break open to damage the retina. More vessels also may grow and start to cover the retina or grow into the fluid that fills the eyeball, further reducing vision.

Researchers estimate that as many as 10 million to 15 million people have diabetes in the United States and 700,000 are at risk of developing diabetic retinopathy. Almost all people with diabetes can show signs of damage to their retina after two or three decades of living with the disease, but not all of them lose their vision. There are no symptoms of diabetic retinopathy at first. As the damage increases, vision becomes blurred. Doctors can see the damage with a device that looks at the retina, which is why annual vision exams are so important for people with diabetes.

The best treatment for diabetic retinopathy is prevention, which means managing diabetes (and high blood pressure, if present) with proper nutrition, exercise, and medications. In some cases, laser treatment may be used to prevent worsening of diabetic retinopathy. People with diabetes also are at higher risk for cataracts and glaucoma.

Glaucoma Glaucoma is a disorder that causes fluid pressure to build up inside the eye, which may cause optic nerve* damage. It may go undetected for many years before its effects on vision are noticed. It is one of the leading causes of blindness in the United States, with elderly people and people of African ancestry at increased risk.

Macular degeneration Macular degeneration is similar to diabetic retinopathy. Changes in the blood vessels supplying the central portion of the retina, known as the macula, cause the vessels to leak and to damage cells that are needed for the central part of the field of vision. Peripheral or side vision usually remains, but without treatment, the damaged field of vision may expand. Doctors sometimes recommend laser surgery to treat the leaking blood vessels when people are in the early stages of macular degeneration in order to prevent or slow progressive vision loss. Others compensate for vision loss by using magnifying devices.

Infections Ocular (OK-yoo-lar) herpes may cause vision loss as a result of herpesvirus infections, usually the herpes simplex virus that causes cold sores or the herpes zoster virus that causes chickenpox and shingles. The U.S. National Eye Institute estimates that ocular herpes affects approximately 400,000 people in the United States.

Infection of the eyes by the *Chlamydia trachomatis* organism is a leading cause of blindness in developing nations. The eyes of newborn babies may become infected during childbirth if the mother has chlamydia.

A BEST FRIEND

Dorothy Harrison Eustis was an American living in Europe when she first saw German shepherd dogs used as guides for people with blindness. The dogs were part of a program to help former soldiers who had been blinded in World War I.

She was impressed. The dogs allowed the retired soldiers to live more independently. With the dogs as their guides, the blind men could walk through and across crowded streets. As Mrs. Eustis wrote in 1927 about one such man, "No longer a care and a responsibility to his family and friends, he can take up his life where he left it off; no longer dependent on a member of the family, he can come and go as he pleases. . . ."

Mrs. Eustis returned to the United States in 1929 and founded the first school to train guide dogs in Nashville, Tennessee. Called the Seeing Eye, the school moved to Morristown, New Jersey, in 1931, where it remains.

German shepherds often are used as guide dogs, although Labrador retrievers, boxers, and even mixed breeds also are used. The dogs begin their training at about 18 months of age with a sighted trainer. Then the dog is matched with a blind person, who spends three or four weeks working with the trainer and the dog.

The dogs learn when to stop and when to go at street corners based on commands from their owners. They do not read traffic signs or lights in part because dogs are color blind. The owner listens to traffic sounds and tells the dog to go when it sounds as if traffic has stopped. But the dog is trained not to go if there is danger. Dogs also steer owners away from people and from objects in their path.

Guide dogs wear a special harness when they work, but may switch to a regular leash during their off-duty hours. It is important not to approach or play with a guide dog when it is working. © *Peter Skinner, Photo Researchers, Inc.*

Helen Keller

Helen Keller (1880–1968) became a writer and activist despite losing her sight and her hearing when she was not even 2 years old. She learned to communicate after she was taught to associate the movements of another person's hands with letters, words, and the objects around her.

During the 1930s, Helen Keller lobbied the U.S. Congress to provide federally funded reading services for people who are blind. Her efforts resulted in the inclusion of Title X in the 1935 Social Security Act, establishing federal grant assistance for the blind.

The story of Helen Keller's life, and the role of her teacher, Anne Sullivan, was made into the movie *The Miracle Worker* (1962), which won Academy Awards for actors Patty Duke and Anne Bancroft. It is available in many video stores and is often broadcast on television.

Accidents About 3 percent of cases of blindness occur from accidents or other injuries that damage the eyes.

How Do People with Vision Loss and Blindness Adapt?

Millions of people with severe vision loss, including more than 1 million people who are blind, can do many of the same things that people with normal vision do. People with partial sight can use powerful eyeglasses and magnifying devices to improve their ability to read and to see objects. People with blindness also can:

- listen to books, newspapers, and magazines on tape
- use computers that read text aloud and respond to spoken commands
- read Braille, a system that translates words into raised patterns of dots that are read by touching them
- use guide dogs to increase their mobility
- take many of the same classes, jobs, and roles as people with sight
- become parents and teachers
- become famous entertainers (if they're talented), like singers Stevie Wonder and Ray Charles.

Resources

The U.S. National Eye Institute, 2020 Vision Place, Bethesda, MD 20892-3655. The National Eye Institute is one of the U.S. National Institutes of Health (NIH). Its website has a search engine that locates information about blindness and vision problems, and its resource list provides links to over 40 other organizations that provide information to the public about eyes and vision.
Telephone 301-496-5248
http://www.nei.nih.gov/

American Council of the Blind, 1155 15 Street NW, Suite 720, Washington, DC 20005. The American Council of the Blind has a monthly radio program called *ACB Reports*, a monthly magazine called the *Braille Forum*, a jobs bank, and "Speech Friendly Software" at its website.
Telephone 800-424-8666
http://www.acb.org

American Foundation for the Blind, 11 Penn Plaza, Suite 300, New York, NY 10001. The American Foundation for the Blind houses the Helen Keller Archive and publishes many print books, talking books, and a *Journal of Visual Impairment and Blindness*.
Telephone 212-502-7661 or 212-502-7662 (TDD)
http://www.afb.org

Lighthouse International, 111 East 59 Street, New York, NY 10022-1202. The Lighthouse offers information, products, and publications about vision and blindness. It includes a Lighthouse National Center for Vision and Child Development, and posts a story called *My Friend Jodi Is Blind* at its website.
Telephone 800-829-0500 or 212-821-9713 (TTY)
http://www.lighthouse.org

National Federation of the Blind, 1800 Johnson Street, Baltimore, MD 21230. The National Federation of the Blind offers many resources for blind children and blind adults. Its website posts an informative fact sheet called *Questions from Kids about Blindness* and a newsletter called *Student Slate: The Voice of Organized Blind Students in America*.
Telephone 410-659-9314
http://www.nfb.org

Research to Prevent Blindness, Inc., 645 Madison Avenue, New York, NY 10022-1010. This is a research organization for scientists, ophthalmologists, and the public.
Telephone 800-621-0026

The Seeing Eye, Inc., P.O. Box 375, Morristown, NJ 07963-0375. This is the pioneer guide dog school in the United States. Its speech-friendly website provides an excellent overview of its history and of guide dog training. It publishes several videos and a *Seeing Eye Guide*.
Telephone 973-539-4425
http://www.seeingeye.org

Boils *See* Abscess

Botulism

Botulism (BOCH-u-liz-em) is food poisoning caused by eating food containing Clostridium botulinum *bacteria or the toxin they produce. Improperly canned foods, fresh produce, and occasionally fish may carry the bacteria.*

Poisoning in Peoria

"I'll have a patty melt on toasted rye, with American cheese and sautéed onions." With those words, 28 patrons in a Peoria, Illinois, restaurant unknowingly exposed themselves to botulism. Without seeing, tasting, or smelling anything unusual, they ate a toxin produced by bacteria spores growing on the onion skins. But these customers were fortunate. They were all hospitalized for treatment and went home healthy.

The U.S. and the World

- 1.1 million people in the United States are legally blind

- 42 million people are blind worldwide

- 100 million people in the United States need eyeglasses to see clearly, and 14 million have eye problems that cannot be corrected with glasses

- Only 3 percent of cases of blindness results from injuries. The remainder occur as a result of eye diseases

- Blindness and eye disabilities may double by the year 2020, because post-war baby boomers are aging and many eye disorders are more likely to occur in old age.

▶ *See also*
Cataracts
Chlamydial Infections
Diabetes
Farsightedness
Glaucoma
Herpes
Nearsightedness
Strabismus

KEYWORDS
for searching the Internet and other reference sources

Botulinum toxin

Food poisoning

*spores are a special form of bacteria that is resistant to heat and disinfectants. Some bacteria become spores during a stage of their life cycle.

When Poison Becomes a Healer

Scientists know that botulism causes muscles to weaken, but recently they wondered whether the poison could be used to relax painfully cramped or tight muscles. Researchers have discovered that botulinum toxin does indeed have healing qualities. It has been used safely and effectively by doctors to:

- reduce wrinkles and frown lines

- relax muscles in the esophagus (the passage between the throat and stomach) to ease the swallowing of food

- treat "writer's cramp," caused by tasks such as writing, using a screwdriver, or playing the piano

- reposition eye muscles in people with "wandering eye," crossed eyes, or problems with eyelid function

- eliminate excessive sweating

- reduce muscle stiffness in people who have had strokes.

What Is Botulism?

Botulism is a rare but serious kind of food poisoning. Most outbreaks are caused by improperly preserved home-canned foods, but some are caused by improperly cooked foods.

Adults and infants are affected differently. In adults, botulism usually is caused by eating the toxin that already has been produced by *Clostridium botulinum* bacteria in the food. In infants, the toxin is produced in the intestine after eating the spores* of the bacteria. Honey is one of the primary sources of infant botulism.

Signs and Symptoms

The symptoms of botulism usually appear 12 to 36 hours after eating the affected food, but the onset can range between 6 hours and 8 days. Blurred vision, difficulty swallowing, body weakness, dry mouth, abdominal pain, vomiting, shortness of breath, and muscle paralysis can occur. Infants with botulism may show signs of weakness, constipation, and breathing difficulties. When death occurs, it is usually caused by paralysis of the respiratory muscles.

Diagnosis

Doctors diagnose botulism by noting the symptoms and conducting laboratory tests on blood or stool to detect the toxin. A doctor might ask about a patient's diet to try to determine the source and possibly test a sample of the suspect food. A brain scan, spinal fluid examination, or electromyography, which measures the activity of the muscles, can be used to help diagnose botulism or to rule out other causes of the symptoms.

Treatment

People who have botulism need to be hospitalized, especially to monitor and support their breathing. The doctor might try to get the poison out of the patient's body by inducing vomiting, rinsing out the stomach, or giving a laxative to flush out the intestines. Adults can be given an antitoxin to counteract the effects of the poison if the diagnosis is made early, within about 72 hours. About 100 cases of botulism occur every year in the United States. Despite improved treatment, 10 to 25 percent of people with botulism still die.

Prevention

Cooking food at high temperatures and using a pressure cooker when canning fruits and vegetables are the best ways to prevent botulism. The toxin can be destroyed by boiling for 10 minutes. Cooked foods should not be left out of the refrigerator for more than 2 hours. Throw out any food that shows signs of spoilage or any cans that are swollen or leaking.

To prevent infant botulism, children younger than 1 year old should not eat honey.

Resources

The U.S. Centers for Disease Control and Prevention (CDC), 1600 Clifton Road NE, Atlanta, GA 30333. CDC posts a fact sheet about botulism at its website.
http://www.cdc.gov/health/diseases.htm

The U.S. Food and Drug Administration (FDA) posts a *Bad Bug Book* at its website that discusses the *Clostridium botulinum* bacterium.
http://vm.cfsan.fda.gov/~mow/intro.html

► *See also*
Food Poisoning
Paralysis

Brain Tumor

A brain tumor is a mass of abnormal cells growing in the brain. Despite its frightening name, not all brain tumors are cancerous or fatal.

KEYWORDS
for searching the Internet and other reference sources

Astrocytoma

Ependymoma

Germinoma

Glioma

Medulloblastoma

Meningioma

Neuroblastoma

Oncology

What Is a Brain Tumor?

A brain tumor is a clump of abnormal tissue that can be found anywhere in the brain. The brain and spinal cord form the central nervous system, which controls everything a person does on purpose (such as walking and talking), or automatically (such as breathing and digesting food). This system also controls people's senses, emotions, thoughts, memory, and personality; it determines who they are.

Brain tumors are categorized in two ways: first, by how they look during imaging tests that create pictures of the brain, and by how the tissue appears under a microscope; and second, according to whether they started in the brain or spread there from another part of the body.

■ **Benign brain tumors** have clearly defined edges and contain cells that look healthy, just like normal cells. They tend to grow slowly, are not likely to spread, and rarely grow back once they are removed. The word "benign" means harmless, although these tumors may cause harm if they start to interfere with normal brain function. Benign brain tumors are not cancerous.

■ **Malignant brain tumors** are also called brain cancer. They can have irregular borders and they are made up of abnormally shaped cells. They tend to spread quickly by sprouting new "roots" into surrounding brain tissue, almost like a plant in the soil. While they may also spread to the spinal cord, they generally do not spread to other parts of the body. In some cases, one tumor may contain a combination of nearly normal and extremely abnormal cells.

- **Primary brain tumors** originate in the tissues of the brain and may be either benign or malignant.

- **Secondary brain tumors** are actually formed from cancer cells that have traveled to the brain from another part of the body. For example, cells from tumors in the lung, breast, or somewhere else can spread to the brain and cause new tumors to grow. Secondary brain tumors are always malignant.

In addition, brain tumors are classified by the type of brain cell that became a tumor, with medical names such as astrocytoma (as-tro-sy-TO-ma), glioma (glee-O-ma), ependymoma (e-pen-di-MO-ma), germinoma (jer-mi-NO-ma), medulloblastoma (med-yoo-lo-blas-TO-ma), meningioma (me-nin-jee-O-ma), and neuroblastoma (noor-o-blas-TO-ma). Their common ending "-oma" means "tumor," and the beginning indicates the part of the brain where the tumor forms. For example, gliomas, the most common type of brain tumor, form in the supportive tissue of the brain, called the glia. The second most common type, meningioma, forms in the meninges, the membranes that cover the brain and spinal cord.

Why Do People Develop Brain Tumors?

Doctors cannot explain why some children and adults develop brain tumors. When it happens, it is not their fault, nor could they have done anything to prevent it. Even though a tumor can spread within the brain, it cannot spread from one person to another; in other words, brain tumors are not contagious.

Researchers have found that some brain tumors are more common in people who are frequently exposed to certain industrial chemicals used to manufacture rubber, pharmaceuticals, crude oil and petroleum, and nuclear fuel and weapons, as well as agricultural chemicals used on farms. They also are investigating whether certain viruses may contribute to brain tumor development.

Heredity is another possible cause under investigation. Because brain tumors sometimes occur in several members of the same family, researchers are investigating whether the tendency to develop them may be inherited.

What Are the Symptoms of a Brain Tumor?

As the tumor grows, it exerts pressure on the brain that often causes headaches, drowsiness, blurred or double vision, or nausea and vomiting. Of course, most times these symptoms are *not* caused by brain tumors. Because different parts of the brain control specific functions in the body, a tumor's symptoms often depend on its location in the brain. Symptoms may include:

- Seizures, or sudden movements or changes in consciousness over which the person has no control.

- Weakness or loss of feeling in the arms or legs.

50 Years Ago: Johnny Gunther

Brain tumors affect people of all ages. Among children and young adults who have tumors, it is one of the more common types diagnosed. Still, childhood brain tumors are relatively rare: the American Brain Tumor Association estimates that only about 4 of every 100,000 children under age 20 will develop a brain tumor.

Back in 1946, one such child was Johnny Gunther, whose father wrote the widely read book *Death Be Not Proud* about Johnny's experiences. At the age of 16, Johnny started experiencing some vision problems and a stiff neck. After a series of tests, he was diagnosed with glioblastoma, a fast-growing tumor that tends to spread quickly within the brain.

The book describes the diagnostic tests that Johnny underwent and his treatments, including surgery and radiation therapy, which was called x-ray therapy at that time. Johnny's father also recounts how the family coped with the disease and the eventual knowledge that Johnny would not get better. Johnny died in 1947 at the age of 17.

Johnny's tumor is not typical of all brain tumors. Some grow much more slowly and do not invade the surrounding tissue. Gunther notes that while his son's tumor looked like a spider stretching out its legs, another type might look more like "a marble stuck in jelly."

Treatment methods for all types of brain tumors have advanced since 1946, making it easier for doctors to remove them and control their growth. Johnny's doctors had to rely on x-rays, vision tests, and a brain wave test called an electroencephalogram to locate his tumor. Now, doctors use CTs, MRIs, and other new computer technologies to create visual "maps" of the brain and pinpoint a tumor's exact location before and during surgery.

- Stumbling or lack of coordination in walking.
- Abnormal eye movements or changes in vision.
- Changes in personality or memory.
- Speech problems.

How Do Doctors Diagnose Brain Tumors?

In addition to asking about symptoms, the doctor performs a neurological exam, which involves different tests of vision and eye movement, hearing, reflexes, balance and coordination, memory, thinking ability, and other functions controlled by the brain.

The doctor is also likely to order imaging tests such as a computerized tomography (CT) scan (a special x-ray that uses a computer to create pictures of the brain), or a magnetic resonance imaging (MRI) scan, which creates a picture of the brain by using a very strong magnetic field instead of x-rays. Another possible type of test, called angiogram imag-

Doctors often use MRIs (magnetic resonance images) as part of the diagnostic process. Here a brain tumor shows up as a roundish spot that differs from the healthy brain tissue nearby. *Visuals Unlimited.*

▶

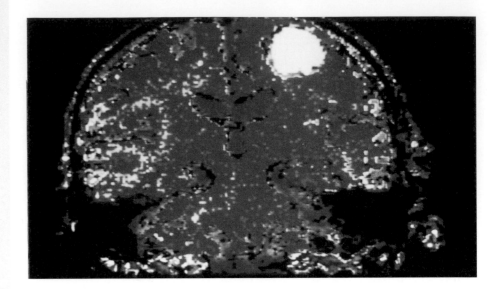

ing, involves injecting dye into a blood vessel and creating a series of images as the dye moves through the brain. This helps doctors to visualize the tumor and the blood vessels leading to it.

Once a tumor is found, doctors often need to gather more information to figure out what type it is. In some cases, the doctor takes a sample of the cerebrospinal fluid that surrounds the brain and spinal cord, and then sends the fluid to be examined under a microscope. More commonly, surgeons will remove part or all of the tumor in a process called a biopsy, and then send the tissue to the laboratory for analysis. To get at the tumor, they open part of the skull (a procedure called craniotomy), or they may drill a small hole in the skull and use a needle to take a tissue sample. Both before and sometimes during the operation, surgeons use computerized images of the brain to help them locate the tumor and avoid the nearby healthy tissues that are essential for normal function.

DR. HARVEY CUSHING

Surgeons performed the first successful removals of brain tumors during the 1880s. Follow-up care was difficult, however, and many patients died afterward.

During the early years of the twentieth century, Dr. Harvey Cushing (1869–1939) pioneered the specialty of neurosurgery in the United States. Dr. Cushing made certain that all types of tumors were classified before surgery based on analysis of the tumor's pattern of growth and on observation of tissue samples. His work also revolutionized post-operative care, which reduced mortality among tumor patients. Dr. Cushing's achievements are reflected in today's surgical techniques, clinical expertise, and laboratory research.

How Do Doctors Treat Brain Tumors?

Surgery, radiation therapy, and chemotherapy are the three most common treatments for a brain tumor. But the type of tumor, its location, and the person's age often determine how these treatments are used. Before the process starts, most patients are given medications to relieve any swelling in the brain and control the seizures that often occur with brain tumors.

Surgery During surgery, surgeons attempt to remove the entire tumor. However, if the tumor cannot be removed completely without damaging vital brain tissue, then they will remove as much as they can. Surgery is usually the only treatment needed for a benign tumor.

Radiation therapy Radiation therapy (also called radiotherapy) is the use of high-powered radiation to destroy cancer cells or stop them from growing. It is often used to destroy tumor tissue that cannot be removed with surgery, or to kill cancer cells that may remain after surgery. Radiation therapy is also used when surgery is not possible. External radiation comes from a large machine, while internal radiation involves implanting radioactive material directly into the tumor. Even though the radiation is focused on the tumor, some of the surrounding healthy tissue is often damaged as well. Therefore, doctors avoid giving radiation to very young children, especially those under age 3, because their brains are still developing. These children are often treated with chemotherapy until they are old enough to have the radiation therapy.

Chemotherapy During chemotherapy, doctors give anticancer drugs by mouth or by injection into a blood vessel or muscle. Because the body automatically tends to prevent chemicals and other foreign substances from entering the brain and spinal cord (a kind of "self-defense" mechanism), doctors may need to inject them right into the spinal fluid.

Stereotactic Surgery

Stereotactic surgery uses a frame attached externally to the skull. The frame allows the surgeon to attach surgical instruments and to position them precisely.

Before surgery, tumor locations are identified using computerized tomography (CT) or magnetic resonance imaging (MRI). The surgeon then drills a small hole in the skull and, using the CT or MRI data, inserts the instruments and navigates to an exact point in the brain. The surgeon can then remove a tumor or perform other procedures.

Doctors often use stereotactic surgery to guide biopsy needles and forceps, to guide electrodes for recording or marking lesions, to guide lasers, to insert endoscopes for looking inside the body, and to guide Gamma knife procedures, which use radiation to do surgery.

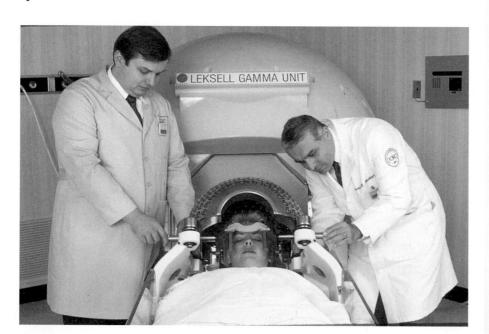

Gamma knife radiosurgery is one of the treatments doctors use for brain tumors. Using technology from linear particle accelerators and cyclotrons to produce a proton beam or gamma radiation, doctors direct the beam for ultra-precise surgery, assisted by three-dimensional computer images constructed by super fast computers. Gamma knife radiosurgery can be performed in a single day, and patients usually can go home the next morning. *© 1990 Custom Medical Stock Photo.*

New treatments Numerous other treatments for brain tumors are being evaluated in research studies called clinical trials. For example, researchers are testing biological therapies that try to "supercharge" the body's disease-fighting immune system against the tumor. They also are testing drugs that would prevent tumors from creating the new blood vessels they need to keep growing. In the United States, the National Cancer Institute has formed groups of doctors nationwide who are working together to find new treatments for brain tumors in children and adults.

Life After a Brain Tumor

Sometimes, the tumor or the treatment damages some of the nearby healthy brain tissue that controls physical and mental function. Patients need to work with a special therapist if they are having trouble using their arms or legs, maintaining balance, speaking, swallowing, or expressing their thoughts. They may feel tired or depressed, and they may experience personality changes. Children may find that they have problems with learning or remembering what they learn when they return to school.

Resources

Books

Gunther, John. *Death Be Not Proud: A Memoir*. New York: HarperPerennial Library, 1998. First published in 1949.

Roloff, Tricia Ann. *Navigating Through a Strange Land: A Book for Brain Tumor Patients and Their Families*. Indigo Press, 1995.

Organizations

U.S. National Cancer Institute (NCI). One of the National Institutes of Health, NCI publishes brochures about cancer, including the fact sheet *What You Need to Know About Brain Tumors*.
Telephone 800-4-CANCER
http://cancernet.nci.nih.gov/wyntk_pubs/index.html

American Brain Tumor Association, 2720 River Road, Des Plaines, IL 60018. The ABTA offers free publications about brain tumors, including *A Primer of Brain Tumors: A Patient's Reference Manual*, *Alex's Journey: The Story of a Child with a Brain Tumor* (especially for children ages 9 to 13), *Dictionary for Brain Tumor Patients*, and many others.
Telephone 800-886-2282
http://www.abta.org

National Brain Tumor Foundation, 785 Market Street, Suite 1600, San Francisco, CA 94103. NBTF publishes *Brain Tumors: A Guide* and its website features descriptions of different brain tumor types, survivors' stories, and a physician interview.
Telephone 800-934-CURE
http://www.nbtf.org.

▶ See also
Cancer
Seizures

Breast Cancer

Breast cancer is a potentially dangerous tumor that develops in the cells of the breast. Cancer cells sometimes spread from the breast to other parts of the body.

KEYWORDS
*for searching the Internet
and other reference sources*

Mammography

Oncology

Tamoxifen

In the United States, breast cancer is a very common cancer among women, second only to skin cancer. Breast cancer also occurs in men, but much more rarely. Deaths from breast cancer have been reduced in recent years because more effective treatments are now available, and because these cancers are found earlier when they are easier to treat.

How Does Breast Cancer Start?

Humans are mammals, and all mammals have breasts, which are the organs that make milk to feed babies. In the breast are lobules (LOB-yools) that look like bunches of grapes. Channels, or ducts, from the lobules enable milk to flow to the nipple. The lobules and ducts are surrounded by fatty tissue and ligaments called stroma (STRO-ma).

Cancer in situ Breast cancer begins when a single cell in a duct or lobule undergoes changes (mutations) that cause it to start growing out of control. At first, even though the cells are growing very rapidly, they stay within the duct or lobule. At this stage the cancer is called cancer in situ. Later, the cells may break out of the duct or lobule into the fat and surrounding tissue, where they continue to divide and multiply. Since a tumor needs nourishment to grow, it sends out signals in the form of proteins that cause new blood vessels to form and support it. Without a blood supply, a tumor will die.

Metastasis Cancer cells may enter the bloodstream, where they may be killed by the immune system (the body's defense against disease). If they are not killed by the immune system, the cancer cells may travel to distant organs of the body, settle there, grow, and divide. This process of spread is called metastasis (me-TAS-ta-sis).

Breast cancer cells are most likely to find their way to the lungs, liver, and bones. Cancer is named for the place where it starts. So even when breast cancer travels to the lungs or the bones, it is still called breast cancer.

Who Gets Breast Cancer?

No one knows yet exactly what causes breast cancer to start. It is impossible to catch it from another person.

Can teenagers get breast cancer? Breast cancer in teenagers is very rare. A girl whose breasts are developing may feel some discomfort from time to time. And once her periods start, she may retain water during the last part of her cycle, which can cause her breasts to ache. But these pains are a normal part of the body's functioning. They are not a sign of cancer.

Anatomy of the breast. Ducts carry milk from the lobules to the nipple. The lobules and ducts are surrounded by fatty tissue and ligaments called stroma.

▶

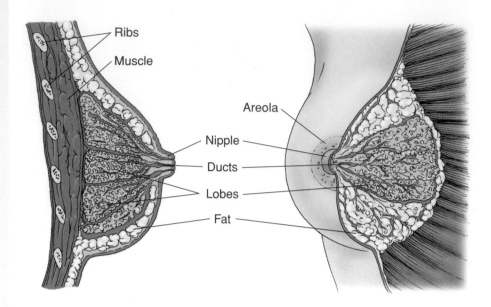

Ribs
Muscle
Areola
Nipple
Ducts
Lobes
Fat

Women, Breast Cancer, and Mammograms

■ All women are at risk for breast cancer. Over 60 percent of U.S. women diagnosed with breast cancer do not have a family history of the disease.

■ Currently, breast cancer occurs in one out of every eight U.S. women.

■ The early detection of breast cancer by mammograms increases the chance of successful treatment.

■ Some doctors believe that every woman should have her first mammogram by age 35. This first mammogram should be saved as a baseline for comparison with future mammograms.

■ Women between the ages of 40 and 50 should have a mammogram every one to two years.

■ Women over the age of 50 should have a mammogram every year.

BRCA1, BRCA2, and estrogen   Women who inherit some mutated genes from their parents are at higher risk of getting breast cancer. These genes, called BRCA1 and BRCA2, are involved in only a small fraction of breast cancer cases. Researchers suspect that natural substances called hormones, especially the female hormone estrogen, play a role in promoting some types of breast cancer.

Family history   A woman whose mother, sister, or daughter has had breast cancer has twice the risk of getting it as a woman with no family history of breast cancer. However, most women diagnosed with breast cancer do not (to their knowledge) have a family history of breast cancer. A woman who has already had breast cancer in one breast is at higher risk of getting it in the other breast.

Age   Age is also a risk factor. Older women have a higher risk of developing breast cancer. Another risk factor is early age for first menstrual period as well as late age for menopause. Women who have their first child after the age of 30, or who do not have any children, also have a higher risk.

Diet and life style   Rates of breast cancer vary around the world, and it appears these differences are related to diet or life style. For example, women in Asia have only one fifth to one tenth the risk of getting breast cancer as women in North America or Western Europe. But when Asian women move to Western countries, their risk increases to the same level as the local population. The reasons why are not clear.

What Happens When Women Have Breast Cancer?

Signs and symptoms   Usually, a woman will notice a painless lump in her breast. Or her doctor may feel the lump during a routine examination. The shape, color, or texture of the breast or nipple may change or the nipple may be tender or have a discharge. Sometimes cancers are found before symptoms occur. In these cases, routine or "screening" mammography (mam-MOG-ra-fee) (x-ray examination of the breasts) shows changes that indicate a possibility of cancer, which must be checked.

Diagnosis   If screening tests or a woman's symptoms suggest cancer, the doctor may request a biopsy (BY-op-see). In this procedure, a small amount of tissue is removed from the abnormal area of the breast and examined under a microscope. Most biopsies show that the woman does not have cancer. If the tissue is benign (be-NINE) (not cancer), no further treatment may be needed. But if the diagnosis is cancer, then the woman will want to learn about the disease and discuss her options for treatment with health professionals, her friends, and family.

Treatment   For tumors that do not appear to have spread, it may be possible to remove only the tumor and leave most of the breast. This is called a lumpectomy (lump-EK-to-mee). Sometimes, however, it may be necessary to perform a mastectomy (mas-TEK-to-mee), an operation that removes the breast. Whether mastectomy or lumpectomy is the best choice depends on the size and sometimes the kind of tumor.

Follow-up treatment may include radiation therapy and anti-cancer medication, called chemotherapy (kee-mo-THER-a-pee), to kill any remaining cancer cells and to prevent them from growing back. The choice of follow-up treatment depends on the kind of tumor and

Men and Breast Cancer

- About 1 percent of all cases of breast cancer occur in men.

- A family history of breast cancer is a risk factor for men as well as for women.

- Breast cancer in men is often not detected until the cancer is advanced and more difficult to treat.

- Breast cancer in men usually shows up as a lump beneath the breast area, fixation of skin to the lump, and discharge from the nipple.

- Treatment usually involves surgical removal of the lump, followed by chemotherapy or radiation therapy.

- Treatment and cure rates for men are similar to those for women.

3,000 YEARS OF BREAST CANCER RESEARCH AND TREATMENT

A description of "bulging tumors" being burned or cut out of the breast can be found in the Edwin Smith papyrus from Thebes, dated 1600 B.C.E.

Ancient Greek women sought help from Aesculapius (es-ku-LA-pe-us), their mythical god of healing. Aesculapian temples were filled with offerings, including carvings of excised tumorous breasts. The women hoped their gifts would prompt an explanation of their disease or convey thanks to the god for his healing power.

The Greek physician Hippocrates (c. 460–c. 375 B.C.E.) emphasized the importance of diet and the environment for the management of breast cancer. During the second century, the Roman physician Galen (130–200 A.D.) focused his research on a theory that excess black bile caused cancer, and that treatment required that the bile be removed by means of bloodletting.

The bloodletting technique prevailed until the 1500s, when medieval doctors began returning to surgical treatment of breast cancer.

***lymph nodes** are bean-sized round or oval masses of immune system tissue that filter bodily fluids before they enter the bloodstream, helping to keep out bacteria and other undesirable substances.

whether it appears to have spread to the lymph nodes* or other parts of the body.

Can Breast Cancer Be Prevented?

There is no sure way to prevent breast cancer. It may be possible for women to reduce their risk of breast cancer by not drinking too much alcohol, by eating a healthy diet, and by getting regular exercise. Because detecting cancer early improves the chance of treating it with a better outcome, or even curing it, women 40 and older should have a screening mammogram and a physical exam to check their breasts every year. Women aged 20 to 39 should have a breast exam every three years. And all women aged 20 and older should learn how to examine their own breasts and check them once a month.

Will There Ever Be a Way of Preventing Breast Cancer?

Because chemotherapy kills healthy cells as well as cancer cells, research efforts in the area of drug treatment are concentrating on drugs that do less damage to healthy cells than current treatments. Researchers also are studying how best to use the information from genetic tests for breast cancer genes to help a woman lower her risk of getting breast cancer.

Tamoxifen research An effective treatment for many women with breast cancer is a drug called tamoxifen. This drug works against the hormones that stimulate the cells in the breast to grow and are believed to be a factor in many breast cancers. Tamoxifen is so effective that it

Support groups

For women with breast cancer, talking to other women who are living with the disease can be a very comforting experience. For women whose breast cancer has come back or spread, it may even do more than that. One study showed that women with metastatic breast cancer who participated in support groups lived an average of almost two years longer than women who did not.

Women who have just been diagnosed with breast cancer also may find it helpful to meet and to talk to women who had breast cancer 10 or 15 years earlier and who are now living happy, healthy lives.

The American Cancer Society and the National Alliance of Breast Cancer Organizations provide information about finding support groups.

IMAGING THE BODY: WILHELM KONRAD RÖNTGEN

In 1895, the German physics professor Wilhelm Konrad Röntgen (1845–1923) discovered a new kind of ray that he found mysterious enough to call "X." Röntgen's "x-rays" (later called "roentgen rays") were an alternative to light that made it possible to see structures within the body. Among the first photographs Röntgen took were of the bones in his wife's hand.

Today, Röntgen's invention is used to take pictures of many parts of the body, including the breast, making early detection of breast cancer possible and saving or extending the lives of millions of women around the world. Röntgen was awarded the Nobel Prize in physics in 1901.

X-ray mammograms are far from perfect. They miss some cancers, and they return uncertain results in some healthy women, causing them to undergo the anxiety and discomfort of biopsies to rule out cancer. Scientists are continuing research efforts to improve breast imaging.

was approved in the late 1990s for use by women who do not have breast cancer but who are at a high risk of getting it. Researchers are investigating similar drugs that do not have the side effects of tamoxifen and might be safe enough for healthy women at lower risk to use as a way of preventing breast cancer.

What Is It Like to Live with Breast Cancer?

Treatment for breast cancer can be very unpleasant. Mastectomy is emotionally difficult, and some women, about 1 in 10, may get serious swelling in their arms as a result of the surgery. As with almost any kind of cancer, a person must learn to live with the fear that the cancer might return. Side effects of chemotherapy may make it impossible for a young woman with breast cancer to have children. Many women lose their hair temporarily. If the cancer has spread, it becomes important to recognize, plan for, and cope with the prospect of dying. And because breasts are a part of the body that we consider very personal and that a woman associates with many things she cherishes, including love and children, she may worry that the people closest to her see her differently. Many women who have had mastectomies are able to have breast reconstructive surgery, which can restore a more normal appearance following breast removal. Many women with breast cancer find support groups very helpful in dealing with the stresses of the illness. It is important for patients, friends, and family to remember that people are much more than the sum of their body parts. No one is to blame for cancer. Love and understanding may help to make even the most difficult situation bearable.

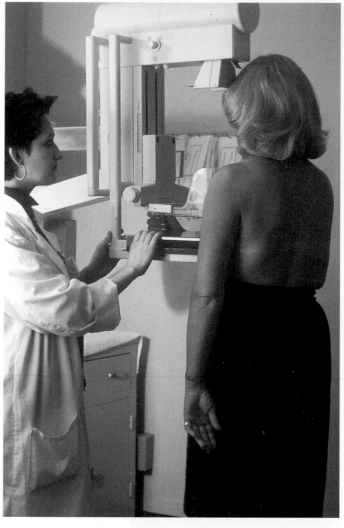

▲ Screening (routine) mammograms contribute to earlier detection of cancer and improved treatment outcomes. © *1991 David Weinstein and Associates/Custom Medical Stock Photo.*

Resources

Books

Love, Susan M. *Dr. Susan Love's Breast Book*, second edition. Reading, Massachusetts: Addison-Wesley, 1995.

Tomlinson, Theresa. *Dancing through the Shadows*. London: Dorling-Kindersly, 1997.

Organizations

U.S. National Cancer Institute, Bethesda, MD 20892. The NCI coordinates the government's cancer research program, and provides information about cancer to patients, their families, and the public. Its fact sheet

What You Need to Know About Breast Cancer is posted at its website.
Telephone 800-4-CANCER
http://www.nci.nih.gov/wyntk_pubs/index.html

American Cancer Society (ACS), 1599 Clifton Road NE, Atlanta, GA
30329-4251. ACS is a national, not-for-profit society whose purpose is to
provide unbiased, accurate, up-to-date health information about cancer.
Telephone 800-ACS-2345
http://www.cancer.org

National Alliance of Breast Cancer Organizations (NABCO).
NABCO's newsletter *NABCO News* publishes information about breast
cancer research, and its website helps people find local support groups.
Telephone 888-806-2226
http://www.nabco.org

Y-Me National Breast Cancer Hotline, 212 West Van Buren, Chicago,
IL 60607. A national organization that offers information and support
to anyone who has been touched by breast cancer.
Telephone 800-221-2141
http://www.y-me.org

University of Pennsylvania Cancer Center. The OncoLink website at the
University of Pennsylvania posts information about all aspects of cancer.
http://www.cancer.med.upenn.edu

▶ *See also*
Cancer
Fibrocystic Breast Disease
Tumor

Breast Lumps *See* **Fibrocystic Breast Disease**

Broken Bones and Fractures

*The bones in the human body are very strong, but they can be broken
(fractured) as a result of trauma. Breaks can range in severity from
hairline fractures that require minimal treatment to shattered bones
that require surgery and may result in permanent damage.*

KEYWORD
*for searching the Internet
and other reference sources*

Orthopedics

Ken's Elbow

Ken knew the steps to the attic were steep, but when his little sister ran
off with his toy airplane, he took the stairs two at a time. Halfway down
he slipped. Ken landed in a heap at the bottom and immediately howled
in pain. When he got up, his arm was twisted in a funny way, and his
elbow would not bend.

Ken's mother rushed him to the emergency room where doctors
took x-rays of his arm. He had broken the bone in the upper part of his
arm as well as his elbow. The breaks were so bad that Ken had to have
surgery that afternoon. The doctor put a metal pin in his elbow to hold
the bones together while they healed. After surgery, Ken's arm had to be

in traction for two weeks. This means that he had to lie on his back in bed while his elbow was held in place by a special device hanging from the ceiling. This device put tension on his arm and elbow in just the right places to allow them to heal properly. After getting out of the hospital, Ken had a plaster cast on his whole arm for another eight weeks. Ken's arm and elbow healed completely, but every so often his elbow aches when he plays baseball.

What Are Bone Fractures?

Bone is the hardest tissue in the human body, but when bones are subjected to forces that exceed their strength, they may break. The terms "break" and "fracture" mean the same thing.

■ A simple fracture is the most common type of break. The bone breaks but does not break through the skin.

■ A compound (open) fracture occurs when the broken bone breaks through the skin. This type of break is serious because, in addition to the damaged bone, bacteria can infect the body through the break in the skin. Sometimes the jagged edges of bone break blood vessels and cause bleeding.

■ A greenstick fracture is a type of incomplete fracture. Greenstick fractures often affect children, whose bones are springy and resilient. The best way to visualize a greenstick fracture is to think of trying to break a small branch off a growing tree. It will not snap off; rather it requires twisting. Twisting of the branch produces splinters. This is similar to what happens in a greenstick bone fracture: the bone cracks and splinters but does not break. If the bone does break into separate pieces, it is called a complete fracture.

Bone is the hardest tissue in the human body, but when bones are subjected to forces that exceed their strength, they may break in several different ways.

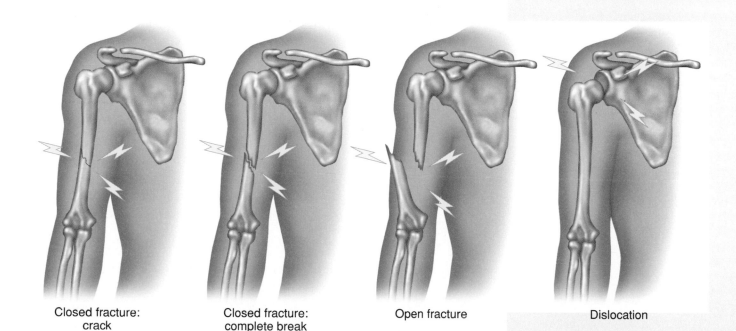

| Closed fracture: crack | Closed fracture: complete break | Open fracture | Dislocation |

Anatomy of Bone

The human skeleton consists of 206 bones that support the body and allow it to move. There are 29 bones in the skull, 27 in each hand, and 26 in each foot.

Bone is living tissue. It consists of cells, blood vessels, connective tissue, proteins, and fibers, as well as minerals such as calcium and phosphorus. Every bone contains both trabecular (tra-BEK-yoo-lar) and cortical (KOR-ti-kal) bone. Trabecular, or cancellous (KAN-sell-us) bone, looks like honeycomb. Despite being porous, it is very strong. Cortical bone is solid and dense. In cross-section, it has circular patterns like those seen in a tree trunk. It forms the outer layer of bones. Many bones also contain bone marrow, where blood cells are made.

The ratio of trabecular to cortical bone varies depending on the type of bone. Trabecular bone surrounded by a thin layer of cortical bone makes up the spine, skull, ribs, and sternum (breast bone), whereas the bones of the arms and legs consist mostly of cortical bone, with only a small amount of trabecular bone at both ends.

- Stress fractures are tiny hairline cracks that can occur when a bone is repeatedly stressed.
- An impacted fracture occurs when a bone breaks and the two pieces ram into each other.
- A comminuted fracture is one in which a bone shatters into pieces.
- Fractures also can occur through joints.
- Sometimes, people tear ligaments (tough bands of connective tissue that hold joints and bones together) even when a bone is not broken. Torn ligaments frequently affect the ankles and knees.
- Dislocations are injuries in which the bones in a joint are pulled apart or displaced in relation to each other. Ligament injuries and fractures often occur with dislocations.

What Causes Breaks and Fractures?

Bones break when they are subjected to extreme force or stress. The likelihood that a bone will break depends on the location of the bone in the body, the thickness of the bone, and the circumstances under which the force was applied. The most commonly broken bones are those in the wrist, hip, and ankle.

Bone is living tissue, and like other living tissue in the body, bone is affected by genetics, hormones, diet, physical activity, disease, and drugs. All of these things can make bones more or less prone to injury. In addition, the strength of bone and the forces acting on bone vary with age, so the types of fractures and the number of people affected by them vary with age as well.

Many types of trauma (for example, skiing or car accidents) can cause a bone to break. However, some people are more prone to breaks

150 YEARS AGO: MILITARY MEDICINE

The practice of military medicine during the U.S. Civil War contributed to the development of medical knowledge. Broken and shattered bones were frequent occurrences on battlefields. Treatment techniques were recorded in detailed reports by military physicians and were published in the *Medical and Surgical History of the War of the Rebellion*, written by Otis A. George and Joseph J. Woodward. The book's case studies of wounded soldiers, and its statistics about the nature of wounds and the effectiveness of various treatments, provided a basis for improved management of wounds and fractures in the decades that followed.

because they have genetic conditions or bone diseases that weaken their bones. For example:

- Osteogenesis imperfecta, which means imperfect bone formation, is also called brittle bone disease. People with this condition have inherited genes that cause a defect in the production of bone. The result is weakened bones that break easily.

- Osteoporosis is a disease that causes a thinning and weakening of the bones, making them prone to fracture. It affects older adults, particularly women after they reach menopause.

- Osteopetrosis is a rare hereditary disease that causes the bones to thicken. Osteopetrosis comes in several forms, some of which cause joint problems. Osteopetrosis congenita is discovered in infancy or childhood and it affects the bone marrow; without a bone marrow transplant, this condition usually is fatal. Marble bone disease also is discovered in infancy. It causes short stature and mental retardation.

- Other diseases, such as bone cancer, osteomalacia (adult rickets), Paget's disease (in which the bones become enlarged, weak, and deformed), and exposure to radiation can weaken bones and make them susceptible to breaks.

How are Fractures Diagnosed and Treated?

Diagnosis A doctor may suspect a broken bone based on the appearance of the injured area. A fractured bone may cause swelling or bruising in the affected area. As in Ken's case, the affected limb might look deformed and it may hurt to move. Sometimes, a break is obvious because the bone has poked through the skin. By touching and pressing on the injured area, the doctor may be able to tell if a bone is broken. X-rays of the injured area usually confirm the diagnosis of a broken bone, although stress fractures or hairline fractures can be difficult to detect on x-rays.

Treatment Broken bones may be treated by realigning the bones back into their proper position, if necessary (a process called "reduction"), and then holding them in place while they heal.

Treating a broken bone depends on where in the body it is located and how severe the break is. In the case of a stress fracture, a device called a splint may be used to immobilize the injured area while it heals. An arm sling also may be used to keep a person from using an injured arm. When a person has a simple fracture, the doctor will guide the bones back into their proper place, if necessary, and then immobilize the injured area with a cast made of plaster or fiberglass.

Other more serious types of fractures can require surgery. For example, in Ken's case, realigning the bones was not a straightforward task. An orthopedic surgeon (bone specialist) needed to open the site of the fracture surgically and use metal pins and plates to hold the bones together temporarily, while they healed. Ken's injury required his arm to be in traction for several weeks before having a cast for another two months.

Is It Broken?

People can break bones anytime and anywhere. To assess the situation, doctors often look for signs of fractures and ask about symptoms. Among the signs doctors look for:

- Is the area swollen and bruised?

- Is the limb hanging at a funny angle?

- Does the limb look out of place?

- Is the bone sticking out through the skin?

Among the symptoms doctors ask about:

- Did the injured person feel or hear anything breaking?

- Can they move the injured area?

- Does it hurt when touched?

Doctors use x-rays to confirm fracture diagnoses. This x-ray shows an open fracture of the fibula, a leg bone. © *1991 Scott Camazine/Photo Researchers, Inc.*

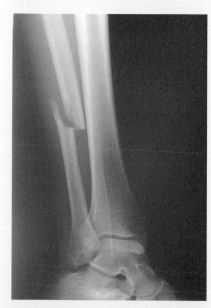

Healing   Splints, casts, and slings are used to keep bones in place while they heal. Healing occurs when the bone tissues produce a substance called callus, which binds the broken pieces together. Healing time varies with age. A fracture that may take three weeks to heal in a four-year-old may take three months to heal in an adult. Casts for simple breaks usually stay on for six to eight weeks, but more severe breaks may require a cast for much longer time periods.

Many people recover completely from breaks and fractures. One possible complication, however, is osteomyelitis, an infection of the bone. Usually, it affects the long bones in the arms and legs but it can be treated with antibiotics. Fractures through joints may increase the risk for arthritis in that joint later on in life, and older people, many of whom have osteoporosis, may not recover well from broken bones.

Resources

Book

Perry, Clayton R., and John Elstrom. *The Handbook of Fractures*. New York: McGraw-Hill, 1998.

Organizations

American Association of Orthopedic Surgeons, 6330 North River Road, Rosemount, IL 60018.
Telephone 708-823-7186

Osteogenesis Imperfecta Foundation, 632 Center Street, Van Wert, OH 45891.

▶ *See also*
Arthritis
Osteomyelitis
Osteoporosis
Rickets
Strains and Sprains
Trauma

KEYWORDS
for searching the Internet and other reference sources

Inflammation

Pulmonary system

Respiratory system

Bronchitis

Bronchitis (brong-KI-tis) is an inflammation of the bronchial tubes, which connect the trachea (windpipe) to the lungs.

Daughter Knows Best

Chrissy's father had been smoking cigarettes since he was Chrissy's age. In the last few years, though, her father had developed a nasty cough that never seemed to go away. Her father said it was just a "smoker's cough" and nothing to worry about, but Chrissy was concerned. Finally, she convinced her father to see a doctor. The doctor said that her father had chronic bronchitis, an illness that affects a large number of smokers. The doctor pointed out that too many smokers do not take this condition seriously until the lungs have been badly damaged. At that point, they can develop life-threatening breathing problems or heart failure. Surprised by what he had learned, Chrissy's father thanked his daughter for urging him to get help before it was too late. The next day, he joined a group for smokers who want to kick the habit.

What Is Bronchitis?

Bronchitis is an inflammation of the lining of the bronchial tubes. These tubes connect the trachea to the lungs. When the tubes become irritated or infected, they swell up inside. This interferes with the flow of air into and out of the lungs. The swollen and inflamed tissues also make large amounts of a thick, slippery substance called mucus*. People with bronchitis bring up mucus when they cough.

There are two types of bronchitis: acute and chronic. Acute bronchitis comes on suddenly and usually clears up in a few days. Chronic bronchitis lasts for a long period of time, and it can come and go over several years.

What Causes Bronchitis?

Acute bronchitis occurs when the bronchial tubes are infected by bacteria or viruses. Almost everyone has acute bronchitis at some point.

Chronic bronchitis occurs when the bronchial tubes are irritated over a long period of time. Cigarette smoke is by far the most common

*__mucus__ (MU-kus) is a kind of body slime. It is thick and slippery, and it lines the inside of many parts of the body. These body linings are called mucous membranes.

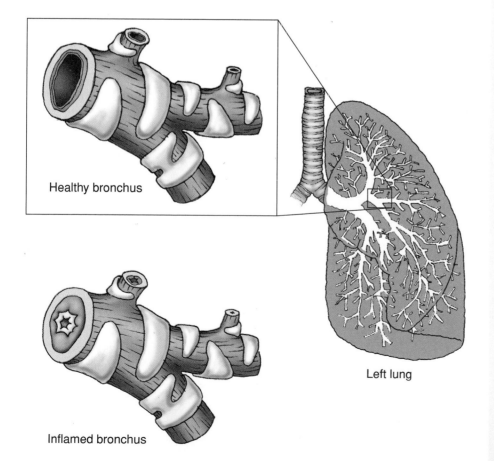

Healthy bronchus

Inflamed bronchus

Left lung

◄ Close-up view of the anatomy of the left lung and of one of its bronchial tubes, which is called a bronchus. Healthy bronchi bring air in and out of the lungs, but people with irritated and inflamed bronchi have mucus clogging up the inside of the tubes. The inflammation interferes with breathing, and it causes coughing that often brings up the mucus.

cause of this irritation, but such things as air pollution, dust, and fumes also can cause it. Once the bronchial tubes have been irritated for a while, the lining begins to thicken, and the tissues start to make excess mucus all the time. This leads to long-lasting problems with coughing and shortness of breath. The irritated bronchial tubes also are an ideal breeding ground for repeated infections. Over 14 million people in the United States have chronic bronchitis.

What Are the Symptoms?

Acute bronchitis Acute bronchitis can lead to chest discomfort, breathlessness, wheezing, and a deep cough that brings up yellow mucus. A person with acute bronchitis may feel tired for a few days and may have a fever. An occasional, brief attack of bronchitis usually goes away in a matter of days without causing long-term health problems.

Chronic bronchitis Chronic bronchitis is a more serious illness. The main symptom is a cough that produces lots of yellow mucus. The problem often begins with coughing that continues after a winter cold. As time goes on, the coughing may continue throughout the year. As the illness gets worse, the person may develop constant shortness of breath.

How Is Bronchitis Diagnosed and Treated?

*stethoscope (STETH-o-skope) is a medical instrument used for listening for sounds produced in the chest, abdomen, and other areas of the body.

Diagnosis To diagnose bronchitis, the doctor asks about symptoms and listens for abnormal breathing sounds with a stethoscope*. The doctor looks for other conditions that may cause coughing: asthma, an inhaled object such as a peanut, or a tumor. In some cases, the doctor may order other tests as well, such as a chest x-ray or a lung function test. But if the person's cough lasts for at least three months of the year, for two or more years in a row, then the doctor probably will diagnose the problem as chronic bronchitis.

Treatment of acute bronchitis Time is often the best healer of acute bronchitis. To help the person feel better, the doctor may advise resting, drinking plenty of fluids, and perhaps taking nonprescription medication for fever and nonprescription cough medicine.

Living with chronic bronchitis The treatment of chronic bronchitis is aimed mainly at cutting down on irritation of the bronchial tubes. This means giving up smoking, avoiding polluted air, and staying away from irritants such as dust, fumes, and cold or dry air. People with chronic bronchitis also should try to avoid anyone with a cold or the flu, as catching such an infection can make the bronchitis worse. To make breathing easier, the doctor may prescribe medications that help relax and open up the air passages in the lungs.

Of course, prevention is always better than treatment of a problem after it has developed. Most cases of chronic bronchitis could be prevented if people did not smoke.

Resource

American Lung Association, 1740 Broadway, New York, NY 10019.
The American Lung Association posts information about chronic bronchitis at its website.
Telephone 800-LUNG-USA
http://www.lungusa.org

▶ See *also*
Asthma
Emphysema
Tobacco-Related Diseases

Bruxism (Jaw Grinding)
See Temporomandibular Joint Syndrome

Bubonic Plague *See* Plague

Bulimia *See* Eating Disorders

Bunions

Bunions (BUN-yunz) are foot deformities caused by displacement of certain bones. A bunion is visible as a bump on the side of the foot at the joint at the base of the big toe.

KEYWORDS
for searching the Internet and other reference sources

Orthopedics

Orthotics

Podiatry

The Price of Style

When Natalie began her job at the bank, she finally could afford to indulge her love of stylish shoes. The higher the heel and the pointier the toe, the better. However, after several months, the inner side of Natalie's right foot, especially around the base of the big toe, began to swell and turn red. As it rubbed against her shoe, the bump on her foot grew bigger. After a few weeks, even sneakers hurt her foot. Natalie knew she had a bunion; bunions ran in her family, and her foot looked just like her mother's and grandmother's feet. She counted the days until her appointment with a podiatrist (po-DY-a-trist), or foot specialist.

What Causes Bunions?

Hallux valgus The medical term for bunion is "hallux valgus": hallux means big toe, and valgus means a deformity pointing away from the middle of the body. A bunion is formed when the first metatarsal (MET-a-tar-sal), which is the long bone along the inner side of the foot, pushes out at the base of the big toe, and the big toe is displaced toward the smaller toes. The first metatarsal and one of the big toe bones meet at the first joint of the big toe; the bump characteristic of a bunion is caused by inflammation and swelling of this joint.

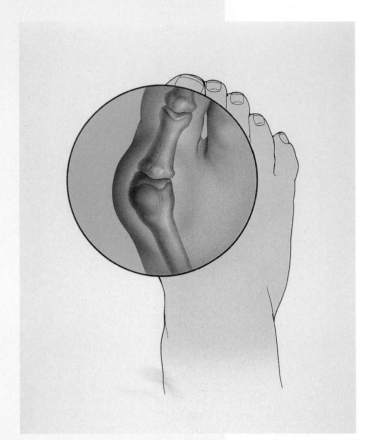

▲

A bunion is formed when the first metatarsal bone (along the inner side of the foot) pushes out at the base of the big toe, and the big toe is displaced toward the smaller toes. The bump that characterizes a bunion is caused by joint inflammation and swelling. © 1998 T. Buck/ Custom Medical Stock Photo.

*orthotic is a support or brace for weak or ineffective joints or muscles.

Anyone can develop a bunion Bunions are a very common and painful foot deformity. Anyone, including children, can develop a bunion. However, bunions are most common in women over 30, possibly because of shoe choice. Narrow, pointy, high-heeled shoes can speed up the formation of a bunion in people who are susceptible to developing them. People who have flat feet or low arches also are more prone to develop bunions than people with higher arches.

Pronation and other foot abnormalities Foot abnormalities are a common cause of bunions. For example, people whose feet are rotated so that the inside edge of the foot hits the ground first when they walk (pronated feet) are prone to bunions. Many people have a genetic susceptibility to developing bunions, and bunions also may develop in association with arthritis.

How Are Bunions Treated?

Natalie had the classic symptoms of a bunion: the inner side of her foot was deformed by a red, swollen, painful lump the size of a large marble; she also had a big callus (an area of hard thick skin) along the inner side of her foot; her other toes overlapped one another; and sometimes the skin over the bunion became infected.

Before treating the bunion, Natalie's podiatrist took x-rays of her foot to examine the foot bones. She had a large and well-developed bunion, and he decided to inject medication into her big toe joint to reduce the swelling. He also prescribed devices called orthotics* that fit into her shoes to help reduce pressure and weight on her big toe. To help reduce swelling, the podiatrist told Natalie to take aspirin, put ice packs on her foot, and soak her foot in mineral salts. She also would have to give up the high heels.

Osteotomy These treatments did not work for Natalie, and ultimately she had bunion surgery. The podiatrist performed an osteotomy (os-tee-OT-o-mee), which means "cutting of bone." After giving Natalie local anesthesia to block pain in her foot, the podiatrist removed areas of the metatarsal that had thickened, and he used a small titanium (ty-TANE-ee-um) screw to hold the bones in their correct position. Like almost all bunion repairs, Natalie's was successful. She was walking again the day of the surgery and was back to work in four days.

Resources

Book

Tremaine, M. David, M.D., and Elias M. Awad, Ph.D. *The Foot and Ankle Sourcebook: Everything You Need to Know.* Lowell House, 1998.

Organizations

American Podiatric Medical Association, 2 Chevy Chase Circle NW, Washington, DC 20005. The APMA's website features information about bunions and other disorders affecting the feet. http://www.apma.org

American College of Foot and Ankle Surgeons, 515 Busse Highway, Park Ridge, Illinois 60068. This organization's website provides information about foot health, foot and ankle deformities, and foot injuries. http://www.acfas.org

▶ See also
Arthritis
Flat Feet

Burns

Burns are tissue injuries caused by fire, sun, steam, hot fluids, heated objects, electricity, lightning, radiation, and other things. Burns may cause a variety of problems ranging from minor discomfort to serious life-threatening conditions.

Why Are Burns a Hot Topic?

The skin is the protective outer surface of the body. Its outer layer is the epidermis, comprising several layers of epithelial cells arranged like shingles on a roof. Its inner layer is the dermis, which contains many types of nerves that sense touch, pain, heat, and cold. Healthy skin renews itself and helps keep body fluids in and unwanted bacteria out. When burns injure the skin, they upset these processes. All burns result in skin cell injury. The most serious burns can result in death.

What Are the Three Classes of Burns?

First degree burns   These burns are the least severe. They affect only the top layer of skin, the epidermis, which turns red at the burn site and hurts when it is touched. First degree burns sometimescause small blisters and mild swelling, but they usually heal rapidly on their own.

Second degree burns   These burns affect both the dermis and the epidermis. They often cause pain, fever, swelling, chills, and blisters,

KEYWORDS
for searching the Internet and other reference sources

Dermatology

Epithelium

Rehabilitation

Trauma

Wounds

Did You Know?

The U.S. National Institute of General Medical Sciences reports that there are more than 2 million burn injuries requiring medical attention each year. Among people with burn injuries:

▪ 70,000 require hospitalization

▪ 20,000 require treatment in special burn units

▪ 10,000 die of burn-related infections

▪ burn research and burn treatments are improving survival rates even among people with burns covering more than 90% of their bodies.

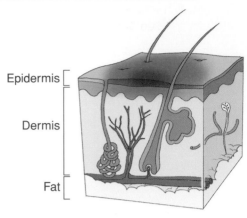

Epidermis

Dermis

Fat

First degree burn   Second degree burn   Third degree burn

First degree burns affect only the top layer of skin (the epidermis). Second degree burns affect the epidermis and the dermis. Third degree burns are the most serious. They affect deeper layers of tissue, including nerves, sweat glands, fat, and hair follicles.

Sunburns

These things can help ease the discomfort of sunburns:

- cool baths or cool compresses

- soothing lotions

- over-the-counter pain medications such as acetaminophen.

These things can make sunburns worse:

- petroleum jelly

- butter

- harsh soaps

- over-the-counter sprays containing benzocaine.

Severe sunburn should be treated by a doctor.

which may be reddish or whitish in color. Severe sunburns often are second degree burns, and it is important to see a doctor about them.

Third degree burns   These are the most serious burns and require immediate medical treatment. They affect all layers of skin and cause damage and cell death to all kinds of tissues, including nerves, sweat glands, fat, and hair follicles. The burn area itself may be free from pain if its nerve endings have been damaged, but the area around the burn will often be extremely painful. The whitish or reddish blisters of second degree burns usually will not be present, but the skin may be blackened or charred. Other complications of third degree burns may include:

- loss of body fluids (dehydration)

- respiratory (breathing) problems

- bacterial infections and pneumonia

- shock.

How Do Doctors Treat Burns?

Treatment depends on how large the burn is and how deeply it has injured skin tissue and underlying organs. Mild burns usually heal on their own when the injured area is kept clean and dry. More serious burns often require treatment in a hospital. The most serious burns may require treatment in a hospital's specialized burn unit or in an intensive care unit. These burns often require skin graft surgery to replace the damaged tissue followed by a long healing period and physical therapy for the injured area. Fire safety, awareness, and prevention are the best defenses against burns.

Resources

U.S. National Institute of General Medical Sciences, 45 Center Drive, MSC 6200, Bethesda, MD 20892-6200. The NIGMS posts resource lists and fact sheets about burns and other injuries at its website.
http://www.nih.gov/nigms

American Burn Association, 625 North Michigan Avenue, Suite 1530, Chicago, IL 60611. The ABA publishes a *Journal of Burn Care and Rehabilitation* and posts burn statistics and a reference bibliography at its website.
http://ameriburn.org

Bursitis *See* **Arthritis**

▶ *See also*
Skin Conditions
Shock
Trauma

C

Campylobacteriosis

Campylobacteriosis is an infection of the intestinal tract that is caused by the Campylobacter *bacterium. The infection may cause diarrhea, nausea and vomiting, and abdominal cramps.*

KEYWORDS
for searching the Internet
and other reference sources

Campylobacter jejuni

Enteritis

Food Poisoning

Guillain-Barré syndrome

What Is *Campylobacter*?

Campylobacter (kamp-pi-lo-BAK-ter) is a type of bacteria that is a normal inhabitant of the digestive tract of many animals. People, however, do not normally carry *Campylobacter*, and exposure to it usually causes an intestinal infection called campylobacteriosis (kamp-pi-lo-bak-ter-ee-O-sis).

The most common source of *Campylobacter* in the United States is chicken. When chickens (and other animals) are killed for food, the bacteria from their digestive tract can contaminate the meat. People get infected when they eat raw or uncooked meats and eggs (thorough cooking kills the bacteria), drink raw (unpasteurized) milk, or drink contaminated water. Oftentimes, juices from raw meats drip and contaminate other foods. In rare cases, contact with people or animals who are infected spreads the illness.

Campylobacter is the most common bacterial cause of diarrhea in the United States, where more than 2 million cases occur each year. The illness most frequently affects infants and children younger than age 10, although anyone can get it. Most cases occur in the summer and fall.

What Happens When People Get Campylobacteriosis?

Within two to five days after exposure to *Campylobacter*, a person may develop diarrhea, fever, abdominal cramps, and blood in the stool. Most people with campylobacteriosis recover within about ten days without any treatment other than drinking lots of fluids to prevent dehydration (a dangerous loss of fluids and salts).

In serious cases, people with campylobacteriosis may require antibiotics* and intravenous* (IV) rehydration. In rare cases, campylobacteriosis may lead to other illnesses, such as colitis, arthritis, meningitis (men-in-JY-tis), and Guillain-Barré (gee-YAN-ba-RAY) syndrome, a disorder that can result in temporary paralysis.

Prevention The best way to prevent infection is to treat all meat and eggs as if they were contaminated: never letting meat drip on other food;

* **antibiotics** (an-ty-by-OT-iks) are drugs that kill bacteria.

* **intravenous** (in-tra-VEE-nus) means injected directly into the veins.

169

always cooking meat thoroughly; always washing cooking utensils and cooking areas thoroughly; and always washing hands after using the bathroom, touching pets, and before handling food.

Resources

Book

Scott, Elizabeth, and Paul Sockett. *How to Prevent Food Poisoning: A Practical Guide to Safe Cooking, Eating, and Food Handling.* New York: John Wiley, 1998.

Organizations

The U.S. Food and Drug Administration (FDA) posts a *Bad Bug Book* at its website with a fact sheet about *Campylobacter jejuni* and campylobacteriosis.
http://vm.cfsan.fda.gov/~mow/chap4.html

The U.S. Centers for Disease Control and Prevention (CDC). CDC has a National Center for Infectious Diseases that posts a fact sheet about *Campylobacter* infections at its website.
http://www.cdc.gov/ncidod/dbmd/diseaseinfo/campylobacter_g.htm

▶ See also
Arthritis
Bacterial Infections
Colitis
Diarrhea
Food Poisoning
Gastroenteritis
Meningitis
Shock

Cancer

Cancer is a group of many related diseases in which abnormal cells grow out of control and spread.

KEYWORDS
for searching the Internet
and other reference sources

Carcinogens

Carcinoma

Metastasis

Oncogenes

Oncology

Osteosarcoma

An Ancient Affliction

The disease we call cancer has been around as long as we have. Evidence of cancerous growths, or tumors, has been found among fossilized bones and in human mummies dating from ancient Egypt. The ancient Greek physician Hippocrates (hi-POK-ra-tees) was the first to use the word "carcinoma" (kar-si-NO-ma) to describe various kinds of tumors. Hippocrates noted that parts sticking out from some tumors looked like the limbs of a crab. The word "cancer" comes from the Latin word for crab. In 1913, only one in nine people had a chance of being alive five years after a diagnosis of cancer. Today, depending on the cancer, more than 50 percent of people with cancer will survive the disease. For many types of cancer, early detection and treatment result in a normal lifespan.

What Is Cancer?

In all forms of cancer, cells grow out of control and may spread. In the United States, half of all men and one third of all women will develop one type of cancer or another during their lifetime. Almost everyone knows someone who has had cancer, and it is natural for children to worry that they might get it. But cancer in children is very rare. Some cancers are more common than others. The cancers that adults get most frequently are cancers of the skin, lungs, and colon and rectum. Breast cancer is a common cancer among women. Childhood cancers include leukemia (loo-KEE-mee-ya), lymphoma (lim-FO-ma), brain cancer, and osteosarcoma (os-tee-o-sar-KOME-a) (bone cancer). Cancer is sometimes referred to as a malignancy or a malignant tumor.

How Does Cancer Begin?

With more than 100 types of cancer, the disease can arise in almost any part of the body. Each cancer is different, but they all start the same way. A healthy body is home to more than 10 trillion cells (at least 100 times as many stars as there are in the entire Milky Way galaxy). Just as neighbors cooperate to maintain an orderly community, cells usually grow, divide, and die in a controlled fashion. But cancer cells are renegades, bad neighbors in the cellular community. Cancer begins when a single cell starts to multiply inappropriately.

What turns a good cell bad? The operating instructions for everything that our cells do are contained in the genes, packets of information that we inherit from our parents. Genes are made of a substance called DNA. The function of genes is to make proteins, the building blocks of life that carry out the work of the genes. When a gene inside a cell is switched on, the cell starts producing the required protein. Sometimes genes become altered, and we say they have mutated. Mutations in a gene can affect how the gene works; for example, a mutated gene might produce too much of a protein, or perhaps none at all.

Life proceeds by cell growth and division, and this process is directed by a collection of genes whose proteins work like traffic cops to encourage growth, or to halt it. When these genes become mutated, the proteins they make may erroneously tell cells to continue growing, like a traffic light stuck on green. The mutated genes are called oncogenes. Normal cells with damaged DNA die. But cancer cells with damaged DNA may not.

Many tumors need 30 to 40 years to develop, which explains why children rarely get cancer. But it is possible for a person to inherit a mutant cancer-causing gene. When that happens, people sometimes get cancer at an earlier age.

Genes can undergo mutations as a result of cancer-causing substances called carcinogens (kar-SIN-o-jens) in the environment as well as chemicals in our own cells. Another source of mutations is copying mistakes that occur when DNA is replicated during cell division. Cells normally have repair systems to correct such errors. But when the repair system slips up, the damage becomes a permanent part of that cell and of the cell's descendants. If a person has a faulty repair system, mutations in the genes will build up rapidly, making the cells more likely to become cancerous. Faulty repair plays a role in certain kinds of colon, skin, and breast cancers.

The U.S. and the World

- The U.S. National Cancer Institute says that 8.4 million people—about 3 percent of the population in 1999—have a history of cancer. The death rates for most major cancers have declined since the 1970s, because of earlier detection and better treatment. About 2 million women are breast cancer survivors and 1 million men are prostate cancer survivors.

- Still, cancers killed 539,577 Americans in 1997. This accounted for 23 percent of all deaths that year, making cancer the second leading cause of death after heart disease. Lung cancer caused the majority of the cancer deaths (29 percent), followed by stomach cancer (23.5 percent).

- Each year, about 150 of every 1 million Americans under age 20 will be diagnosed with cancer. But the chances for surviving at least five years with cancer increased for children between the early 1980s (64 percent survived) and the early 1990s (74 percent). That is better than the five-year survival rate for all cancers, which was about 60 percent in the 1990s.

- Worldwide, cancer caused an estimated 7.2 million deaths in 1998, which accounts for 13 percent of all deaths. Lung cancer was the leading cause, accounting for 17 percent of all cancer deaths.

- Cancer deaths worldwide have increased slightly since 1993, when about 6 million people died of cancer. That represented 12 percent of all deaths worldwide in 1993.

- About 81 million people worldwide were living with cancer in 1998. The World Health Organization (WHO) expects the prevalence of cancer cases to increase in the first 25 years of the twenty-first century in developing nations.

The body's defenses are impressive, and it is difficult for cancer to get started. But imagine that a renegade cell has managed to evade every one of the cell's checkpoints and has formed a tumor. Now what? To grow larger than a millimeter (about the size of a pinhead), a tumor needs a blood supply, so it sends out a chemical signal to cause blood vessels to grow.

How Does Cancer Spread?

Normal cells do not wander. But some types of cancer cells do, which is what makes them so dangerous. The process is called metastasis (meh-TAS-ta-sis). Although it may be fairly easy to remove the main, or primary, tumor in cancer, metastasis cannot usually be cured by surgery alone.

In order for cancer to spread to other parts of the body, it must detach from its original location, invade a blood vessel, travel through the circulation to a far-away site, and set up a new cellular colony. At every one of these steps, it must outsmart the many controls the body has to keep cells where they belong.

New techniques show that abnormal cells from a tumor often are circulating even when doctors can find no evidence of spread. We call this undetectable spread micrometastasis (MY-kro-meh-TAS-ta-sis). Once a cancer cell has found a new home, it must reverse all the steps it took in liberating itself. It has to attach to the inner lining of a blood vessel, cross through it, invade the tissue beyond, and multiply. Probably fewer than 1 in 1,000,000 of the cancer cells that make it into the bloodstream survive to take up residence elsewhere.

Cancer cells "prefer" small blood vessels, and the first small blood vessels a freed cancer cell encounters are those of the lungs. So the lungs are the most common site of spread for cancer, followed by the liver. Much of how cancer spreads is still a mystery. Some tissues—for example, cartilage and brain tissue—seem more resistant to cancer. And some animals almost never have cancer.

What Causes Cancer?

A risk factor is anything that increases a person's chance of getting a disease. But having a risk factor does not mean that a person will get the disease for sure. People get cancer as a result of a complex set of interactions between their genes and the environment. We are just beginning to understand these reactions.

Tobacco   Tobacco is a lethal cancer-causing substance. It causes 30 percent of total cancer deaths every year in the United States, affecting the lungs and other organs of the body. Almost all lung cancer is the result of smoking. The younger a person starts to smoke, the greater the risk of cancer.

Food and alcohol   In the United States, diet has been associated with certain cancers, particularly diets containing high amounts of animal (saturated) fat and red meat. After years of studies, coffee has not been proved to cause cancer, nor have artificial sweeteners. Eating insufficient quantities of fruits and vegetables appears to contribute to cancer, for reasons no one understands. It may be that fruits and vegetables help to block the cancer-causing effects of our own bodies. Drinking large amounts of alcohol increases the risk of cancer of the upper respiratory and digestive tracts, and alcoholic liver disease can lead to liver cancer. Even moderate drinking may contribute to breast and colon and rectal cancer.

Radiation   Some forms of radiation cause cancer. But most cancer deaths from radiation are caused by natural sources such as the sun's ultraviolet rays. For example, sunburns during childhood are a key factor in causing a kind of skin cancer called melanoma (mel-a-NO-ma). But electric power lines, household appliances, and cellular telephones have so far not been proven to cause cancer. Radiation from nuclear materials and reactions does cause cancer, but most people are not exposed to levels high enough to harm them.

Chemicals   In the past, some people who worked with certain chemical substances such as asbestos (az-BES-tos) and benzene (BEN-zeen) had a greater chance of getting lung cancers and other kinds of cancers. But strict government regulations have limited the use of these substances and sharply reduced the numbers of these cancers.

How Do People Know They Have Cancer?

Many symptoms of cancer such as weight loss, fever, fatigue, and various kinds of lumps could also be caused by other diseases. Some cancers may cause no symptoms until they have spread. Based on the most commonly occurring cancers, the American Cancer Society publishes a list

AMERICAN CANCER SOCIETY

The American Society for the Control of Cancer (ASCC) was founded in 1911 to educate the public about the dangers of cancer. In 1943, Mary Lasker, the wife of an advertising tycoon who himself would die of cancer, walked into the office of Clarence C. Little, the managing director of the ASCC, and asked him how much money the society was spending on research. Nothing, Little told her.

Lasker immediately began a campaign to raise funds for the renamed American Cancer Society (ACS). A granting program was begun in 1946. By 1948, the ACS had raised around $14 million. Today, the ACS has chartered divisions throughout the country and over 3,400 local units. ACS is the largest source of private, not-for-profit research funds in the United States, second only to the federal government in total dollars spent.

- The World Health Organization estimates about 15 million new cases of cancer will develop in the year 2020, compared with 10 million new cases a year in the late 1990s. Reasons include increased smoking in developing nations, unhealthy diets, and more people living to old age, when cancer risk is higher.

- The World Health Organization estimated in the mid-1990s that 15 percent of all cancers worldwide could be prevented by controlling infections. For example, more than 400,000 cases of liver cancer were tied to infection with hepatitis in the mid-1990s. Parasites in food also can lead to stomach cancers.

- Other trends to watch between 1999 and 2025, according to WHO: Lung cancer and colorectal cancer cases and deaths will increase, largely because of increased smoking and unhealthy diet. Women will die in higher numbers from lung cancer in almost all industrialized countries. Stomach cancer is expected to become less common, because of improved food conservation, changes in diet, and declining infection. Cervical cancer is predicted to decrease in industrialized countries because of increased screening and it might decrease in the developed world if a vaccine is developed. And, finally, liver cancer will decrease as the rates of immunization and screenings for hepatitis increase.

Eating for Health

The American Cancer Society recommends the following general nutritional guidelines to help people stay healthy:

- Choosing most foods from plant sources such as vegetables, fruits, and grains

- Limiting intake of high-fat foods, especially from animal sources

- Staying physically active

- Maintaining a healthy weight

- Limiting consumption of alcoholic beverages

of seven warning signs of cancer. These symptoms do not mean that a person has cancer, but if they occur, a person should see the doctor:

- Change in bowel or bladder habits (for instance diarrhea that does not go away or pain on urination)

- A sore anywhere on the skin that does not heal

- Unusual bleeding or discharge from the nose, mouth, skin, nipple, or vagina

- A thickening or lump in the breast or elsewhere

- Indigestion or difficulty in swallowing

- Obvious changes in a wart or mole

- Nagging cough, particularly if these symptoms occur in a cigarette smoker.

How Is Cancer Diagnosed and Treated?

Diagnosis Diagnosing cancer involves removing some tissue for evaluation. This procedure is called a biopsy (BY-op-see). Once the diagnosis is made, a treatment plan is put together. To do that, it is necessary to determine how widespread the disease is, and how serious. "Staging" the disease means assigning letters and numbers to it as a way of indicating whether it has spread and how far. There are several systems for staging, depending on the type of cancer. Generally speaking, the smaller the tumor, the more curable it is, although some cancer can be unpredictable. The outlook for some cancers, for example, leukemia and lymphoma, is judged according to other criteria. Cancer is classified by the part of the body in which it began and by how it looks under a microscope.

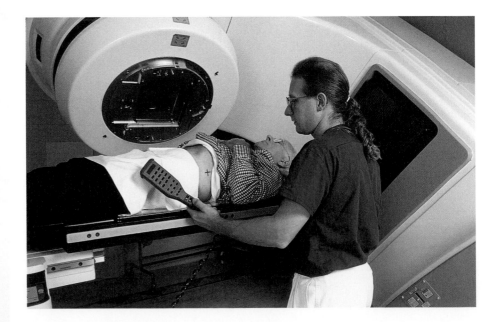

Radiation therapy uses high-energy particles or waves to destroy cancer cells that surgery cannot catch because they are too small to be seen and removed. © *1996 L. Steinmark/Custom Medical Stock Photo.*

174

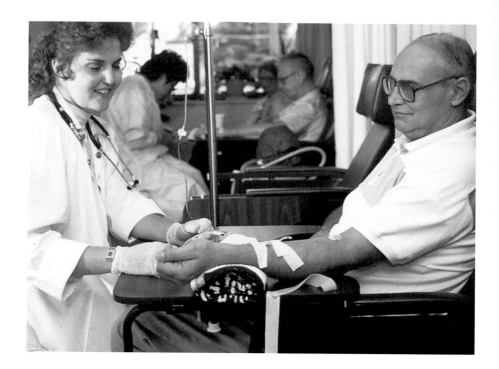

Chemotherapy uses anticancer drugs to treat cancer. Chemotherapy drugs are given through a vein or by mouth as pills. These drugs enter the bloodstream and reach places in the body that surgery and radiation cannot reach. Chemotherapy often is given for cancer that has spread. © 1992 Science Photo Library/Custom Medical Stock Photo.

Treatment   Treatment for cancer includes surgery, radiation, and chemotherapy (kee-mo-THER-a-pee), alone or together. Because different types of cancer vary in how fast they grow, where they spread, and how they respond to treatment, treatment is specifically tailored to the kind of cancer a person has.

- **Surgery** is the oldest form of treatment for cancer, and it still offers the greatest chance of cure for many kinds of cancer. About 60 percent of patients with cancer will have some type of surgery.

- **Radiation therapy** uses high-energy particles or waves to damage cancer cells that surgery cannot catch because they are too small.

- **Chemotherapy** uses anticancer drugs to treat cancer. Chemotherapy drugs are given through a vein (also called an intravenous or IV line) or by mouth as pills. These drugs enter the bloodstream and reach places in the body that surgery and radiation cannot reach. Chemotherapy is often given for cancer that has spread.

Another kind of therapy interferes with the production of substances in the blood called hormones (HOR-mones) that stimulate certain kinds of cells (for example, cells in the breast) to grow.

Will There Ever Be a Cure for All Cancers?

Every day researchers learn a little more about how the cell works, and many of these discoveries are being applied to cancer research. Many current therapies have side effects because they kill healthy cells as well as cancer cells or affect the function of other parts of the body. So one area of research scientists are working on is therapies that will kill only cancer cells and that will leave healthy cells alone. Another area of

Clinical Trials and New Cancer Treatments

Studies of new or experimental treatments in patients are known as clinical trials. Research in cancer could not move forward without them because drugs may work very differently in people than in the animals in which the drugs first proved successful.

Clinical trials seek to answer such questions as:

- Does this new treatment work?

- Does it work better than other treatments already available?

- Do the benefits outweigh the risks, including side effects?

Although there are risks to new treatments, clinical trials are done only when there is some reason to believe that the treatment will be of value to the patient.

Participating in a clinical trial is completely up to the patient. The doctor may suggest it, or patients can request information about clinical trials from the U.S. National Cancer Institute.

research is investigating ways of helping the body's own defense system to fight cancer. Scientists are also exploring substances in food or drugs that will prevent cancer from developing in the first place.

Can Cancer Be Prevented?

In the United States, 1.2 million people are diagnosed with cancer each year. There is no way to prevent cancers children get. But many cancers that occur in adults could be prevented by changes in a person's lifestyle. For example, cancers caused by cigarette smoking and drinking a lot of alcohol could be prevented completely. Limiting certain kinds of foods, such as red meats and animal fats, and eating lots of fruits and legumes (such as peas and lentils) may help reduce the risk of getting many cancers. Physical activity helps to avoid obesity and may have other protective effects against cancer. Most of the one million skin cancers that are diagnosed each year could be avoided by staying out of the sun.

Regular cancer checks, called screenings, for cancer of the breast, colon, rectum, cervix, prostate, testes, mouth, and skin are an effective way of detecting cancer early enough to be treated successfully. In addition, self-examination for breast and skin cancers also helps to detect tumors at earlier stages. The American Cancer Society estimates that if all Americans participated in regular cancer screenings, survival would be dramatically improved.

Living with Cancer

A cancer diagnosis is usually shocking and frightening. A person's life is suddenly disrupted by surgery, treatment, visits to the doctors, and changing personal relationships. Children with cancer may have to miss school for a time or to give up sports or other activities. A person may feel anger at themselves or others, or at God. Children especially may feel that something they did caused the cancer, especially if it is a brother or sister who is sick. Family, physician, friends and organizations, religious groups and clergy, and self-help groups all may be an important source of support. Each person's way of dealing with cancer is unique. Even with cancers that will cause death, a person may live for many years. And more than 70 percent of children and adolescents with cancer are successfully treated.

Alternative and complementary therapies   Many patients seek out other kinds of therapies during their treatment. Cancer is a frightening word, and some people will do anything, no matter how unlikely to work. A number of alternative treatments are themselves dangerous, and can distract from effective treatment. Some can be costly as well. These therapies generally are of two kinds:

- Alternative therapies are often promoted in the mass media as cancer cures. Patients should be aware that these therapies have either not been tested for safety and effectiveness, or have been tested and found to be ineffective.

- Complementary therapies, on the other hand, are used in addition to standard therapy. They may help to relieve symptoms of the disease or side effects of treatment, or they just may make patients feel better. Examples of complementary therapies are meditation to relieve stress and peppermint tea to combat nausea (stomach upset) from chemotherapy.

Patients who are thinking of using alternative or complementary therapies should first discuss it with their health care team.

Resources

U.S. National Cancer Institute, Bethesda, MD 20892. The NCI coordinates the government's cancer research program, and provides information about cancer to patients, their families, and the public. Its Cancer Information Service posts a *What You Need to Know About Cancer* series of fact sheets at its website, and its "kidscontents" fact sheet *When Someone in Your Family Has Cancer* can help with resources and referrals.
Telephone 800-4-CANCER
http://www.nci.nih.gov/wyntk_pubs/index.html
http://rex.nci.nih.gov/NCI_Pub_Interface/guide_for_kids/kidscontents.html

American Cancer Society (ACS), 1599 Clifton Road NE, Atlanta GA 30329-4251. ACS is a national, not-for-profit society that provides up-to-date health information about cancer.
Telephone 800-ACS-2345
http://www.cancer.org

KidsHealth.org and the Nemours Foundation publish *Childhood Cancer* and *What Is Cancer and What Happens When Kids Get It?*, offering practical, straightforward advice for parents and children on the kinds of cancer children get.
http://www.KidsHealth.org

University of Pennsylvania Cancer Center. The OncoLink website at the University of Pennsylvania posts information about all aspects of cancer.
http://www.cancer.med.upenn.edu

The World Health Organization posts information at its website about cancer and other noncommunicable diseases worldwide.
http://www.who.org

▶ *See also*

Bladder Cancer

Brain Tumor

Breast Cancer

Colorectal Cancer

Fibrocystic Breast Disease

Hepatitis

Kidney Cancer

Leukemia

Lung Cancer

Lymphoma/Hodgkin's Disease

Mouth Cancer

Pancreatic Cancer

Polyps

Prostate Cancer

Stomach Cancer

Skin Cancer

Testicular Cancer

Tumor

Uterine/Cervical Cancer

Viral Infections

| **Candidiasis** *See* **Yeast Infection, Vaginal** |

Canker Sores (Aphthous Ulcers)

Canker sores, or aphthous (AF-thus) ulcers, are small, round sores in the mouth that quickly turn white and usually are painful.

KEYWORDS
for searching the Internet and other reference sources

Aphthous ulcers

Oral inflammation

Stomatitis

Ashley's Story

Ashley first noticed a slight tingle in her mouth one morning as she was brushing her teeth before school. It was inside her lower lip, on the soft, fleshy part in front of her bottom teeth. By the next morning, she felt a bump that hurt when her tongue touched it and when she tried to drink orange juice with her breakfast. By dinner time, when Ashley pulled down her lip (gently) to look at the small, round blister in her mouth, she saw that it was white and rimmed with a red ring that looked like a halo. It was Ashley's first canker sore, but it probably would not be her last.

What Is a Canker Sore?

Canker sores are small, round sores that are found where Ashley discovered hers: inside the mouth. They may occur on the inside of the lips, on the tongue, on the roof or floor of the mouth, or inside the cheeks. They may appear as one small sore or in groups, and they can be quite irritating and painful to even the slightest touch. Contact with acidic, salty, or spicy foods and fluids, like chips or orange juice, can be particularly painful for people with canker sores.

Canker sores are not contagious*. They cannot be passed along from one person to another by kissing or by sharing food. It is important, however, to distinguish canker sores from other kinds of mouth sores, which may be caused by viral infections*, trauma, vitamin deficiencies, and sometimes, but not often, cancer. If a mouth sore has not healed within a week or two, it is important to see a doctor.

What Causes Canker Sores?

No one is sure what causes canker sores, although they occur more frequently when people are experiencing stress. Often, the first sores appear as children near middle school age. Canker sores are more common among women.

How Are Canker Sores Treated?

Ashley's canker sore disappeared on its own two weeks after she first noticed that sore feeling inside her mouth. Most canker sores clear up the same way, without treatment, although some people use over-the-counter medications to numb canker sores during the first four or five days when they are most painful. It also helps to avoid the sore while brushing teeth and to cut out foods that aggravate the pain, such as salty chips, citrus fruits, or spicy foods.

If canker sores recur or return, or if they do not heal on their own within two weeks, they may need to be seen by a doctor or dentist. But usually, canker sores go away on their own.

Resource

U.S. National Institute of Dental Research (NIDR), Building 31, Room 2C35, 31 Center Drive, MSC 2290, Bethesda, MD 20892-2290. The U.S. National Institute of Dental Research publishes information about canker sores, fever blisters, and mouth care.

* **contagious** means transmittable from one person to another.

* **viral infections** cause mouth sores that are called fever blisters or cold sores. These are often caused by the herpesvirus, and they usually appear on the gums or around the mouth and lips. Unlike canker sores, fever blisters and cold sores are contagious.

▶ *See also*

Herpes

178

Carbon Monoxide Poisoning

Carbon monoxide is a colorless, tasteless, odorless gas that results from incomplete burning of solid, liquid, and gaseous fuels. This gas can cause dizziness, nausea, coma, or death if breathed in sufficient amounts.

KEYWORDS
for searching the Internet
and other reference sources

Anoxia

Environmental health

Hypoxia

Hyperbaric oxygen

Toxicology

A Close Call

The neighbors could set a clock by Dr. Smith's morning routine. He turned off the porch light at 6:00 a.m., picked up the newspaper from the driveway at 6:15, and took the dog for a walk at 6:30. One winter morning, Dr. Smith's next-door neighbor noticed that none of these things had happened. He knew the Smiths were home, but they did not answer the doorbell or the telephone.

The neighbor called the police, who broke into the house and found four unconscious people. The gas heater had shut off during the night and had been giving off carbon monoxide gas for many hours. The Smiths were rushed to the hospital and treated for carbon monoxide poisoning. Dr. Smith and his wife and children were lucky; they were found in time and recovered completely after several weeks.

What is Carbon Monoxide (CO) Poisoning?

Carbon monoxide (CO) is a chemical created when some fuels, such as coal and gas, are burned. CO is toxic because it reduces the amount of oxygen received by the body's cells. Red blood cells contain a protein called hemoglobin that carries oxygen to the body's cells. Because CO binds much more easily and tightly to hemoglobin than does oxygen, CO will replace oxygen in the bloodstream when inhaled. When that happens, the cells that need lots of oxygen, such as those of the heart, skeletal muscles, and central nervous system, cannot function properly.

Acute CO poisoning   Dr. Smith and his family suffered acute* CO poisoning, in which a large amount of CO was breathed at one time. This kind of poisoning can lead to death: it kills 25 to 40 percent of those exposed. Survivors may feel symptoms for days, months, or years.

* **acute** means sudden.

Chronic CO poisoning   CO poisoning also can be chronic*. A small amount of CO inhaled continuously or frequently over a long period of time does not kill, but it does impair oxygen flow to the brain and may cause long-term nervous system problems, such as headaches, dizziness, weakness, sleepiness, nausea, and vomiting. Low-level chronic exposure to CO is especially serious for people with heart, lung, or circulatory problems, and for infants and older adults. Developing fetuses also can be affected by CO poisoning.

* **chronic** (KRON-ik) means continuing for a long period of time.

Carbon monoxide detectors for the home look like smoke detectors and can be installed to monitor for CO fumes. © *Tony Freeman/PhotoEdit.*

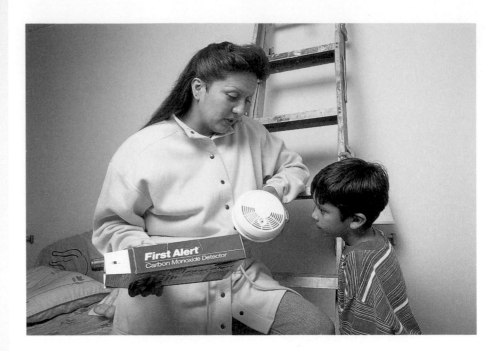

Carbon Monoxide and the Environment

CO is one of the most prevalent poisons in the environment. It can get into buildings, homes, and vehicles in many ways. Sources of CO include car exhaust, gas or oil furnaces, kerosene lamps, space heaters, improperly installed appliances, wood stoves, wood-burning fireplaces, and tobacco smoke. CO poisoning most often occurs during winter months, when people use heaters and fireplaces.

How Is CO Poisoning Treated?

A person with acute CO poisoning requires extra oxygen as soon as possible. The individual may be given pure oxygen to breathe. A hyperbaric (hy-per-BARE-ik) oxygen chamber also may be used to treat CO poisoning. This is a large chamber that holds the patient, and sometimes the medical team. The chamber is filled with 100 percent oxygen, and the pressure is increased to three atmospheres (three times the pressure of the air near the earth's surface, or the pressure the body feels about 90 feet under water). Pressure and pure oxygen help the oxygen molecules displace the CO attached to hemoglobin. Diagnosis and treatment of chronic CO poisoning may be more difficult, because its symptoms are similar to flu and many other conditions.

Can CO Poisoning Be Prevented?

CO poisoning is usually preventable. Basic safety guidelines include:

- Never burning charcoal in a tent or camper to keep warm.
- Installing water heaters and gas appliances properly and checking them often to make sure they are operating correctly.
- Keeping chimneys and wood-burning fireplaces clean.

- Never letting a car idle inside a garage, especially if the garage is attached to the house.
- Installing commercial CO detectors (similar in design to smoke detectors) for the home.

Resources

The U.S. National Center for Environmental Health at the Centers for Disease Control and Prevention (CDC) posts a *Checklist for the Prevention of Carbon Monoxide (CO) Poisoning* at its website. http://www.cdc.gov/nceh/programs/heeh/monxide/cocklst.htm

The U.S. National Institute of Neurological Disorders and Stroke posts a fact sheet at its website about anoxia and hypoxia from carbon monoxide inhalation and other causes. http://www.ninds.nih.gov/patients/Disorder/anoxia/anoxia.htm

▶ See also
Environmental Diseases

Cardiovascular Disease *See* Heart Disease

Carpal Tunnel Syndrome

Carpal tunnel syndrome is a painful condition affecting the hand and wrist caused by a pinched nerve in the wrist.

What Is Carpal Tunnel Syndrome and Who Gets It?

Carpal tunnel syndrome (CTS) occurs when the median nerve in the wrist is compressed by other structures in the "tunnel" formed by ligaments* and the carpal (or wrist) bones. The median nerve provides feeling to the palm, thumb, and middle fingers, and irritation of this nerve causes numbness, weakness, and pain.

Hundreds of thousands of people in the United States have CTS. Many are people who use their hands and wrists too much (repetitive motion) or in ways that are not ergonomically* correct, but there are other causes too. CTS also affects some people who have synovitis*, arthritis, diabetes, obesity, or thyroid disease, and sometimes women who are pregnant or going through menopause*.

What Happens When People Have CTS?

John's father loved coaching Little League, but after spending all week clicking away on his computer keyboard, his hands hurt too much to throw a baseball or grip a bat. John's father went to the doctor and complained of burning, tingling, and aching in his hands. He told the doctor that it hurt to cross his thumb over the palm of his hand and that the pain came and went but was worse at night.

KEYWORDS
for searching the Internet and other reference sources

Ergonomics

Musculoskeletal system

Orthopedics

* **ligaments** (LIG-a-ments) are bands of fibrous tissue that connect bones or cartilage, supporting and strengthening the joints.

* **ergonomics** (er-go-NOM-iks) is a science that helps people to know the best postures and movements to use while working, in order to avoid injury and discomfort.

* **synovitis** (sin-o-VY-tis) is inflammation of the membrane surrounding a joint.

* **menopause** (MEN-o-pawz) is the end of menstruation.

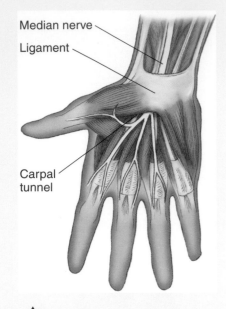

Anatomy of the wrist and palm.

Median nerve
Ligament
Carpal tunnel

* **cortisone** (KOR-ti-zone) is a medication used to relieve inflammation.

High-Risk Jobs for CTS

- Assembly line workers
- Butchers
- Carpenters
- Computer users, especially word processors and data entry clerks
- Draftsmen
- Dental hygienists
- Grocery store checkers
- Musicians
- Typists
- Writers

▶ *See also*

Repetitive Stress Syndrome

Strains and Sprains

KEYWORDS
for searching the Internet and other reference sources

Bartonella henselae

Retinitis

Mild CTS   The doctor suspected CTS and did some tests on the median nerve in both wrists. The doctor diagnosed a mild case of CTS, and told John's father to wear splints on his wrists, to take aspirin, and to take lots of breaks during the day when working on the computer.

John's father did some research about ergonomics and repetitive stress syndromes, and decided to reposition his computer keyboard. He lowered the keyboard so that his hands arched down at the wrist, and he stopped resting his wrists at the edge of his desk.

Advanced CTS   John's father had only a mild case of CTS. In cases with more serious symptoms, the doctor may have to inject a medication called cortisone* into the wrists. In severe cases of CTS, the doctor may recommend a surgical procedure, called carpal tunnel release, to relieve the pain. If left untreated, CTS can cause permanent nerve damage. With early treatment most people achieve pain relief and, like John's father, can return to coaching baseball and other active pursuits.

Resources

The U.S. National Institute of Neurological Disorders and Stroke (NINDS) posts a fact sheet about CTS at its website. http://www.ninds.nih.gov/patients/Disorder/CARPAL/carpal.htm

American Academy of Orthopaedic Surgeons, 6300 North River Road, Rosemont, IL 60018-4262. The AAOS is a physician group that posts a fact sheet about CTS at its website.
Telephone 800-346-AAOS
http://www.aaos.org

Association for Repetitive Motion Syndromes (ARMS), P.O. Box 471973, Aurora, CO 80047-1973
Telephone 303-369-0803

Canadian Centre for Occupational Health and Safety, 250 Main Street, Hamilton, Ontario, Canada L8N 1H6.
Telephone 800-263-8466
http://www.cohs.ca/oshanswers/diseases/carpal.html

Cat Scratch Disease

Cat scratch disease is an infection by Bartonella henselae *bacteria. It causes swollen glands, usually after a scratch or a bite from a cat.*

Where Is *Bartonella henselae* Found?

Bartonella henselae, the bacterium that causes cat scratch disease, is found all over the world. Cats and kittens carry the bacterium in their saliva. Although the infection does not make cats or kittens sick, they can transmit the infection to people, most often through a bite or a scratch. People cannot pass along the infection to other people.

What Happens When People Get Cat Scratch Disease?

Symptoms   Cat scratch disease usually results in a sore appearing at the site of the bite or scratch a few days afterward, followed a week or two later by swelling of the lymph nodes* (swollen glands) near the bite or the scratch as the body's immune system fights off the infection. Adults will sometimes run a low fever, or have a headache and joint pain, or feel more tired than usual. Most people get better within about three weeks. People with weakened immune systems are at risk for more serious complications, which may include:

lymph nodes are bean-sized round or oval masses of immune system tissue that filter bodily fluids before they enter the bloodstream, helping to keep out bacteria and other undesirable substances.

- retinitis (re-ti-NY-tis): inflammation of the retina of the eye, which can cause blindness

- encephalitis (en-sef-a-LY-tis): inflammation of the brain

- seizures

- infections of the liver, spleen, bones, or other organs.

Diagnosis   The doctor usually starts with a physical exam and a medical history, which should include information about contact with cats. The doctor may diagnose cat scratch disease if the person has fever, is feeling unwell, and has enlarged lymph nodes accompanied by a blister. Other ways to identify the disease include testing the blood for antibodies to *Bartonella* or performing a biopsy on an enlarged lymph node.

Treatment   Most people get better on their own. The doctor may prescribe antibiotics to help fight the bacterial infection, and the doctor may drain fluid from lymph nodes that are severely enlarged. People with weakened immune systems need continuing care from their doctors to minimize the risk of complications.

Preventing Cat Scratch Disease

It is important to teach children to stay away from stray cats and unknown cats. It is also important to teach them to be careful with their own pets, who may bite and scratch when provoked. Whenever cats bite or scratch people, it is a good idea to check with a doctor (about the person) and with a veterinarian (about the pet).

Resources

The Association of State and Territorial Directors of Health Promotion and Public Health Education (ASTDHPPHE) posts a fact sheet about cat scratch disease at its website.
http://www.astdhpphe.org/infect/catscratch.htm

Did You Know?

- There are more than 60 million pet cats in the United States.

- Approximately 24,000 people get cat scratch disease in the U.S. each year.

- Kittens transmit cat scratch disease to people more often than adult cats do.

- Kittens who have fleas are 29 times likelier to carry *Bartonella henselae* bacteria than kittens without fleas.

- Fewer than 5 percent of people with cat scratch disease develop severe symptoms.

KidsHealth.org (The Nemours Foundation) is a website that posts fact sheets about many different conditions, including cat scratch disease. http://KidsHealth.org

American Academy of Family Physicians, 8880 Ward Parkway, Kansas City, MO 64114-2797. The AAFP's familydoctor.org website posts fact sheets about many different conditions, including cat scratch disease.
Telephone 800-274-2237
http://familydoctor.org/handouts/024.html

▶ *See also*
Bacterial Infections
Conjunctivitis
Fever
Infection
Seizures
Zoonoses

Cataracts

Cataracts develop when the lens of the eye becomes cloudy. They usually impair vision and sometimes occur as people get older.

KEYWORDS
for searching the Internet and other reference sources

Ophthalmology

Vision

Many people who live to an old age will develop cataracts, often without noticing the effects until they are past age 70. For some, it might mean only a slight change in vision. Others, however, will find they need surgery to remove the cloudy lens.

A cataract results when the clear lens in the eye becomes cloudy. Like frost on a window, the cataract makes it more difficult to see clearly. The reason is that the light passing through the cloudy lens is distorted before it reaches the visual receptors in the retina* at the inside rear of the eyeball.

*****retina** lines the inner surface of the back of the eyeball. It contains millions of light-sensitive cells that change light into nerve signals that the brain can interpret.

Cataracts develop slowly, causing the eye's clear lens to become cloudy. Cataracts can be removed surgically.

▶

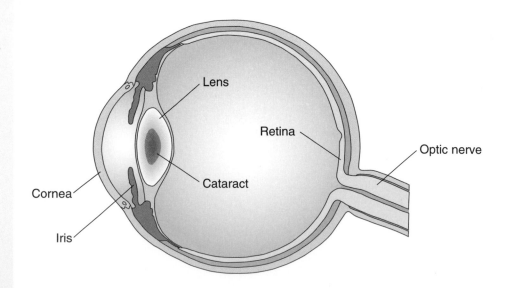

Lens
Retina
Optic nerve
Cataract
Cornea
Iris

What Happens When People Get Cataracts?

Researchers believe that cataracts develop because the proteins in the eye change as people age. The changes cause the lens to become cloudy. Other factors, such as smoking, poor nutrition, eye injury, exposure to excessive sunlight, and certain medical conditions such as diabetes, also may be factors that put people at higher risk of developing cataracts.

Cataracts develop slowly. At first, people notice difficulty reading the newspaper, or they experience blurry vision. The eyes become more sensitive to light, and seeing at night becomes especially difficult. People with cataracts often say they feel they have a film over their eyes, as if they are looking through a piece of gauze.

For a short time, the condition actually may benefit some people who always had trouble seeing things that are near them, such as the words on this page. The cloudiness of a cataract changes how light is focused and temporarily results in better vision for such people. They may find themselves able to read for the first time without eyeglasses, a condition sometimes called "second sight." As the cataracts worsen, however, eventually these people will experience increasing visual difficulties.

How Do Doctors Diagnose and Treat Cataracts?

An ophthalmologist's* eye exam can detect a cataract and follow its progress. When cataracts are detected, the doctor can evaluate the symptoms and decide on the best course of treatment.

* **ophthalmologist** is a medical doctor who specializes in treating diseases of the eye.

Many people can live with the condition untreated. For others, surgery may be recommended to remove the cloudy lens and to replace it with a clear artificial lens that is smaller in size than a dime. Cataract surgery improves vision in 90 to 95 percent of the people who have it. It is one of the most common operations, with more than 1 million performed each year. Surgery generally is done when the lens has become so opaque or cloudy that reading, driving, or watching television become major problems.

Can Cataracts Be Prevented?

Some studies suggest that vitamins C and E may lower the likelihood of developing cataracts. That is because these vitamins appear to reduce damage to the proteins that are linked to the development of cataracts. Also, using sunglasses that block ultraviolet light may lower a person's risk of developing cataracts, because studies strongly suggest that sunlight plays a role in their development. Avoiding cataracts is another important reason to avoid smoking, as smokers appear to have an increased risk of developing cataracts.

Resources

Book

Cassel, Gary H., M.D., Michael D. Billig, O.D., and Harry G. Randall, M.D. *The Eye Book: A Complete Guide to Eye Disorders and*

Health. Baltimore: Johns Hopkins University Press, 1998. A good general reference on eye problems.

Organization

The U.S. National Eye Institute posts a fact sheet about cataracts at its website.
http://www.nei.nih.gov/TextSite/publications/cataract.htm

▶ *See also*
Presbyopia

* **bacteria** (bak-TEER-ee-a) are round, spiral, or rod-shaped single-celled microorganisms without a distinct nucleus that commonly multiply by cell division. Some types may cause disease in humans, animals or plants.

* **mucus** (MYOO-kus) is a kind of body slime. It is thick and slippery, and it lines the inside of many parts of the body.

Cavities

Cavities are areas of tooth decay caused by bacteria.

Grin, Don't Bear It

Michael's friend Ashley always said that she loved his smile, and Michael wanted to keep it that way. However, Michael was unaware that he had a small cavity starting in one of his front teeth. Even though Michael had felt a little twinge now and then when he ate ice cream and candy, his favorite foods, he had not paid much attention. Michael never would have known that he had a cavity if he had not gone to the dentist for a regular checkup. Luckily, the dentist was able to drill out the decay and fill the cavity before it got worse. Michael vowed to do a better job in the future of brushing, flossing, and cutting back on sugary snacks.

What Are Cavities?

Cavities, also known as caries (KARE-eez), are areas of decay on the teeth that are caused by bacteria*. They are one of the most common of all human diseases. Almost half of American children have had a cavity by age four. Not only children have cavities, however. Teenagers and adults also are prone to tooth decay. Fortunately, most cavities can be prevented by taking good care of the teeth, eating a healthy diet, and getting regular dental care.

What Causes Cavities?

The human mouth is home to a host of bacteria. The type of bacteria that causes cavities most often is *Streptococcus mutans* (strep-to-KOK-us MU-tanz), but other types play a role, too. Such bacteria in the mouth change the sugars and starches in food to acid. The bacteria and acid combine with mucus* and food particles, forming a sticky mass called plaque on the teeth. Plaque is the rough substance that people feel when running their tongue over their teeth several hours after brushing.

The acid in plaque can eat a hole in a tooth's enamel, the hard substance that covers and protects the outside surfaces of the tooth. People hardly notice the cavity at this stage, or they might feel a slight twinge when eating foods that are sweet, very cold, or very hot. However, bacteria that enter the hole in the enamel can make their way through the softer inside parts of the tooth. Eventually, the bacteria may reach the tooth's pulp, the soft tissue in the center of the tooth that contains nerves and blood vessels. When this happens, the blood vessels can swell and press on the nerves, causing a painful toothache. Left untreated, infection of the pulp by bacteria can cause the blood vessels and nerves in the tooth to die.

Plaque sticks best in the pits and grooves of the back teeth, just above the gums, between the teeth, and around the edges of earlier fillings. Cavities are most likely to form in these areas.

Who Gets Cavities?

Anyone can get cavities. They are most common in children, young adults, and the elderly. People who eat a diet filled with sugary foods also have a high risk of developing cavities, since the more sugar people eat, the more cavity-causing acid they make. People who already have a lot of fillings have an increased risk as well, since the area around fillings is an ideal spot for decay to start.

How Are Cavities Treated?

Cavities are usually painless during the early stages. Most are found during regular dental checkups. A dental x-ray can find cavities that are hard to see. Treating cavities early can prevent later pain and tooth loss.

If a cavity is found, the decay process can be stopped by removing the decayed part of the tooth with a special drill. If there is a lot of decay, or if a tooth is very sensitive, the dentist may give the person a shot of anesthetic* or have the person breathe an anesthetic gas before drilling. The decayed material is then replaced with a filling. Such fillings can be made from a number of materials. The most common is silver amalgam (a-MAL-gam), an alloy of silver and other metals, which is used mainly in back teeth. Fillings in the front usually are made of other materials that match the color of the teeth.

Sometimes, there is so much decay that removing it all leaves a tooth weak and easily broken. In that case, the dentist may fit the person with a crown, an artificial replacement for the part of the tooth above the gum. The crown is made in a laboratory, and then it is cemented to what is left of the tooth.

If the tooth is very seriously decayed or infected, the dentist may perform a root canal. This is a procedure in which the pulp is removed from the root, which is the part of the tooth that anchors it to the gums. The empty space is then cleaned and filled with a special material. The root and the tooth stay in place, but the tooth structure is not as strong as before. To shore it up, the person may need a crown.

How Can Cavities Be Prevented?

People can take several steps to stop most cavities. They can brush twice a day and floss every day. Brushing and flossing help remove plaque. They can use a soft-bristled toothbrush. People should pick a brush that feels

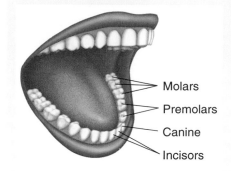

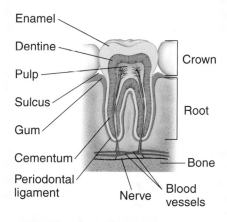

Cavities are most likely to form in the areas where plaque sticks to the teeth. The acid in plaque can eat a hole in a tooth's enamel, allowing bacteria to reach the tooth's pulp. Left untreated, infection of the pulp can cause the blood vessels and nerves in the tooth to die.

*__anesthetic__ (an-es-THET-ik) is a medicine that deadens the sensation of pain.

A Flurry of Fluoridation

Fluoride is a mineral that occurs naturally in all water sources. Many areas, especially in the southern states, have a water supply that is well fluoridated naturally.

Scientists as far back as the early 1900s noted fluoride's role in preventing tooth decay. Fluoride can even reverse the early decay process. Since the 1940s, some communities in areas where natural fluoride is low have been adding extra fluoride to their water. This is a very effective and inexpensive way to help prevent cavities on a large scale.

Today, about 60 percent of the U.S. water supply is fluoridated. In places where the water is not fluoridated, or in families who drink unfluoridated bottled water instead of tap water, dentists may prescribe fluoride supplements for children.

▶ *See also*

Abscess

Bacterial Infections

Gum Disease

Halitosis

comfortable and will reach all the teeth, even those in back. They should replace the toothbrush when the bristles show signs of wear. People should use a toothpaste that contains fluoride, a mineral that helps protect against tooth decay. To clean the teeth, they should brush with a short, gentle, back-and-forth motion. People should not forget the inside surfaces, the back teeth, and the tongue. They should floss to reach plaque between the teeth and under the gum line, where a brush cannot go. Finally, people should cut down on sweets and between-meal snacks. Damaging acid forms in the mouth each time a person eats a sugary or starchy food. The acid continues to affect the teeth for at least 20 minutes afterward. The more often people eat these kinds of food, the more times they feed the bacteria that cause cavities. In addition, some sugary foods do more harm than others. Sticky or chewy sweets may cling to the teeth, staying in the mouth and causing problems longer than other foods.

People should see their dentist regularly for checkups and cleanings. Dentists may apply extra fluoride (FLOOR-eyed) in the form of a gel, foam, or rinse. In addition, dentists may apply dental sealants, thin plastic coatings that are put on the chewing surface of back teeth. Such sealants are painted on as a liquid, but they quickly harden to form a shield over the teeth that keeps out the food and bacteria that cause decay. Dentists say that children should get sealants on their permanent back teeth as soon as they come in. In some cases, sealants are also put on baby teeth or on the teeth of teenagers or adults.

Resources

Book

Smith, Rebecca W. *The Columbia University School of Dental and Oral Surgery's Guide to Family Dental Care.* New York: W. W. Norton, 1997.

Organizations

American Dental Association, 211 East Chicago Avenue, Chicago, IL 60611. The leading national organization for dentists has information about tooth decay and dental care on its website.
Telephone 312-440-2500
http://www.ada.org

U.S. National Institute of Dental and Craniofacial Research, 31 Center Drive, MSC 2290, Bethesda, MD 20892-2290. Part of the U.S. National Institutes of Health (NIH), this agency provides information on tooth decay and dental care.
Telephone 301-496-4261
http://www.nidcr.nih.gov

Cellulitis *See* **Abscess**

Cerebral Palsy

Cerebral palsy refers to several different conditions. They are caused by prenatal injury to the brain and affect a person's ability to move.

KEYWORDS
for searching the Internet and other reference sources

Cerebellum

Movement disorders

Spastic paraplegia

"Why Isn't Our Baby Walking?"

Rob and Carol were the first to notice that something was wrong with their eleven-month-old daughter Nancy. Nancy was an alert, happy baby. But unlike other children they knew, she did not reach for her toys at five or six months, and now she was barely sitting up on her own. When Carol would bend down to hug Nancy, she noticed that the child remained stiff. Left on her own in her crib, or on a blanket on the floor, Nancy did not crawl around like other children do. Rob and Carol scheduled a visit with Nancy's pediatrician (a doctor who specializes in treating children). They described Nancy's behavior, and asked the doctor whether she might have cerebral palsy.

How Brains and Muscles Communicate

Every gesture we make, from scratching our nose to jumping down the stairs, is the result of a complex set of messages that travel between our brains and our muscles. When we decide we want to do something, our brains tell our muscles how to do it. Brushing our teeth, throwing a ball, crossing the street, and even talking are different kinds of movements that are all controlled by special centers in the brain.

What Is Cerebral Palsy?

Sometimes the centers in the brain that control movement become damaged. When that happens, the messages from the brain to the muscles seem to be "scrambled." For children with this condition, which is called cerebral palsy, ordinary movements may be difficult or impossible. About 500,000 Americans have cerebral palsy.

Are There Different Types of Cerebral Palsy?

Every person with cerebral palsy will be affected differently, depending on which part of the brain was injured and how much damage occurred. A person's movements may be spastic (SPAS-stik), which means that the person moves in a stiff or jerky way. Other people may not be able to control their movements, and they must struggle just to hold themselves upright or to hold things. Some people with cerebral palsy move very shakily. One-fourth of people with cerebral palsy have a mix of these problems. Cerebral palsy may affect both arms and both legs or only one side of the body. Sometimes only the legs are affected. People with severe cerebral palsy may need a wheelchair to get around; others who are more mildly affected may be able to walk and run with only a slight limp.

150 Years Ago: "Lame Duck"

William John Little (1810–1894) developed a deformity in his foot at a young age as a result of polio infection. His schoolmates nicknamed him "lame duck." At the age of 16, Little decided to pursue a career in medicine, hoping to find a cure for his condition. Although Little never found his cure, his research did lead to the description of another disease.

In 1853, Little published *On the Deformities of the Human Frame*, in which he first described cerebral palsy. Little's medical practice focused on the musculoskeletal system, and his research contributed to advances in both neurology and orthopedics.

"Little's Disease" is the name now used to designate a congenital form of cerebral palsy.

Do People with Cerebral Palsy Have Other Difficulties?

Cerebral palsy can cause weakness in other muscles in the body. For example, people with cerebral palsy may have trouble talking or swallowing food, and sometimes they drool. Some may also suffer from seizures, which are storms of electrical activity in the brain that may cause a person abruptly to stop what they are doing, lose control of their body movements, and sometimes become confused or unconscious. About one-fourth to one-half of children with cerebral palsy have some kind of learning problem. This is because the damage to the brain that causes problems in controlling the muscles can also affect the parts of the brain that control how a person learns. One child might simply have trouble with reading or math; another might need special learning help. But most people with cerebral palsy have normal intelligence, even when their physical disabilities are severe.

What Causes Cerebral Palsy?

Cerebral palsy is mostly a condition that people are born with, caused by injury to the developing brain. It is not contagious, like a cold or measles. Cerebral palsy does not get worse, but it also does not go away. In some cases, ill health in the mother while she is pregnant may lead to cerebral palsy in the newborn infant. Infants who are born prematurely have a higher risk of developing cerebral palsy. And sometimes a serious accident, such as almost drowning, might cause brain damage and cerebral palsy in a small child. Although many believe that injury to the brain occurring during the birth process is a common cause of cerebral palsy, that is not the case. In 80 percent of cases, there is no identifiable cause for cerebral palsy. There is no way to test for cerebral palsy before a baby is born.

How Is Cerebral Palsy Diagnosed?

It is not always easy for doctors to tell whether an infant or young child like Nancy has cerebral palsy. When parents bring their child in, the doctor will ask the parents questions about the child, and will look for anything unusual about the child's muscles and movements. The doctor will especially check the child's reflexes to see if the child's brain and nervous system are functioning properly. For example, the doctor will tap the child's knee with a small rubber mallet to test for reflexes in the legs. If a child does have cerebral palsy, a team of specialist doctors and therapists will work with the parents to set up a program of treatment.

How Is Cerebral Palsy Treated?

Having cerebral palsy does not mean that a person cannot have a happy life. It does mean that people with cerebral palsy may face more challenges in day-to-day living than other people without cerebral palsy. Treatment, also called therapy, may help children with cerebral palsy to cope with everyday tasks that the rest of us take for granted. Each child is different, so the mix of therapies will vary from child to child. For instance, therapy can be given to strengthen parts of the body needed for walking and climbing stairs, to strengthen the mouth muscles needed for talking, and to help a child to master ordinary but important activities like getting dressed and eating. Medications (such as those used to control seizures), surgical techniques, and special equipment (such as wheelchairs, braces, and communication devices), are also available to help people with cerebral palsy lead more normal lives. Parents of children with cerebral palsy and people with the condition themselves must work closely with their doctors, therapists, and teachers to decide on the best treatment plan for each individual.

Is It Possible to Prevent Cerebral Palsy?

Since the cause of cerebral palsy is unknown in the majority of cases, there is no way to prevent it. An expectant mother can increase the chances that her baby will be healthy by eating properly, getting regular checkups, and not smoking, drinking, or abusing drugs. Protecting infants from accident or injury can help to avoid the brain damage that sometimes causes cerebral palsy after birth. But for now there is no real solution to the mystery of cerebral palsy. The hope of overcoming it lies in continuing medical research.

Living with Cerebral Palsy

Children who have cerebral palsy may not be able to do all the things that other children do, or at least, not in the same way. But most children with cerebral palsy can:

- Go to school
- Have friends
- Go on class trips and to summer camp
- Listen to music

Tools That Help

Many different kinds of equipment are available to help people with cerebral palsy to do everyday things. Wheelchairs with and without motors help those who cannot walk to get around. People who can walk but who are unsteady on their feet can use walkers, which look a little like four-wheel cycles with no seat. Spoons, toothbrushes, and pencils with special handles and shapes make it easier to hold and to use things. Alphabet boards make it possible for people who have trouble speaking to spell out words. There is even a computer that talks for people who cannot.

■ Play on the computer

■ Read books

■ Enjoy sports

Many people with cerebral palsy will eventually be able to go to college, hold a job, get married, and raise families.

Resources

Books

Killilea, Marie. *Karen*. New York: Prentice Hall, 1952. For young readers and their parents, this classic book is an intelligent, very human account of what it is like to have cerebral palsy. *Karen* is out of print, but is worth searching for in the library. A volume called *Wren* for younger children also is out of print but worth searching for.

Miller, Freeman, and Steven Bachrach. *Cerebral Palsy: A Complete Guide for Caregiving*. Baltimore: Johns Hopkins University Press, 1995.

Organizations

United Cerebral Palsy, 1660 L Street NW, Suite 700, Washington, DC 20036. United Cerebral Palsy is the leading source in the United States for information about cerebral palsy and other disabilities. http://www.acpa.org

The U.S. Centers for Disease Control, located in Atlanta, Georgia, posts information about cerebral palsy on its website at: http://www.cdc.gov/nceh/programs/cddh/ddcp/htm

Tutorial

Cerebral Palsy: A Multimedia Tutorial for Children and Parents. A friendly, informative introduction to cerebral palsy from the Children's Medical Center at the University of Virginia. http://www.med.virginia.edu/cmc/tutorials/cp/cp.htm

▶ See also
Epilepsy

| **Cervical Cancer** *See* Uterine/Cervical Cancer |

Chagas' Disease

Chagas' (SHAH-gas) disease is a parasitic infection common in South and Central America. It is chronic (long-lasting) and can seriously damage the heart and the digestive system many years after a person gets infected. Another name for it is American trypanoso-miasis (tri-pan-o-so-MY-a-sis).

KEYWORDS
for searching the Internet
and other reference sources

American trypanosomiasis

Infection

Trypanosoma cruzi

Reduviidae

Chagas' disease is an infection with a protozoan (pro-to-ZO-an), a tiny parasite called *Trypanosoma cruzi*. This parasite infects many kinds of mammals in South and Central America. It is spread to people by blood-sucking insects called reduviid (re-DOO-vi-id) bugs. These bugs, also called kissing or assassin bugs, pick up the parasite when they bite an infected person or animal. The parasites multiply inside the bugs. When the bugs bite other people, they deposit parasite-laden feces on the skin. If the people accidentally rub the feces into a cut or scratch, or into their eyes or mouth, they can get infected too.

▲

Reduviid bugs, like the assassin bug shown here, live in the cracks and crevices of poorly built houses. Reduviid bugs can pick up the *Trypanosoma cruzi* parasite that causes Chagas' disease when they bite an infected person or animal and then pass along the parasite to the next person they bite. © *Tom Boyden/Visuals Unlimited.*

Reduviid bugs tend to live in the cracks and crevices of poorly built houses in rural South and Central America and in Mexico. So Chagas' disease used to be largely an illness of the rural poor in those areas. But in the 1970s and 1980s, many people moved from the countryside to Latin American cities, bringing the infection with them. In the cities, it started to spread through transfusions of contaminated blood. More rarely, it can also spread from a pregnant woman to her fetus. Chagas' disease is estimated to kill up to 50,000 people a year.

What Are the Symptoms of Chagas' Disease?

Chagas' disease has acute, indeterminate, and chronic phases.

Acute phase People usually get infected as children. Most have no symptoms, but some have fever, swelling of the lymph nodes, or swelling around the eyes, if that was where the parasite entered the body. Symptoms usually go away in four to eight weeks. In rare cases, there may be heart damage or seizures. In people with weakened immune systems, such as those with AIDS, the acute stage can recur later, in a very severe form.

Indeterminate phase The parasite is still present in the body but causes no symptoms. This stage lasts a lifetime in most infected people.

Chronic phase In about one third of infected people, serious symptoms develop 10 to 20 years or more after they became infected. The most common problems are:

- enlargement and weakening of the heart, a condition called cardiomyopathy (kard-ee-o-my-OP-a-thee), which can make a person feel weak and short of breath

- ventricular dysrhythmias (dis-RITH-me-as)—a form of irregular heartbeat that can cause sudden death

- megacolon—an enlargement of the colon (large intestine) that can cause extreme constipation and require surgical treatment

- enlargement of the esophagus (the tube carrying food from the throat to the stomach), which can make eating difficult.

The U.S. and the World

Chagas' disease occurs only in the Americas, mainly in South and Central America and in Mexico. It is believed to create a greater economic burden than any other tropical disease except malaria and schistosomiasis.

- In South and Central America, about 16 million to 18 million people are infected with Chagas' disease. Many live in thatch, mud, or adobe houses in poor areas.

- In the United States, many people who emigrated from South and Central America are thought to be infected with Chagas' disease, chiefly in the indeterminate or chronic stages. But it is extremely rare for someone to catch the disease in the United States. In a recent 20-year period, fewer than 20 newly acquired U.S. cases were reported, including three from blood transfusions.

- About 50,000 people die each year from the disease.

- The World Health Organization (WHO) reports that about 100 million people are at risk of developing Chagas' disease.

▶ See also
Dysrhythmia
Parasitic Diseases

KEYWORDS
for searching the Internet and other reference sources

Immunization

Varicella

How Is Chagas' Disease Diagnosed and Treated?

In the acute stage, the parasites can be seen when blood is examined under a microscope. In the later stages, diagnosis is more difficult, and an array of different blood tests is used.

In the acute stage, the parasites often can be eliminated by prescription medication taken for several months. In later stages, there is no proven cure. Instead, doctors try to treat the symptoms of the organ damage the parasites cause.

How Is Chagas' Disease Prevented?

In Latin America, many countries are taking part in a campaign to wipe out Chagas' disease. They are using pesticides to kill the bugs that transmit the disease, and they are upgrading housing so the bugs cannot hide in cracked walls and thatched roofs. They also are trying to screen blood supplies more thoroughly.

This campaign is farthest along in the countries of the "Southern Cone": Argentina, Brazil, Chile, Paraguay, and Uruguay. In this area, new infections of children and young adults reportedly were reduced by almost 70 percent in the late 1990s.

Travelers to areas where Chagas' disease is common should use insect repellent (bug spray). If possible, they should avoid sleeping in thatch, mud, or adobe homes, or they should use bed nets at night.

Resources

The World Health Organization posts information about Chagas' disease at its website.
http://www.who.int/ctd/html/chag.html

The U.S. Centers for Disease Control and Prevention (CDC) has a Division of Parasitic Diseases that posts information about Chagas' disease at its website.
http://www.cdc.gov/ncidod/dpd/chagas.htm

Chickenpox

Chickenpox (varicella) is a common childhood disease caused by the herpes varicella virus that causes a blister-like rash, itching, tiredness, and fever.

What Is Chickenpox?

With its rash and fever, chickenpox is common in children and usually mild. But it can be serious, especially in infants, adults, and people with weak immune systems*. Chickenpox is caused by varicella (var-i-SELL-a), a virus in the herpesvirus family.

* **immune system** is the body's defense system for fighting off attacks by viruses, bacteria, fungi, and other foreign substances that can cause illness or hurt the body.

The chickenpox virus spreads from person to person by contact with the fluid in chickenpox blisters or through droplets in the air. It is very contagious. About 4 million people in the United States get chickenpox each year; about 10,000 of these people get sick enough to go to the hospital, and about 100 die. Chickenpox is most common in children under the age of 15, but anyone can get it. Most cases occur in the late winter or spring.

Immunization of children with the chickenpox vaccine now available is expected to decrease cases of the disease dramatically over the next few years.

What Are the Symptoms of Chickenpox?

The first sign of chickenpox may be a cough, an achy feeling, or a runny nose. Then a rash develops that looks like red spots. This rash forms blisters that dry and become scabs within four to five days. The rash usually starts on the chest, back, and face, but it usually spreads over the whole body. A person may have anywhere from just a few itchy spots to more than 500. Along with the rash, the person may have a fever and feel tired. Symptoms are usually more severe in adults.

Serious problems resulting from chickenpox are also more common in adults. In some people, the chickenpox virus can lead to pneumonia (noo-MO-nee-a), an inflammation of the lungs. In other people, it can lead to encephalitis (en-sef-a-LY-tis), an inflammation of the brain. In rare cases, the result can be brain damage or even death. Scratching the itchy rash can cause scars and sometimes a bacterial germ infection of the skin that can spread through the body and cause high fever.

A person can give chickenpox to someone else from one or two days before the rash starts until all the blisters have formed scabs. The disease will show up 10 to 21 days after contact with the sick person.

A boy with chickenpox. © *John D. Cunningham, Visuals Unlimited*

What Are the Long-Term Risks?

Even after a person gets over chickenpox, the virus does not go away. It lives on in an inactive or dormant state within the nerve roots of the person's body. The virus can reawaken many years later to cause shingles, a disease that usually starts with a tingling feeling, itching, or severe pain in the skin. Within days, a blister-like rash forms. The pain can last for weeks, months, or years after the rash heals. A person can catch chickenpox from someone with shingles, but can't catch shingles itself.

When Is a Doctor Needed?

Chickenpox is usually a mild disease. However, there are still times when it is important to talk to a doctor:

■ If a fever lasts longer than four days

■ If a fever rises above 102 degrees Fahrenheit

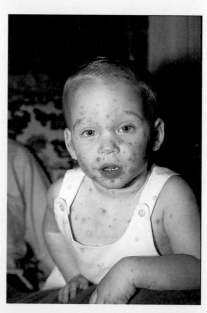

■ If an area of rash leaks pus or becomes more red, warm, swollen, or sore.

It is important to call a doctor right away if the person with chickenpox seems extremely ill or develops any of these problems:

■ Trouble waking up

■ Confusion

■ Trouble walking

■ Stiff neck

■ Repeated vomiting

■ Severe cough

■ Trouble breathing

A young child may develop chickenpox blisters in his or her mouth and throat. This makes eating and drinking very uncomfortable. Refusing to drink can lead to dehydration*, especially in very small children with a fever, and this must be treated by a doctor.

*__dehydration__ (dee-hy-DRAY-shun) is loss of fluid from the body.

How Is Chickenpox Treated?

To treat a fever, people who have chickenpox should take only non-aspirin medicines such as acetaminophen (a-set-a-MIN-o-fen). They should never take aspirin or products that contain aspirin. The use of aspirin by people with a virus-caused illness such as chickenpox has been linked to Reye's (RIZE) syndrome, a serious disease that affects the whole body, especially the liver and brain.

Scratching a chickenpox rash can cause a skin infection. People with chickenpox should try not to scratch, and they should keep their fingernails clean and cut short. Oatmeal baths and a soothing lotion called calamine (KAL-a-mine) lotion may help relieve the itching.

Acyclovir (ay-SY-klo-veer) is a drug that fights the chickenpox virus. Because this drug can have side effects, doctors usually prescribe it for people who are at high risk for severe symptoms. This includes people with long-term skin or lung diseases, those with diseases or taking medicines that weaken the immune system, and anyone over age 12, since at that age chickenpox can be more severe than for younger children. To be helpful, this drug must be started very soon after the rash first appears.

Can Chickenpox Be Prevented?

In the past, almost everyone got chickenpox by the time they reached adulthood. Since 1995, however, there has been a vaccine against chickenpox. A vaccine is a preparation given to people to prevent a disease. This vaccine does not give 100 percent protection, but eight or nine out of every ten people who get it are protected from the disease. People who do catch chickenpox after getting the vaccine usually have a very mild case with few itchy spots, a mild fever, and a fast recovery.

The vaccine is recommended as part of the usual immunizations of childhood. Also, people 13 years old and older who have not had chickenpox should get this vaccine. People who have already had chickenpox do not need the vaccine, because they cannot get the disease again.

Many adults do not remember if they have had chickenpox. These people can have a blood test to check for signs that they have had the disease. If this test is not available, though, it is usually safe to receive the vaccine, even if a person has already had chickenpox.

Some people should not take the vaccine, however. These include women who are pregnant, people who currently have a serious illness, those who have a weak immune system, and people who have received a blood transfusion in the past five months.

Resources

Book

Silverstein, Alvin, Virginia Silverstein, Laura Nunn. *Chickenpox and Shingles*. Springfield, NJ: Enslow Publishers, 1998.

Organizations

U.S. Centers for Disease Control and Prevention (CDC), National Immunization Program, 1600 Clifton Road N.E., Atlanta, GA 30333. A government agency that offers information on chickenpox. Telephone 800-CDC-SHOT
http://www.cdc.gov/nip

American Academy of Pediatrics, 141 Northwest Point Boulevard, Elk Grove Village, IL 60007-1098. The American Academy of Pediatrics posts a fact sheet about chickenpox vaccine at its website. Telephone 847-228-5005
http://www.aap.org/family/chckpox.htm

VZV Research Foundation, 40 East 72nd Street, New York, NY 10021. This is a group that studies chickenpox and shingles. Telephone 800-472-VIRUS

▶ See also
Herpes
Immunodeficiency
Reye's Syndrome
Shingles
Viral Infections

Chlamydial Infections

Chlamydial (kla-MID-ee-al) infections are caused by three species of microorganisms. Chlamydia trachomatis *can cause eye or lung infections and can also infect the urinary and genital areas of both men and women.* Chlamydia pneumoniae *causes infections of the respiratory tract, and* Chlamydia psittaci *causes an illness, known as parrot fever, that is similar to the flu.*

KEYWORDS
for searching the Internet
and other reference sources

Trachoma

Psittacosis

197

What Are the Diseases Caused by Chlamydial Infections?

Chlamydia trachomatis   In the United States, *Chlamydia trachomatis* (tra-KO-ma-tis) is responsible for more cases of sexually transmitted diseases (STDs) than any other organism. Sexually transmitted diseases are passed from one partner to another during sexual activity. It is estimated that between 4 and 8 million people are infected in the United States by *Chlamydia trachomatis* every year.

Chlamydia trachomatis also causes an eye infection called trachoma (tra-KO-ma), which is an inflammation of the membrane covering the eye. It causes the eye to become irritated and red with a thick discharge. Infants whose mothers' have *Chlamydia* infections may become infected during birth. These infants can develop eye infections a few days after birth or pneumonia several weeks after birth.

Chlamydia pneumoniae   *Chlamydia pneumoniae* (noo-MO-nee-eye) can cause infections in the respiratory tract. The result can be bronchitis, pneumonia, or pharyngitis*. In the United States it is one of the leading causes of pneumonia in people between the ages of 5 and 35.

Chlamydia psittaci   The illness psittacosis (sit-a-KO-sis) or parrot fever, is caused by *Chlamydia psittaci* carried by birds (mainly parrots, parakeets, and lovebirds). In human beings it causes an illness that is like the flu. Only people who work closely with birds, such as pet-store workers or those who train carrier pigeons, are liable to contract this disease.

How Are Chlamydial Infections Transmitted?

Chlamydial infections are passed from one person to another through direct contact. Sexually transmitted chlamydia is passed from one person to another by direct sexual contact, and the people at most risk are those who have unprotected sex or multiple sex partners.

Parrot fever is caused by inhalation of dust from feathers and droppings or by the bite of an infected bird. Trachoma is transmitted by eye-to-eye or hand-to-eye contact, eye-seeking flies, or by sharing contaminated articles such as towels, handkerchiefs, or eye makeup.

Who Is at Risk for Chlamydial Infections?

Those most at risk for *Chlamydia trachomatis* infections are people who are sexually active with someone who is infected. Unborn babies of mothers with the disease are also at risk of infection during birth. People who work with birds that are illegally brought into the United States are at risk of infection with *Chlamydia psittaci*.

What Are the Symptoms of Chlamydial Infections?

The most common symptom of chlamydia trachomatis infections in men or women is a burning sensation during urination. Unfortunately, many women who are infected do not have any symptoms. If they are

*__pharyngitis__ (far-in-JI-tis) is inflammation of the pharynx, part of the throat.

pregnant and do not know that they have been infected, they may unknowingly pass the disease on to their baby at birth. Besides a burning sensation when urinating, a person with chlamydia trachomatis may have an abnormal discharge from the genital area. The genital area may become inflamed, and in women the inflammation can spread to the internal reproductive organs. Women then may develop a disease called pelvic inflammatory disease (PID). This can cause a woman to become infertile, that is, unable to become pregnant and have children.

Trachoma is still found in poor areas of the southeast United States and in poor areas of other countries around the world. Trachoma infection causes eyelid swelling, tearing, and sensitivity to light. Seven to ten days after the symptoms start, small lumps develop inside the eyelid and gradually increase in size and number. If not treated, scarring of the cornea* occurs, and vision is diminished or completely lost.

Parrot fever has an incubation period of one to three weeks. There is then a sudden onset of fever, chills, loss of appetite, and fatigue. Later a cough develops that progresses to pneumonia. Up to 30 percent of people who have untreated parrot fever die.

*cornea (KOR-ne-a) is the transparent structure covering the front chamber of the eye.

How Are Chlamydial Infections Treated?

Chlamydial infections can be successfully treated with antibiotics. Because untreated chlamydial infections can lead to serious and permanent problems, possible infections should be treated and evaluated by a doctor as soon as possible. If a person is being treated for genital infections due to chlamydia, his or her partner should also be tested and treated. Parents of newborn children should be alert to the condition of the baby's eyes. If they become red, swollen, or have a thick discharge, a physician should be contacted immediately. Persistent coughing by a newborn is also a signal to call a doctor.

Can Chlamydial Infections Be Prevented?

The best prevention for genital infection by chlamydia is to avoid sexual contact with an infected person. Abstaining from sexual relations is the only certain way to avoid contracting *Chlamydia trachomatis* since it is common for infected people not to know they have the infection.

Parrot fever can be prevented by buying birds from reputable pet stores or breeders who sell imported birds that have been quarantined*, examined, and fed antibiotic-treated bird feed for 45 days.

*quarantine is the enforced isolation (for a fixed period) of apparently well persons or animals who may have been exposed to infectious disease.

Resources

Books

Stoffman, Phyllis. *Family Guide to Preventing and Treating 100 Infectious Illnesses.* New York: John Wiley & Sons, 1995.

Thacker, John, and Rachel Kranz. *Straight Talk about Sexually Transmitted Diseases.* New York: Facts on File, 1993.

► *See also*
Pelvic Inflammatory Disease
Pneumonia
Sexually Transmitted Diseases
Zoonoses

KEYWORDS
*for searching the Internet
and other reference sources*

Enteritis

Enterotoxins

Infection

Organizations

KidsHealth.org website has dozens of articles on many types of infections, including chlamydia.
http://KidsHealth.org

American Social Health Association (ASHA), P.O. Box 13827, Research Triangle Park, NC 27709.
Telephone 919-361-8400
http://sunsite.unc.edu/ASHA/

Cholera

Cholera (KOL-er-a) is an illness that results from infection of the large intestine by Vibrio cholerae *bacteria. Cholera causes watery diarrhea and vomiting.*

Outbreak!

In January 1991, an outbreak of cholera, a disease that can cause life-threatening diarrhea, began in several towns along the seacoast of Peru. Within months, the disease had spread to many countries in Central and South America. Within two years, more than 700,000 cases and 6,000 deaths had been reported in the western hemisphere. Although cholera usually is not a problem in the United States, some cases occurred in American travelers. In February 1992, 75 people became ill after they were served seafood salad containing cholera bacteria on an airplane flight from South America to Los Angeles.

Cholera bacteria live in water. At this crossroads near Capetown in South Africa, human waste contaminates the drinking water and the water used for cleaning and cooking food.
© *M. Courtney-Clarke, Photo Researchers, Inc.*

What Is Cholera?

Cholera is an illness that leads to large, frequent, watery stools (bowel movements). It is caused by infection of the large intestine by *Vibrio cholerae* bacteria, which secrete a toxin* that inflames the large intestine and prevents it from reabsorbing water. The illness often is mild, but it can be severe. In about 1 out of 20 cases, severe diarrhea and vomiting lead to rapid loss of water from the body, known as dehydration. Without treatment, death can occur within hours.

Cholera is spread by drinking contaminated water and by eating raw or undercooked food. The disease is rare in the United States, Canada, Europe, Australia, and New Zealand, thanks to modern treatment of drinking water and sewage, but it is prevalent in Central and South America, Africa, and Asia. Travelers may run into the disease, as happened in the United States when air passengers ate contaminated seafood. The disease does not spread easily from person to person, and casual contact with an infected person does not pose a threat.

What Happens When People Get Cholera?

Symptoms Most people infected with cholera bacteria do not become ill. When illness does occur, it usually appears within a few days of infection and causes only mild diarrhea. About 5 percent of people with cholera become very sick, however, with lots of watery diarrhea as well as vomiting and leg cramps. The result can be severe dehydration. If these people are not given replacement fluids, they can die in a matter of hours.

The U.S. and the World

The World Health Organization reports that cholera is found most often in these parts of the world:

- Central America: Belize, El Salvador, Guatemala, Honduras, Mexico, Nicaragua

- South America: Bolivia, Brazil, Chile, Colombia, Ecuador, Peru, Venezuela

- Africa: Benin, Burkina Faso, Burundi, Cameroon, Cape Verde, Central African Republic, Chad, Comoros, Democratic Republic of Congo, Djibouti, Ghana, Guinea, Guinea Bissau, Kenya, Liberia, Malawi, Mozambique, Nigeria, Rwanda, Sierra Leone, Somalia, South Africa, Swaziland, Tanzania, Togo, Uganda, Zambia, Zimbabwe

- Asia: Afghanistan, Armenia, Bhutan, Cambodia, Hong Kong, India, Iran, Iraq, Japan, Malaysia, Nepal, Philippines, Singapore, Sri Lanka, Vietnam

*****toxins** (TOK-sinz) are poisonous substances.

150 YEARS AGO: EPIDEMIOLOGY

Epidemiology is the science that studies how diseases spread and how to control their spread effectively. An early epidemiologist was the British physician John Snow (1813–1858), who hypothesized that contaminated water was responsible for the spread of cholera.

In 1854, during one of many cholera epidemics, Snow observed that a significant number of people with cholera in the Golden Square area of London all shared something in common: they all used the same water pump on Broad Street. Snow demonstrated that sewage had seeped into the pump's well, contaminating the water, and infecting the community.

Thanks to Snow's demonstration that cholera was a waterborne disease, doctors abandoned their belief that "miasma" (a noxious airborne substance) was the cause of cholera. The German bacteriologist Robert Koch (1843–1910) later identified the *Vibrio cholerae* bacterium as the waterborne agent that causes cholera.

Diagnosis Cholera is diagnosed by checking a person's stools for *Vibrio cholerae* bacteria.

Treatment People with cholera need fluids and salts to replace those lost through diarrhea and vomiting. The person may be asked to drink large amounts of a solution that is made from a prepackaged mixture of sugar and salts mixed with water. If the person is too sick to drink, fluids can be given intravenously*. Without such treatment, severe cholera can kill up to half or more of those who become ill. With prompt treatment, however, fewer than 1 percent of people with cholera die. Sometimes antibiotic medications are given as well to decrease the length and severity of the illness.

** **intravenous** (in-tra-VEEN-us) fluids are injected directly into the veins.*

Tips for Travelers on Preventing Cholera

A cholera vaccine is available to help prevent the disease. The vaccine, however, gives only partial protection for a limited time and, as a result, it may not be recommended for travelers. By taking simple steps, though, travelers can reduce their risk of getting the disease, even when visiting areas where cholera is widespread. The U.S. Centers for Disease Control and Prevention (CDC) recommends the following for people planning to travel to areas where cholera is found:

- Drinking only water that has been boiled or treated with chlorine or iodine. Other safe drinks include tea and coffee made with boiled water and bottled soft drinks served with no ice.
- Eating only foods that have been thoroughly cooked and are still hot. Also safe are fruits that a person peels himself just before eating.
- Avoiding other raw fruits and vegetables, including salads.
- Not eating undercooked or raw shellfish or fish.
- Not buying foods or drinks from street vendors.
- Not bringing perishable seafood back to the United States.

The *Vibrio cholerae* bacterium under an electron microscope. Color has been added to show the nucleic acid (orange) and the flagellum (tail), which is used by the bacterium to move. *CNRI/Science Photo Library, Photo Researchers, Inc.*

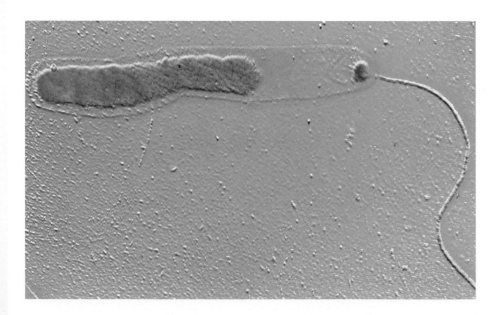

CHOLERA IN THE U.S.

During the nineteenth century, cholera epidemics killed thousands of people in the United States.

In 1832, cholera swept through the slave population in Richmond, Virginia. The next year, an epidemic in New Orleans killed almost one quarter of the city's population.

Another epidemic occurred in the United States in 1849, and during the 1850s, thousands of pioneers who headed for Oregon or California died on the trail from cholera.

The third major cholera pandemic in the United States occurred in 1866. No major U.S. outbreaks have occurred since the 1890s, mainly because government officials learned the value of keeping public water supplies clean.

Resources

Books

García Márquez, Gabriel. *Love in the Time of Cholera*. New York: Penguin, 1999. Originally published in Spanish in 1985 as *El amor en los tiempos del cólera*, this is a complex novel set in a Central American seaport that experiences periodic cholera outbreaks. The author was awarded the Nobel Prize for Literature in 1982.

Poe, Edgar Allan. *The Masque of the Red Death*. A classic tale of terror about the "red death," available in many audiocassette, paperback, and hardcover editions.

Organizations

U.S. Centers for Disease Control and Prevention (CDC), 1600 Clifton Road N.E., Atlanta, GA 30333. CDC posts fact sheets about cholera and information for travelers at its website.
Telephone 800-311-3435
http://www.cdc.gov

World Health Organization (WHO), 525 23rd Street N.W., Washington, DC 20037. WHO's Communicable Disease Surveillance and Response (CSR) division posts a global cholera update at its website to report numbers of cholera cases and deaths worldwide.
Telephone 202-974-3000
http://www.who.int/emc/diseases/cholera

 See also
Bacterial Infections
Diarrhea

Chorea *See* **Huntington's Disease**

Chronic Fatigue Syndrome

Chronic fatigue syndrome, also called CFS, is a disorder marked by intense exhaustion.

KEYWORDS
for searching the Internet
and other reference sources

Myalgia

Neuromyasthenia

"It Just Hit Me Like Lightning"

In November 1996, the enormously popular American jazz pianist Keith Jarrett found himself completely drained of energy in the middle of a concert tour in Italy. The only way he could get through his performances was to stay in bed most of the day and get up just for the concert at night. Too tired even to cross the street, Jarrett would not play in public again for 2 years. The illness was so severe that he said he felt as though aliens had entered his body. He was eventually diagnosed with chronic fatigue syndrome.

What Is Chronic Fatigue Syndrome?

Chronic fatigue syndrome (CFS) is a condition of severe fatigue and other symptoms of weakness. For many years, patients with CFS were told that their illness was probably psychological or mental in origin. Since the 1980s, however, most doctors have come to recognize CFS as a physical condition. Still, efforts to find an easily identifiable cause, such as a bacterium or a virus, have so far been unsuccessful, and CFS is diagnosed and defined primarily by how it makes people feel.

The precise number of people with CFS is difficult to know, but one study by the U.S. Centers for Disease Control and Prevention (CDC), a major public health agency in the United States, suggested that 200 out of every 100,000 Americans between the ages of 18 and 69 have the condition. CFS is more common among women than among men, but it affects all racial and ethnic groups. Although adolescents can have CFS, their cases have been less well studied.

Because there are no specific tests for the disorder, in 1988 the CDC drew up a list of symptoms that define it. This set of symptoms provides a standard to guide doctors in diagnosing and treating the condition.

CFS is defined as fatigue that begins very suddenly and continues or recurs over a period of 6 months. In addition to fatigue, cases of CFS must include four or more of the following symptoms:

- Forgetfulness or difficulty concentrating
- Sore throat
- Tender lymph (LIMF) nodes* in the neck or armpit
- Muscle pain
- Pain in the joints without joint swelling or redness
- Unusual headaches

* **lymph nodes** are bean-sized round or oval masses of immune system tissue that filter bodily fluids before they enter the bloodstream, helping to keep out bacteria and other undesirable substances.

- Unrefreshing sleep

- A vague feeling of illness or depression that lasts more than 24 hours following exercise.

What Causes CFS?

There are many different opinions about what causes CFS. There is no evidence that CFS is contagious. Some doctors believe that CFS is caused by a virus. In fact, symptoms of CFS may begin after a viral infection, but this does not mean that a viral infection explains the persisting symptoms and long-term effects of the condition. It is possible that CFS may be caused by a malfunction in the immune system, that is, the body's defenses against disease. Other doctors think that some imbalance of chemicals in the brain might cause CFS. Many people with CFS also suffer from depression. Consequently, some doctors argue that CFS is a psychiatric condition, and the physical symptoms follow from that.

Diagnosing CFS Is Hard

It is very difficult for doctors to diagnose CFS. Although they take a medical history, examine the patient, and request routine laboratory tests of blood and other bodily substances, there are no specific findings that define CFS or laboratory tests that indicate a clear diagnosis. Instead, the diagnosis of CFS is made when other causes of the characteristic symptoms cannot be found. A wide number of medical conditions have many of the same symptoms: viral infections, depression, kidney disease, heart disease, and many others. Before diagnosing CFS, these other possible causes must be ruled out.

What Are the Symptoms of CFS?

The hallmark of CFS is intense fatigue that comes on very suddenly. Other symptoms vary from person to person, and they may come and go.

NEURASTHENIA

Chronic Fatigue Syndrome (CFS) is a relatively new name for this condition. In the 1800s, doctors usually diagnosed "neurasthenia" (nervous exhaustion) instead. They believed that nervous exhaustion was a result of the stressful and demanding nature of "modern" nineteenth century society, and blamed "new" technologies such as steam power and the telegraph for stressing the nervous system.

For example, patients may have trouble concentrating or remembering things such as a story they have just read in the newspaper. Eye problems such as blurry vision are common, as are chills, night sweats, and diarrhea. Patients may complain that their weight has changed even though they have not changed their diet. Some people with CFS say they feel as though they are in a fog. The symptoms that the CDC lists for CFS are the ones most commonly seen among the long list of those which have been reported.

Can CFS Be Treated?

CFS has no known specific cause, so there is no specific treatment for it, but usually people do not get worse. Most get better over time, and some will eventually become completely well again.

Although CFS itself is not treatable, some of the symptoms can be helped—for example, headache and pain. Antidepressants may be prescribed to relieve anxiety and depression. Patients with CFS should avoid heavy meals, alcoholic drinks, and caffeine. Although they may not feel like moving around very much, moderate exercise may bring benefits.

In their quest for a cure, patients may be tempted to try unproven treatments. Such treatments are often expensive, however, and they may be of little value or even harmful.

What Is It Like to Live with CFS?

CFS profoundly alters the ability of patients to work, study, and enjoy themselves. Patients may feel driven to seek consultations from many different kinds of doctors and practitioners of alternative medicine to find an answer. Most people are able to keep on with their lives, but some are unable to work, and others need help with day-to-day activities. Many of the symptoms of CFS are hard for others, including employers, to understand, and patients may feel isolated and frustrated when family and friends make jokes about being tired. They may become angry at their physicians, too, for not understanding or being able to help them. Periods of relative good health may alternate with times when patients do not feel very well at all. Research efforts are continuing with the goals of identifying the cause of the condition and finding ways to prevent, cure, or lessen the symptoms and disability caused by this disorder.

Resources

Book

Bell, David S. *The Doctor's Guide to Chronic Fatigue Syndrome: Understanding, Treating, and Living with CFS*. Reading, MA: Addison-Wesley, 1994.

Organizations

The National Institutes of Health posts information about chronic fatigue syndrome on its website at:
http://www.niaid.nih.gov/publications/cfs/contents.htm

U.S. Centers for Disease Control and Prevention (CDC), 1600 Clifton Road, NE, Atlanta GA 30333. The United States government authority for information about infectious and other diseases. http://www.cdc.gov/ncidod/diseases/cfs/facts.htm

▶ *See also*
Depressive Disorders
Fibromyalgia

Cirrhosis of the Liver

Cirrhosis (sir-RO-sis) damages liver cells and replaces them with scar tissue that prevents the normal flow of blood through the liver and interferes with many of the liver's vital functions.

KEYWORDS
for searching the Internet and other reference sources

Biliary atresia

Digestive system

Gastrointestinal system

Wilson's disease

Many people believe that only heavy drinkers can get cirrhosis of the liver. Although it is true that the number one cause of cirrhosis in the United States is drinking alcohol, a person need not be a heavy drinker to get the disease. The chance of developing cirrhosis depends on the amount and frequency that a person drinks, as well as their weight and height, and their body's ability to metabolize, or process, alcoholic products in the blood stream.

What Is Cirrhosis of the Liver?

Cirrhosis is a chronic* liver disease in which normal liver cells are damaged and replaced by scar tissue. The disease prevents the normal flow of blood through the liver and prevents the liver from functioning properly. It is most often (but not always) the result of severe liver damage or chronic liver disease. Although some liver tissue can regenerate or repair itself when injured, the extent to which damaged cells are able to regenerate

* **chronic** (KRON-ik) means continuing for a long period of time.

A healthy liver in adults weighs about 3 pounds (left). A liver damaged by alcoholism shows a buildup of fatty tissue (middle), and a liver with cirrhosis is enlarged and swollen (right). © *A. Glauberman/Science Source, Photo Researchers, Inc.*

* **bile** is a greenish-brown fluid manufactured in the liver that is essential for digesting food. Bile is stored in the gallbladder, which contracts and discharges bile into the intestine to aid digestion of fats after a person eats.

* **clotting** is a process in which blood changes into a jellylike mass that stops the flow of blood.

varies with each person. If cirrhosis is not treated, it can eventually lead to liver failure, or death.

The liver is a large, complex organ, about the size of a football and weighing around three pounds. It is located beneath the ribs in the upper right side of the abdomen, and is connected to the small intestine by the bile duct, which transports bile* from the liver to the intestines. A healthy liver is soft and smooth.

The liver is one of the most important organs, serving as the body's most comprehensive chemical factory and refinery. Almost all of the blood that leaves the stomach and intestines passes through the liver. The liver is responsible for cleansing the body of toxic or poisonous substances; processing nutrients, hormones, and medications; and for making proteins and clotting* factors that are crucial to healing. In a person with cirrhosis, toxic substances and bile remain in the bloodstream, because the liver has not removed them.

What Causes Cirrhosis?

Cirrhosis is not contagious; it cannot be passed on from one person to another. Cirrhosis has many possible causes:

- Drinking alcohol: The most frequent cause. About one third of all heavy drinkers eventually will develop cirrhosis; the rest may suffer from other forms of liver disease, but not cirrhosis.

- Chronic viral hepatitis (inflammation of the liver): Hepatitis (usually types B, C, and D) is the second most common cause of cirrhosis.

- Wilson's disease, which causes a buildup of copper in the liver, brain, kidneys, and eyes.

- Cystic fibrosis, which causes a buildup of mucus in the lungs, liver, pancreas, and intestines.

- Hemochromatosis (he-mo-kro-ma-TO-sis), which causes a buildup of iron in the liver and other organs.

- Blockages or inflammation of the bile ducts, called biliary (BIL-ee-ar-ee) cirrhosis.

- Congestive heart failure.

- Glycogen storage disorders, which prevent the body from using sugars properly.

- Parasitic infections.

- Reactions to prescription drugs, environmental toxins, and inhalant abuse (sniffing toxic substances).

What Are the Signs and Symptoms of Cirrhosis?

In the early stages, cirrhosis is considered a "silent" disease, because people show few symptoms. Over time, however, people with cirrhosis begin to experience fatigue, weakness, exhaustion, and loss of appetite. Weight loss and nausea are common. As cirrhosis worsens, the liver manufactures fewer of the proteins that the body needs and other symptoms develop:

- As less of the protein albumin (al-BYOO-min) is made, water will accumulate in the person's legs (a condition called edema) or abdomen (a condition called ascites) (a-SITE-eez).

- A slowing down of the production of plasma proteins such as fibrinogen (fy-BRIN-o-jen), essential for blood to clot, makes it easier for a person with cirrhosis to bruise or to bleed.

- Jaundice, a yellowing of the whites of the eyes or skin, may occur in a person with cirrhosis. This is caused by the buildup of bilirubin (bil-e-ROO-bin) or bile pigment that is normally passed by the liver into the intestines.

- Some people with cirrhosis also experience intense itching due to the bile products deposited in the skin.

- Cirrhosis prevents the liver from cleansing toxins, poisons, or drugs from the bloodstream. As these build up, they can lead to changes in mental function and personality. Early signs of cirrhosis may include neglect of personal appearance, forgetfulness, trouble concentrating, or changes in sleeping patterns. Later signs may include loss of consciousness or coma*.

- Cirrhosis also can affect abdominal blood vessels. Normally, the huge portal vein transports blood from the intestines and spleen through the liver. Cirrhosis blocks the flow, causing a condition called portal hypertension. As the spleen swells, the body attempts to divert blood through other blood vessels. But these new vessels are often not strong enough for the job. If they break, people can vomit blood, a highly dangerous situation.

How Do Doctors Diagnose and Treat Cirrhosis?

Diagnosis   Doctors always begin with a medical history and a physical exam. Evidence of an enlarged or swollen liver; evidence of edema or ascites; and signs of mental confusion caused by the buildup of toxic substances in the brain all can lead a doctor toward a diagnosis of cirrhosis.

The doctor also may order CT* or ultrasound* scans of the liver to see if it is scarred. A needle biopsy, in which a needle is put through the skin to take a sample of tissue from the liver, can be useful in diagnosing cirrhosis. The liver also can be inspected through a laparoscope (LAP-a-ro-skope), a viewing device inserted through a tiny incision in the abdomen. The presence of telangiectasia (tel-an-je-ek-TAY-ze-a), which are tiny, expanded, "spidery" blood vessels in the skin, particularly in the face and upper chest, may indicate cirrhosis.

Treatment   Treatment depends on the type and stage of the cirrhosis. The goal is to stop the progress of the disease while trying to reverse

Did You Know?

- About 25,000 people die in the United States each year from cirrhosis.

- Cirrhosis is the fourth disease-related cause of death in the United States for people aged 24 to 44.

- Experts estimate that more than half of all liver diseases could be prevented if people acted upon knowledge that is already available.

*coma is an unconscious state, like a very deep sleep. A person in a coma cannot be awakened, and cannot move, see, speak, or hear.

*CT scans are the short form for computerized axial tomography, which uses computers to view structures inside the body.

*ultrasound (sonography) uses sound waves to create images of the inside of the body.

damage to the liver. If the cirrhosis is caused by alcohol, stopping drinking will be the first step.

At the present time, there is no one treatment to "cure" cirrhosis. Symptoms such as itching can be treated with medications. Diuretics (drugs that help remove excess salt and water from the body) also may be prescribed to treat edema or ascites. In severe cases of liver failure, when the liver cells have completely stopped working, a liver transplant may be the only solution.

How Is Cirrhosis Prevented?

Adults who eat a nutritious diet and limit their alcohol consumption can help prevent destruction of healthy liver cells. Other tips that can help prevent the disease include:

- Never mixing drugs, in particular alcohol and over-the-counter medications.

- Closely following label directions when using chemicals: ensuring good ventilation, never mixing chemicals, avoiding inhaling any chemical products, avoiding getting chemicals on the skin, promptly washing any accidentally exposed area, and wearing protective clothing.

- Avoiding any type of inhalant abuse.

- Avoiding intravenous drug use by which hepatitis B, C, and D may spread.

Living with Cirrhosis

People with cirrhosis can live for many years. Even when complications develop, they usually can be treated. Many people with cirrhosis have undergone successful liver transplantation and gone on to live healthy lives.

People recovering from cirrhosis are advised not to drink alcohol. Poor nutrition, particularly associated with alcohol or drug abuse, is believed to play a role in how cirrhosis develops, although physicians have yet to understand this completely. In the meanwhile, eating a healthful, well-balanced diet is recommended.

Resources

U.S. National Digestive Diseases Information Clearinghouse, 2 Information Way, Bethesda, MD 20892-3570. This division of the National Institutes of Health posts a fact sheet about cirrhosis at its website. http://www.niddk.nih.gov/health/digest/pubs/cirrhosi/cirrhosi.htm

American Liver Foundation, 1425 Pompton Avenue, Cedar Grove, NJ 07009. The ALF publishes brochures and fact sheets about cirrhosis, biliary atresia, and liver transplantation.
Telephone 800-223-0179

The Primary Biliary Cirrhosis Support Group. This is a large internet support group.
http://members.aol.com/_ht_a/pbcers/pbcers.htm

Cleft Palate

A cleft palate is a gap or split in the roof of the mouth (the palate). It occurs when the palate of a fetus does not develop properly during the first months of pregnancy.

Mixed Feelings

Tonya and Phil were excited to hear their newborn son's first cry, but they were shocked when they saw him for the first time; baby Philip's upper lip was split up the middle. The doctor told them that Philip had a cleft palate as well as a cleft lip, and that both are fairly common birth defects. The doctor reassured Philip's parents that Philip was otherwise a very healthy baby—the cleft lip and palate would cause Philip some problems, but none that could not be overcome. A plastic surgeon would repair Philip's lip and palate, and a team of specialists would work on problems with his teeth, ears, and speech.

What Is a Cleft Palate?

Cleft means gap or split, and the palate is the roof of the mouth. A cleft palate occurs when the roof of the mouth in a fetus* does not develop properly during pregnancy, leaving a hole between the nose and the mouth.

The palate extends from the top teeth to the uvula (YOOV-u-la), which is the little piece of tissue that hangs in the back of the throat. There is a bony hard palate (which can be felt just behind the top teeth) and a muscular soft palate (just behind the hard palate). A fully formed palate is necessary to close off the nose and throat from the mouth. It keeps food from going up the nose, and it pushes food to the back of the throat when a person is swallowing. The palate also is important for speaking because it keeps air from going out of the nose instead of the mouth.

The mouth and nose of a fetus develop early during pregnancy: between 5 and 12 weeks. Three developing areas must fuse (close) together to form the face. The pieces that form the palate usually come together like a zipper—when the growth process is disturbed for some reason, the zipper does not close all the way, leaving a cleft. Formation of the palate and the upper lip are separate processes, but they are linked, and many children born with a cleft palate also have a cleft lip. A cleft lip impairs sucking, speech, and appearance. The size and severity of a cleft depends on how much of the palate or lip has fused together. Clefts can consist of one split down the middle (a unilateral cleft) or two splits (a bilateral cleft).

▶ *See also*

Alcoholism

Cystic Fibrosis

Gallstones

Heart Disease

Hepatitis

Jaundice

Parasitic Diseases

KEYWORDS
for searching the Internet and other reference sources

Craniofacial syndromes

Otolaryngology

Reconstructive surgery

* **fetus** (FEE-tus) is the term for an unborn human offspring during the period after it is an embryo, from 9 weeks after fertilization, until childbirth.

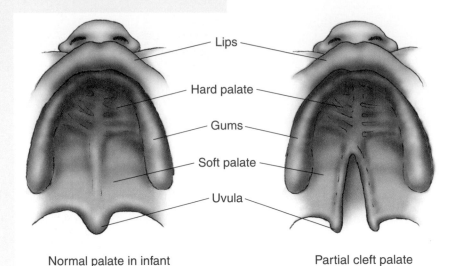
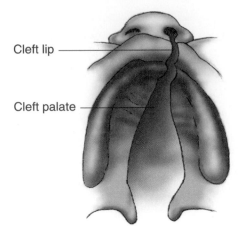

Lips

Hard palate

Gums

Soft palate

Uvula

Cleft lip

Cleft palate

Normal palate in infant

Partial cleft palate

Complete cleft palate and cleft lip

A cleft palate is a gap or split in the roof of the mouth (palate). The palate fuses closed (left) as a normal part of fetal development. If the palate does not fuse correctly, it can result in a partial cleft palate (middle), or a complete cleft palate and cleft lip (right).

As a baby, Shantell had surgery to repair her complete cleft palate and cleft lip. Here she is before (left) and after (right). *Courtesy of Janet Salomonson, M.D., Santa Monica, CA/Cleft Palate Foundation.*

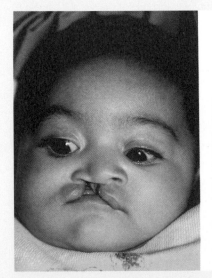
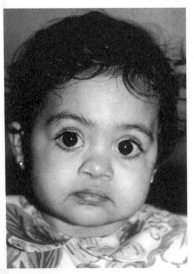

Why Are Babies Born with Cleft Palates and Cleft Lips?

Cleft palates and lips probably are the result of a number of factors acting together. One in five cases is inherited, probably through the interaction of many different genes*. In most cases, however, clefts seem to be caused by environmental factors that the fetus is exposed to early in pregnancy. The German measles (rubella) virus, other infections, vitamin deficiencies, some medications, alcohol and drug use during pregnancy, all seem to increase the likelihood of a child being born with a cleft lip or palate. Prevention efforts are focused on teaching the public about these risk factors during pregnancy.

What Happens to Children with Cleft Palate and Cleft Lip?

Symptoms   An improperly formed palate and/or upper lip affects a child's physical and emotional health in many different ways:

■ A cleft lip is a highly visible disfigurement, and a cleft palate can cause abnormal growth of the face. Uncorrected, they can lead to serious self-esteem problems.

■ When a person speaks, sounds are made by directing air through the nose or the mouth. A complete upper lip also is required to make certain sounds. A cleft palate, however, lets air escape out the nose all of the time, resulting in unusual sounds.

■ A hole in the palate can allow food or liquid to come out of the nose. Usually, the palate acts as a barrier and prevents this problem.

- Because a cleft palate allows liquid to invade the sinuses and ear tubes, children with cleft palates are prone to ear and sinus infections.

- Many children with cleft palates and/or cleft lips have dental problems such as missing bone, missing or malformed teeth, and malocclusion (top and bottom teeth that do not fit together properly). Such problems interfere with chewing and cause facial disfigurement.

- Some children with clefts also have congenital heart problems, growth disorders, or learning problems.

Treatment   Fixing Philip's cleft lip and palate will require several surgeries. When he is about three months old, a plastic surgeon will repair his lip by stitching the edges together using flaps of skin from other parts of his mouth. Philip's cleft palate will be repaired when he is between six months and a year old. If Philip is prone to ear infections, the doctor will put tubes in his ears to help drain them of the fluid that leads to infection. These repairs are done as early as possible to prevent hearing and speech problems.

Philip also may require several cosmetic surgeries to adjust his facial features as he grows older. He may need dental work to encourage jawbone growth and to straighten his teeth. He will have his hearing checked frequently by a hearing specialist (an audiologist), and he will work regularly with a speech therapist to learn how to train his palate muscles to work properly.

Philip and his parents will have a lot to deal with over the next several years, but his prognosis is good. The doctor expects that when Philip enters first grade, he will be speaking well, and he will have barely a scar where his cleft lip once was.

Resources

Books

Berkowitz, Samuel. *The Cleft Palate Story: A Primer for Parents of Children with Cleft Lip and Palate.* Chicago: Quintessence Press, 1994.

Charkins, Hope. *Children with Facial Difference: A Parent's Guide.* Bethesda: Woodbine House, Inc., 1996.

Organizations

U.S. National Institute of Dental and Craniofacial Research, Building 31, Room 2C35, 31 Center Drive, MSC 2290, Bethesda, MD 20892-2290.
http://www.nidcr.nih.gov

American Cleft Palate-Craniofacial Association, 104 South Estes Drive, Suite 204, Chapel Hill, NC 27514.
Telephone 800-24-CLEFT or 800-242-5338
http://www.cleft.com

*genes are chemicals in the body that help determine a person's characteristics, such as hair or eye color. They are inherited from a person's parents and are contained in the chromosomes found in the cells of the body.

The U.S. and the World

- Clefts are one of the most common birth defects in the world. Approximately 1 in 700 babies is born with a cleft palate and/or cleft lip.

- More than 5,000 babies are born in the U.S. each year with these problems.

- Among people with clefts, 50 percent have both a cleft palate and a cleft lip; 30 percent have only a cleft palate; and 20 percent have only a cleft lip.

- Boys are twice as likely as girls to have a cleft lip or a cleft lip and palate, whereas girls are twice as likely as boys to have just the cleft palate.

- People of Asian, European, and Native American ancestry are more prone to clefts than other ethnic groups.

- Clefts are least likely to occur in people of African ancestry.

Operation Smile

Cleft palate repair requires multiple surgeries, and many people do not have access to or money for the medical care they need. In 1982, Dr. William P. Magee (a plastic surgeon) and his wife Kathleen (a nurse and social worker) founded Operation Smile to help make a difference.

Operation Smile and its volunteers provide free reconstructive (repair and rebuilding) surgery and other medical services for children in the United States and in 20 developing countries. Operation Smile volunteers have performed facial surgery on 50,000 children since 1982. In 1999, Operation Smile's "World Journey of Hope '99" helped 5,000 children in 19 countries.

KEYWORDS
*for searching the Internet
and other reference sources*

Circulatory system

Thrombus

* **pulmonary embolism** is a blockage of the pulmonary artery or one of its branches that is frequently caused by thrombosis, or formation of a blood clot, in the lower extremities.

* **hemophilia** (hee-mo-FIL-e-a) is a hereditary disease that results in abnormal bleeding because the blood fails to clot. It occurs almost exclusively in males.

KEYWORDS
*for searching the Internet
and other reference sources*

Respiratory infections

Rhinitis

American Speech-Language-Hearing Association, 10801 Rockville Pike, Rockville, MD 20852.
Telephone 800-638-8255 or 301-897-5700 (TTY)
http://www.asha.org

Operation Smile, 6435 Tidewater Drive, Norfolk, VA 23509. (757) 321-7645.
http://www.operationsmile.org

Clotting

Clotting is the process that changes blood in the body from a free-flowing liquid into a thick, jellylike substance that stops bleeding.

Almost as soon as blood starts to flow from a cut finger or scraped knee, platelets begin to gather. Platelets are clear blood cells that start the process of clotting. But like a towel used to wrap a leaky drainpipe, the disc-shaped platelets cannot completely stop the flow of blood.

As many as 20 different proteins in the blood come together in the clotting process. The proteins are in the plasma, which is the yellow-tinted portion of the blood that also contains water and other substances and carries blood cells and nutrients. These proteins in plasma are called "clotting factors." The protein clotting factors react with calcium and with other substances in the body's tissues and platelets to create a thick mass of jellylike material that plugs up the cut.

Clotting helps to stop bleeding from wounds. But blood may clot in the wrong places and times, such as the veins in the leg. This causes a condition known as "thrombosis." Clots in veins may break free and travel to the heart and lungs, where they may cause a pulmonary embolism*, which can cause death.

Some people have blood that does not clot well. Perhaps the best known clotting disorder is hemophilia*. People with liver disorders also may have blood that does not clot well since the liver produces some of the most important clotting factors found in the blood.

Cold

A cold is a short-term viral infection that usually occurs in the winter. It causes inflammation of the tissues lining the inside of the nose, which produces a stuffy nose and difficulty breathing. It also causes sore throat, sneezing, and a runny nose. Along with these symptoms, people sometimes complain about headache and fatigue.

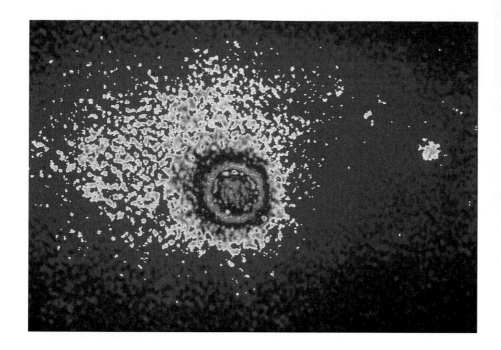

The rhinovirus, photographed at 100,000 times its actual size. © *1991 Custom Medical Stock Photo*

What Is a Virus?

A virus is the smallest type of infectious agent. It is anywhere from one-half to one-hundredth the size of the smallest bacteria. Viruses are responsible for a wide range of diseases, from the common cold and warts, to AIDS, chickenpox, and influenza.

What Are the Different Types of Viruses That Cause Colds?

There are about 200 viruses that can cause the common cold. The ones that cause colds most frequently belong to two major groups—rhinoviruses and coronaviruses.

2,500 YEARS AGO: PHLEGM

Hippocrates of Cos (c. 460–c. 375 B.C.E.) was the ancient Greek physician often called the father of medicine. He believed that the body contained four primary fluids ("humors"): yellow bile, black bile, blood, and phlegm.

According to Hippocrates, sickness resulted when the bodily humors became unbalanced; the common cold, for example, resulted from an excess of the humor "phlegm." Hippocratic physicians thought that mucus discharges from the nose were a sign of the body's effort to heal itself by releasing the excess humor.

Who Is at Risk for Colds?

Some people will say they have never had a cold, but almost everyone is at risk for catching colds. School children and young children in day care get the most colds. Some children have as many as ten colds a year.

Young children have not yet been exposed to and had the time to build up immunity to cold viruses the way older people have. Since school children are so close to each other in large numbers, they pass cold viruses along to each other. As children grow older, they get fewer colds.

A young adult may only have two or three colds a year. Older people may have only one or no colds at all.

The winter months are times when most people catch their colds. One of the reasons that winter is a time for colds is that people crowd together indoors in warm places. They tend to go to the movies, parties, and the mall in cold weather, and pass the cold viruses around to other people.

How Are Cold Viruses Transmitted?

There are three main ways cold viruses spread from one person to another:

1. When someone sneezes or coughs they spray little moisture droplets containing virus particles into the surrounding air. Others nearby may inhale these droplets and then become infected as well.

2. A person with a cold rubs his nose and then shakes hands with someone. The virus can be passed on if the person touches his eyes or nose or touches food with his hands. This way of catching a cold is called "via hand contact."

3. When people handle objects that have recently been handled by someone with a cold, they may have contact with the viruses. For example, picking up a book that has been handled by someone with a cold or playing cards with someone who has a cold can result in a person catching a cold.

What Parts of the Body Do Cold Viruses Affect?

Cold viruses attack the mucous linings of the nose and throat, and sometimes the eye. The tissues in the nose and throat become inflamed from the infection. The nose is stuffy, and it is hard to breathe.

What Are Symptoms of a Cold?

Some of the other symptoms of colds are:

- A tickling sensation in the throat
- Sneezing
- Sore throat
- Stuffy and/or runny nose
- Watery eyes
- Cough

- Headache
- Fatigue
- Low grade fever, up to 101 degrees Fahrenheit

Influenza, or "flu," shares many of the symptoms of the common cold, but with the flu the fever is usually higher, and the symptoms are worse.

What Are Some Complications That Can Follow a Cold?

Sometimes rather than starting to feel better after three or four days, a person gets worse or develops new symptoms such as an earache, a worsening cough with chest pains, or a very sore throat. This may be because a bacterial infection has occurred. Sinuses may become infected with bacteria. The middle ear is another site that can become infected by bacteria. Such infections are called secondary infections.

What Is the Treatment for a Cold?

It takes about a week for a cold to clear up on its own. If it lasts much longer than that, a doctor should be consulted. Other symptoms might have to be treated if an infection spreads beyond the usual areas affected by the cold. If there is pain in the chest as a result of the infection or in other places such as the ears, a secondary bacterial infection may be present. Unlike the cold, which should *not* be treated with antibiotics, the bacterial infection may require the use of them.

Antibiotics and colds Some people think that using antibiotics for a cold will help them recover more quickly or reduce the discomfort of their symptoms. Colds are caused by viruses, not bacteria. Antibiotics are effective against bacteria, not against viruses!

Overuse of antibiotics has led to the development of bacteria that are resistant to them. These new strains of bacteria have developed the ability to inactivate antibiotics or to continue to grow in spite of the presence of the antibiotic. Therefore, antibiotics should be used only when a doctor is reasonably certain that the antibiotic will be effective and that the infection is likely caused by a bacterium and not a virus.

Can the Common Cold Be Prevented?

There are many beliefs people have about preventing colds. Two of the most common:

- Can colds be prevented by keeping away from damp places or chilly drafts? In the past, people thought that drafts that chilled the body caused colds. But Ben Franklin knew better. Over 200 years ago, he wrote that colds came from contact with other people, not from chills.
- Can a cold be prevented by taking lots of vitamin C supplements? While many people believe that vitamin supplements prevent colds, there is no clear scientific evidence proving this.

There are still common sense measures that can be taken, such as resting, drinking lots of liquids, and eating a healthy diet. Aspirin should not be given to children with viral infections, since this has been linked with the risk of Reye's syndrome (a potentially fatal condition that affects the liver and brain).

Some people recommend over-the-counter cold medicines for nasal stuffiness and coughs. These medicines often have unpleasant side effects such as sleepiness and dry mouth. Cough medicine should be used only if coughing is interfering with sleep. Use of over-the-counter medicines will not affect the amount of time of time it takes for the cold to get better and the side effects of the medication may be worse than the symptoms of the cold itself.

Resources

Books

Kittredge, Mary. *The Common Cold.* New York: Chelsea House Publishers, 1989.

Silverstein, Alvin. *The Common Cold and Influenza.* Hillside, NJ: Enslow Publishers, 1994.

Organization

KidsHealth.org., the website created by The Nemours Foundation, has information on many infections, including the cold. http://KidsHealth.org.

▶ *See also*
Bacterial Infections
Influenza
Reye's Syndrome
Viral Infections

Cold Sores *See* **Herpes**

Cold-Related Injuries

Cold-related injuries, such as hypothermia and frostbite, occur when low temperatures damage the body. In hypothermia, the body's internal temperature falls, causing blood flow and breathing to get dangerously slow. In frostbite, outer parts of the body, such as fingers and toes, start to freeze. Other cold-related injuries include chilblains and trench foot.

KEYWORD
for searching the Internet and other reference sources

Hypothermia

Who Is at Risk for Cold-Related Injuries?

Anyone who spends time outdoors in cold weather can be at risk for cold-related injuries. That includes people who fish, hunt, or hike, especially in the mountains, where temperatures can drop quickly and icy rain or

WEATHER AND WARFARE

Throughout history armies faced the perils of winter weather. George Washington at Valley Forge (1777–1778) lost many men to the cold. Napoleon, after first successfully invading Russia in 1812, was forced to retreat from the walls of Moscow when his army faced the terrible Russian winter.

snow can blow in with little warning. In snowstorms, people trapped in their cars can suffer permanent injury or even death, if they cannot keep warm until help arrives.

In cities, homeless people who remain outdoors in the cold are at special risk. So are poor people who cannot afford to heat their homes or whose landlords do not provide heat.

Indoors or outdoors, elderly people, the very young, and those who abuse alcohol or drugs also are at extra risk. Hypothermia, in which body temperature falls, is most common in cold, wet weather. But with elderly people, especially, it can occur at temperatures as high as 65 degrees Fahrenheit, coming on gradually over days. That's because aging can reduce the body's ability to conserve heat and maintain an internal (core) temperature of about 98.6 degrees. In addition, elderly people may not feel the cold as much and so may not take steps to get warm.

In the United States, from 500 to 1,000 people are known to die each year from the cold. But doctors suspect that thousands of elderly people may be hospitalized each year for problems caused by undiagnosed hypothermia.

What Is Frostbite?

Frostbite is the freezing of any part of the body. Ice crystals form within or between the cells. Red blood cells and platelets clump and restrict blood flow, especially to the ears, fingers, toes and nose. These areas usually are the first to turn cold, white, hard, and numb. Frostbite can be deceptive—because it causes numbness, rather than pain, people may not know it is happening in time to prevent serious damage.

How Is Frostbite Treated?

In dealing with frostbite, doctors usually recommend that the affected body parts be warmed rapidly in warm, not hot, water. Rubbing the frostbitten parts is not advisable because more tissue damage can be caused by this process. Another myth is that the frostbitten area should be rubbed with snow. This can also cause more damage.

219

A doctor treats a mountain climber's frostbitten hands. *Corbis/Jason Burke; Eye Ubiquitous*

▶

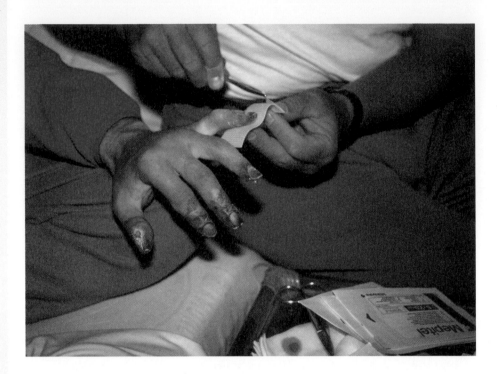

Thawing is occurring when the affected part begins to become pink or red. If it remains white that means more time has to be allowed for thawing in the warm water.

Small blisters appear right after the rapid thawing. They break in about a week. A black scab forms after the blisters rupture. Normal tissue may have already formed below. The thawed part is usually protected to avoid both refreezing and excessive heat. Usually neither bandages nor dressings are used, and the area is cleaned with mild soaps.

A doctor will recommend exercises to preserve joint motion in hands and feet. Early surgical removal of the dead tissue may save the part from amputation. Antibiotics are prescribed, if necessary.

The Wind-Chill Factor

The wind-chill factor can increase heat loss from the body. If the skin is wet, there is an even greater transfer of heat to the surrounding air from the body. Those who are at risk from these circumstances are people who fish on ice, hunters, skiers, campers, and hikers in the mountains. Anyone exposed to wind and low temperatures can develop serious frostbite.

The actual temperature and the wind speed determine the wind-chill temperature. The lower the wind-chill temperature, the greater risk to human beings.

Temperature	35°F	15°F	0°F	−15°F
Wind Speed	10 mph	20 mph	30 mph	45 mph
Wind Chill				
Temperature	22°F	−17°F	−49°F	−78°F

What Is Hypothermia?

Hypothermia (hy-po-THER-mee-a) is the lowering of the body temperature below 35 degrees Centigrade. It results from prolonged exposure to cold when the body heat loss is greater than heat production. Hypothermia can be life-threatening. As in the case of frostbite, the sooner the affected person receives treatment the better the chances for survival.

What Are the Symptoms of Hypothermia?

Some of the symptoms of hypothermia are slurred or incoherent speech, a drop in the level of awareness, irritability, slowed rate of breathing, and violent shivering. When shivering stops, it indicates exhaustion, and the body temperature drops even more rapidly. Children and the elderly are more susceptible to hypothermia, because their body temperature drops more rapidly.

A COLD RIDE

A description of what it might feel like to freeze can be found in *These Happy Golden Years* by Laura Ingalls Wilder, which takes place in the Dakota Territory in the early 1880s. Almanzo Wilder, a young man who owns a sleigh and two horses, undertakes to drive Laura Ingalls home for the weekend from the place where she teaches school. Unfortunately a storm is brewing; the wind blows hard, and the thermometer has dropped to 40 below zero and is frozen there:

The cold was piercing through the buffalo robes. It crept through Laura's wool coat and woolen dress, through all her flannel petticoats and the two pairs of woolen stockings drawn over the folded legs of her warm flannel union suit. . . . In spite of all she could do, Laura shook all over. Pressing her knees tight together did not stop their shaking. The lantern beside her feet under the fur robes seemed to give no warmth. The pains bored into her temples, and a knot of pain tightened in her middle.

But Almanzo does not get worried about her until she starts to feel sleepy:

She was growing more used to the cold. It did not hurt so much. Only the pain in her middle kept tightening, but it was duller. The sound of the wind and the bells and the cutter's runners on the snow all blended into one monotonous sound, rather pleasant. . . .
"All right?" he asked. She nodded. It was too much trouble to speak.
"Laura!" he said, taking hold of her shoulder and shaking her a little. The shaking hurt; it made her feel the cold again. "You sleepy?"
"A little," she answered.
"Don't go to sleep. You hear me?"
"I won't," she said. She knew what he meant. If you go to sleep in such cold, you freeze to death.

In reality, going to sleep in the cold does not cause a person to freeze to death, although moving the body, more likely to occur when a person is awake, helps generate body heat. The sleepiness is a symptom of severe hypothermia (low body temperature), and asleep or not, Laura and Almanzo are certainly in danger of freezing.

One reason that Laura Ingalls Wilder excelled at describing the cold realistically is that her stories are true; she is recording her own experience. Another one of her novels is called *The Long Cold Winter*.

Irritable behavior may be a sign of hypothermia. Aside from comments about being cold, hypothermia symptoms may emerge in the form of anger or inability to perform physical movements. Severe hypothermia may produce rigid muscles, dark and puffy skin, irregular heart and respiratory (breathing) rates, unconsciousness, and eventually death.

How Is Hypothermia Treated?

Hypothermia is treated by keeping the patient warm and by getting immediate medical attention. If wet, the clothes are removed carefully. The skin is not rubbed. If the person is unconscious and not breathing, cardiopulmonary resuscitation (CPR) should be attempted by someone who has been trained in this revival technique.

What Are Trench Foot and Chilblains?

Trench foot is a painful disorder of the foot involving damage to the skin, nerves, and muscle that is caused by prolonged exposure to cold or dampness or by prolonged immersion in cold water. The soldiers fighting in the trenches during World War I developed this painful condition because they did not have access to clean, dry socks and boots.

Chilblain (CHILL-blain; often referred to in the plural, "chilblains") usually affects the fingers and is characterized by redness, swelling, and itchiness caused by exposure to damp cold. Tissue damage is less severe with chilblains than with frostbite, where the skin is actually frozen. Chilblains do not cause permanent damage.

Can Frostbite and Hypothermia Be Prevented?

It is important to dress properly in cold, damp weather. Wearing several layers of dry, loose-fitting clothing that allow perspiration to evaporate is important. Exposed flesh should be protected from the wind. Face masks, hoods, and ear muffs are helpful. Hats are important because 30 percent of the body's heat is lost through the head. Gloves and socks should be kept dry. Consuming adequate amounts of food and fluid will help the body to generate heat.

It is also important to listen to highway department advisories about driving during snowstorms, since getting caught in a stalled car in a snowstorm can easily lead to frostbite and hypothermia.

Resources

"Climate and Weather," *Universal Almanac*. Kansas City, MO, 1994.

Mosby's Outdoor Emergency Medical Guide. St. Louis, MO: Mosby Yearbook, 1996

Survival: How to Prevail in Hostile Environments. New York: Facts on File, 1994.

Wilkerson, James A. *Hypothermia, Frostbite and Other Cold Injuries*. Seattle, WA: The Mountaineers, 1986.

▶ *See also*

Gangrene
Heat-Related Injuries

Colitis

Colitis (ko-LY-tis) is the general term meaning inflammation of the lining of the colon (the lower part of the large intestine) and the rectum.

What Is Colitis?

Colitis is a type of inflammatory* bowel disease that affects mainly the large intestine and the rectum*. Different types of colitis may be chronic or acute and may have different causes, but they have many symptoms in common, including diarrhea that may be bloody. Many people also feel abdominal pain and cramping.

Acute colitis   Acute colitis has many different causes, including:

- Bacteria from contaminated food and water: As the bacteria grow, they release poisons (toxins) that cause the lining of the bowel to become sore and inflamed.

- Antibiotics: Antibiotics used to treat specific bacterial infections also may kill helpful bacteria that occur naturally in the intestines. This can allow harmful intestinal bacteria to grow more abundantly and to cause acute colitis.

- Insufficient blood flow to the colon: This is known as ischemic colitis and may have a wide range of causes.

- Heavy doses of radiation to the lower abdomen: Called radiation enterocolitis, this may occur long after radiation therapy has been completed.

Acute colitis lasts for a short time, then goes away on its own or is cured by treatment.

Chronic colitis   The exact causes of chronic colitis are not always known. Scientists think that the body's immune system may react inappropriately to a virus or bacteria, causing the lining of the intestine to become and to remain inflamed. Chronic colitis is ongoing and long-lasting. In many cases it cannot be cured, although treatments are available that may help relieve a person's symptoms.

Ulcerative colitis is an example of chronic colitis. Persistent, small, bloody sores (ulcers) usually form on the inside lining of the colon or rectum. Many people with ulcerative colitis have mild symptoms, but others may have frequent, severe symptoms that can disrupt their daily lives.

How Is Colitis Diagnosed and Treated?

The symptoms of colitis are similar to those of other inflammatory bowel diseases such as Crohn's disease (ileitis).

Diagnosis   A thorough physical examination, medical history, and diagnostic tests are needed to make an accurate diagnosis of colitis. Stool

KEYWORDS
for searching the Internet and other reference sources

Digestive system

Enteritis

Gastroenterology

Inflammation

* **inflammation** is the body's reaction to irritation, infection, or injury that often involves swelling, pain, redness, and warmth.

* **rectum** is the final portion of the large intestine, connecting the colon to the outside opening of the anus.

samples are usually examined for evidence of blood or infection. Often the colon is examined through a procedure called colonoscopy (kol-on-OS-ko-pee). An endoscope, or lighted flexible tube and camera attached to a television monitor, is inserted through the anus. This allows the doctor to see the inside lining of the colon and rectum. During the colonoscopy, the doctor may remove a tissue sample (called a biopsy) from the intestinal lining for further examination under the microscope.

Treatment Treatment for acute colitis depends on its cause. Although chronic colitis may not be cured, many people's symptoms are treated effectively with prescription medications that reduce inflammation in the colon and rectum and control diarrhea.

Some people find their symptoms improve if they change their diet. Many people with chronic colitis have periods of months or years when their symptoms go into remission (go away). Very severe cases of colitis may require surgery to remove the damaged portion of the colon and limit intestinal bleeding.

Resources

U.S. National Digestive Diseases Information Clearinghouse, 2 Information Way, Bethesda, MD 20892-3570. This division of the National Institutes of Health posts fact sheets about ulcerative colitis and Crohn's disease at its website.
http://www.niddk.nih.gov/health/digest/pubs/colitis/colitis.htm
http://www.niddk.nih.gov/health/digest/pubs/crohns/crohns.htm

Crohn's and Colitis Foundation of America, Inc., 386 Park Avenue South, New York, NY 10016-8804.
Telephone 800-932-2423
http://www.ccfa.org

▶ *See also*
Colorectal cancer
Diarrhea
Diverticulitis and Diverticulosis
Gastroenteritis
Inflammatory Bowel Disease
Irritable Bowel Syndrom

KEYWORDS
*for searching the Internet
and other reference sources*

Autoimmunity

Dermatomyositis

Inflammation

Lupus

Polyarteritis nodosa

Polymyositis

Rheumatology

Scleroderma

Sjögren's syndrome

Collagen Vascular Diseases

Collagen vascular diseases are a diverse group of diseases in which the body reacts against its own tissues, often causing joint pain and inflammation, fever, rash, fatigue, and difficulty swallowing.

Collagen vascular diseases have been recognized for a long time. Rheumatoid arthritis is a chronic inflammatory* disease that causes stiffness in the joints (places where bones meet), and can lead to disfigurement. It is an ancient disease; bone changes showing this condition have been identified in skeletons thousands of years old. Systemic lupus erythematosus (er-i-thee-ma-TO-sis), which affects multiple organs and tissues throughout the body, was first described in 1828.

What are Collagen Vascular Diseases?

Collagen vascular diseases, sometimes called connective tissue diseases (CTDs) or autoimmune diseases, cover a wide array of disorders in which the body's natural immune or self-protection system fails to recognize its own tissues and goes on attack against itself. Some of these diseases limit their damage to a single organ, and others spread problems throughout the body.

Immune responses to foreign bodies In a healthy immune system, antigens (foreign bodies such as viruses and bacteria) are recognized as different from regular body tissues. When an antigen enters the bloodstream, it triggers the production of antibodies, substances that attack the alien substance. Lymphocytes (LIM-fo-sites) and leukocytes (LOO-ko-sites) are the special white blood cells responsible for creating these antibodies.

Lymphocytes include two subtypes (T cells and B cells), which have the unique ability to recognize the invading alien and alert the immune system to destroy it. The process is highly specialized: different lymphocytes recognize specific antigens and produce antibodies against only that particular antigen.

Autoimmune responses In collagen vascular diseases, this immune system malfunctions. Rather than responding to foreign antigens, the body produces antibodies (autoantibodies) against its own antigens and normal proteins. Researchers do not understand what gets this autoimmune process started, but they have a fairly good idea of how it proceeds once it begins.

Systemic lupus erythematosus (SLE) People with lupus develop antibodies to their own nucleic (noo-KLAY-ic) acids* and cell structures,

*****inflammation** is the body's reaction to irritation, infection, or injury that often involves swelling, pain, redness, and warmth.

*****nucleic acids** are the cell structures that transfer genetic information: DNA (deoxyribonucleic acid) transfers information to RNA (ribonucleic acid), which leads to the production of body proteins.

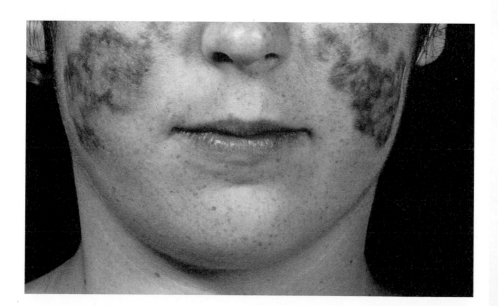

◄

Systemic lupus erythematosus (SLE) may cause a distinctive butterfly-shaped rash on the face. © *1993 Custom Medical Stock Photo.*

225

including those in the heart, kidneys, and joints. As a result of a faulty interaction between lymphocyte B and T cells, the cells fail to identify a protein as normal, mistake it for a foreign antigen, and then move on to produce autoantibodies called antinuclear antibodies. These antinuclear antibodies attack the nucleus and DNA (genetic material) in healthy cells. Immune complexes are the result of this mistaken battle. When they accumulate in the kidney, blood vessels, joints, and other sites, they cause inflammation and tissue damage.

Rheumatoid arthritis   In rheumatoid arthritis, the autoimmune process begins in connective tissue and the cushiony membranes that surround joints and the ends of bones. Collagen (KOL-a-jen) is the tough glue-like protein that gives joints their support and flexibility, and it represents 30 percent of the body's protein. Rheumatoid arthritis is thought to begin when T cells mistake the body's own collagen cells for foreign antigens and alert B cells to produce antibodies to fight the invader. The leukocytes rush in and produce cytokines (SY-to-kines), small proteins that are essential in healing the body but that cause serious damage in large doses. The inflammation and joint damage that result can lead to joint deformities and can spread throughout the body, wherever there is connective tissue.

Causes   Researchers are studying the causes of autoimmune diseases. Some autoimmune diseases have strong genetic components and may be passed down from parents to children. Environmental factors may act to trigger these diseases in some way. Fatigue, stress, and higher levels of certain antibodies also may lead to these diseases. Even ultraviolet rays of sunlight have been suggested as possible contributing causes. Collagen vascular diseases are not contagious; people cannot catch these diseases from one another.

What Happens When People Have Collagen Vascular Diseases?

Symptoms   Symptoms differ depending on the illness, but they often include joint pain, fever, rash, recurrent infections, fatigue, mouth ulcers, dry mouth and dry eyes, hair loss, difficulty swallowing, swollen glands, or fingers and toes that get overly cold when exposed to cooler temperatures. In addition to systemic lupus erythematosus and rheumatoid arthritis, collagen vascular diseases include:

- **Scleroderma:** This progressive and systemic sclerosis (skle-RO-sis) causes skin to thicken and tough fibrous tissue to form in the internal organs of the digestive tract, kidneys, heart, and lungs.
- **Sjögren's syndrome:** This causes dry mouth, dry eyes, and other symptoms.
- **Polymyositis and dermatomyositis:** These are inflammatory muscle disorders that may also affect the skin, the heart, and the lungs.
- **Mixed connective tissue diseases:** These combine features of lupus, scleroderma, and polymyositis.

■ **Polyarteritis nodosa:** This disorder can damage small and medium-sized arteries of almost any organ, including the kidneys, heart, and intestines.

Diagnosis   A complete medical history and a physical examination are the basis for the diagnosis of autoimmune disease. A number of laboratory tests can be used to help diagnose collagen vascular diseases. Blood tests can check levels of autoantibodies. Other tests include rheumatoid factor tests, urinalysis, blood counts, liver and kidney tests, and a sedimentation rate, which will give a nonspecific indicator of inflammation. A chest x-ray and other tests of specific lung function also may be done, since collagen vascular disorders occasionally produce breathing difficulties.

Treatment   At present, there are no cures for autoimmune diseases, although some may go into remission as symptoms disappear for periods of time. Treatment depends on the extent of the disease. Doctors may prescribe steroid creams or anti-inflammatory medications to ease discomfort. In advanced cases, immunosuppressant drugs may help lessen the immune system's over-reaction.

Living with Collagen Vascular Diseases

These serious diseases often require adjustments in activities of daily living. People with rheumatoid arthritis often have early morning stiffness that lasts for about an hour, after which they can go on about their day. Avoiding certain foods, and reducing physical and emotional stresses, also seem to reduce symptoms for some people.

Resources

American Autoimmune Related Diseases Association, 15475 Gratiot Avenue, Detroit, MI 48205
Telephone 313-371-8600
http://www.aarda.org

Lupus Foundation of America, 1300 Piccard Drive, Suite 200, Rockville, MD 20850-4303
Telephone 301-670-9292
http://www.lupus.org

Sjögren's Syndrome Foundation, 333 North Broadway, Jericho, NY 11753
Telephone 800-4-SJOGRENS
http://sjogrens.com

Scleroderma Foundation, 89 Newbury Street, Suite 201, Danvers, MA 01923
Telephone 800-722-HOPE
http://www.scleroderma.org

▶ *See also*
Arthritis
Fever
Hair Loss
Immunodeficiency
Infection
Lupus

227

Colon Cancer *See* Colorectal Cancer

Color Blindness

Color blindness is a condition in which a person has a defect in the eye that causes an inability to identify various colors and shades.

KEYWORDS
for searching the Internet and other reference sources

Chroma

Color saturation

Hue

Ophthalmology

Vision

Red means stop. Green means go. It is one of the earliest lessons a child learns. But for more than 10 million people in the United States, this is not as simple as it sounds. These people usually are called "color blind," although it is more accurate to say that they have poor color vision.

How Does Color Blindness Happen?

Color blindness almost always is inherited from the mother's genes. It affects boys most often, as girls usually have additional genetic material that overrides the vision problem. About 1 in 12 males has some degree of color blindness, whereas only about 1 in 100 females has it. People with color blindness often have no other vision problems, but color blindness is sometimes a result of other eye diseases and vision problems.

Eight million colors   The human eye can identify more than 8 million shades of colors. But the ability to distinguish among the colors begins with the three primary colors* of light: red, green, and blue. Just as a person can mix the color brown by coloring the same area with red and green crayons, the eye sees various colors by combining primary colors.

As light passes through the eye, it focuses the image on the retina. The retina contains layers of cells at the inside rear of the eyeball and acts a little like the photographic film in a camera. The retina contains millions of receptors called "rods" that help see light and "cones" that help see light and colors. When light strikes the rods and cones, chemicals are released.

Red and green   People with poor color vision have cones that do not function properly, because they do not release some of the chemicals when they are struck by light. As a result, these people see only certain colors and shades. The most common form of color blindness is difficulty in seeing the colors red and green properly, or the same way most people see them. The condition can range from mild to severe. Sometimes a person simply cannot see the colors as vividly as a person who has normal color vision. Other times, there are areas that seem to lack color and to appear in shades of gray. Rarely does color blindness mean that people see everything in shades of gray, as in black-and-white photographs, movies, or television shows.

*primary colors are sets of colors that can be mixed to create all other colors. There are two kinds of primary colors: subtractive or colorant primaries (red, blue, and yellow), which refer to pigments like crayons; and additive or light primaries (red, blue, and green), which refer to light.

How Is Color Blindness Diagnosed and Treated?

The first signs of poor color vision may be noticed in school, when a child starts to learn to identify colors. A simple vision test can determine if the problem is color blindness. An image made up of dots is shown to the child. It may be a number (4, for example, as in the illustration at right) made up of green dots on a background of yellow and orange dots. If the child cannot see the green numeral 4 distinctly because it appears to blend in with the background, he may have color blindness.

There is no treatment or cure for color blindness. People are often taught to recognize colors in other ways. For example, traffic lights usually have the red light on top and green on the bottom.

Resource

Lighthouse International, 111 East 59 Street, New York, NY 10022. The Lighthouse International website posts fact sheets about vision problems, color contrast, and partial sight.
Telephone 800-829-0500 or 212-821-9713 (TTY)
http://www.lighthouse.org/color_contrast.htm

Here is a test. People with color blindness may see only colored dots. People without color blindness probably will see the number 4. ▼

▶ See also
Blindness
Genetic Disorders

KEYWORDS
for searching the Internet
and other reference sources

Digestive system

Oncology

Colorectal Cancer

Colorectal cancer (colon cancer) is a dangerous growth that starts in the parts of the digestive tract called the colon and rectum and may spread.

A Painful Surprise

In October 1998, New York Yankees outfielder Darryl Strawberry went to see his doctor because of pains in his stomach. Surprisingly, the cause turned out to be colon cancer. Many people think of colon cancer as a disease that affects only older people or only men, but anyone can be at risk. When colon cancer is discovered early, it is highly curable. Colon cancer is not contagious.

What Is Colorectal Cancer?

The colon and rectum   Colorectal cancer begins in either the colon or the rectum. Both are part of the digestive tract, which is a series of tubes and organs that process the food we eat. Digestion begins in the stomach. From the stomach, partly digested food passes into the small intestine, the longest section of the digestive tract, which absorbs most of the nutrients. The food then continues into the large intestine (the colon), which is a muscular tube approximately 5 feet long. In the colon,

Did You Know?

The American Cancer Society reports the number of cases of colon and rectal cancer in the U.S. for 1999 as follows:

- 43,000 men and 51,700 women diagnosed with colon cancer

- 19,400 men and 15,300 women diagnosed with rectal cancer

- 9 out of every 10 people diagnosed with colorectal cancer are older than age 50

- The number of people who die from colorectal cancer has been going down for the past 20 years

Doctors can use a special viewing instrument called an endoscope to view the inside of the colon. © *1992 G-I Associates/Custom Medical Stock Photo.*

▼

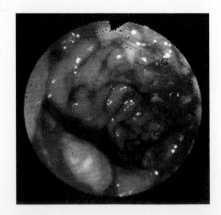

the remaining water and nutrients are extracted from the food and the rest is stored as waste. The waste moves from the colon into the rectum, and then passes out of the body through the anus during a bowel movement. Cancer is similar in the colon and the rectum, so they often are discussed together.

Polyps and adenocarcinoma Colorectal cancer does not happen overnight. It can take many years to develop, and it usually is preceded by changes in the lining of the colon or rectum that occur over several years. One of these changes is a growth of tissue into the center of the colon or rectum, called a polyp (POL-ip). Not all polyps develop into cancer, but some do. Removing a polyp early can prevent it from becoming cancer.

Ninety-five percent of colorectal cancers are of the particular kind called adenocarcinoma (AD-e-no-kar-si-NO-ma). These cancers begin in the lining of the colon or rectum and can grow either into the center of the colon or rectum, or outward through the wall. If the cancer is not treated, cancerous cells can break away into the circulatory system and travel to other parts of the body. When a cancer spreads in this way, it is said to have metastasized (me-TAS-ta-sized).

Risk factors No one knows for sure what causes colorectal cancer, although there are a number of risk factors that may increase a person's chances of developing it. Sometimes people inherit colorectal conditions that increase their chances of developing cancer. Having certain types of polyps (particularly large and numerous ones) also increase the risk. People who already have had colon cancer are at greater risk of developing new cancers in other areas of the colon and rectum.

To reduce risk, experts recommend eating a diet high in fruits, vegetables, and whole grain foods. Similarly, regular exercise may help to prevent colorectal cancer.

What Happens When People Have Colorectal Cancer?

Signs and symptoms The symptom that brought Darryl Strawberry to the doctor was gnawing pains in his abdomen. Another symptom a person might notice is a change in bowel habits, for example, diarrhea or constipation that lasts for more than a few days. Or a person might feel the need to have a bowel movement even after they have had one, or one might notice bleeding from the rectum or blood in the stool.

Diagnosis Just because people have symptoms does not mean that they have colorectal cancer. But the only way to be sure is to consult a doctor. It also is possible to have colon or rectal cancer and not to have any symptoms at all. For this reason, tests to screen for colorectal cancer are recommended for people over 50, whose age puts them at greater risk for developing the disease.

The simplest test is a digital rectal exam. The doctor inserts a gloved finger into the rectum to feel for anything that is not normal. People often are shy at the thought o;f such a test, but it is very effective in detecting certain kinds of cancers. Other tests use special instruments to examine parts of the colon. If the doctor finds anything unusual, he or she may remove a small amount of tissue for examination under the microscope (a biopsy) to see whether the tissue is cancerous or benign (harmless).

How Is Colorectal Cancer Treated?

If cancer is found, the next step is to do tests to see whether it has spread. Doctors use a system of numbers or letters to stage, or classify, the cancer. The lower the number or letter, the less the cancer has spread. A higher number, for example, stage IV, means a more serious stage of the disease. The three main types of treatment for colorectal cancer are surgery, radiation therapy, and chemotherapy:

- **Surgery** is the main treatment for both colon and rectal cancer. In some more advanced instances of rectal cancer, a person may need to have a colostomy*. Colostomies usually are not needed in colon cancer.

- **Radiation therapy** uses high-energy radiation to kill cancer cells. It is used to kill small areas of cancer that might not have been removed during surgery.

- **Chemotherapy** (kee-mo-THER-a-pee) refers to the use of anti-cancer drugs to kill cancer cells. The drugs may be given through a vein in the arm or as pills, which means that they can enter the bloodstream and can reach any area of the body where metastasized cancer cells may have traveled.

*__colostomy__ (ko-LOS-to-mee) is a surgical procedure in which a part of the large intestine is removed, and the end of the intestine is attached to an opening made in the abdomen. The stool is passed through this opening into a special bag.

Can Colorectal Cancer Be Prevented?

Scientists do not know how to prevent colorectal cancer, but there are steps people can take to reduce their risk.

Screening   Because finding colorectal cancer early often means it can be cured, people age 50 and older should follow the screening guidelines established by the American Cancer Society. Younger people whose close relatives (mother, father, sister, or brother) have had colorectal cancer or physical conditions that increase the risk for colorectal cancer should begin screening earlier than age 50. Younger people who have had colorectal cancer already must be particularly careful to follow up with their doctors regularly to make sure the cancer does not return. Eating a healthy diet, getting plenty of exercise, and never smoking are other things people can do to decrease their risk.

Research   If detected and treated early, colorectal cancer can be cured. Researchers now are studying the use of natural or man-made chemicals to lower a person's risk of ever developing colorectal cancer. Another area of investigation is in the kinds of changes to DNA that people inherit or acquire during the lifespan that might cause the cells of the colon and rectum to become cancerous. Such studies could lead to new drugs and new therapies for correcting those problems. Researchers

Sigmoidoscopy and Colonoscopy

Colorectal cancer is highly curable if it is caught early. Two tests can help to prevent or cure many cases of colon cancer.

The first is called sigmoidoscopy (sig-moyd-OS-ko-pee). In this test, the doctor uses a slender, lighted tube linked to a video camera to examine the rectum and lower part of the colon. This is where most cancers and polyps are found.

Another test is called colonoscopy (ko-lon-OS-ko-pee). In this test, a long, thin, flexible tube linked to a video camera allows the doctor to examine the entire length of the colon. If polyps are found, they can be removed using a wire loop. Because polyps take 6 to 10 years to develop into cancers, removing them early can help prevent them from becoming cancerous.

▶ *See also*
Cancer
Inflammatory Bowel Disease
Polyps
Tumor

KEYWORDS
for searching the Internet and other reference sources

Brain stem

Consciousness

Coma

also are working to develop colorectal screening methods that are faster and more comfortable than the ones available now. Experimental treatments that enlist the body's own defenses in the fight against cancer also are being tested.

What Is It Like to Live with Colorectal Cancer?

Caught in the early stages, colorectal cancer is one of the most curable cancers. People recover from surgery and resume their normal lives. Many people feel shame about colorectal cancer, however, because it involves a part of the body they do not usually talk about. Moreover, people who have had permanent colostomies may feel different from everyone else. Everyone's reaction to cancer and to treatment is different. There is no single right way to handle it. Support groups can be particularly helpful for people who are living with this very curable form of cancer.

Resources

U.S. National Cancer Institute (NCI), Bethesda, MD 20892. NCI coordinates the government's cancer research program. Its Cancer Information Service posts the fact sheet *What You Need to Know About Cancer of the Colon and Rectum* at its website, along with many other factsheets.
http://cancernet.nci.nih.gov/wyntk_pubs/index.html

American Cancer Society, 1599 Clifton Road N.E., Atlanta, GA 30329-4251. This national, not-for-profit society posts accurate and up-to-date health information about cancer at its website.
http://www3.cancer.org

Concussion

Concussion, or brain concussion, is an injury to the brain caused by a blow to the head or by violent jarring or shaking. It is a form of head trauma that often involves loss of consciousness, which may be momentary or may last for several hours. Brain concussion is a common injury that may sometimes have serious consequences.

Most people who watch sporting events on television have seen team physicians run out to the playing field to examine athletes who receive blows to the head. The doctors often ask the injured players if they know where they are or what day of the week it is. That is one way that doctors find out whether people have concussion.

What Causes Concussion?

A blow to the head, an injury, a fall, or sudden severe shaking may cause the brain to hit the inside of the skull. If the impact affects the consciousness centers in the brain stem*, then the person with concussion loses consciousness. This may happen if, for example, one boxer's knockout punch makes the other boxer's head accelerate sharply, or if someone's head decelerates suddenly, as when it strikes the ground during a fall.

Sports are among the most common causes of concussion, and sports with the most physical contact, such as football, boxing, and hockey, are most likely to produce head injuries that involve concussion. Concussions may also occur during collisions or falls in basketball, soccer, and baseball, or while riding motorcycles or bicycles.

About half of all head injuries are caused by motor vehicle accidents. A large percentage of these accidents involve drivers who have been drinking alcohol. Other causes include fights and industrial accidents.

What Happens to People with Concussion?

Concussion does not always cause complete loss of consciousness. People who get mild concussions may be temporarily stunned or dazed. They may feel dizzy, light-headed, or confused for a brief time. With loss of consciousness may also come nausea or vomiting, numbness, blurred vision or temporary blindness, or amnesia, which means loss of memory for events just before or just after the injury that caused the concussion.

The longer the period of unconsciousness, the more severe the symptoms may be, which is why a doctor should examine people with concussion

*__brain stem__ is the part of the brain that connects to the spinal cord. The brain stem controls the basic functions of life, such as breathing and blood pressure.

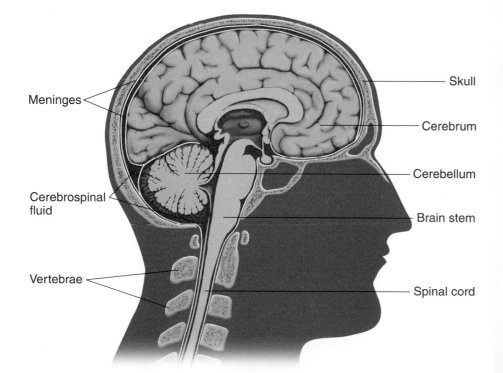

Concussion may result from sudden traumas, such as motor vehicle accidents or sports injuries, that cause the brain to hit the inside of the skull.

Skull — Cerebrum — Cerebellum — Brain stem — Spinal cord — Meninges — Cerebrospinal fluid — Vertebrae

as soon as possible. The symptoms of concussion usually do not last long, but in rare cases they may persist for several weeks or longer.

Do People with Concussion Need Medical Treatment?

Permanent brain damage does not normally result from a single mild concussion, but a doctor must first make sure that there has not been a more serious head injury, such as contusion (bruise) or laceration of the brain. The doctor usually asks about the injury that caused the concussion and notes the person's signs and symptoms.

Sometimes people worry that it is unsafe to fall asleep after a concussion, but doctors usually advise a period of bed rest, either at home or in a hospital, and no sports or riding a bicycle until recovery is complete. If headache is a symptom, the doctor may suggest pain medication. People with concussion should not drink alcohol or take sedatives*.

If unconsciousness, headache, or drowsiness return several hours or days after the injury, it is important to see the doctor again. The doctor may recommend hospital treatment or may diagnose postconcussion syndrome. People who have had a concussion are at higher risk of severe injury, or even sudden death, if they get a second concussion within a short time after the first injury. Under these circumstances, avoiding possible head trauma becomes vitally important.

What Is Postconcussion Syndrome?

Headache, dizziness, and other symptoms of concussion usually go away in a few minutes or days. Occasionally, however, they may persist much longer, even for years. The person may complain of a group of symptoms including not only headache and dizziness, but also confusion, poor memory, anxiety, sleeplessness, irritability, lack of energy, and depression. A person with this group of lasting symptoms following a concussion is said to have postconcussion syndrome*.

Although postconcussion syndrome is not well understood, many medical researchers believe it may be the result of subtle changes in the brain that do not show up in medical tests. Because brain tests are normal, people sometimes believe that postconcussion syndrome is due to psychological factors or that people with postconcussion syndrome are faking their symptoms, especially if they are attempting to win damages in a lawsuit. This may be so in some cases, but often postconcussion symptoms exist in the absence of a lawsuit or persist after a settlement has been reached.

How Do People Prevent Concussion?

Wearing a helmet Wearing a helmet is the best way to prevent a concussion in most situations where it might occur. Boxers are at high risk to receive this type of injury, and that is why they always wear protective headgear during training matches. The same is true in football, hockey, and other sports where there is a lot of physical contact, or where falls are likely. Bicycle and motorcycle riders also need to wear helmets to protect against serious head injury in case of a fall or collision.

*****sedatives** are medications that calm people and reduce excitement and irritability.

*****syndrome** means a group or pattern of symptoms that occur together.

Seat belts, air bags, and designated drivers In automobile accidents, seat belts and air bags can prevent riders from banging their heads against the windshield or dashboard. Many accidents can be prevented if adults who drink alcohol designate (choose) a nondrinking friend to drive them home after they have been drinking; this person is called a "designated driver."

Resources

Kulstad, Scott. *Sports Medicine for Young Athletes: A Guide for Parents, Teachers, and Coaches.* Minneapolis, MN: Institute for Athletic Medicine, Fairview Press, 1998. A useful book that includes a section on concussions.

Levy, Allan M., and Mark L. Fuerst. *Sports Injury Handbook: Professional Advice for Amateur Athletes.* New York: John Wiley and Sons, 1993. Covers head and neck injuries, with separate chapters on sports with the highest risks of concussion.

Micheli, Lyle J., with Mark Jenkins. *The Sports Medicine Bible: Prevent, Detect, and Treat Your Sports Injuries Through the Latest Medical Techniques.* New York: Harper Perennial, 1995. Discusses head injuries and preventive measures.

Congestive Heart Failure *See* Heart Disease

Conjunctivitis

Conjunctivitis is an inflammation of the conjunctiva (kon-junk-TY-va), which is the thin membrane that lines the inside of the eye-lids and covers the sclera, or white surface of the eye. Conjunctivitis is often called pinkeye.

How Do People Get Conjunctivitis?

Conjunctivitis is a common disorder in the United States, affecting one in every 50 people each year. Conjunctivitis has many different causes, including infections and allergies.

Acute conjunctivitis This form of conjunctivitis is most often called pinkeye. It is contagious*, often the result of infection from bacteria, such as *Haemophilus influenzae* (he-MOF-i-lus in-floo-ENZ-eye), or viruses, such as adenovirus (AD-e-no-vi-rus), which can cause the common cold. This is the kind of conjunctivitis that often spreads rapidly in schools during the spring or fall.

What does "punch drunk" mean?

Boxers are sometimes called "punch drunk" if they develop slurred speech and poor concentration after receiving repeated punches and blows to the head during their careers. Repeated concussions can cause an accumulation of injuries to the brain and may result in permanent damage.

▶ See also
Amnesia
Trauma

KEYWORDS
for searching the Internet and other reference sources

Inflammation

Ophthalmology

*****contagious** means transmittable from one person to another.

* **neonatal** refers to newborn.

* **allergens** are substances that provoke a response by the body's immune system or cause a hypersensitive reaction.

* **ophthalmologist** is a medical doctor who specializes in treating diseases of the eye.

Neonatal conjunctivitis   Neonatal* (nee-o-NAY-tal) conjunctivitis occurs when mothers with gonorrheal or chlamydial infections transmit them to their babies during childbirth. This form of conjunctivitis is also called neonatal ophthalmia (off-THAL-mee-a) and is treated with antibiotics.

Allergic conjunctivitis   Allergies and irritant substances can also cause conjunctivitis. This type of conjunctivitis is not contagious and is more common in adults. Irritants and allergens* may include cosmetics (including mascara), pollen, air pollutants, smoke, dust, plant poisons, and animal danders from household pets.

What Are the Signs and Symptoms of Conjunctivitis?

The characteristic sign of conjunctivitis is a redness or pink color in the white of the eye and lining of the eyelids. Sometimes the eyelids are also swollen. A watery discharge or pus may sometimes be seen coming out between the eyelids. Sometimes the lids are temporarily stuck together upon wakening in the morning. The eyes often feel itchy, but vision usually is not affected.

Do People with Conjunctivitis Need to See a Doctor?

People who suspect they have conjunctivitis should consult with a family doctor or an ophthalmologist*.

Diagnosis   By examining a person's eyes, a doctor can tell whether redness and irritation are caused by conjunctivitis or by something else. If the diagnosis is conjunctivitis, and the infectious type is suspected, the physician may take a small swab sample from the inside of the eyelids. When tested in the laboratory, such samples can be used to determine the type of organism causing the infection. This will be important for treatment, especially if bacteria are found to be the cause.

Treatment   Treatment of conjunctivitis depends entirely on what is causing a particular case. If bacteria are the cause, the doctor may prescribe

In conjunctivitis, the membrane that lines the eyelids and covers the eye becomes inflamed and swollen.

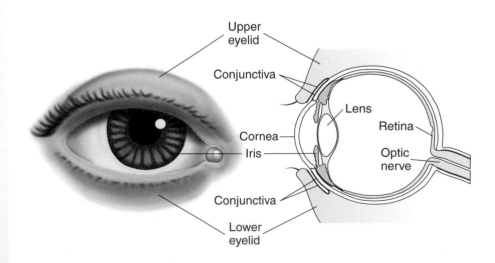

antibiotics. Or, the doctor may prescribe other medications, such as anti-histamines (ant-e-HISS-ta-meens), to treat conjunctivitis caused by allergies. Other helpful treatments include using warm water to wash away discharge around the eyes, and applying anti-inflammatory ointments or eyedrops inside the eyelids.

How Is Conjunctivitis Prevented?

People with the infectious type of conjunctivitis, which is contagious and thus can be spread, should wash their hands often. They also should use their own separate washcloths and towels rather than sharing with others. In addition, it is important that they avoid rubbing the eye affected, because this may spread the condition to the other eye.

Resources

Books

Cassel, Gary H., M.D., Michael D. Billig, O.D., and Harry G. Randall, M.D. *The Eye Book: A Complete Guide to Eye Disorders and Health*. Baltimore: Johns Hopkins University Press, 1998. A good book that is easy to read. It has a chapter on conjunctivitis and contains more information about other eye conditions.

Collins, James F. *Your Eyes: An Owner's Guide*. Englewood Cliffs, NJ: Prentice Hall, 1995. A useful nontechnical book on the subject.

Organization

The U.S. National Eye Institute posts a fact sheet about the cornea, corneal diseases, and conjunctivitis at its website. http://www.nei.nih.gov/textsite/publications/cornea.htm

▶ *See also*
Allergies
Cold

Constipation

Constipation is a condition that involves difficulty in having a bowel movement or involves having stools (solid waste material from the body) that are dry and hard.

KEYWORDS
for searching the Internet and other reference sources

Cathartics

Digestion

Fecal impaction

Intestines

Laxatives

What Is Constipation?

Normal bowel movement patterns vary from person to person. Some people move their bowels as often as after every meal. Other people may move their bowels every 3 days or so. Both of these patterns may be normal.

With constipation a person feels discomfort and has irregular bowel movements. The difficulty comes from the dry, hard condition of the stool. Constipation may be associated with many medical illnesses.

What Causes Constipation?

Several factors can contribute to constipation, such as not eating enough fiber or drinking enough fluids, inactivity, or not developing regular toilet habits. Certain medical conditions such as irritable bowel syndrome or hypothyroidism are associated with constipation. Sometimes the medicine people take for other illnesses causes them to become constipated. Pregnant women frequently develop constipation, also.

Constipation can occur when a person "withholds" stool and the intestines reabsorb the water in the stool, causing it to become harder. Withholding the stool can happen if a person is not comfortable having a bowel movement, for example, when traveling or if the toilet area is considered unsafe or unpleasant.

What Is the Treatment for Constipation?

Although many people take laxatives (LAK-sa-tivs) for constipation, doctors warn that these should not be taken regularly because the intestines may become sluggish and dependent on laxatives. Instead, it is recommended that people eat a diet that is rich in fiber. Foods that have fiber are whole grains, like bran or whole wheat, beans, fruits, and vegetables. Eating mostly foods that contain a lot of starch or sugar, like cookies and cakes, doesn't give the body enough fiber for good digestion and proper elimination. Also, it is important to drink sufficient amounts of water.

In serious cases of constipation, a person may need to be examined by a doctor and possibly be given an enema (EN-e-ma). This is a process of putting fluid into the rectum to loosen the stool. The doctor also may prescribe medication to help the patient regain regular bowel habits.

For a child who develops a serious case of constipation, the doctor may help by providing a habit-training program. In addition to being instructed about proper diet and increased water intake, the child may be given medicine to help develop regular toilet habits.

Can Constipation Be Prevented?

Most people can prevent constipation by following a regular routine for bowel movements. Here are some things that help prevent constipation:

- Eating foods rich in fiber
- Avoiding junk foods
- Drinking sufficient water every day
- Regular toilet habits
- Regular exercise
- Plenty of rest

Resources

Office of Disease Prevention and Health Promotion, National Health Information Center, Washington, DC. This office offers information on many diseases and disorders.
Telephone 800-336-4797 or 202-429-9091
http://odphp.osophs.dhhs.gov

The U.S. National Institutes of Health posts information about constipation on its website.
http://www.nih.gov/nia/health/pubpub/const.htm

▶ See also
Diarrhea
Hemorrhoids
Irritable Bowel Syndrome

Consumption *See* Tuberculosis

Convulsions *See* Seizures

Coronary *See* Heart Disease

Cretinism *See* Thyroid Disease

Creutzfeldt-Jakob Disease (CJD)

Creutzfeldt-Jakob disease (CJD) is a fatal disease that affects the brain. It is a form of human spongiform encephalopathy (SPUN-ji-form en-sef-a-LOP-a-thee), which means it causes the brain to become sponge-like as it deteriorates.

KEYWORDS
for searching the Internet and other reference sources

Infection

Dementia

Myoclonus

Neuromuscular system

Prions

Scrapie

Spongiform encephalopathies

What Is Creutzfeldt-Jakob Disease (CJD)?

Creutzfeldt-Jakob disease is a slowly progressing disease of the brain. While most people who contract the disease die within several months, some people decline slowly and may live several years after they are diagnosed. Creutzfeldt-Jakob disease usually affects older people.

Since Creutzfeldt-Jakob disease affects the brain, its primary symptom is dementia (de-MEN-sha). Some signs of dementia are disorientation, neglect of personal hygiene and grooming, and irritability. Other symptoms include fatigue, insomnia, and muscle twitching or sudden contractions. Medical treatment focuses on making people with CJD as comfortable as possible as a cure does not exist yet.

How Widespread Is Creutzfeldt-Jakob Disease?

Creutzfeldt-Jakob disease is rare. About 200 people are reported to have the disease in the United States, and it affects approximately 1 person per million worldwide. Mostly, if affects older people: approximately 6 people in every million worldwide between the ages of 70 to 74, with the mean age of death from CJD now at 67 years. About 90 percent of cases are reported to lead to death within 1 year after symptoms begin, with the remaining 10 percent of people with CJD declining over a 1- to 2-year period. Because CJD usually is a slowly progressing disease, symptoms may not begin for as long as 20 years after infection.

What Causes Creutzfeldt-Jakob Disease?

Creutzfeldt-Jakob disease is caused when a molecule called the prion protein, which is normally found in the brain, becomes abnormal. Scientists are not sure how prions ("proteinaceous infectious particles") work or how they cause disease.

Scientists are studying several types of CJD:

* genes are chemicals in the body that help determine a person's characteristics, such as hair or eye color. They are inherited from a person's parents and are contained in the chromosomes found in the cells of the body.

- In **sporadic** CJD, the gene* coding for the prion protein mutates (changes) spontaneously and begins to produce the abnormal prion protein. This protein can infect other brain cells.

- In **genetic** CJD, a mutated gene for the prion protein is inherited and passed from one generation to the next.

- In **iatrogenic** (i-at-ro-JEN-ik) CJD, the disease is transmitted from an infected person to a healthy person during a medical procedure such as transplant surgery or from receiving human growth hormone derived from the pituitary gland of an infected person.

"Mad Cow Disease"

In 1986, a brain disease called bovine (BO-vyne) spongiform encephalopathy (BSE) was discovered in cows. Termed "mad cow disease" because the infected cows stumbled and lost muscular coordination, the disease had been transmitted to the cows from feed made from ground sheep bones and parts. The sheep had a disease called scrapie (SCRAP-ee), which had been passed on to the cattle.

It was thought that mad cow disease could not be passed on to people, but the British Ministry of Health discovered a variant form of BSE in people younger than the average age for CJD cases. Countries all over Europe and other parts of the world began to ban the import of beef from Britain, and millions of cattle in Britain were killed in order to avoid spreading the disease. Many people turned to vegetarian diets, and many restaurants stopped serving beef.

Resources

U.S. National Institute of Neurological Disorders and Stroke (NINDS), Bethesda, MD 20892. NINDS posts a fact sheet about CJD at its website. The fact sheet includes referrals to other resources. http://www.ninds.nih.gov/patients/disorder/creutjab/cjd.htm

Creutzfeldt-Jakob Disease Foundation, P.O. Box 611625, North Miami, FL 33261-1625.

▶ *See also*
Alzheimer's Disease
Encephalitis
Kuru
Zoonoses

Crohn's Disease *See* Inflammatory Bowel Disease

Cross Eyes *See* Strabismus

Croup

Croup (KROOP) is a children's disease that is marked by a barking cough and loud noise when a child with croup inhales. Children with croup have difficulty breathing; parents often are worried by the dramatic sound effects at the beginning of the illness, but complete recovery from the viral infection that usually causes croup can be expected.

KEYWORDS
for searching the Internet and other reference sources

Angina trachealis

Epiglottitis

Infection

Respiratory system

What Is Croup?

The word croup is used to describe several conditions that cause a loud, barking cough and difficulty with breathing. Some croup-like conditions are caused by allergy, others may be caused by bacterial infections, but the majority of cases, about 75 percent, are caused by parainfluenza or other types of viruses.

All three types of croup cause the vocal cords and areas below them to become swollen and inflamed. As the swelling causes the upper airways to become narrower and more constricted, the pitch of the breathing sounds and the barking cough may become higher.

Adults are at risk for croup, but it is mainly a children's disease, affecting infants and toddlers especially, and children up to about age 12 years. Adult croup does not lead to the same narrowing of the upper airways as in children, because the airways of adults are wider and the supporting tissue is firmer than in children.

What Happens to People with Croup?

Diagnosis   The degree of obstruction of the airways is the doctor's most important consideration in diagnosing and treating croup. If the bronchi

Vaporizers

A cool mist vaporizer is a device that uses water and sometimes medication to create an aerosol vapor. The vaporizer can keep bedrooms humid (moist), which is helpful for croup or other respiratory conditions that benefit from moisture rather than dry air.

A steam vaporizer is a device that is filled with water. The water gives off steam when it is boiled. Steam vaporizers can cause burns and should not be used near children.

▶ *See also*
Infection

Influenza

Laryngitis

Pneumonia

Viral Infections

Whooping Cough

KEYWORDS
for searching the Internet and other reference sources

Adrenocorticotropin (ACTH)

Corticotropin-releasing hormone (CRH)

Cortisol

Endocrine system

Hormones

(breathing tubes), the lungs, or the epiglottis (the little finger-like tissue extension at the back of the throat) become infected, a child may be unable to breathe or swallow adequately and that is a true medical emergency. Most cases of croup, however, can be treated at home.

Mild croup   Cases of mild croup are treated at home with vaporizers and humidifiers. A makeshift steam room can be set up by closing the door of the bathroom and running hot water from a shower. The steam from the shower will put moisture into the child's airway, which can help open up the airway and relieve the child's cough. A cool-mist humidifier can be run in the child's room throughout the night.

Serious cases of croup   Signs of more serious croup infection are muscles of the neck or chest that sink in with each breath taken by the child. Serious croup infections require immediate medical treatment. Hospitals sometimes use mist therapy to increase room humidity. The child may be kept in what is called a croup tent to maximize the effect of the cool mist therapy. Inhaled medications may be prescribed to help control spasms and swellings in the upper airways.

How Dangerous Is Croup?

Most cases of croup clear up by themselves in five to six days or less with the hoarseness, cough, and other sounds of labored breathing subsiding gradually. Some cases may take longer. Stridor (STRY-dor), the high-pitched breathing sound, may persist, and ear infections or pneumonia are possible complications in some cases. When croup interferes with breathing, hospital care is usually needed. Ear infections or pneumonia are possible complications in some cases. Outbreaks of croup usually occur in the late fall or winter.

Cryptosporidiosis *See* Cyclosporiasis and Cryptosporidiosis

Cushing's Syndrome

Cushing's syndrome is a condition that occurs when the body is exposed to high levels of the hormone cortisol. Symptoms may include muscle weakness, extra body fat, excess hair, and emotional problems.

What Is Cushing's Syndrome?

Cushing's syndrome is an endocrine, or hormone*, condition. It occurs when the body is exposed to high levels of the hormone cortisol for long periods of time.

Cortisol and the endocrine system Cortisol is a hormone essential for life. It is involved in maintaining blood pressure and the immune system and in the body's handling of proteins, carbohydrates, and fats. It also helps the body respond to stress. However, too much cortisol has negative effects on the body.

Usually, cortisol production is tightly regulated by the interactions of three parts of the endocrine system:

1. A part of the brain called the hypothalamus (hy-po-THAL-mus) secretes corticotropin-releasing hormone (CRH).

2. CRH signals gland attached to the brain, the pituitary gland, to release adrenocorticotropin (ACTH).

3. ACTH signals the adrenal glands to make cortisol and release it into the bloodstream. The adrenal glands are a pair of organs located just above the kidneys in the abdominal cavity.

If something goes wrong with any of these glands or with the signaling system, the body may produce too much cortisol.

Tumors Certain tumors, either cancerous or noncancerous, can cause Cushing's syndrome. For example, noncancerous pituitary tumors that secrete ACTH are a cause of the condition. Tumors elsewhere in the body, such as in the lungs, also can produce ACTH, and tumors of the adrenal glands can cause overproduction of cortisol. Most cases of Cushing's syndrome are not inherited, but the tendency to develop tumors can be inherited.

Cortisone-based therapies Treatment with high doses of cortisone-based hormone medications for asthma, rheumatoid arthritis, lupus, and other inflammatory diseases is the most common reason people develop Cushing's syndrome.

What Are the Signs and Symptoms of Cushing's Syndrome?

In 1932, the American neurosurgeon Harvey Williams Cushing (1869–1939) described eight patients with symptoms of what later was named Cushing's syndrome. Dr. Cushing described how too much cortisol led to:

- obesity, especially of the face, neck, and upper body
- purplish stretch marks associated with weight gain
- thin and fragile skin that bruises easily
- slow wound healing
- weakened bones (osteoporosis)
- fatigue and weak muscles
- problems with sugar metabolism, which may lead to diabetes

* **hormones** are chemicals that are produced by different glands in the body. Hormones are like the body's ambassadors: they are created in one place but are sent through the body to have specific regulatory effects in different places.

The adrenal glands are a pair of organs located just above the kidneys in the abdominal cavity. In some people with Cushing's syndrome, the adrenal glands produce too much of the hormone cortisol.

▼

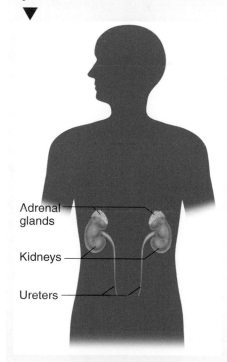

Adrenal glands

Kidneys

Ureters

- menstrual irregularities
- growth of excess hair
- high blood pressure
- irritability and depression.

How Is Cushing's Syndrome Diagnosed and Treated?

Diagnosis A doctor who sees a patient with symptoms suggestive of Cushing's syndrome will ask questions about the person's medical history and perform a physical exam. Laboratory tests, such as analysis of blood and urine, are used to measure cortisol levels. If cortisol levels are high, other tests are done to find out why. For example, imaging techniques for looking inside the body (such as CT scans* and MRIs*) can be used to look for tumors.

Treatment Treatment of tumors varies depending on the type. A tumor may be removed surgically, or it may be treated with radiation or chemotherapy. Sometimes Cushing's syndrome is treated with drugs to inhibit cortisol production. If Cushing's syndrome occurs as a side effect of hormone therapy, doctors can alter the dosage to minimize the side effects of the medication.

Altering hormone dosage and removal of tumors can lead to a full recovery, although sometimes the tumors come back. Because Cushing's syndrome can be difficult to diagnose, affected people sometimes live with the condition for years before it is diagnosed and treated.

Resources

The U.S. National Institute of Diabetes and Digestive and Kidney Diseases (NIDDK) posts a fact sheet about Cushing's syndrome at its website.
http://www.niddk.nih.gov/health/endo/pubs/cushings/cushings.htm

Cushing's Support and Research Foundation, Inc., 65 East India Row 22B, Boston, MA 02110.
Telephone 617-723-3824
http://world.std.com/~csrf/

Pituitary Tumor Network Association, 16350 Ventura Boulevard, Number 231, Encino, CA 91436.
Telephone 805-499-9973
http://www.pituitary.com

* **CT scans** or CAT scans are the shortened names for computerized axial tomography, which uses computers to view cross sections inside the body.

* **MRI** means magnetic resonance imaging, which uses magnets to view inside the body.

▶ *See also*
Hypertension
Metabolic Disease
Obesity
Osteoporosis
Stress-Related Illness

Cyclosporiasis and Cryptosporidiosis

Cyclosporiasis (sy-klo-spor-I-a-sis) and Cryptosporidiosis (krip-to-spo-rid-e-O-sis) are infections in the intestines that result from eating or drinking food or water contaminated by the parasites Cyclospora cayetanensis *and* Cryptosporidium parvum. *These infections can result in diarrhea, stomach cramps, and nausea.*

KEYWORDS
for searching the Internet
and other reference sources

Crypto

Infestation

Parasites

Protozoa

Thousands of people in Milwaukee, Wisconsin, started to get sick in early 1993. They had stomach pains, nausea, fever, and diarrhea, as if perhaps they had influenza. But authorities soon discovered that dangerous one-celled parasites* were in the city's water supply. When people drank water, the parasite caused cryptosporidiosis, one of several infections that parasites can cause.

In the end, more than 400,000 people came down with symptoms of cryptosporidiosis. More than 100 people died, including many who had other diseases like AIDS. The parasite had entered the water system from human waste in Lake Michigan, a water source for the city. Filters on the city's water plant had not removed the parasite. That problem has been remedied.

* **parasites** are creatures that live in and feed on the bodies of other organisms. The animal or plant harboring the parasite is called its host.

How Do People Get Cyclosporiasis and Cryptosporidiosis?

Cryptosporidiosis and cyclosporiasis, a closely related illness, are two of the most common infections that result from contaminated water and food. They (and similar illnesses) affect millions of people worldwide and are especially dangerous to children, the elderly, and people with other illnesses, especially those (like AIDS) that weaken the immune system. The infections are common in developing nations, but they also are found increasingly in developed nations like the United States that import food. For example, a 1996 outbreak of cyclosporiasis in Houston, Texas, was linked with raspberries imported from Guatemala.

Both cyclosporiasis and cryptosporidiosis result when humans eat food or drink water containing microscopic parasites from infected human or animal waste. The *Cyclospora cayetanensis* and *Cryptosporidium parvum* parasites also can enter the human body when people touch objects that have come in contact with infected fecal matter and then place fingers in their mouths. Fresh fruits and vegetables can become contaminated if they are irrigated with water that contains the parasites.

What Happens When People Get Cyclosporiasis and Cryptosporidiosis?

Symptoms   Although caused by different parasites, cyclosporiasis and cryptosporidiosis cause many of the same symptoms: watery diarrhea,

245

Did You Know?

Intestinal infections like cyclosporiasis and cryptosporidiosis are among the most common illnesses in the world. More than 2.2 million people worldwide died from illnesses that cause severe diarrhea, making it the sixth leading cause of death in 1998. All but 7,000 of those deaths occurred in low- and middle-income nations.

stomach pain, nausea, fever, and vomiting. Weight loss is common, because of the diarrhea and loss of appetite. The first symptoms of cyclosporiasis often appear a week after the parasite enters the body, but the first symptoms of cryptosporidiosis may appear as soon as two days after infection or as long as ten days after. The illnesses can last for a few days to two weeks. Infections from cyclosporiasis sometimes can last more than a month and return one or more times.

Diagnosis It can be hard to diagnose cyclosporiasis and cryptosporidiosis, because many illnesses can cause similar symptoms. If doctors suspect these infections, they may order tests to examine patients' stool for signs of the parasites.

Treatment The danger of intestinal infections like cyclosporiasis and cryptosporidiosis is dehydration from the loss of water through diarrhea. Doctors will remind patients to drink plenty of fluids, like water and sports drinks. Cyclosporiasis also can be treated with antibiotics. Cryptosporidiosis, however, has no special drug cure. Usually people will completely recover from either illness in a week or two. People with AIDS and other diseases that weaken the immune system need extra medical attention, because they are at higher risk of severe infections.

How Are These Infections Prevented?

Intestinal infections like cyclosporiasis and cryptosporidiosis are among the most common illnesses in the world. Several activities can lower the chances of getting these or similar intestinal illnesses:

- Washing hands frequently and thoroughly with hot water, especially after going to the bathroom, changing diapers, playing with animals or cleaning up after them, and gardening, because the soil can be contaminated by animal or human waste. It also is important to clean hands before eating.

- Washing fresh fruits and vegetables thoroughly before eating. Even fruit that can be peeled should be washed.

- Avoiding unfiltered water from lakes, rivers, and other sources. Even a sparkling spring might be contaminated and should not be used for drinking water. It also is important to avoid swallowing water in lakes and rivers as well as in swimming pools and spas, because chlorine might not be enough to kill the parasites.

Water quality varies, even in industrialized nations like the United States. Tap water led to the 1993 outbreak of cryptosporidiosis in Milwaukee. Some people choose to drink only bottled water or use special filters for drinking water and ice. When overseas, and especially when in developing nations, it is never a good idea to drink tap water or use ice made from tap water. It also is recommended that fruits and vegetables be avoided when traveling outside the United States, unless they can be cooked or peeled.

Resources

The U.S. National Center for Infectious Diseases has a Division of Parasitic Diseases that posts fact sheets about cyclosporiasis and crypto-sporidiosis at its website.
http://www.cdc.gov/ncidod/dpd/crypto.htm
http://www.cdc.gov/ncidod/diseases/cyclospo/cyclogen.htm

The U.S. Food and Drug Administration posts a *Bad Bug Book* at its website with fact sheets about *Cyclospora cayetanensis*, *Cryptosporidium parvum*, and other parasitic protozoa.
http://vm.cfsan.fda.gov/~mow/intro.html

▶ *See also*
AIDS and HIV
Diarrhea
Giardiasis
Parasitic Diseases

Cyst

A cyst is a small, balloon-like swelling anywhere in the body. A cyst may contain air, fluid, or solid content contained within a sac. Usually, cysts are harmless, but they may be removed surgically if they cause discomfort or distress to the people who have them.

KEYWORD
for searching the Internet and other reference sources

Dermatology

Where Are Cysts Found in the Body?

Cysts may develop in many areas on the inside or outside of the body. They may be found in the mouth around a developing tooth, in the skin around a hair follicle or sweat gland, in other glands, in the spinal cord, in the liver, in bone tissue, in ovaries*, and in other parts of the body.

Cysts form most often when fluid in a gland* becomes blocked in the ducts or tubes leading out of the gland. Sometimes cysts form because the glands are overactive and produce more fluid than the tissues can absorb. Another cause of cyst formation is the presence of parasites in vital organs, like the liver or brain.

* **ovaries** are the sexual glands in which eggs are formed in women.

* **glands** are organs that produce substances like hormones and chemicals that regulate body functions.

What Are the Different Types of Cysts?

Cysts are classified mainly by their location in the body. Some of the most common are:

- Alveolodental (al-vee-o-lo-DEN-tal) cysts form around a developing tooth

- Baker's cysts form around the knee joint

- Chocolate cysts form in the ovary (named for their dark brown fluid)

- Corpus luteum (KOR-pus LOO-tee-um) cysts (plural form is corpora lutea) are yellow bodies that form in the ovary when an egg is released during the normal reproductive cycle

▶ *See also*

Abscess

Tumor

KEYWORDS
for searching the Internet and other reference sources

Chest physical therapy

Gene therapy

Mucoviscidosis

Phenylalanine

Pulmonary system

*pneumonia is an inflammation of the lungs, usually caused by bacteria, viruses, or chemical irritants.

- Ependymal (e-PEN-di-mal) cysts form in the central canal of the spinal cord
- Ganglion (GANG-lee-on) cysts usually develops around the tendons or joints
- Lacteal (LAK-tee-al) or milk cysts form in the breast
- Sebaceous (se-BAY-shus) cysts form under the skin from plugged oil glands
- Solitary bone cysts form in long bones of children and adults
- Wens are sebaceous cysts that form on the scalp.

How Are Cysts Treated?

Most cysts do not need treatment. If cysts become painful, or if they form on visible parts of the body like the hand or around the ears, the doctor may remove them. Cysts can be removed by sucking out the fluid with a needle and syringe (aspiration) or with surgery. Surgery is more effective. When the fluid is removed with a needle, there is a tendency for the cyst to return. Sometimes cysts disappear without any treatment.

Cystic Fibrosis

Cystic fibrosis is an inherited condition in which glands produce excessively sticky mucus. The sticky material clogs the lungs, liver, pancreas, and intestines and makes it difficult to breathe and to digest food properly.

Rachel's Story

Rachel's parents were worried. They believed they provided all the proper care Rachel needed, just as they had for their older daughter when she was a baby. But Rachel failed to gain as much weight as other children her age, even though she seemed to have the typical appetite of an infant. Rachel also seemed to have more colds than other children had and a lot more colds than her older sister ever had. She coughed often and breathed with a wheezing sound. Then, around the time of her second birthday, Rachel developed pneumonia*.

Rachel's failure to gain weight and her frequent respiratory infections led her doctor to suspect that Rachel had cystic fibrosis (SIS-tik fy-BRO-sis), which is usually known by its initials, CF. Tests confirmed the diagnosis.

CF is a hereditary disease that affects about 30,000 children and adults in the United States. It is the most common hereditary condition that affects people of European ancestry, occurring in 1 of every 2,000

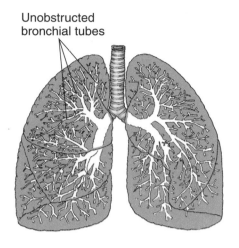

Unobstructed bronchial tubes

Healthy lungs

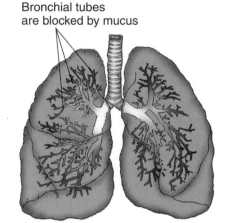

Bronchial tubes are blocked by mucus

Lungs with cystic fibrosis

Cystic fibrosis is a chronic disease in which the glands produce excessively sticky mucus that can clog the bronchial tubes in the lungs, making it difficult to breathe.

◀

live births. About 1,000 new cases of CF are diagnosed each year in the United States, usually by the time children reach their third birthday.

What Is Cystic Fibrosis?

Cystic fibrosis is a chronic, hereditary disease that affects many of the body's organ systems. In CF, some of the thin, easy-flowing mucus* in the body's respiratory and digestive systems become thicker. Glands* in the body produce mucus to do such things as lubricate the lungs, trap dust and bacteria that is inhaled through the nose, and protect the lining of the intestines from the acidic fluids that help digest food.

The glands in people with CF, however, produce sticky mucus that clogs the passageways in the lungs, which makes it difficult to breathe and leads to infections. The sticky mucus also blocks the easy flow of digestive acids and enzymes from the pancreas* and liver* to the intestines. Without adequate amounts of these digestive fluids in the intestines, people with CF cannot break down their food into the substances the body needs for nourishment.

What Causes Cystic Fibrosis?

CF is caused by a mutation in a gene* on chromosome 7. Chromosome 7 is one of 23 pairs of chromosomes that are part of each person's genetic makeup. The CF gene causes the production of a protein that lacks an important amino acid*, phenylalanine (fen-il-AL-a-neen). Without that amino acid, the protein hinders the ability of mucus to obtain the proper amounts of water and salt from the body, which the mucus needs to maintain its thin and easy-flowing texture. This turns the mucus into a dense, sticky substance that clogs the respiratory and digestive systems.

The obstructions in the lungs make it hard to breathe and can increase the risk of infections. The problems in the digestive system prevent the body from getting all the nutrients it needs from food. It also means people

* **mucus** is a combination of water, salt, cells, and other material that forms a coating that lines the respiratory and digestive systems.

* **glands** are groups of cells that act on substances in the bloodstream to change them for use in other parts of the body or to remove them from the body.

* **pancreas** is an organ in the upper abdomen that secretes enzymes to help with digestion.

* **liver** is a large organ with many functions, including secreting the digestive fluid bile.

* **genes** are chemicals in the body that help determine a person's characteristics, such as hair or eye color. They are inherited from a person's parents and are contained in the chromosomes found in the cells of the body.

* **amino acids** are the chief components of proteins.

249

Cystic fibrosis is a chronic disease caused by a mutation in a gene located on chromosome 7. If both parents carry the CF gene, there is a 50 percent chance that their child may carry the gene too, and a 25 percent chance that their child may have CF. ▶

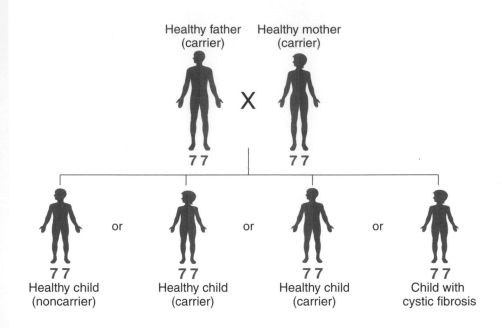

Healthy father (carrier)   Healthy mother (carrier)

7 7   7 7

or   or   or

7 7   7 7   7 7   7 7
Healthy child   Healthy child   Healthy child   Child with
(noncarrier)   (carrier)   (carrier)   cystic fibrosis

*carriers are people who have the genes for a disease without having the disease itself.

with CF often have thicker, foul-smelling bowel movements, because fat in food cannot be broken down by digestive fluids and absorbed.

A person may carry the CF gene on one of the two copies of chromosome 7 and not have any signs of CF. This person is called a carrier*. Parents can pass the CF gene to many generations of offspring. When a person has the CF gene on both copies of chromosome 7, then that person will have CF. When parents are both carriers, such as Rachel's parents, their children have a one in four chance of having CF. Estimates are that 10 million Americans, or 1 out of 29, carry the CF gene.

How Do Doctors Know Someone Has CF?

As far back as the 1600s, there were descriptions of children with symptoms of cystic fibrosis. It was not until 1938 that it was recognized as a separate disease, because lung infections are common to many conditions. Even today, the symptoms of CF sometimes can be confused with pneumonia or asthma.

Symptoms   Cystic fibrosis affects each person differently. Many people with CF do not appear to be severely ill. In general, people with CF have some or all of these symptoms:

▶

Lung infections are common in cystic fibrosis. Seen under a light microscope are tissue samples from a healthy lung (left) and from a lung affected by cystic fibrosis (right). © *1998 Custom Medical Stock Photo.*

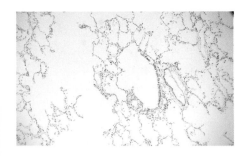
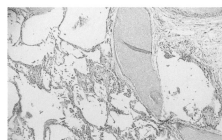

250

- Salty-tasting skin and sweat
- Persistent cough or wheezing
- Many respiratory infections
- Bulky, smelly stools or bowel movements
- Nasal polyps (small growths in the nose)
- Enlargement of the fingertips and toes (clubbing)

Also, people with CF may eat large amounts of food but still be hungry. The food is not being digested properly, because the mucus is blocking the ability of digestive enzymes* and acids to break down food and absorb nutrients. Large portions of the poorly digested food are passed out during bowel movements. The individual may lose weight.

*enzymes are natural substances that speed up specific chemical reactions in the body.

Later the pancreas may clog up and fail to secrete the enzymes essential to normal digestion. The liver becomes clogged, which may lead to cirrhosis (si-RO-sis), a condition in which the liver becomes hardened and fails. Diabetes also develops frequently in people with CF as they get older.

Diagnosis   Doctors may begin to suspect CF soon after birth when the baby becomes ill with repeated respiratory infections, fails to gain weight despite a healthy appetite, and shows other symptoms of CF. In addition, about 10 percent of infants with CF have intestinal blockage due to thick mucus that is apparent at birth. Many of the symptoms of CF are common in people who do not have the disease, but there are tests to confirm a person has CF.

A sweat test is considered the best method to diagnose cystic fibrosis because it is relatively easy to perform and is accurate. The test determines the salt content of perspiration. Although sweat can seem salty in people without CF, the level of salt in the perspiration of people with CF is higher. A more complicated test looks for the CF gene on both copies of chromosome 7.

People with CF can use a device called a nebulizer to inhale medication that helps loosen mucus secretions in the lungs. *Simon Fraser/RVI, Newcastle-upon-Tyne, Science Photo Library/Custom Medical Stock Photo.*

A Morning Ritual for Rachel

After her doctor determined that Rachel had cystic fibrosis, her parents worried she would not have a chance to do many of the same things as her older sister or other children. But as she grew, Rachel went to school, participated in sports, and did many other everyday activities.

Most people with CF get treatment that involves helping them breathe more easily and digest food better, which makes day-to-day activities less difficult. Although their symptoms can range from mild to severe, many people with CF receive treatments similar to Rachel's.

For example, Rachel receives chest physical therapy. Each morning, her parents vigorously thump Rachel's back and chest to help loosen the thick mucus in her lungs so she can cough it out. They learned the technique from a physical therapist after Rachel was diagnosed with CF.

Coughing is one of the main ways that people with CF can clear the mucus from their lungs. In school, Rachel's teachers were told to expect her to cough often. Although the teacher and the students knew Rachel

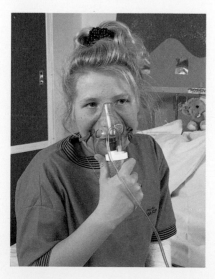

Turning on the CF Gene

In 1989, scientists discovered the location of the CF gene. If they could replace the defective gene with a normal gene, then they would be able to cure the cells that produce the defective CF protein. This would mean the mucus in the respiratory and digestive systems would be thin and easy flowing as opposed to thick and sticky.

In 1990, two teams of researchers were able to correct CF cells in lab dishes, by adding normal copies of the gene. In the spring of 1993 the first experimental dose was given to a person with CF. In October 1993, scientists determined that gene treatment had repaired a damaged gene in a human patient.

Gene therapy is a complicated experimental process. Scientists are beginning to understand what methods can be used to deliver the gene to the parts of the body where it can do its work. And they are studying how often the treatment would need to be repeated to assure the best results.

It could be that the gene therapy never would be able fix all of the defective genes, but it might cause enough of them to work properly to improve the quality of life for people with CF.

Boomer Fights Back

When Gunnar Esaison was diagnosed in 1993 with cystic fibrosis, his father, Boomer Esaison, decided to fight back. The Cincinnati Bengals quarterback, National Football League star, and television sports reporter had been a fierce competitor for many years. Now, his greatest battle became the fight against CF.

The NFL star started the Boomer Esaison Foundation, with the main goal being to find a cure for CF. The Foundation supports basic research and clinical trials for new CF treatments.

had CF, they did not make a big deal about her coughing. Rachel kept her own box of tissues on her desk, so she could cough the mucus into it and toss it into a nearby garbage can.

Rachel also participated in physical education classes. Exercise is another way that people with CF loosen the mucus in their lungs. Sometimes Rachel got tired more quickly than the other children, because she could not breathe as easily. But she joined in many of the exercises and games on most days.

At lunch and other times she ate a meal or snacks, Rachel took pills. The pills contained enzymes to help her digest food. Without them, the mucus in her digestive system would prevent her from getting the nutrients she needs from food. Even with the enzyme pills, Rachel and others with CF often need to take vitamin supplements and eat a diet rich in nutrients to assure they get the proper nourishment.

Rachel and others with CF also take antibiotics to prevent or treat lung infections. Sometimes, the antibiotics are taken as pills or inhaled into the lungs using a device called a nebulizer. People with CF also sometimes take prescription medications that thin the mucus and help reduce lung inflammation, which makes breathing easier and helps reduce the number of lung infections.

Perhaps the most exciting news for people with CF like Rachel was the discovery of the CF gene in 1989. It has led to research into gene therapy.

Living with CF

Once, CF almost always caused death in childhood. But treatments in recent decades have allowed many people with cystic fibrosis to live into adulthood. As with children, the symptoms for an adult can range from mild to severe, but eventually the recurring infections in the lungs begin to damage the lung's ability to function. This is the usual reason people with CF eventually die.

The Cystic Fibrosis Foundation says that now the average life expectancy of people with CF is 31 years. That is many years longer than in the past, but it still means only half of the people with CF will live that long. About half will live longer. With treatment, people with CF are able to do many of the things that other people do. And with work continuing in gene therapy, there is optimism that CF research is advancing toward a cure.

Resources

Books

Grinshaw, Joshua. *My Heart Is Full of Wishes*. Austin, TX: Raintree-Steck-Vaughn, 1995. A young boy with CF describes his dreams.

Harris, Ann. *Cystic Fibrosis: The Facts*. New York: Oxford University Press, 1995.

Silverstein, Alvin. *Cystic Fibrosis*. New York: Venture Books, 1994.

Organization

Cystic Fibrosis Foundation, 6931 Arlington Rd., Bethesda, MD 20814
http://www.cff.org

Cystitis *See* Urinary Tract Infection

Cytomegalovirus

Cytomegalovirus (CMV) is a very common virus. In most cases, its presence causes few or no symptoms at all. In people with weakened immune systems, however, it may cause severe illness. In fetuses, it may cause brain damage or birth defects.

What Is Cytomegalovirus (CMV)?

Cytomegalovirus (sy-to-MEG-a-lo-vy-rus) is a very common virus, with close to 85 percent of the U.S. population carrying antibodies to it, according to the U.S. National Institutes of Health. That means most Americans have been exposed to this virus. CMV may be present in urine, saliva, blood, breast milk, or semen. CMV can remain in the body for a long time without causing symptoms of illness, and most people who carry the virus probably picked it up during childhood.

Groups at risk for health problems   CMV infections can cause serious problems for people with immune disorders or weakened immune systems, such as people having organ transplants or cancer chemotherapy, or people with AIDS. About 40 percent of HIV and AIDS patients develop CMV retinitis (re-ti-NY-tis), an eye disease that can cause blindness. The virus also can be dangerous to fetuses, if transmitted during pregnancy, or to babies after birth if transmitted from the mother's milk. People who need blood transfusions or bone marrow transplantation also are at risk for CMV infection, and blood and bone marrow must be screened for the virus before use. The same blood screening is done for newborn infants who have a low weight at birth.

What Happens When People Have CMV Infections?

Symptoms   Newborn infants who survive a prenatal infection from cytomegalovirus may not weigh very much at birth. The infant may have fever and may appear yellowish, which indicates the child may have jaundice (a sign of liver disease). This infection can be very serious for an infant because it can cause many complications and disabilities. In older children and adults, CMV usually does not cause symptoms. When it does, symptoms may vary from mild to serious, and include fever lasting from one to two weeks, an illness that seems like mononucleosis, hepatitis, and sometimes a rash.

▶ *See also*
Asthma
Cirrhosis
Genetic Diseases
Pneumonia

KEYWORDS
for searching the Internet and other reference sources

Ganciclovir

Foscarnet

Infection

Retinitis

Diagnosis Cytomegalovirus is diagnosed by isolating CMV antibodies from urine, blood, or tissues. CMV can remain in the body for months or years after initial infection, however, so the presence of the antibodies indicates only that the person has been infected at some point in the past. The doctor usually interprets the lab findings as part of an overall examination, review of symptoms, and complete medical history.

Treatment Cytomegalovirus infections are treated with antiviral drugs. When illnesses are acute (severe), treatment may require intravenous (through a vein) injections for up to two weeks. People with CMV retinitis must remain on antiviral drugs for their lifetime.

Prevention Many people acquire CMV during childhood by sharing toys or by touching the mouth with unwashed hands. Frequent handwashing by children and by adults can help reduce transmission.

Resource

The U.S. National Institute of Allergy and Infectious Diseases (NIAID) posts a fact sheet about cytomegalovirus infection at its website. http://www.niaid.nih.gov/factsheets/cmv.htm

▶ *See also*

AIDS and HIV

Blindness

Hepatitis

Immunodeficiency

Jaundice

Mononucleosis, Infectious

Pneumonia

Pregnancy, Complications of

Viral Infections

D

Dandruff *See* **Skin Conditions**

Deafness and Hearing Loss

Deafness is the partial or complete loss of hearing. Hearing loss and deafness may be present from birth, as a result of many possible causes, or may begin later in life as a result of age-related changes in the ear, disease, injury, or excessive exposure to noise.

KEYWORDS
for searching the Internet and other reference sources

Audiology

Audiometry

Cochlear implant

Otology

Otolaryngology

Kathy Peck was a guitarist in the 1970s and 1980s in a rock band known as the Contractions. They played a mix of punk and new wave music in San Francisco and toured across the United States. The band gained some critical and popular success, playing shows with such groups as Duran Duran. But in the mid-1980s, Peck realized she was losing some of her hearing. All those years of playing loud music and attending concerts had damaged her ears, as had happened also to musician Pete Townshend of the Who. When Kathy Peck and F. Gordon, M.D., attended an especially loud concert in 1988, they decided to make a difference. They started H.E.A.R. (Hearing Education and Awareness for Rockers), a group that aims to prevent hearing loss among musicians and their fans. H.E.A.R.

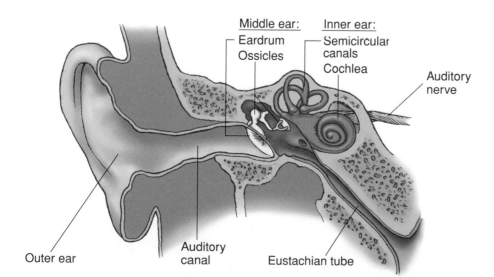

Anatomy of the ear. As sound waves travel through the ear, they are converted into electrochemical messages that are sent along more than 30,000 nerve connections to the brain. The brain then interprets these messages as words and other sounds.

Anatomy of the Ear

- **Pinna** (PIN-na) is the medical term for what most people mean when they say "ear": the part of the ear that protrudes from the head and is used to hold up eyeglasses and to wear earrings.

- **Eardrum** (tympanic membrane) is the thin, flexible layer of semi-transparent tissue that forms the dividing wall between the outer ear and the middle ear.

- **Ossicles** (OSS-i-kulz) are the three smallest, most delicate bones in the body: the malleus (MAL-ee-uss) looks like a hammer; the incus (ING-kuss) looks like an anvil; and the stapes (STAY-peez) looks like a stirrup.

- **Cochlea** (KOKE-lee-a) is the organ of hearing that resembles the shell of a snail.

- **Cilia** (SILL-ee-a) are the delicate hairs in the inner ear.

* **earwax,** also known as cerumen (se-ROO-men), is the waxlike substance in the ear that traps dust and other particles to prevent them from damaging the inner ear.

promotes wearing earplugs to reduce loud music to a level that does not damage the ear.

Rock music is not the only cause of noise-related ear damage: excessive exposure to power tools and other forms of machinery is one of the most common causes of deafness and hearing loss in the United States. Overall, more than 28 million Americans have some form of hearing loss.

What Is Hearing?

Hearing depends on the ability of sound waves to travel through the various parts of the ear. As sound waves travel through the ear, they are converted into electrochemical messages that are sent along more than 30,000 nerve connections to the brain. The brain then interprets these messages as words and other sounds.

How sounds are heard   Sounds actually are waves of energy that move through the air. Sometimes it is even possible to feel them, as when a hand is placed for a few moments next to a loudspeaker.

The pinna* is the fleshy, visible part of the outer ear that captures the sound waves. It directs sound waves down a short tunnel, called the ear canal. The canal ends at the eardrum*, which vibrates when sound waves reach it.

The vibrating eardrum causes the bones (ossicles*) that are connected to it to begin vibrating as well. The ossicles are three tiny bones in the air-filled middle ear. As the bones move, the sound waves are transferred through another thin layer of tissue into the inner ear.

The most complex action in the ear occurs in the inner ear, deep within the skull. The sound waves first enter the cochlea, which contains liquid and is lined with cilia (tiny strands of hair). The liquid in the cochlea begins to vibrate and causes the microscopic hairs to move, too. The movement of the hairs stimulates nerves that are connected to the brain, which interprets the signal as a particular word or sound.

Hearing loss and deafness   People with total deafness can hear no sounds at all. Others have partial deafness, which means they may have trouble hearing certain sounds unless someone is speaking close to them. Some people slowly start to lose their ability to hear, and the problem gets worse as time passes. Hearing loss may be temporary, such as when ear wax* builds up. If the wax is removed properly by a health professional, hearing returns. But some forms of total or partial hearing loss are permanent.

What Causes Hearing Loss?

There are basically three types of hearing loss: conductive, sensorineural (sen-sor-i-NOOR-al), and a mixed form that combines conductive and sensorineural hearing loss.

Conductive hearing loss   Conductive hearing loss occurs when sound waves are not transferred (conducted) completely from the outer and middle ear to the inner ear. If sound is imagined as waves of water, then conductive hearing loss occurs when something is creating a "dam" that blocks the sound waves. This dam can be many things, such as the buildup of earwax in the ear, water from swimming in the ear canal, or an infection that causes part of the ear to malfunction. Other causes include:

- Damaged eardrums: Sometimes the eardrum gets a tear or hole in it, which causes it to lose some or all of its ability to vibrate properly. Such damage may occur if a cotton swab or other object is placed too far inside the ear; if an explosion or gunshot or other extremely loud sound occurs too close to the ear; or as a result of an ear infection, a head injury, or a sudden or extreme change in air pressure.

- Abnormal bone growth: The ossicles (OSS-i-kulz) are the tiny bones in the middle ear that work together in a very small space to conduct sound from the ear drum to the inner ear. If they grow too much or too little or are damaged, they cannot do their jobs well. This problem may be present from birth or it may occur as children grow.

Sensorineural hearing loss   Sensorineural hearing loss occurs when there is a problem with some part of the inner ear or with the nerves that send messages from the inner ear to the brain. This type of hearing loss is more common than conductive hearing loss and more difficult to treat. Some estimates say that about 90 percent of hearing loss results from sensorineural problems. The most common cause of sensorineural hearing loss is change in the inner ear as people age. Not all older people experience sensorineural hearing loss, but many do. Common forms include:

- Presbycusis (press-bi-KOO-sis), the most common form, starts gradually for many people when they are in their forties or fifties.

200 YEARS AGO: LUDWIG VAN BEETHOVEN

The composer Ludwig van Beethoven (1770–1827) created some of music's most important symphonies even though he spent most of his life struggling with hearing loss and deafness. He began to experience mild episodes of hearing loss when he was about 28 years old. His hearing loss grew progressively worse until he was left completely deaf at the age of 44.

Beethoven continued to compose great works. Contemporaries reported that he placed his ear to the piano while he played in order to sense the vibrations of his compositions. Medical historians are uncertain as to how Beethoven became deaf, although they believe nerve damage and otosclerosis (o-to-skler-O-sis), which damages the bones in the ears, are the likeliest causes.

Watching the Volume Control

Loud music is fun but it can damage the hair in the inner ear and lead to permanent hearing loss. It can be a special problem for those who listen to music through earphones.

Even two hours of loud music can damage the ear. Doctors advise those who listen to music to keep the volume at a level where other sounds and conversation still can be heard. If other people can hear the music from earphones, then it is too loud to be safe. At concerts, ear plugs can lower damaging sound levels.

The same advice about protecting the ears applies to those who work regularly with loud machines, including power tools, lawn mowers, and leaf blowers.

More than 50 percent of people age 75 and older have some form of presbycusis.

- Damage to the cilia (SILL-ee-a), the delicate hairs in the inner ear. Loud noises can damage the cilia, as can poor blood supply to the inner ear resulting from high blood pressure, heart disease, smoking, or poor nutrition. Infections, tumors, and some medications also may damage the cilia and nearby parts of the inner ear or nerves to the brain.

- Genetic disorders may cause deafness from birth by interfering with the proper development of the inner ear or nerves to the brain.

- Injuries to the ear or head, such as a skull fracture, may cause sensorineural hearing loss.

- Ménière's (men-YERZ) disease affects more than 3 million people in the United States, many of them between the ages of 30 and 60. It can cause sensorineural hearing loss, vertigo and dizziness, and a ringing in the ears called tinnitus (ti-NY-tis).

Mixed hearing loss   Mixed hearing loss involves any combination of conductive hearing loss and sensorineural hearing loss. For example, loud noise can damage the ear drum, which would cause conductive hearing loss. But loud noise also can damage the hairs in the inner ear, which would be sensorineural hearing loss. If both occur, people are said to have mixed hearing loss.

When Sounds Begin to Fade

Hearing loss or deafness that is present from birth usually is first discovered by parents. They might begin to notice that loud sounds do not startle the baby or cause the baby to turn toward them. By school age, all children should have had their hearing tested, either by the family doctor or in school.

Hearing loss at later ages often is not recognized at first. People may find they can hear almost as well by increasing the volume on the television set or by moving closer to someone who is speaking, but they may not realize they are doing these things. Other signs of hearing loss include needing people to repeat what they have said; complaining that other people are mumbling; misunderstanding what people have said; and not hearing the phone, doorbell, or voices calling from other rooms. Often, the voices of women and children cause earlier problems, because the hair cells that recognize their higher-pitched voices are the first to fail.

Diagnosis   Doctors use several tests to diagnose hearing loss. One involves patients listening on earphones for a variety of tones and signaling when they are heard and when they disappear. A related test involves a special device that is placed behind the ear and transmits tones directly to the inner ear through the skullbone called the mastoid. If these tones are recognized better than those from the earphone test, it usually means the hearing problem is in the middle ear. Another test involves understanding various words as they are spoken through earphones.

Treating Hearing Loss

Treatment for ear wax buildup or infections can reverse some forms of hearing loss. Surgery to repair damaged ear drums or the bones of the middle ear also is possible.

Hearing aids   The most common device used to amplify sound is the hearing aid. Aids come in various forms that fit in or behind the ear and can help make sounds louder and clearer. They cannot completely restore lost hearing, but they can make it easier for many people to hear sounds. Audiologists are trained specialists who help select, fit, and monitor the use of hearing aids for both children and adults.

Cochlear implants   A cochlear (KOKE-lee-ar) implant is a complex device that replaces the work of the delicate hair cells (cilia) of the inner ear. A receiver worn behind the ear captures sound waves and transmits them to a receiver that is surgically placed inside the skull. This receiver then stimulates the nerves that the brain uses to interpret sounds. The surgery can be expensive, and it does not work for everyone, but for some it can be an effective way to partially restore hearing.

Living with Deafness and Hearing Loss

People with deafness and hearing loss usually learn to read lips and to use sign language for conversation. Other ways to improve activities of daily living include:

- Closed caption televisions that display words as people speak.
- Lights that flash when the phone or doorbell rings.
- Enhanced telephone services and telephones.
- Dogs trained to alert their human companions to sounds, like the phone ringing, a baby crying, or the person's name being called.

Many people with deafness and hearing loss take pride in the many ways that deafness education and deaf culture enrich the lives of people who can hear.

Resources

Books

Carmen, Richard. *Consumer Handbook on Hearing Loss and Hearing Aids: A Bridge to Healing.* Auricle Ink Publishers, 1998.

Turkington, Carol A. *The Hearing Loss Sourcebook: A Complete Guide to Coping With Hearing Loss and Where to Get Help.* New York: Plume, 1997.

Organizations

U.S. National Institute on Deafness and Other Communication Disorders, National Institutes of Health, 31 Center Drive, MSC 2320,

Bethesda, MD 20892-2320. NIDCD publishes brochures, posts fact sheets, provides referrals to other organizations, and offers a *Kids and Teachers* section at its website.
Telephone 301-496-7243 (voice) or 301-402-0252 (TTY)
http://www.nih.gov/nidcd/

American Speech-Language-Hearing Association, 10801 Rockville Pike, Rockville, MD 20852.
Telephone 800-638-8255 or 301-897-5700 (TTY)
http://www.asha.org

American Society for Deaf Children (ASDC), P.O. Box 1510, Olney, MD 20830-1510. ASDC supports parents and families of deaf children and the professionals who work with them, stressing the use of sign language in the home, school, and community.
Telephone 800-942-ASDC
http://www.deafchildren.org

H.E.A.R. (Hearing Education and Awareness for Rockers), P.O. Box 460847, San Francisco, CA 94146. Information on safe volume levels for music, and on ear plugs for both musicians and fans.
Telephone 415-773-9590
http://www.hearnet.com

Dehydration *See* Shock

Dementia *See* Alzheimer's Disease

Dengue Fever

Dengue, or dengue fever, is an infectious tropical disease caused by a virus passed from person to person by a mosquito. Also sometimes called Aden fever or breakbone fever, dengue causes severe pain in the bones, joints, and muscles. In most cases, dengue fever goes away in a week or two without treatment, but sometimes it causes shock, hemorrhaging, and death.

Who Gets Dengue?

Dengue (DENG-gee, English; DAIN-gay, Spanish) affects millions of people each year in tropical and subtropical regions. It is especially common in southeastern Asia and is also found in Latin America and the Caribbean, including Puerto Rico. Sometimes dengue may also appear in temperate climates in summer. Only very rarely does it occur in the United States.

Although dengue sometimes breaks out in epidemics, it is not spread directly from person to person. Instead, it is spread by the bite of a

▶ *See also*
Dietary Deficiencies
Ear Infections
German Measles
Heart Disease
Infection
Tinnitus
Tumor
Vertigo

KEYWORDS
for searching the Internet and other reference sources

Aden fever

Aëdes mosquitoes

Breakbone fever

Hemorrhagic fevers

tropical mosquito whose scientific name is *Aëdes* (a-EE-dez). The *Aëdes* mosquito picks up the dengue arbovirus* by biting a person who has dengue (people are the main source of the virus), and when the mosquito bites someone else, it infects the next person with the virus. The virus then multiplies in the new person's body, causing the disease symptoms.

Does Dengue Cause Broken Bones?

Dengue does not cause broken bones, but the severe pain that often accompanies it may be the reason why it is called "breakbone fever." Its symptoms begin very abruptly, several days after infection. In addition to bone, joint, and muscle pain, there may be high fever, a rash, headache, and pain behind the eyes. The symptoms usually subside after five to seven days, return a few days later, and then go away entirely.

After recovery from dengue, people may feel weak and psychologically* depressed. These feelings may last for days or weeks, but dengue is rarely fatal. In a small percentage of cases, people get a severe form of the disease, called dengue hemorrhagic* fever, which causes internal bleeding. This sometimes turns into an even more dangerous condition called dengue shock syndrome. According to the World Health Organization, these severe forms of dengue kill approximately 24,000 children in tropical countries each year, although most people who get these diseases recover.

What Is the "Dengue Triad"?

In diagnosing dengue fever, doctors look for three main signs or symptoms called the "dengue triad": (1) fever, (2) rash, and (3) pain, including headache. Blood tests may be done to help in the diagnosis. In areas where dengue is uncommon, the physician may also ask if the patient has recently been in a tropical country.

How Do Doctors Treat Dengue?

There is no specific treatment for a typical case of dengue fever, which runs its course and clears up by itself. Doctors usually recommend bed rest and drinking plenty of fluids. They may also prescribe pain-relieving medications to ease symptoms.

How Is Dengue Prevented?

Prevention requires control or eradication of *Aëdes* mosquitoes, and protection against their bites. The *Aëdes* mosquito also spreads other diseases, such as yellow fever, making public health improvements especially important. There is no available drug or vaccine that is effective against the dengue virus.

Resources

The U.S. National Center for Infectious Diseases at the Centers for Disease Control and Prevention (CDC) posts a fact sheet about dengue at its website.

http://www.cdc.gov/ncidod/dvbid/dhfacts.htm

The U.S. and the World

- Dengue fever exists in more than 100 countries, but occurs mostly in tropical and subtropical areas of Asia, Africa, and Central and South America. Overall, as many as 2.5 billion people worldwide are at risk.

- Some cases have occurred in the United States, but most often in people who have traveled recently to other countries. The *Aëdes* mosquito also can be found along the border between Texas and Mexico.

- The World Health Organization reports that approximately 500,000 people worldwide—almost 90 percent under age 15—are hospitalized every year with dengue fever. Millions more are infected but are not hospitalized.

- Approximately 24,000 people die from dengue each year, most of them children or young adults.

* **arbovirus** is a virus that multiplies inside blood-feeding insects and is transferred from host to host by insect bites.

* **psychological** refers to mental processes including feelings and emotions.

* **hemorrhage** means heavy and uncontrolled bleeding, often in the internal organs.

The *Aëdes* mosquito picks up the dengue virus by biting a person who has it and then transfers the virus to the next person it bites. © *1991 Science Photo Library. All rights reserved. Custom Medical Stock Photo.*

Why Is Dengue on the Return?

Dengue fever seemed to be disappearing, but by the late 1970s it had reemerged as an infectious disease that was spreading rapidly worldwide and growing in number of cases, making an especially dramatic reappearance in Latin America. Researchers see several possible reasons for the return of dengue and its spread, including:

- Mosquito-eradication programs may have lapsed due to lack of funding and possible concerns about pesticides.

- More people have crowded into cities with poor sanitation.

- More people are traveling internationally.

- Global warming may be allowing the *Aëdes* mosquito to increase its range.

According to a 1998 estimate by the World Health Organization, dengue is now prevalent in over 100 countries, with tens of millions of people infected each year.

▶ See also
  Viral Infections
  Yellow Fever

The World Health Organization (WHO) posts a fact sheet about dengue at its website.
http://www.who.int/ctd/html/dengue.html

Depression *See* Depressive Disorders

Depressive Disorders

Depressive (de-PRES-iv) disorders are mental disorders that cause long periods of excessive sadness and affect a person's feelings, thoughts, and behavior.

Jodie's Story

Even when the sun shines brightly, Jodie feels darkness everywhere she looks. She used to sleep so soundly that her father said he needed a cannon blast to wake her. In recent weeks, however, she rises unexpectedly in the gray light before dawn. She lies awake, staring at shadows from the headlights of passing cars and crying as the shapes slowly cross her ceiling.

Why would Jodie cry over a thing like that? Lately, so many odd things bring tears to her eyes. She is tired constantly. She cannot concentrate. Sometimes when she tries to solve a simple math problem in class or decide what to have for lunch, it seems as if her brain will not work. Jodie used to love to go with her friends to get a soda after school. Now all she wants to do is get home to her room and be alone. Nothing is fun, not her favorite books or television shows or even foods. Sometimes Jodie is annoyed at things and people, but she cannot explain why. Mostly, she feels sadder than she ever has felt.

For weeks, Jodie's friends have told her to snap out of it. She thinks to herself, "I want to, but what would the point be? I wish I knew what was wrong!"

What Are Depressive Disorders?

Jodie has depression (de-PRESH-un), a disorder that affects more than 17 million people in the United States. Although people often say that they are "depressed" when they feel down, this is not the same thing as the mental disorder called depression. Award-winning author William Styron, who wrote the book *Sophie's Choice*, suffered from depression. In *Darkness Visible*, Styron's book about his depression, he calls the disorder a "veritable howling tempest in the brain." He compares depression to a storm that blows away all of a person's usual feelings and abilities to cope with life.

All children and adults, and even apparently some animals, feel sad at times. Perhaps it is because a relative has died or a person's favorite team has lost an important game. For most people, the mood passes after a while. Within a short time, they find themselves getting excited about a day at the beach, a visit from a favorite aunt, or a good grade on a test. They even might forget what made them so sad. If someone breaks a promise or has an argument with a friend, the sadness may return, but only for a few hours or a couple of days. These are all examples of the regular ups and downs of life.

However, people with depression have long periods when nothing seems to make their mood better. It affects their whole body and mind: how they feel, think, and behave. The good news is that, if they get professional help, more than 80 percent of people with depression will feel better, often within a few weeks.

Major depression Depression comes in many forms. One is called major depression, also known as clinical (KLIN-i-kal) depression. This type involves excessive sadness and/or loss of interest in activities. The symptoms must last for at least two weeks and go along with other mental and physical symptoms. In some cases, the down period lasts for many weeks or months. At times, a person with major depression may feel as if the disease has gone away on its own. "Normal" feelings return, like the ones they used to experience. But like a tide that moves in and

KEYWORDS
*for searching the Internet
and other reference sources*

Bipolar disorder

Dysthymia

Major depression

Mental disorders

Mood disorders

Suicide

Did You Know?

- As many as 1 in 33 children may have depression, according to the Center for Mental Health Services, a U.S. government agency.

- For teenagers, the rate of depression may be as high as 1 in 8.

- The majority of people who commit suicide have a depressive disorder.

DEPRESSION AND CREATIVITY

Many famous writers, composers, and artists suffered through periods of depression. These include the writers Herman Melville (*Moby-Dick*) and Mary Shelley (*Frankenstein*) and the artists Vincent van Gogh and Michelangelo.

Manic depression, with its swings between intense sadness and extreme happiness, has been a particular problem for many people with great creative talent. One reason artists sometimes are called "temperamental" may be because many have struggled with a disorder that made them seem extremely moody. Of course, not all writers, artists, and musicians experience depression. Still, some studies suggest that people in these careers are more likely to show signs of depressive disorders than people in other fields.

- Does the depression of creative people put them in touch with feelings that they then express creatively in books, poems, music, and art?
- Does creative talent make a person more likely to act or to seem depressed?
- Do healthy creative people simply act differently from the rest of society?

Different people have different answers for these questions. The discussion about the possible link between depression and creativity goes on.

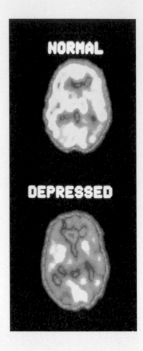

▲

Doctors and researchers use computer-generated positron emission tomography (PET) scans to study how the brain functions. Here a PET scan (top) shows the brain of a healthy person in contrast to the brain of a person with untreated depression. *ASAP/Photo Researchers, NIH/Science Source, Photo Researchers, Inc.*

*neurotransmitters are chemicals in the nervous system that transmit nerve impulses.

*genes are chemicals in the body that help determine a person's characteristics, such as hair or eye color. They are inherited from a person's parents and are contained in the chromosomes found in the cells of the body.

out at the beach, the suffering usually comes back if the person does not get treatment. About 8 percent of people experience this type of depression at some point in their lives.

Chronic depression   Chronic (KRON-ik) depression, also known as dysthymia (dis-THI-me-a), is a form of depression that lasts for two years or more. People with chronic depression do not experience the severe down feelings of someone with major depression. Instead, they suffer from a nagging feeling of emptiness that never seems to go away. They often are said to have a negative view of life or to feel "down in the dumps." About 15 to 20 percent of people who get a depressive disorder have chronic depression.

Major depression and chronic depression also are called unipolar depression (yoo-ni-PO-lar de-PRESH-un). Unipolar means the person experiences one type of feeling; in this case, sadness.

Bipolar disorder (manic depression)   Manic (MAN-ik) depression is another type of depressive disorder. People with manic depression have periods of almost unlimited energy, wild happiness, and hyperactivity that are followed by periods of depression. The mood extremes may be mild or severe, and the mood changes may occur slowly or quickly. Because this type of depression involves two different feelings, it is called bipolar (by-POL-ar) depression, to distinguish it from unipolar depression. Only about 1 percent of people with a depressive disorder have bipolar disorder.

What Causes Depressive Disorders?

Researchers learned much about the causes of depression in the 1980s and 1990s. It seems that many different factors about a person's biological makeup and life experience can trigger the start of depression. It also seems that a combination of factors often must exist together, both within a person's body and during day-to-day activities, for depression to occur. Unlike a cold, this illness cannot be caught from another person.

Researchers studying depression and the brain have found links between depression and an imbalance in certain chemicals in the nervous system, known as neurotransmitters*. These chemicals let brain cells communicate with each other and, therefore, allow the brain to function normally. In people with depression, the nervous system may have either too much or too little of these chemicals.

Researchers also know that depression and manic depression can occur in several members of the same family. This is because certain genes* that are passed from parent to child might increase the chance of getting the disorder. Even if someone's parent, brother, or sister has depression, however, it does not mean that the person will. For example, identical twins have the same genes, but sometimes one gets depression and the other does not.

Certain situations a person faces in life also can cause depression or make it worse. One of the toughest experiences for anyone is loss of a loved one, such as a grandparent who dies or a parent who moves away because of a divorce. It is natural to feel sadness on such occasions. For some people, however, the sadness does not go away. Instead, it develops into depression. There are many other situations that are linked with depression. For children and young adults, there could be school-related problems, difficulties with friends or family, or physical or sexual abuse. For adults, there could be money problems, separation or divorce, or the loss of a job.

Researchers say that certain people seem more vulnerable to depression because of how they think about themselves and their lives. For example, people with low self-esteem might be more likely to develop depression. They might think that they are ugly, stupid, or always saying the wrong things, even if family and friends tell them differently. Also, people who are always pessimistic can become overwhelmed by depressed feelings. Such people see the negative in almost every situation. They think that it does not matter what they do or how hard they try, because nothing will work out right anyway.

Any one of these factors might lead to depression. Often, however, depression occurs for a combination of reasons. For example, it is normal for a teenager who loses a parent to feel sad. However, if the teenager already thinks that the world is a terrible place and nothing good ever happens, the stress of the loss might be worse for this teenager than for other people. If the teenager also inherited a gene linked to depression, it might be difficult to bounce back from the loss without treatment.

How Do People Know They Have a Depressive Disorder?

Unipolar disorders Major depression and chronic depression involve a variety of symptoms. Some people experience only a few symptoms, while others feel most of them. Possible symptoms include:

- Ongoing feelings of sadness, hopelessness, or emptiness. In children, the mood can appear more as irritability than as sadness.

- Loss of interest in family, friends, favorite hobbies, and other things that usually make the person happy.

- Crying easily or frequently.

- Change in sleeping habits. Some people have trouble sleeping. Others find themselves sleeping too much.

- Change in eating habits. Some people lose their appetite or lose weight without dieting. Others overeat or gain weight.

- Extreme fatigue or a feeling of slowness.

- Inability to concentrate or make decisions.

- Increased interest in death or thoughts of suicide.

Diagnosing Depression

In 1952, the American Psychiatric Association created a book that helps psychiatrists and others determine if someone has depression and other mental disorders. It is called the *Diagnostic and Statistical Manual*. As psychiatrists and researchers learn more about mental disorders, the manual is revised and updated. The fourth edition, called *DSM-IV* for short, was released in 1994.

These symptoms must last for at least two weeks and be present every day for most of the day before depression is diagnosed. If the person has recently experienced a major loss, the symptoms must last for two months or longer before it is considered depression. For people with major depression, the symptoms might occur once, or they might return over and over. For those with chronic depression, the symptoms linger for a long time.

Bipolar disorder Manic depression also involves periods during which the person has the symptoms described above. However, the bouts of depression take turns with manic periods that last for a week or longer. Possible signs of a manic period include:

- Exaggerated increase in happiness. At first, the person may feel better than ever, but the elated mood is not connected to a special event, such as getting a good grade or winning a big game. The person may be wildly happy just "because it's Tuesday."

- Boundless energy and restlessness. The person might seem to be moving or fidgeting constantly.

- Decreased need for sleep. The person might be awake for most of the night or even for days on end without feeling tired.

- Rapid or racing thoughts. The person might jump from one topic of conversation to the next, often without an apparent connection between the thoughts. In addition, the person might talk a lot more than usual and become distracted easily.

► A counseling session. Psychiatrists, psychologists, and mental health counselors often play important roles in the diagnosis and treatment of depression. *Michael Newman/PhotoEdit.*

- Inappropriate behavior, such as abuse of drugs and alcohol.

- Poor judgment. The person might spend lots of money or run up high debts using credit cards.

- Increased sexual desires that can become abusive or inappropriate.

- Unreasonable feelings of power over events and people.

How Are Depressive Disorders Diagnosed?

Depression is not always an easy condition to diagnose. When a person cannot move one arm after a fall, the doctor can order an x-ray to check for a broken bone. However, the symptoms of depression may not be so obvious.

Often, people with depression do not realize that they have the disorder. They might sense that things are wrong, but often it is a family member, friend, coworker, family doctor, or teacher who notices the problem. That is when a professional who specializes in mental health, such as a psychiatrist* or clinical psychologist*, should be consulted. Such professionals are trained to observe how a person acts and talks. They look for symptoms of depression and decide what to do based on what they see and hear from the person and the person's family.

How Are Depressive Disorders Treated?

Almost all people who get depression can be helped. Statistics show that about 8 of every 10 people who get help find that their symptoms improve.

Depressed people may benefit from talking with a psychiatrist, clinical psychologist, or other mental health counselor. Mental health counseling* can help them learn how to cope better with stressful situations, such as moving to a new town or experiencing problems at home. Counseling also can help a person understand how current situations or past experiences might be causing the depression or preventing its relief. Family members sometimes also take part in counseling.

There are several antidepressant medications* that psychiatrists and other physicians can prescribe to affect the way that neurotransmitters work in the brain. These medications correct the imbalance that causes the symptoms of depression and allow a person to feel better. The drugs usually start working within a few weeks, although people often need to keep taking them to prevent the symptoms from returning. If one medication does not work in a matter of weeks or has side effects, another can be tried. Medications work best when used with counseling.

Medications and mental health counseling do not work for everyone. About 20 percent of people with the worst symptoms of depression do not respond well to these treatments, either used alone or in combination.

Some severe cases of depression require the person to spend time in a hospital for more intensive observation and treatment. In addition, psychiatrists sometimes treat such severe cases with electroconvulsive therapy*.

* **psychiatrist** refers to a medical doctor who has completed specialized training in the diagnosis and treatment of mental illness. Psychiatrists can prescribe medications, diagnose mental illnesses, and provide mental health counseling and therapy.

* **clinical psychologist** refers to a mental health professional who has earned a non-medical doctoral degree. Clinical psychologists can do psychological evaluation and provide mental health counseling and therapy.

* **mental health counseling,** also known as psychotherapy, involves talking about feelings with a trained professional. The counselor can help the person change thoughts, actions, or relationships that play a part in the illness.

* **antidepressant medications** are used for the treatment and prevention of depression.

* **electroconvulsive therapy,** popularly known as "shock therapy," involves sending small, carefully controlled pulses of electric current to the brain, which leads to brief seizures. It is a fast treatment for severe depression.

267

This involves passing a small amount of electricity through the brain after the person has been put to sleep with a drug. Although a controversial procedure, many who receive the treatment report feeling better.

Some people have claimed that their depressed feelings improved after they took an herb called St. John's wort*, which is sold over the counter in many stores. Although physicians prescribe the herb in Europe, the National Institute of Mental Health in the United States says that not enough scientific studies have been done to know if the herb really works and is safe. In the late 1990s, NIMH began a large-scale, three-year study to help answer these questions. Until the study is completed, the institute does not recommend that people use the herb.

Many people with depression and their family members have found that joining a support group helps them cope with the problems caused by depression. It often helps to know that other people are going through the same things.

Living with a Depressive Disorder

About two-thirds of the people with symptoms of depression do not seek or get the proper help. The disorder often makes it hard for them to

St. John's wort is the common name for hypericum, an herb that is being studied as a possible treatment for depression.

Nerve cells (neurons) use chemicals called neurotransmitters to send messages. The message (neural signal) travels in a specific direction from one cell to the next across a connecting synapse (SIN-aps), often transmitted from the axon terminal of one cell (the presynaptic neuron) across the synapse to the dendrites of the next (the postsynaptic neuron). Some antidepressant medications work by targeting levels of serotonin and other neurotransmitters in the synapses.

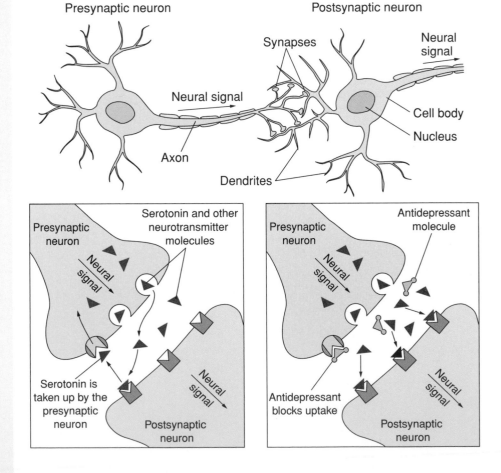

recognize what is wrong. Some people try to mask depression by using alcohol or illicit drugs, but such "self-medication" usually just makes their depression worse. Other people might believe that their mood problem is a sign of weakness and think that they can overcome it without outside help.

Such people need to understand that depression is an illness, not a character flaw. Just as something can go wrong with the heart or lungs, people can have something go wrong in their brain. This makes them ill, not "crazy."

For anyone who has a long period of sadness or other symptoms of depression, it is important to seek help. A young person should talk with parents, relatives, teachers, school counselors, or a close adult friend about these feelings, especially if they include thoughts of suicide. In most cases, people with depressive disorders can be helped with proper treatment.

Resources

Books

Jamison, Kay Redfield. *An Unquiet Mind: A Memoir of Moods and Madness*. New York: Knopf, 1995. A clinical psychologist writes about her lifelong struggle with manic depression.

Smith, Linda Wasmer. *Depression: What It Is, How to Beat It*. Berkeley Heights, NJ: Enslow, 2000. A book for teenagers about depression and manic depression.

Styron, William. *Darkness Visible: A Memoir of Madness*. New York: Random House, 1990. An excellent short book about the well-known author's battle with depression.

Organizations

American Psychiatric Association, 1400 K Street Northwest, Washington, DC 20005. A professional organization that provides information about depressive disorders on its website. http://www.psych.org

Depression-Fighting Drugs

Among the medications prescribed for depression, one of the best-known is Prozac (the brand name for fluoxetine). Prozac became the most widely prescribed antidepressant in the world soon after it was introduced in the late 1980s. It was the first in a new class of antidepressants known as selective serotonin reuptake inhibitors (called SSRIs for short). Such drugs work by acting on a neurotransmitter, or brain chemical, called serotonin. Other SSRIs have been introduced since Prozac.

Other classes of antidepressants include heterocyclic antidepressants (once called tricyclic antidepressants) and monoamine oxidase inhibitors (called MAOIs for short). The most widely prescribed drug for treating the manic period in bipolar disorder is lithium carbonate (called lithium for short).

DEPRESSION IN HISTORY

Ancient Egyptians and Greeks described a disorder that sounds like depression 4,000 years ago. In past centuries, people tried treatments that seem cruel today, such as removing parts of the brain or dropping depressed people into freezing water to "shock" them.

National Depressive and Manic Depressive Association, 730 Franklin Street, Suite 501, Chicago, IL 60610. A national support organization for people with depressive disorders and their families.
Telephone 800-82-NDMDA
http://www.ndmda.org

U.S. National Institute of Mental Health, 6001 Executive Boulevard, Room 8184, MSC 9663, Bethesda, MD 20892-9663. A government institute that provides information about depressive disorders.
Telephone 800-421-4211
http://www.nimh.nih.gov

▶ *See also*
Alcoholism
Mental Disorders
Substance Abuse

| **Dermatitis** *See* **Skin Conditions** |

| **Developmental Disabilities** *See* Autism; Cerebral Palsy; Mental Retardation |

Diabetes

Diabetes mellitus is a condition that results when the pancreas produces little or no insulin, or when the cells of the body cannot use the insulin produced effectively. When insulin is absent or ineffective, the cells of the body cannot absorb glucose (sugar) from blood to provide the body with energy.

KEYWORDS
for searching the Internet and other reference sources

Carbohydrate metabolism

Insulin resistance

Polyuria

Melinda's Story

Melinda had just turned twelve and felt hungry all the time. Her stomach growled in class and her after-school snack no longer held her until dinner. No matter how many trips she made to the school water fountain, she was always thirsty. Even worse, she could not believe how often she needed to go to the bathroom. One of her teachers, after signing Melinda's seventh bathroom pass for the day, suggested that Melinda ask her parents to take her to the doctor. She thought that Melinda might have diabetes, and she was right.

What Is Diabetes?

Diabetes is a group of related diseases characterized by elevated levels of glucose (sugar) in the blood. It is caused by the failure of the pancreas to produce sufficient insulin, or any insulin at all. It can also be caused by the failure of the body's cells to make proper use of the insulin that is produced.

The pancreas, the site of insulin production, is a large gland near the stomach. It contains groups of cells that function like tiny factories, producing different hormones* at exactly the right time and in the right amount. These groups (or "islands") of cells are called islet (EYE-let) cells.

* **hormones** are chemicals that are produced by different glands in the body. Hormones are like the body's ambassadors: they are created in one place but are sent through the body to have specific regulatory effects in different places.

One type of islet cell is called a beta (BAY-ta) cell. Beta cells are responsible for producing a hormone called insulin. The human body needs insulin to function, because insulin helps the body use food for energy.

When people eat, their bodies break food down and convert it into sugars and other fuels. The main fuel is a sugar called glucose (GLOO-kose). When it is in the blood, it is called "blood glucose" or sometimes "blood sugar." Glucose provides the energy people need to carry out almost every task, from pumping blood to walking to reading a book. But glucose cannot get too far on its own—insulin must be there to allow it to pass into the body's cells.

Insulin works like a key, "unlocking" the door to cells. When insulin production stops or slows down in the beta cell factory, the body's cells cannot take in the glucose they need for energy. People with diabetes get glucose from their food, but no matter how much they eat, if the insulin "key" is absent or not working properly, their glucose fuel is "locked out" of the body's cells.

The pancreas is one of the most important organs in the body. It has several functions as part of the endocrine (hormone-producing) system and the digestive system.

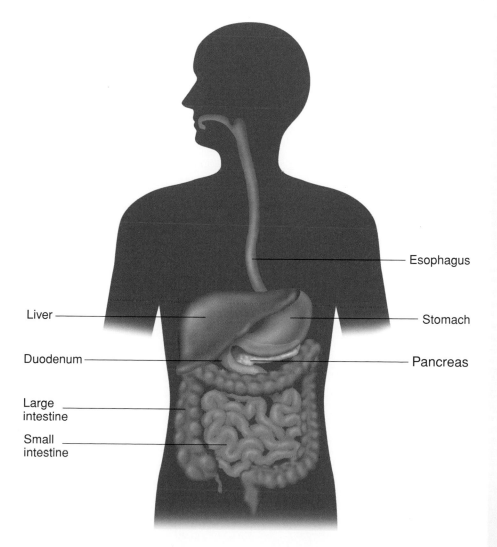

Esophagus

Liver

Stomach

Duodenum

Pancreas

Large intestine

Small intestine

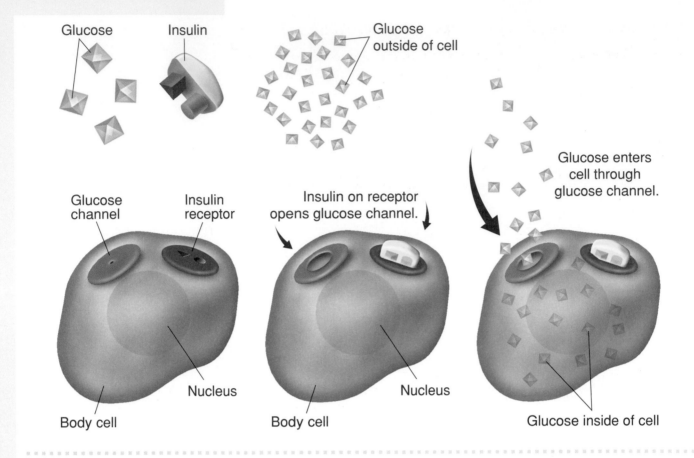

Glucose   Insulin

Glucose
outside of cell

Glucose enters
cell through
glucose channel.

Glucose   Insulin
channel   receptor

Insulin on receptor
opens glucose channel.

Nucleus

Body cell

Nucleus

Body cell

Glucose inside of cell

▲

The hormone insulin is the key that
unlocks the body cell's glucose channel,
allowing glucose ("blood sugar") to enter
the cell and refuel it. Without the insulin
key, glucose is locked out of the cell and
must remain in the bloodstream.

What Are the Different Types of Diabetes?

More than fifteen million people in the United States have diabetes, but
fewer than one million of those people (about 750,000) have the type that
Melinda has. This type is known as Type 1 diabetes. It is also called immune-
mediated diabetes or insulin-dependent diabetes mellitus (IDDM).

Type 1 diabetes is usually diagnosed before a person turns 19, and is
therefore also referred to as "juvenile" diabetes. About 125,000 children
and teenagers in the United States today have Type 1 diabetes. They
make little or no insulin of their own, so they depend on injections of
insulin to stay healthy. They also need to make lifestyle changes, such as
when and what they eat.

The other fourteen-plus million Americans with diabetes have what
is called Type 2 diabetes. Other names for this kind of diabetes include
non-insulin-dependent diabetes mellitus (NIDDM) or adult-onset diabetes. Type 2 diabetes occurs when the cells of the body do not respond
to insulin the way they should. This type of diabetes usually affects people who are over 40 years old. Extra body fat often contributes to this
condition and, many times, weight loss can help remedy it. A person
with Type 2 diabetes is not necessarily dependent on insulin injections
the way a person with Type 1 diabetes is. Type 2 diabetes can also be treated
with pills in addition to a change in diet.

What Causes the Different Types of Diabetes?

Type 1 diabetes   Type 1 diabetes is not contagious like a cold or chickenpox: people cannot catch it from one another. Nor do people get Type 1 diabetes suddenly. It usually takes months or years to develop in a person's body. Despite what many people think, Type 1 diabetes isn't caused by eating too many sweets.

Although scientists do not know exactly what causes Type 1 diabetes, they have enough evidence to suggest that there are at least a couple of different reasons why one person might develop it while another would not: genes and environmental triggers.

- **Genes.** People with Type 1 diabetes are born with certain genes for the illness, just as they are born with genes for blue eyes or brown eyes. Genes are something people inherit from their parents before they are born. In some families, the genes for Type 1 diabetes are passed from parents to more than one child; a sibling of someone with Type 1 diabetes has about a 5 percent chance of also developing it.

- **Environmental triggers.** Some people have Type 1 diabetes set in motion by an environmental trigger, like a virus. The trigger will make the person's immune system attack and destroy the beta cells, with the result that insulin can no longer be produced. However, for an environmental trigger to have this effect, people probably have to have a genetic predisposition to it. Most people do not just suddenly develop diabetes because they get the flu.

Type 2 diabetes   Just as with Type 1 diabetes, people with Type 2 diabetes are not contagious. Two major factors seem to play a role in why people develop Type 2 diabetes: genes and obesity (or being overweight).

- **Genes.** Just as certain genes may mean that a person may be more likely to develop Type 1 diabetes, other genes play an important part in people who develop Type 2 diabetes.

- **Obesity.** Many people who have Type 2 diabetes are obese. Scientists think that this extra weight may impair the body's ability to use insulin effectively.

How Do People Know If They Have Diabetes?

Symptoms   When the body does not have adequate amounts of insulin, symptoms like Melinda's result. Frequent urination is very common in a person with Type 1 diabetes. This happens because glucose cannot get into the body's cells and builds up in the blood instead. Normally, the kidneys do not allow glucose to get into the urine. But in the case of diabetes, the high level of blood glucose spills into the urine, pulling extra water out of the body along with it.

Feeling very thirsty is also common, because the body needs to make up for all the liquid lost through urination. Feeling hungry and eating a

Diabetes at a Glance

Diabetes Type	Treatment	Age
Type 1	insulin	babies to adults
Type 2	diet, exercise, pills; in some cases insulin	most common in overweight adults over 40, but increasing among children and young adults

lot are also common symptoms; the body is looking for a way to get the energy that it is missing. But even with all the extra eating, people with undiagnosed diabetes may lose weight, because their bodies start to use fat for energy instead of sugar. In the case of growing children and teenagers, the fact that they are not gaining weight at a time in their lives when they should be may be a sign that diabetes may be present.

These symptoms are common to both Type 1 and Type 2 diabetes, although usually less severe in the latter. Type 2 diabetes may sometimes present with other symptoms, such as repeated or hard-to-heal infections, blurred vision, and dry, itchy skin. But often these symptoms are quite mild, and due attention is not paid to them.

Diagnosis If a doctor suspects that a patient has diabetes, usually he or she will first do a urine test. The test is simple: it involves a small sample of the patient's urine and special strips of paper that are treated with a chemical to detect glucose. If the immersed strip shows that glucose is present, the doctor will want to confirm the test by checking the patient's blood sugar with a blood test. If the doctor feels sure that there is too much glucose in the patient's blood, further evaluation and testing will be done, and treatment will be started if the diagnosis of diabetes is confirmed.

Because people with Type 2 diabetes continue to make insulin that is functioning to a certain extent, they may develop symptoms over a period of months or years without facing immediate danger. They may

TWO MILLENNIA OF MEDICINE

The ancient Greek physician Aretaeus (ar-e-TE-us) of Cappadocia (c. 81–c. 138) described diabetes as a "melting down of the flesh and limbs into urine." Throughout history, many people with the disease died at an early age by wasting away, although the disease was probably not as prevalent in ancient times as it is now.

Treatments frequently involved dietary changes. Aretaeus recommended milks, cereals, and starches. In 1797, John Rollo recommended a meat diet high in proteins. These diets were not cures for diabetes, but they did allow people with diabetes to live longer than if they had remained on standard diets.

The first truly successful treatment for diabetes was finally made available in the 1920s when Frederick Banting, Charles Best, and John James Macleod first isolated insulin for use through therapeutic injections.

feel tired, worn out, or thirsty much of the time, without thinking that it could be diabetes. In many cases, Type 2 diabetes is actually discovered by accident, during a routine physical exam or screening blood or urine test.

How Is Type 1 Diabetes Treated?

A person who has been diagnosed with Type 1 diabetes needs to do a number of things to function well. These include taking insulin, following a food plan, exercising, monitoring blood glucose levels, and taking urine tests. All of these things contribute toward achieving the major goal: keeping the amount of glucose in the blood as close to normal as possible, so the person with diabetes stays healthy and feels good, now and in the future.

Insulin   People with Type 1 diabetes must get the correct amount of insulin into their blood. Different sources of insulin have been used to treat diabetes. Pork insulin is extracted from the pancreas of a pig, but human insulin does not come from the pancreas of a human. Instead, human insulin is synthetic. It is made in a laboratory, and is the type most commonly used to treat diabetes today.

Insulin comes in liquid form (dissolved in water) in a bottle and must be injected into the body. Unlike a lot of medications, insulin cannot be swallowed in pill form because the hormone insulin is a protein. Like other proteins, it would be digested and broken apart in the stomach, just like the protein contained in food.

Most people take insulin by using a needle to inject it into the layer of fat beneath the skin. The most common places where people take insulin are in their arms, legs, stomach, and hips—all places where people have some fat. The injection does not hurt very much, since the needle is very thin. Usually, a person needs to inject insulin this way two or more times a day, on a set schedule, coordinated with meals.

Some people with Type 1 diabetes use an insulin pump. It is about the same size as a beeper, with a small container filled with insulin. The insulin gets automatically "pumped" into the person's body through a small tube attached to a needle inserted into the skin. The insulin is pumped in at a slow rate all the time, with an extra "boost" pumped in before meals to prepare the body for the incoming sugar.

However people with Type 1 diabetes take insulin, one thing stays constant: they must take insulin every single day to allow the body's cells to take in and use glucose properly. They cannot take a break or decide to stop taking it, or they will become ill.

Food   Proper nutrition is a very important part of staying healthy—for everyone—and especially for a person with Type 1 diabetes. Since food affects how much glucose is in the blood, people with Type 1 diabetes must pay careful attention to the food they eat, how much they eat, and when they eat it. In particular, since carbohydrates are the body's main source of glucose, many people with diabetes estimate the amount of carbohydrates in each meal to determine if they are getting the right amount of sugar.

Sports Stars with Type 1 Diabetes

These outstanding athletes were all diagnosed with Type 1 diabetes at an early age:

- **Jackie Robinson** Robinson was the baseball immortal who broke the color barrier in 1947. In his 10-year career with the Brooklyn Dodgers, Robinson was a batting champion, the League MVP, and a member of six championship teams. He was elected to the Hall of Fame in 1962, his first year of eligibility.

- **Bobby Clarke** The tenacious leader of hockey's Philadelphia Flyers for 15 seasons, Bobby Clarke was first diagnosed with diabetes at the age of 15. Undeterred, he went on to win three Hart Trophies as league MVP.

- **Wade Wilson** An NFL quarterback for over 16 years, beginning in 1981, Wilson led the Minnesota Vikings to three playoffs and the 1987 NFC Championship game.

All that does not mean that the eating habits of someone with diabetes are so very different from other people. The food itself can be the same as that eaten by most people. But in most cases, their meal plans must be on some sort of schedule, include snacks, and limit sweets because of the large amount of sugar they contain.

Exercise   Just like healthy eating, exercise is something that is important for everyone and especially for people with Type 1 diabetes. It was not too long ago that some doctors thought people with Type 1 diabetes should not exercise, but that opinion has changed. Exercise helps insulin work better to control the level of glucose in the blood. Exercise also helps keep people with diabetes at the right weight, and it helps maintain a healthy heart and blood vessels. In addition, exercise helps people feel good about themselves.

When people with Type 1 diabetes exercise, they use glucose at a faster-than-normal rate, so they must pay special attention to ensure that their blood glucose level does not drop too low. This may mean taking less insulin, eating more before exercise, or having snacks during and after exercise.

Blood glucose and urine testing   People who have Type 1 diabetes usually test their blood glucose three or more times a day. This involves pricking the finger with a tiny, sharp device to get a drop of blood. The blood drop is put on a chemical strip and inserted into a testing meter that "reads" the amount of sugar in the blood. The person then records the blood glucose numbers in a diary. This monitoring helps to determine if the level of glucose in the blood is where it should be and guides adjustment in the treatment plan.

Urine testing is another helpful form of monitoring. It is especially important when a person with Type 1 diabetes is sick (with the flu, for example). Any kind of physical stress, such as an infection, tends to interfere with the body's cells taking in and using glucose properly. When this happens, the cells begin to break down fat for energy. A potentially harmful byproduct of this process is the production of ketones*. Urine testing is an effective means of determining if ketones are building up in the blood.

Hypoglycemia, Hyperglycemia, and Ketoacidosis

Sometimes, even with insulin, proper nutrition, and exercise, it can be difficult to control diabetes completely. Blood glucose levels can become either too high or too low in some cases, and blood levels of ketones can rise to toxic levels.

Hypoglycemia   If the level of glucose in the blood is too low, this is called hypoglycemia (hy-po-gly-SEE-mee-a). This can result when someone takes too much insulin, misses a meal or snack, or exercises too hard without taking special precautions. In its beginning stages, hypoglycemia can make someone weak, shaky, dizzy, and sweaty. A person with diabetes learns to be very aware of these warning signs and almost always takes action

* **ketones** (KEE-tones) are the chemicals produced when the body breaks down fat for energy. In large amounts, ketones are poisonous; as they build up in the blood, they become increasingly toxic.

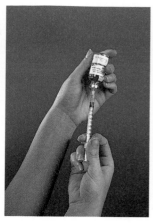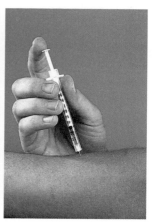

A girl with diabetes removes a vial of insulin from the refrigerator (left). The insulin is drawn out of the bottle with a small insulin syringe (center). The needle is thin and lubricated, so it hardly hurts at all when it goes in (right).

to treat them, by drinking some juice or taking glucose tablets, before they become severe. If left untreated, a person may become disoriented, sleepy, or have a hard time talking. Eventually, he may become very confused and uncoordinated and, in extreme cases, go into a coma*. The treatment for an extreme case of hypoglycemia is to give the person sugar as soon as possible, by intravenous* injection if necessary.

***coma** is an unconscious state, like a very deep sleep. A person in a coma cannot be awakened, and cannot move, see, speak, or hear.

***intravenous** (in-tra-VEE-nus) means injected directly into the veins

Hyperglycemia   Another problem that people with Type 1 diabetes can have is too much glucose in the blood, called hyperglycemia (hy-per-gly-SEE-mee-a). When there is too much sugar in the blood, it is often because the person has taken too little insulin, has eaten too much high-sugar food, or is ill with an infection or stressed for other reasons. Symptoms include very frequent urination, extreme thirst, weakness, and tiredness.

Ketoacidosis   In uncontrolled diabetes, when the blood becomes too acidic because of high levels of ketones in it, the condition that results is called ketoacidosis (ke-to-a-si-DO-sis). A person in ketoacidosis may be nauseated or vomiting and breathing very deeply. If he does not get treatment, he will become dehydrated and go into a coma. Emergency treatment involves insulin and lots of fluids, usually by intravenous injection. Fortunately, ketoacidosis is almost always preventable in people whose diabetes has been diagnosed, and who take care to manage their diabetes properly.

How Is Type 2 Diabetes Treated?

People who have Type 2 diabetes are often able to treat their diabetes with dietary changes and a weight-control program, if needed. This consists of balancing a healthy combination of foods and exercise.

In some cases, people with Type 2 diabetes are treated with pills. These pills do not contain insulin, but they help the body to make more insulin or respond to insulin more normally. Sometimes, a person with Type 2 diabetes will need to take insulin injections, like a person with Type 1 diabetes.

There are many similarities in the treatments for Type 1 and Type 2 diabetes, but the main difference is the role of insulin. If a person with

Diabetes Research

Clinical trials are research projects undertaken by scientists, pharmaceutical companies, and government researchers to investigate whether medications and treatment plans are safe and effective.

To evaluate the effectiveness of careful self-management in reducing the long-term complications of diabetes, in 1983 the U.S. National Institute of Diabetes and Digestive and Kidney Diseases (NIDDK) undertook a large ten-year study, called the Diabetes Control and Complications Trial (DCCT for short).

People with diabetes took part in the DCCT and followed instructions for testing their blood glucose three or four times a day, taking more frequent insulin injections or using an insulin pump, and following a healthy meal plan. The test results showed that the people who maintained near-normal blood glucose levels had fewer long-term complications, such as problems with their hearts, eyes, or kidneys. It proved that for a person with diabetes, paying close attention to small things on a daily basis has a big payoff later on.

The U.S. and the World

Globally, there were approximately 135 million adults with diabetes in 1995. By the year 2025, that number is expected to rise to 300 million.

- By the year 2025, it is estimated that the number of persons with diabetes will be over 57 million in India, 37 million in China, and 22 million in the United States.

- In 1997, there were more than 15 million people with diabetes in the U.S. Of those, more than 5 million had not been diagnosed.

- Over 90 percent of diabetes cases are Type 2 diabetes. While Type 1 (the type that affects most children and teenagers with diabetes) is most common in Americans of European descent, the prevalence of Type 2 diabetes is 2 to 4 times higher in Americans of African, Hispanic, and Asian heritage. The highest incidence of all is among Native Americans.

- In 1997, the average cost of health care for each American with diabetes was over $10,000 per year, compared to approximately $2,500 per year for Americans without diabetes.

*__retina__ is the back inner surface of the eyeball that plays a key role in vision. This surface contains millions of light-sensitive cells that change light into nerve signals that the brain can interpret.

Type 2 diabetes forgets to take his insulin, he will not go into ketoacidosis. And while a doctor might say it is all right for a person with Type 2 diabetes to stop taking insulin completely and just take pills, this would not be possible for a person with Type 1 diabetes.

What Is It Like to Live With Type 1 or Type 2 Diabetes?

Between taking insulin, following a meal plan, testing blood sugar levels, and the rest, living with Type 1 diabetes can sound like a big job—and it can be—especially in the beginning. Luckily, many people who have been diagnosed with Type 1 diabetes have an entire diabetes treatment team to help them along. This team usually includes a doctor, a diabetes nurse, a dietician, a psychologist, and a social worker. Ideally, the entire team works to become partners with the patient and the patient's family, so that they can maintain as normal a life as possible.

People with diabetes can do almost everything that people without diabetes can. They can:

- go to school
- play sports
- spend time with friends
- eat food at parties
- do almost every kind of job
- go to college
- get married

A person with diabetes may have to eat an extra snack before competing in a track meet, or duck out of a party for a minute to take insulin, or have only a small bit of ice cream when everyone else is going for the Super Sundae. But people who control their diabetes lead normal lives. And women with diabetes who want to have babies can usually do so, with the support of their diabetes treatment team.

How Can Diabetes Affect a Person's Life in the Future?

Both Type 1 and Type 2 diabetes can have negative long-term effects on a person's health. These effects tend to develop very slowly and gradually. Because a person with diabetes may not process fat properly, there tends to be damage to the blood vessels in the body, which increases the chances for high blood pressure, heart attacks, and strokes. Diabetes can also have long-term effects on the eyes, because tiny blood vessels in the retina* become weakened. If these blood vessels burst, they can cause bleeding and scarring in the eye, or even blindness. The chance of nerve damage, and of developing kidney disease, is also increased in a person with diabetes. Finally, foot health can become an issue for people with diabetes: because the condition can affect circulation to the feet, small cuts or wounds can turn into serious infections without proper care.

People with diabetes can take steps to help prevent or lessen the effects of these long-term problems. Recent research has shown that blood sugar control is a key factor. It is very important for people with diabetes to have regular physical checkups, when a doctor can monitor blood pressure and foot health, check fat levels in the blood, and look for problems with the kidneys. Annual trips to the eye doctor are crucial for people with diabetes. If the ophthalmologist* discovers problems with the blood vessels in the retina, vision problems often can be prevented or lessened with laser surgery.

While people with diabetes must depend on doctors and other medical professionals to help them, they can also do quite a bit to help themselves. Continued education about proper diabetes management is a key part of helping people with diabetes stay healthy.

Will There Ever Be a Cure?

Diabetes research is an active field. Much of the scientific work is concerned with insulin: how to get it into the body, or how to get the body to produce it on its own. Since insulin cannot be swallowed, researchers

Medic Alert Tags

People with diabetes often wear metal tags or bracelets imprinted or inscribed with important medical information. In the event of an accident or diabetic coma, the information on the tag can alert medical personnel about the patient's condition.

Some companies offer medical alert tags that have an identification number that is unique to the individual so that a doctor who doesn't know the person can retrieve the patient's medical history in the event of emergency.

* **ophthalmologist** is a medical doctor who specializes in treating diseases of the eye.

BANTING, BEST, AND THE DOG WITH DIABETES

Two scientists and a dog may sound like characters in a movie, but it was just such a threesome who were involved in discovering insulin. Shortly after World War I had ended, a Canadian surgeon named Frederick Banting (1891–1941) became very interested in diabetes and how the pancreas functions in a person with diabetes. A neighborhood child had died from diabetes, and this helped pique Banting's interest in making discoveries about the condition.

In his University of Toronto laboratory, assisted by a graduate student named Charles Best, Banting took out the pancreas glands of several dogs (which caused the dogs to develop diabetes), extracted their insulin, and began investigating the properties of insulin. Banting and Best discovered that insulin brought down the level of blood glucose in the dogs' blood; the dogs who had their pancreas glands removed could now survive, as long as they had insulin injections. A famous photo was taken of the two scientists in 1921, and between them stands the very first dog with diabetes that was kept alive with insulin.

In 1923, Sir Frederick Banting and the Scottish scientist John James Macleod (1876–1935) were awarded the Nobel Prize for medicine and physiology for their discovery of insulin.

Best, Banting, and one of the dogs they treated with insulin, April 1922. *Courtesy Banting House National Historic Site Collection.*

Greek Speak: A Diabetes Dictionary

Many English words come from Greek. These include many of the words used to describe diabetes, as well as the word "diabetes" itself.

Diabetes Greek for "passing through," because Greek doctors noticed how much liquid people with diabetes drank, and how often they needed to urinate.

Mellitus Greek for "honey-like" or "sweet," because it was noticed that the urine of people with diabetes smelled sweet, due to its high sugar content.

Insulin Greek for "island." The groups of islet cells in the pancreas that are responsible for making insulin and other hormones look like tiny islands under a microscope.

Hypo Greek for "below," and thus "too little."

Hyper Greek for "above," and thus "too much."

Glyk Greek for "sugar."

Emia Greek for "blood."

▶ *See also*
Genetic Diseases
Hypoglycemia
Kidney Disease
Obesity

have been investigating other ways to get it into the bloodstream without an injection, such as eye drops, nasal sprays, and inhalers. They have also experimented with pancreas transplantation, as well as transplantation of the islet cells that make insulin. Until there is a cure for diabetes, however, people must live with it and control it using the information and equipment available to them now.

Resources

Books

Betschart, Jean, and Susan Thom. *In Control: A Guide for Teens with Diabetes*. Minneapolis: Chronimed Publishing, 1995.

Chase, H. Peter. *Understanding Insulin Dependent Diabetes*. Denver: The Guild of the Children's Diabetes Foundation, 1995. Also available online at the website for the Barbara Davis Center for Childhood Diabetes. http://www.uchsc.edu/misc/diabetes/UIDDM.html

Silverstein, Alvin, Virginia B. Silverstein, and Robert A Silverstein. *Diabetes*. Springfield, New Jersey: Enslow Publishing, 1994.

Magazines

Diabetes Forecast. A magazine published by the American Diabetes Association.

Diabetes Self-Management. A magazine published by R.A. Rapaport Publishing, Inc. Available online at http://www.diabetes-self-mgmt.com/

Organizations

American Diabetes Association, 1660 Duke Street, Alexandria, VA 22314. The American Diabetes Association website offers trustworthy reviews of many other diabetes-related sites on the web. http://www.diabetes.org

Children With Diabetes. Produced by the Juvenile Diabetes Foundation, this site is an online community for children and young adults with Type I diabetes. http://childrenwithdiabetes.com/

Juvenile Diabetes Foundation, 120 Watts Street, New York, NY 10005. http://www.jdfcure.org

Information about Frederick Banting and Charles Best may be found at the website devoted to the work of Frederick Banting. http://www.diabetes.ca/atoz/banting/banting.htm.

Diarrhea

Diarrhea is a condition in which bowel movements are abnormally frequent and stools are abnormally liquidy. It is not itself a disease but is usually a symptom of some other underlying disorder. Diarrhea may be a result of food poisoning, diseases such as dysentery or cholera, emotional upsets, or many other conditions.

What Is Diarrhea?

Diarrhea is very common, a condition with which almost everyone is familiar. Usually, it is little more than an unpleasant nuisance that briefly interferes with work or play. Sometimes, however, severe attacks can seriously endanger a person's health by causing dehydration*. Diarrhea can last different lengths of time: it may be either acute (coming and going quickly) or chronic (long-lasting).

Diarrhea develops in the small or large intestines. The intestines may become irritated and inflamed by an infection or by certain foods. The inflamed intestine does not reabsorb as much water from the stool (bowel contents) as it normally would. In some infections, the intestines actually add more water to the stool. This extra water makes the stools very loose.

What Are the Symptoms of Diarrhea?

Although diarrhea may occur by itself, often it is accompanied by abdominal pain, gurgling bowel sounds, nausea, vomiting, and general weakness. The stools, or bowel movements, are loose or watery and may contain blood, pus, mucus, or droplets of fat. Sometimes attacks of diarrhea alternate with periods of constipation.

What Causes Diarrhea?

Bouts of diarrhea that range from mild to severe can be caused by several types of infectious microorganisms* (my-kro-OR-gan-iz-ims) in contaminated food or water. Diarrhea can also result from the body having trouble digesting dairy products or other foods. Mild cases of diarrhea can be caused by eating spicy food or by anxiety about something stressful, like having to give a speech in front of a lot of people.

Food poisoning We all have heard of a party at which a lot of people got sick after eating the same food. Foods that are not cooked thoroughly or kept refrigerated until just before serving can cause food poisoning. Also, it is important to make sure that raw meat or poultry does not come in contact with cooked foods, that the hands are washed thoroughly before handling any foods, and that all dishes and utensils are thoroughly washed after they have been in contact with raw meat or poultry.

Bacteria such as staphylococcus (staf-i-lo-KOK-us) can cause digestive upsets of this kind. Certain strains of a common intestinal bacterium

KEYWORD
for searching the Internet and other reference sources

Digestion

* **dehydration** (dee-hy-DRAY-shun) is loss of fluid from the body.

* **microorganisms** are living organisms that can only be seen using a microscope. Examples of microorganisms are bacteria and viruses.

known as *E. coli* (EE KO-ly) can cause very serious illness with symptoms that include diarrhea. A group of bacteria called salmonella (sal-mo-NEL-la) also are often responsible for food poisoning. Salmonella causes gastroenteritis (gas-tro-en-ter-I-tis), or inflammation of the gastrointestinal tract. Salmonella infection can cause diarrhea for a week or longer.

Dysentery Dysentery is an intestinal infection that causes severe diarrhea, often with blood, pus, and mucus in the stools. It is especially common in developing (poor) countries with poor sanitation facilities, causing the food and water supply to become contaminated. The most common causes of dysentery are bacteria and amebas*. Amebic dysentery can cause chronic diarrhea that comes and goes.

Cholera Outbreaks of cholera often accompany natural disasters such as earthquakes and great storms that disrupt sanitation and cause food and water to become contaminated. It also is widespread in refugee camps and other wartime situations in which people live in severely overcrowded conditions. Food and water contaminated by the cholera bacteria cause a watery form of diarrhea that can rapidly lead to death from severe dehydration.

Giardiasis A mainly tropical disease that can give rise to severe diarrhea is giardiasis (jee-ar-DY-a-sis). Caused by a parasite*, it usually enters the body in contaminated drinking water.

In recent years, giardiasis has become increasingly prevalent in developed countries such as the United States, especially among preschool children. In settings such as households and day-care centers, where children are in close contact, giardiasis can be caught by touching stool-contaminated objects or from hand-to-hand contact.

Traveler's Diarrhea Traveling to foreign countries and drinking water or eating foods washed in the local water supply can also cause

***amebas** (a-MEE-buz) are small, one-celled animals that live in fresh and salt water. Amebas can be seen only with a microscope.

***parasites** are creatures that live in and feed on the bodies of other organisms. The animal or plant harboring the parasite is called its host. Two parasitic infections, cyclosporiasis and cryptosporidiosis (discussed elsewhere), are major causes of diarrhea worldwide.

An open sewer overflows a walkway in Abidjan, Ivory Coast, in West Africa. Unsanitary conditions like these often result in widespread dysentery and cholera outbreaks. © 1995 Charles O. Cecil, Visuals Unlimited

digestive upsets that include diarrhea; these are sometimes called traveler's diarrhea.

Often, the exact cause of traveler's diarrhea cannot be determined. Likely suspects are certain viruses and strains of bacteria such as *E. coli* that are present in the local water supply. Other causes may include changes in diet, excessive alcohol intake, and salmonella or shigella bacteria.

Lactose Intolerance   Sometimes people get diarrhea from eating dairy products like milk, cheese, and ice cream. This is because there is a sugar in milk and milk products called lactose (LAK-tos). To be able to digest this sugar, there must be an enzyme* in the body called lactase (LAK-tays). Some people do not make enough of this enzyme, and when they eat milk or milk products they get diarrhea.

*enzymes are natural substances that speed up specific chemical reactions in the body.

Malabsorption   Many diseases can interfere with the intestine's ability to absorb or take up digested foods. This is called malabsorption (mal-ab-SORP-shun). When foods are not digested and absorbed properly, it can cause diarrhea.

Antibiotic-Induced Diarrhea   Antibiotics kill not only the bacteria that make us sick, but also kill the "good" bacteria that normally live in the intestines and help us digest food. This can allow the overgrowth of certain bacteria that cause diarrhea.

What If Diarrhea Lasts a Long Time?

Diarrhea caused by parasites, such as in amebic dysentery and giardiasis, can become chronic (long-lasting). Infestation with worms also can produce lasting diarrhea.

More often, the cause of chronic diarrhea is not an infection. Instead, it may be the result of inflammatory bowel disease, which includes ulcerative colitis (ko-LY-tis) and Crohn's disease. A disorder known as diverticulitis (di-ver-tik-yoo-LY-tis), in which abnormal pouches in the walls of the intestines become inflamed, can also cause chronic diarrhea. Other causes include cancer of the intestine, a condition called irritable bowel syndrome, and inability to digest certain foods.

Diarrhea in Infants

Infants and young children commonly get diarrhea from viral infection or giardiasis. When a baby has diarrhea, usually the condition is more serious than in adults or older children. An infant with these symptoms can lose body fluids so rapidly that his life can be endangered, especially if he also is vomiting. Signs of dehydration in infants, such as a dry mouth, lack of urine production, or unresponsiveness, require immediate medical attention. Bacterial intestinal infections such as cholera cause many infant fatalities in developing countries.

How Is Diarrhea Treated?

Most cases of diarrhea are mild and do not require medical attention. For bouts that last more than a few days, recur, or show blood in the

▶ *See also*

Cancer

Cholera

Constipation

Cyclosporiasis and Cryptosporidiosis

Diverticulitis

Food poisoning

Gastroenteritis

Giardia

Inflammatory Bowel Disease

Irritable Bowel Syndrome

Lactose intolerance

Worms

KEYWORDS
for searching the Internet and other reference sources

Antioxidants

Minerals

Nutraceuticals

Nutrition

Phytochemicals

Protein

Vitamins

stool, a doctor should be consulted. For infants, medical advice should be sought if the diarrhea lasts more than 48 hours. Medical tests that may be used in diagnosis may include examination and culture of stool samples (for bacteria, viruses, or parasites), x-rays, or use of a colonoscope (ko-LON-o-skope), an instrument for viewing the lining of the colon.

Treatment of mild diarrhea consists mainly of drinking liquids to prevent dehydration. In some cases, doctors may prescribe medications that ease symptoms. Treatment of severe diarrhea depends largely upon the cause. For example, antibiotics may be prescribed for dysentery or certain kinds of food poisoning.

Can Diarrhea Be Avoided?

Washing one's hands thoroughly after using the toilet is always important, but especially so where contagious forms of diarrhea such as giardiasis can be spread. Travelers in foreign countries should use bottled (not tap) water, and avoid eating raw fruits and vegetables.

Resources

Rosenthal, M. Sara. *The Gastrointestinal Sourcebook.* Los Angeles: Lowell House, 1997. This book is easy to read and tells how to take care of the digestive system and its upsets.

Janowitz, Henry D. *Your Gut Feelings.* New York: Oxford University Press, 1994. This is a well-written, illustrated book that includes a chapter on diarrhea.

Peikin, Steven. *Gastrointestinal Health.* New York: HarperCollins, 1991.

Dietary Deficiencies

Dietary deficiencies are disorders that occur because of a lack of essential nutrients in the diet, or because the body cannot absorb and process those nutrients once they are eaten. Most dietary deficiency diseases are caused by a lack of protein, vitamins, or minerals.

What Are Dietary Deficiencies?

The human diet is divided into five nutritional groups: proteins, carbohydrates, fats, vitamins, and minerals. These five groups include about 50 nutritional items that are necessary for good health and growth. Each of these items plays a vital role in the functioning of the human body. The amount of nutrients needed for good health varies from individual to individual. Age, gender, and overall health condition affect how much of these nutrients a person needs for good health.

Whenever a person does not get enough of an essential nutrient, they are at risk for a dietary deficiency disease. Most dietary deficiency diseases are caused by a lack of protein, vitamins, or minerals. Protein deficiency diseases occur when a person does not eat enough protein; these diseases are prevalent in developing countries where people are too poor to buy protein-rich foods or where such foods are hard to find. Generally speaking, vitamin and mineral deficiencies are due to diets that lack some of the nutrients found in fresh vegetables and fruit, as well as milk, cheese, or eggs. In some cases, genetic* disorders, metabolic* disorders, or illnesses that prevent the body from digesting or absorbing particular nutrients will cause the deficiencies.

The Supplement Habit

A trend toward taking vitamin and mineral supplements has been growing in the United States. It is estimated that anywhere from 30 to 40 million people in the United States alone are using nutritional supplements on a daily basis. The potency of small amounts of vitamins to cure deficiency diseases may have led to the unrealistic expectation that vitamins and minerals can ensure good health when taken in large amounts as supplements. Despite this widespread habit, very few scientific studies exist to prove these supplements can make a difference.

It is important to check with a doctor before adding nutritional supplements to the diet, and to keep in mind the following facts:

* genetic (je-NET-ik) pertains to genes, which are chemicals in the body that help determine a person's characteristics, such as hair or eye color. They are inherited from a person's parents and are contained in the chromosomes found in the cells of the body.

* metabolic (met-a-BOL-ik) pertains to the process in the body that converts food into energy and the chemical processes necessary for growth, maintenance, and function of body tissues.

- Most vitamins are water-soluble. The body can absorb only so much of a vitamin, and the rest is excreted in the urine throughout the day.

- Large doses of some vitamins, such as A and D, can be harmful. Vitamins A and D are fat-soluble vitamins and can accumulate in the liver to the point of becoming toxic.

- Too much of certain trace elements, like zinc, copper, fluoride, and selenium, can be toxic.

- Most nutritionists recommend eating a well-balanced diet as the most effective and least expensive way of getting the nutrients needed to stay healthy.

- Vitamin supplements are warranted for certain people, such as pregnant women, newborns, and people on special diets.

- The health-food and vitamin industries that market supplements claim that the minimum daily amounts recommended by the U.S. Food and Drug Administration (FDA) are too low. The American Dietetic Association (ADA) recommends that doctors or licensed dietitians be the source of supplement prescriptions.

Protein Deficiencies

Proteins are the essential components of all organs and chemical activities. Proteins make up body tissues such as muscle, connective tissue, and skin. Other proteins are enzymes, chemicals that cause reactions to occur that allow the body to function. For example, some enzymes digest food or convert sugar into energy. Proteins are composed of building blocks called amino acids. When proteins are eaten and digested, they are broken down into amino acids that are then redistributed throughout the body, where they form new proteins and enzymes. When protein is missing from the diet, the body cannot function properly. Milk, meat, and legumes are important sources of dietary protein.

Protein-energy malnutrition (PEM) The term protein-energy malnutrition (PEM) is used to describe the range of conditions related to calorie (energy) and protein deficiency disorders. These diseases are prevalent in developing countries where people lack sufficient food. In this category of malnutrition are the diseases kwashiorkor (kwash-e-OR-kor) and marasmus (ma-RAZ-mus). These diseases affect mainly children, with as many as half of the children in starvation-prone countries not surviving to their fifth birthdays. Adults rarely suffer from protein deficiency diseases unless there is a problem in the intestines that prevents absorption of amino acids.

Kwashiorkor Kwashiorkor is a disease caused specifically by a lack of protein in the diet. The term originates from an African word that describes the situation of an infant being weaned* from breast milk to make room for the next baby. When weaning occurs and protein-rich food (such as milk, meat, or legumes) is not available, the baby experiences tiredness, muscular wasting, and edema (water retention). The hair and skin lose color, the skin becomes scaly, and the child may experience diarrhea and anemia.

Marasmus Marasmus is a wasting away of body tissue from a lack of both calories and protein in the diet. A child with marasmus is cranky and irritable, and is skinny rather than swollen with edema.

Vitamin Deficiencies

There are 13 vitamins essential for healthy growth, development, cell function, and metabolism: vitamins A, C, D, E, K, and eight B vitamins (together they are called the B complex vitamins). All vitamins must be taken into the body from outside food sources, except for vitamins D and K, which can be made under specific circumstances by the body.

Vitamin A, night blindness, and xerophthalmia Vitamin A is necessary to protect the retina*, and for the normal growth and health of skin and membrane cells. A deficiency of vitamin A can cause night blindness, a condition in which the eyes fail to adjust to the dark because of problems with the retina. The deficiency also may cause "glare" blindness, or problems seeing when the eye is exposed to too much light or to a sudden change in the amount of light when entering a darkened room.

Vitamin A deficiency also can cause a disease called xerophthalmia (zeer-off-THAL-mee-a). The symptoms of this disease are eye dryness

* **weaning** means accustoming a child to take food other than by breastfeeding.

* **retina** (RET-i-na) is a structure lining the back of the eye that is necessary for vision.

and thickening of the surface of parts of the eye. If left untreated, xerophthalmia may lead to blindness.

Vitamin A can be obtained directly from foods such as milk, eggs, and liver, as well as from carotene, a chemical that is found in green and yellow fruits and vegetables such as apricots, cantaloupe, oranges, peaches, collards, broccoli, turnip greens, kale, carrots, sweet potatoes, and squash. Carotene is converted to vitamin A in the body.

Vitamin B1 and beriberi   Beriberi (BER-ee-BER-ee) is a disease that affects the heart, digestive system, and nervous system. It results from a lack of vitamin B1 (also called thiamin) in the diet. Thiamin is used to help the body make energy. Food sources for this vitamin are meats, wheat germ, whole grain and enriched bread, legumes, nuts, peanuts, and peanut butter. The early stages of beriberi are characterized by fatigue, loss of appetite, and a numb, tingling feeling in the legs.

There are three forms of beriberi:

- Infantile beriberi: Although a nursing mother may not have the disease herself, her infant gets sick from not getting enough thiamin in the breast milk. The child may die in infancy, or the child may develop wet or dry beriberi.

- Wet beriberi: This is characterized by an accumulation of fluid throughout the body, and a rapid heart rate that can lead to sudden death.

- Dry beriberi: In this form of beriberi there is no fluid accumulation, but there is a loss of sensation and a weakness in the legs. People with dry beriberi often need to walk with the aid of a cane and may become bedridden and susceptible to infectious diseases.

Beriberi is still found in Japan, Indonesia, China, Malaysia, India, Burma, the Philippines, Brazil, Thailand, and Vietnam. In the United States and other developed nations, it usually occurs in a milder form, often accompanying malnutrition and alcoholism. Beriberi also may affect pregnant women who have a poor diet, and people in institutions where there is poor nutritional planning, such as some prisons, geriatric hospitals, or institutions for the mentally ill.

Vitamin B3 and pellagra   A deficiency of vitamin B3 (also called niacin) leads to a disease called pellagra (pe-LAG-ra). Good sources of niacin include liver, lean meat, whole wheat products, fish, eggs, roasted peanuts, the white meat of poultry, avocados, dates, figs, prunes, kidney, wheat germ, and brewer's yeast.

Pellagra affects the skin, nervous system, and digestion, and can cause the "four Ds": diarrhea, dermatitis, dementia, and death. A person who is developing pellagra may feel weak and tired, may have trouble sleeping, and may lose weight. The skin that is exposed to the sun may become scaly, rough, and reddened, and painful sores may develop in the mouth. There is a loss of appetite accompanied by indigestion and diarrhea. A

Beta-Carotene and Vitamin A Research

As of 1999, 22,000 physicians under the supervision of the Department of Medicine at Harvard University were studying the long-term effects on the body of beta-carotene (vitamin A).

Among the questions about beta-carotene that researchers hope to answer:

- Can it lower the incidence of cancer?
- Can it boost resistance to infection?
- Can it be useful in the treatment of AIDS?

85 YEARS AGO:
JOSEPH GOLDBERGER

Joseph Goldberger (1881–1929) was a member of the United States Public Health Service. In 1914, he joined a commission to study the high number of pellagra cases in the southern United States. Goldberger determined that pellagra was not an infectious disease, and that a pellagra-preventing factor in certain foods could prevent its occurrence. In 1928, niacin (vitamin B3) was accepted as the factor that prevented pellagra.

Niacin is also known as nicotinic acid. The active form of niacin used by the body is called niacinamide.

person with pellagra also might experience headaches, dizziness, and muscular tremors. Sometimes mental disorders (or dementia) appear.

Pellagra is common around the world, although the "fortification" of processed wheat with vitamin B in the United States keeps the numbers low. Pellagra is seen in people who eat mostly corn rather than wheat and in people whose diets lack enough protein. People with gastrointestinal diseases that prevent their bodies from using B vitamins properly also may develop pellagra.

Other B complex vitamins Cobalamin (B12) provides protection against certain types of anemia and mental disturbances. Vitamin B6 can protect against anemia, skin problems, and irritability.

Vitamin C and scurvy Vitamin C affects blood vessels, skin, gums, connective tissue, red blood cells, wound healing, and the absorption of iron. A deficiency of vitamin C leads to scurvy. The main symptom of scurvy is hemorrhaging, or bleeding under the skin, which results in the appearance of many bruises. A person with scurvy also may have swollen and infected gums. Wounds heal slowly, and bleeding in or around vital organs can be fatal.

Scurvy is one of the oldest deficiency diseases recorded and the first one to be cured by adding a vitamin to the diet. It was a common malady of sailors during the age of exploration of the New World. In the modern world, people whose diets lack vitamin C-rich foods, such as citrus fruits, are still at risk of developing scurvy. Those most at risk are infants, the elderly, and people on fad diets.

Vitamin D, rickets, and osteomalacia Vitamin D is essential for proper bone formation because it helps regulate the amounts of certain bone-forming minerals (calcium and phosphate) in the bloodstream. Vitamin D is added to milk and infant formula and is found in other foods, like sardines, salmon, and tuna. Vitamin D also is made by the skin in response to exposure to sunlight.

Without enough vitamin D, a person can develop a disease called rickets, which is characterized by bone deformities. Rickets affects mainly children, because bone growth occurs during childhood. Rickets can cause the legs to become bowed by the weight of the body, and can cause the wrists and ankles to become thickened. Teeth are badly affected and take a longer time than usual to come in. All the bones are affected by not having sufficient calcium and phosphorous for their growth and development. Childhood rickets once was a common disease of infants and children, but is rarely seen today because milk and infant formulas have vitamin D added to them.

An adult version of rickets caused by a deficiency of Vitamin D, calcium, and phosphorous is called osteomalacia (os-tee-o-ma-LAY-sha). The bones become soft, deformed, and painful. This disease is seen more often in the Middle East and Asia than in Western countries.

Vitamins E and K   Vitamin E helps prevent reproductive problems and promotes good skin health. Vitamin K promotes normal blood clotting by aiding in the manufacture of fibrinogen (fy-BRIN-o-jen) and other proteins needed for clotting. Vitamin E deficiencies are not very common, and Vitamin K deficiencies are rare except in newborns. To prevent newborn bleeding, newborns are given a shot of vitamin K.

Folate and birth defects   A deficiency in folate (also known as folic acid or folacin) in pregnant women can result in some central nervous system birth defects in their babies. To help prevent these birth defects, it is important for pregnant women to supplement their diets with folate very early in their pregnancies. The best food sources for folate include deep green leafy vegetables, carrots, liver, egg yolk, cantaloupe, apricot, pumpkin, avocado, beans, and whole wheat and dark rye flours.

Mineral Deficiencies

There are about 25 mineral elements in the body that usually appear in the form of simple salts. Those minerals that appear in large amounts are called macrominerals, whereas those that are in small or trace amounts are called microminerals. Minerals known to be essential to a healthy body include calcium, phosphorous, cobalt, copper, fluorine, iodine, iron, and sodium. The result of a mineral deficiency depends on the particular mineral that is missing from the diet.

Iodine, goiter, and hypothyroidism   Iodine is necessary for the proper functioning of the thyroid, a gland that controls the body's metabolic rate and producing essential hormones*. Without sufficient iodine in the diet, the thyroid begins to enlarge its cells in an effort to produce its hormones, and this activity may produce a goiter, which is a swelling in the front of the neck. Most goiters in countries with high standards of living result from diseases of the thyroid rather than from a dietary deficiency of iodine.

Vitamin C Megadoses and Linus Pauling

Two-time Nobel laureate Linus Pauling believed that vitamin C was effective in preventing and lessening the effects of colds. He also proposed the use of vitamin C in the treatment of cancer. Pauling's program called for extremely large doses (megadoses) of Vitamin C, from 2,000 to 9,000 milligrams (mg), which greatly exceeds the government's recommended daily requirements. The National Research Council recommends 60 mg daily for non-smoking adults and 100 mg daily for smokers.

Many people follow Pauling's vitamin C regimen when they feel a cold coming on, despite the lack of supporting evidence for his theory.

*hormones are chemicals that are produced by different glands in the body. Hormones are like the body's ambassadors: they are created in one place but are sent through the body to have specific regulatory effects in different places.

Some geographic regions lack iodine in the soil, which can lead to hypothyroidism (underactive thyroid) and to arrested physical and mental development in infants. One very common source of iodine is iodized salt. Another excellent source of iodine is the sea vegetable kelp.

Iron and anemia   Iron is necessary for the formation of certain proteins and enzymes. Hemoglobin (HE-mo-glo-bin), which is the oxygen-carrying protein in the blood, is one such iron-dependent protein. Iron deficiency can lead to anemia, a lack of oxygen in the blood, which in turn can lead to fatigue and other complications. Good food sources of iron are liver, lean meats, legumes, dried fruits, and green leafy vegetables.

Other minerals   A zinc deficiency can lead to prostate* and skin disorders, while a copper deficiency can lead to metabolic disorders. Deficiencies of calcium and phosphorus lead to softening of the bones or to hypercalcemia (hy-per-kal-SEE-mee-a), a condition in which too much calcium leads to a surplus formation of bone.

Zinc and copper are trace elements that are found in a variety of foods. Deficiencies of these minerals are rare. Dairy products, green vegetables, sunflower seeds, cooked dried beans, walnuts, sardines, salmon, and soy products are good sources of calcium. Phosphorous is found in many foods, including fish, poultry, meat, whole grains, eggs, nuts, and seeds.

* **prostate** (PROS-tate) is a gland in the male. Located near the bladder and urethra, it secretes the fluid component of semen.

How Are Dietary Deficiency Diseases Treated and Prevented?

In most cases, dietary deficiency diseases are treated by giving the affected person foods rich in the missing nutrient and/or by giving them supplements. A person's recovery (none, partial, or full) depends on the particular disease, at what age the disease developed, and whether the effects are reversible once they have occurred.

Most dietary deficiency diseases can be prevented by eating a well-balanced diet comprising a diversity of foods. Ongoing medical care can help prevent dietary deficiency diseases caused by genetic problems and by metabolic problems that prevent the body from absorbing or utilizing nutrients properly.

In countries where food and money are scarce, however, dietary deficiency diseases remain all too common among children and adults.

Resources

Books

Mindell, Earl and Hester Mundis. *Earl Mindell's Vitamin Bible for the 21st Century*. New York: Warner Books, 1999.

Pressman, Alan H., Sheila Buff, and Gary Null. *The Complete Idiot's Guide to Vitamins and Minerals*. New York: Alpha Books, 1998.

Tamborlane, William V., Janet Z. Weiswasser, Teresa Fung, and Jane E. Brody. *The Yale Guide to Children's Nutrition.* New Haven: Yale University Press, 1997.

Organizations

The U.S. Food and Drug Administration (FDA) posts many useful fact sheets at its website, along with a food pyramid to guide dietary choices. http://vm.cfsan.fda.gov

The U.S. National Institutes of Health (NIH) and its member institutes have a *Consumer Health Information* website, with links to many different fact sheets about diet. http://www.nih.gov/health/consumer/conkey.htm

The World Health Organization (WHO) posts fact sheets about *Food and Nutrition* at its website. http://www.who.org/home/map_ht.html

The International Food Information Council, 1100 Connecticut Avenue N.W., Suite 430, Washington, D.C. 20036. This group's website posts information about nutrition for adults and for children along with an online glossary of nutrition-related terms. http://ificinfo.health.org

▶ *See also*
Anemia
Eating Disorders
Genetic Diseases
Kwashiorkor
Metabolic Diseases
Osteoporosis
Rickets
Scurvy
Skin Conditions
Thyroid Disease

Diphtheria

Diphtheria (dif-THEE-ree-a) is a serious, sometimes fatal bacterial disease caused by Corynebacteria diphtheriae *that begins with nose and throat symptoms.*

KEYWORDS
for searching the Internet
and other reference sources

Antitoxin

Corynebacterium diphtheriae

Respiratory system

Vaccination

What Is Diphtheria?

Descriptions of diphtheria date from antiquity. The microorganism that causes it, a bacterium called *Corynebacterium diphtheriae* (ko-rin-ee-bak-TEE-ree-um dif-THEE-ree-eye), enters the body through the tonsils, nose, and throat, and multiplies there, producing a thick, gray membrane made of bacteria, dead cells, and a tough protein called fibrin that can eventually block breathing and swallowing. The word *diphtheria* comes from the Greek for "leather hide." The bacteria also produce a toxin, or poison, called diphtheria exotoxin, which spreads by way of the blood to other tissues of the body, such as the heart and nerves. In severe cases, the damage the toxin causes can result in heart failure and paralysis leading to death.

How Is Diphtheria Caught?

Diphtheria is highly contagious*. Although it is now rare in the United States and Europe, it was a leading cause of death in infants and children

* **contagious** means transmittable from one person to another.

291

until the twentieth century. It still occurs in other places in the world, and in 1993 and 1994, some 50,000 cases were reported in the former Soviet Union.

Diphtheria is spread when a person breathes in particles that someone with diphtheria releases into the air when sneezing or even talking. People with diphtheria can infect others for up to 4 weeks. Unimmunized people at greatest risk of catching diphtheria are children under 5 and adults over 60, as well as people who live in crowded, unsanitary conditions or who do not get adequate nutrition.

What Are the Symptoms of Diphtheria?

Symptoms of diphtheria usually appear 2 to 4 days after infection. At first, the infection feels like a bad sore throat. A person may also have a mild fever and swollen glands. Children frequently have nausea, vomit-

75 YEARS AGO: NOME, ALASKA

In 1925, an epidemic of diphtheria struck the small Alaskan town of Nome. There was not enough antitoxin to treat all the townspeople, and severe winter weather prevented airplanes from delivering the serum. So a relay of sled dog teams from Nenana (675 miles away) rushed the antitoxin to Nome, arriving in just under 27.5 hours and saving the lives of many people. The Iditarod Sled Dog Race from Anchorage to Nome commemorates this historic serum run each year.

A statue in New York City's Central Park honors Balto, one of the sled dogs who carried diphtheria antitoxin to Nome in 1925. © *Kim Heacox/Peter Arnold, Inc.*

DOCTOR'S DILEMMA

I n Sinclair Lewis's novel *Arrowsmith*, the inexperienced young doctor Martin Arrowsmith must choose between cutting an opening in the windpipe of a girl dying of diphtheria or making a long trip to try to fetch antitoxin that will lessen the effects of the disease.

ing, chills, headache, and fever. The thick coating that forms in the nose, throat, or airway can make it hard to breathe or to swallow.

A doctor diagnoses diphtheria by taking a swab from the throat and doing laboratory tests to detect the bacterium, or by doing blood tests for antibodies to diphtheria toxin, that is, substances produced by the body to protect it from the toxin.

How Is Diphtheria Treated?

Children and adults with diphtheria are treated in the hospital. An antitoxin is given to neutralize the diphtheria toxin in the body and to keep the disease from progressing. Antibiotics are given to destroy the diphtheria bacteria. Patients are kept isolated, and doctors will also examine members of their families who may have been exposed to the bacteria, and recommend appropriate treatment.

How Can Diphtheria Be Prevented?

With treatment, most people recover from diphtheria. But unlike diseases such as measles or chickenpox, getting diphtheria once does not mean a person will never get it again. So the best way to prevent the disease is to be vaccinated against it. Diphtheria vaccine is usually given together with vaccines that protect against two other diseases: tetanus (also called lockjaw) and pertussis (also known as whooping cough). This DTP vaccine is given at 2, 4, and 6 months of age, with additional shots given at 12 to 18 months and again at 4 to 6 years to boost the body's defenses. After age 11 to 16, booster vaccinations against diphtheria and tetanus should be given every 10 years.

Resources

Organizations

U.S. Centers for Disease Control and Prevention (CDC), 1600 Clifton Road, NE, Atlanta, GA 30333. The United States government authority for information about infectious and other diseases, the CDC posts information about diphtheria on its website at: http://www.cdc.gov/nip/vaccine/hip-dtp.htm

The World Health Organization (WHO), Avenue Appia 20, 1211 Geneva 27, Switzerland. This group's website posts a fact sheet about diphtheria at:
http://www.who.int/inf-fs/en/fact089.htm

Short Story

Williams, William Carlos. "The Use of Force." In *Telling Stories: An Anthology for Writers*, edited by Joyce Carol Oates. New York: Norton, 1998.

Tutorial

"Childhood Infections: Diphtheria." Helpful information for parents about diphtheria from the Nemours Foundation.
www.kidshealth.org/parent/common/diphtheria.html

▶ *See also*
Bacterial Infections
Tetanus
Whooping Cough

Dissociative Identity Disorder *See* Multiple Personality Disorder

---

Diverticulitis/Diverticulosis

Diverticulosis is the presence of diverticula (dy-ver-TIK-yoo-la) in the colon (large intestine). Diverticula are small sacs or pouches that bulge outward from the inside surface of intestinal wall. If diverticula become inflamed or infected, the resulting disease is called diverticulitis.

KEYWORDS
for searching the Internet and other reference sources

Gastrointestinal tract

Inflammation

The cause of diverticulosis is not known with certainty, but many physicians believe that it is related to too little roughage in the diet. Roughage is coarse, bulky food that is rich in plant fiber. It has been observed that people in developing countries whose diets include large amounts of plant materials (fruits and vegetables) almost never have diverticulosis.

Diverticulosis is common in the United States and in other developed countries, where refined foods often lack significant amounts of fiber. Young people rarely have diverticulosis, but it is more likely to occur as people age. By the time a person in the United States reaches the age of 80, there is more than a 50 percent chance that he or she will have diverticulosis.

What Do Diverticula Look Like?

Diverticula occur most commonly in the sigmoid colon, which is the part of the large intestine closest to the rectum. There are usually many of them, ranging from pea size or smaller to about 1 inch across. Doctors believe these pouches may form due to pressure in the lower intestine, as

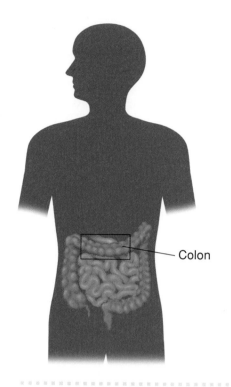

Colon

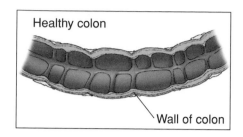

Healthy colon

Wall of colon

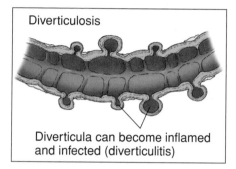

Diverticulosis

Diverticula can become inflamed
and infected (diverticulitis)

Diverticula are small pouches bulging
from the wall of the intestines.

occurs in constipation. That is why a high-fiber diet, which keeps wastes
moving smoothly through the bowel and distributes pressure more
evenly, is thought to reduce the likelihood of developing diverticulosis
or diverticulitis.

How Do Doctors Diagnose and Treat Diverticula?

Symptoms People with diverticulosis may never know they have it,
because it does not always cause symptoms. Sometimes, however, the
diverticula may become inflamed, causing diverticulitis. This may happen when the diverticula become plugged with wastes. The symptoms of
diverticulitis include abdominal pain, fever, gas, diarrhea or constipation, and bleeding from the rectum.

Diagnosis A doctor can find out if a person has diverticula by x-ray
examination or by looking inside the colon through a viewing instrument
like a sigmoidoscope (sig-MOI-do-skope) or a colonoscope (ko-LON-o-
skope). Diverticula that have not caused symptoms are sometimes discovered during routine medical checkups.

Treatment Diverticulosis does not usually require special treatment,
although doctors may recommend increasing roughage in the diet. In
mild cases of diverticulitis, treatment may include drinking more fluids,
bed rest, and antibiotics to control infection. Sometimes doctors recommend intravenous (in-tra-VEE-nus) or IV fluids*.

    Occasionally, diverticulitis may be accompanied by serious complica-
tions. If diverticula rupture (RUP-chur) or break open, intestinal contents
may leak or spill out and cause an infection in the surrounding abdomen.

* **intravenous** (IV) fluids are fluids
given through a flexible plastic
tube into a person's vein.

Sometimes the intestine may become blocked or narrowed, in which case surgery may be needed.

How Are Diverticula Prevented?

Including adequate amounts of vegetable fiber in the diet is often recommended as a way to avoid diverticulosis and diverticulitis. Bran, cabbage, beans, and whole-grain breads are examples of foods high in dietary fiber. Fiber supplements are often used, particularly by older adults, to maintain regular bowel habits and to reduce the risk of diverticulitis.

Resource

Janowitz, Henry D. *Your Gut Feelings*. New York: Oxford University Press, 1994. A nontechnical book that includes helpful information about intestinal disorders, with a separate chapter on diverticulitis and diverticulosis.

▶ *See also*

Constipation

KEYWORDS
for searching the Internet and other reference sources

Chromosomes

Mosaicism

Trisomy 21

Down Syndrome

Down Syndrome is a genetic condition that occurs when a person has three copies of chromosome 21 rather than the usual two. People with Down Syndrome usually have a characteristic physical appearance, significantly lowered intellectual abilities, and sometimes a number of physical problems, such as heart defects.

Jason's Sister Anna: A Look at Someone with Down Syndrome

First and foremost, Jason's sister Anna is a happy, active, five-year-old girl. But she also is a girl with Down Syndrome, and Jason feels more protective of his sister than do most big brothers. When they are out at the mall, everyone says how adorable Anna is, but they also stare at her. Anna has many of the characteristic features of people with Down Syndrome. These features may include:

- a flattened face
- up-slanted eyes
- low-set ears
- a protruding tongue
- a short neck

- a single, straight crease across the palm
- characteristic patterns of the ridges of the skin on her fingers, palms, and soles
- short arms and legs
- poor muscle tone
- mental retardation
- certain other health problems

All of these characteristics vary among affected people, and some people with Down Syndrome have fewer of these features than do others. Anna is somewhere in the middle of the range. She is moderately mentally retarded.

Jason researched Down Syndrome for a school report and now worries about Anna's health. Many people with Down Syndrome have health problems such as heart defects, increased susceptibility* to infection, respiratory problems, and digestive problems. Childhood leukemia occurs slightly more frequently in children with Down Syndrome than in other children, and adults with the syndrome are at increased risk for Alzheimer's disease.

*__susceptibility__ (su-sep-ti-BIL-i-tee) means having less resistance to and higher risk for infection or disease.

What Is Down Syndrome?

People have Down Syndrome when they have three copies of chromosome 21 (or parts of chromosome 21). Chromosomes provide all of the genetic information needed for the cells of the body to work properly. Normally, most of a person's cells contain 23 pairs of chromosomes, for a total of 46. The exceptions are eggs and sperm cells, which have only one set of 23 chromosomes. Most people with Down Syndrome have 47 chromosomes, instead of the usual 46, and the extra genetic material causes developmental problems. Down Syndrome can occur in three ways.

Nondisjunction   Ninety-five percent of people with Down Syndrome have Trisomy 21, meaning they have three copies of chromosome 21. This

---

A BRIEF HISTORY OF DOWN SYNDROME RESEARCH

1866: An English physician, John Langdon Haydon Down (1828-1896), published the first description in the medical literature of a person with Down Syndrome.

1959: Jerome Lejeune, a French physician, found the extra chromosome 21.

1990: Chromosome 21 was the first chromosome to be fully mapped*.

*__mapping__ locates the positions of all the genes on a chromosome.

*replicate (REP-li-kate) means to create an identical copy.

occurs because of an error in cell division called nondisjunction. Normally, an egg or a sperm cell has only 23 chromosomes. During the cell divisions that form these reproductive cells, the 23 chromosomes first replicate* and then separate, with one set of 23 going to each new cell. If the two copies of chromosome 21 do not separate, however, the result is an egg or a sperm cell with two copies of the chromosome instead of the usual one. At least 95 percent of the time, trisomy 21 occurs when a normal sperm fertilizes an egg with two copies of chromosome 21. When cell division begins to form an embryo, the extra chromosome is then replicated in every cell of the body.

Translocation   When the extra chromosome 21 breaks off during cell division and attaches to another chromosome, it is called translocation. In this case, the total number of chromosomes is 46, but the genetic material from the extra chromosome 21 that is attached to another chromosome causes the features of Down Syndrome. Translocation accounts for 3 to 4 percent of Down Syndrome cases.

Mosaicism   The third type of Down Syndrome is called mosaicism (mo-ZAY-i-siz-im). This occurs when nondisjunction of chromosome 21 takes place in one of the initial cell divisions after the egg is fertilized, causing some cells to have 46 chromosomes and others to have 47. Only 1 to 2 percent of people with Down Syndrome have mosaicism.

What Causes Down Syndrome?

No one knows what causes the chromosomal abnormality that results in Down Syndrome, a condition that affects approximately 1 in 1,000 babies. Any woman can have a baby with Down Syndrome. It is not associated with a person's culture, race, where they live, or how rich or poor they are.

*correlated means linked in a way that can be measured and predicted.

A mother's age, however, does seem to be correlated* with her risk of having a child with Down Syndrome. While 80 percent of children with Down Syndrome are born to women younger than 35, this means that 20 percent are born to women older than 35. But women over 35 only have 5 to 8 percent of all babies. In other words, older women have a greater chance of giving birth to a baby with Down Syndrome, and the risks increase as women grow older. Researchers estimate the chance of having a baby with Down Syndrome to be:

- approximately 1 in 1,250 for a 25-year-old woman
- approximately 1 in 378 for a 35-year-old woman
- approximately 1 in 30 for a 45-year-old woman.

Can a Pregnant Woman Find Out if Her Baby Has Down Syndrome?

Down Syndrome is the most common chromosomal abnormality in humans, and there are several ways to test for it.

Screening tests   The triple screen test and the alpha-fetoprotein (AFP) test are commonly used to predict whether a woman is carrying a baby with Down Syndrome. They arc called screening tests because they do not give a definite answer. Instead, they measure the amounts of certain substances in the mother's blood that can indicate a problem. If one of these tests is positive, it does not necessarily mean that the fetus (the developing baby) has Down Syndrome, but it does indicate that more tests should be done. Sometimes the test results are false-negatives, meaning that the test did not indicate Down Syndrome even though the fetus has it. Low levels of AFP in the mother's blood are correlated with Down Syndrome in the fetus, but the test detects only about 35 percent of cases. The triple test, which measures levels of three substances, is correct about 60 percent of the time.

Diagnostic tests   Pregnant women over 35, and women with positive results of screening tests, can be tested using several different diagnostic tests, such as amniocentesis (am-nee-o-sen-TEE-sis), in which the chromosomes from the fetus's cells are examined. Diagnostic tests give a definite answer, which means they are correct 98 to 99 percent of the time. For these tests, samples are extracted from the tissue or fluid surrounding the fetus or from the umbilical cord. On rare occasions, these procedures cause the mother to have a miscarriage (lose the baby before birth). Women who plan to have diagnostic tests performed should receive information and have emotional support available to help them understand the procedures and cope with test results indicating Down Syndrome and with the possibility of miscarriage.

What Does Life Hold for Anna and Her Family?

In 1910, most children with Down Syndrome did not live past the age of nine. When antibiotics were developed in the 1940s, the average child with Down Syndrome survived to age 19 or 20. By the start of the twenty-first

Most people with Down Syndrome have some degree of mental retardation, but many are able to go to school and to live at home with their families or in group homes that help them work independently. *CORBIS/Lester V. Bergman.*

century, because of advances in clinical medicine, about 80 percent of people with Down Syndrome are expected to live to age 55 or longer.

Anna's family learned all they could about Down Syndrome as soon as she was born. They knew Anna would learn to sit, walk, and talk somewhat later than her peers. Anna's family is providing her with a stimulating home environment, good medical care, and good educational programs. They are teaching her to be a happy productive member of the community. Whether she will ever be able to go to school or to work or live independently depends on the level of her mental development. However, Anna's family knows that the Americans with Disabilities Act of 1991 (ADA) will help protect Anna's right to live her life free of unnecessary limitations or discrimination due to her disabilities.

Resources

Books

Cunningham, Cliff. *Down Syndrome: An Introduction for Parents*. Boston: Brookline Books, 1995.

Hassold, Terry J., and David Patterson. *Down Syndrome: A Promising Future, Together*. New York: John Wiley, 1998.

Selikowitz, Mark. *Down Syndrome: The Facts*. New York: Oxford University Press, 1997.

Organizations

National Down Syndrome Society, 666 Broadway, 8th Floor, New York, NY 10012-2317.
Telephone 800-221-4602

National Down Syndrome Congress, 1800 Dempster Street, Park Ridge, IL 60068-1146.
Telephone 800-232-NDSC

▶ *See also*
Genetic Diseases
Mental Retardation

Drug Abuse/Addiction *See* Substance Abuse

Dwarfism

Dwarfism and other types of short stature have many different causes.

Life As a Little Person

Don is an energetic and outgoing young man in his twenties, and when people stare he never misses the opportunity to explain that he has achondroplasia (a-kon-dro-PLAY-zee-a), a genetic condition that affects his skeletal system and causes his unusual appearance.

KEYWORDS
*for searching the Internet
and other reference sources*

Achondroplasia

Endocrinology

Genetics

Human growth hormone

Musculoskeletal system

Don is 4 feet 5 inches tall, his arms and legs are very short, his head looks big for his body, his forehead bulges, and his jaw sticks out. Don tells people that the proper term for people with achondroplasia is dwarf or little person (although he prefers just plain Don). Don likes to show kids who are the same size he is that he can drive a car because the pedals have been equipped with extensions.

Don does not consider himself disabled, although dwarfism is recognized as a disability under the Americans with Disabilities Act. Don endured a lot of teasing as a child, but he attributes his self-esteem to a supportive family and to a peer group called Little People of America (LPA).

What Is Dwarfism?

Dwarfism is a condition that causes people to be unusually short. Many types of dwarfism are caused by an underlying genetic problem. Gene* mutations (changes) that cause dwarfism can be spontaneous (not carried by the parents), and most people with dwarfism are born to average-sized parents. In some cases, however, dwarfism is inherited.

There are over 100 causes of short stature, many of which fall into the following categories:

* **genes** are chemicals in the body that help determine a person's characteristics, such as hair or eye color. They are inherited from a person's parents and are contained in the chromosomes found in the cells of the body.

- Mutations (changes) in certain genes cause skeletal disorders in which the bones, especially the arms and leg bones, do not develop properly. Achondroplasia, the most common form of dwarfism, affects about 1 in 25,000 people. The average adult height of people with achondroplasia is 4 feet tall.

- Metabolic and hormonal disorders can cause proportional short stature, a condition in which people are small but all of their body parts are proportional to each other. Malnutrition, kidney disease, or diseases in which the body cannot absorb food properly can cause this type of short stature. More commonly, it occurs when the pituitary gland, a hormone-secreting gland attached to the brain, does not secrete enough growth hormone.

- Disorders of certain chromosomes also can cause short stature. For example, the average height of adult women with Turner syndrome, a genetic condition caused by a missing or partially missing X chromosome, falls between 4 feet 6 inches and 4 feet 8 inches without treatment. Down Syndrome, a condition that occurs when a person has three copies of chromosome 21, also results in arms and legs that are shorter than usual.

What Are the Signs of Dwarfism?

Unusually short stature and very short legs and arms are the most visible signs of dwarfism. Some people also are affected by other problems, which may include:

- Late development of motor skills

- Increased susceptibility to middle ear infections

Diego Rodríguez de Silva Velázquez (1599–1660) painted this portrait of the Spanish royal family in 1656. The royal court included two ladies-in-waiting with dwarfism. The painting now hangs in the Museo del Prado in Madrid. *Erich Lessing, Scala/Art Resource, New York.*

- Pressure on the brain and spinal cord, resulting in nerve and breathing problems

- Hydrocephalus (hy-dro-SEF-a-lus), excess fluid in the brain

- Crowding of teeth in the jaw

- Weight problems

- Curvature of the spine and bowed legs

- Fatigue, numbness in the back and thighs, back pain

- Problems with joints

How Is Dwarfism Diagnosed and Treated?

Diagnosis Once dwarfism is suspected in a developing child (for instance because of outward appearance, failure to grow, or how bones look in x-rays), doctors must find the underlying cause. Scientists know which genes cause some forms of dwarfism, so genetic tests can confirm or rule out those specific conditions. Growth hormone deficiency and certain other growth disorders should be looked for.

Treatment Dwarfism caused by a deficiency of growth hormone is treated by giving the child growth hormone injections; many patients receiving this treatment grow several inches per year faster than they did before treatment. The growth of girls with Turner syndrome can also be improved with growth hormone therapy. There is no proven way yet to successfully promote growth in people with many other forms of dwarfism, but medical care is essential to prevent and treat complications caused by skeletal abnormalities.

Surgery Joint replacement surgery can help improve mobility for some people with dwarfism. Sometimes, people with achondroplasia opt for an experimental surgical procedure that lengthens the arms and legs. It involves cutting a bone, inserting a scaffold between the bone segments, and allowing new bone to grow and fill in the gaps. Limb-lengthening surgery is not a common treatment; it is controversial; it is painful; it requires repeated surgeries; and it can lead to complications such as nerve damage.

Resources

Book

Roloff, Matt, and Tracy Sumner. *Against Tall Odds: Being a David in a Goliath World*. Sisters, OR: Multnomah, 1999.

Organizations

Human Growth Foundation (HGF), 997 Glen Cove Avenue, Glen Head, NY 11545
Telephone 800-451-6434
http://www.hgfound.org

Little People of America (LPA) National Headquarters, Box 745, Lubbock, TX 79408
Telephone: 888-LPA-2001
http://www.lpaonline.org

▶ See also
Birth Defects
Dietary Deficiencies
Down Syndrome
Ear Infections
Genetic Diseases
Growth Disorders
Hydrocephalus
Kidney Disease
Obesity
Turner Syndrome

Dysentery *See* Diarrhea

Dyslexia

Dyslexia (dis-LEX-ee-a) is a learning disability that affects a person's ability to interpret written words and write and spell properly.

What Is Dyslexia?

Dyslexia is a learning disability* that makes a person unable to recognize written words properly. It comes from the combination of two Greek

KEYWORDS
for searching the Internet and other reference sources

Language disorders

Learning disabilities

Special education

Specific reading disability

303

learning disability refers to a disorder in the basic mental processes used for language or math. The disorder occurs in people of normal or above-normal intelligence. It is not the result of an emotional disturbance or of an impairment in sight or hearing.

genetic refers to a trait that is passed from parent to child through the genes, the hereditary material that helps determine many physical and mental characteristics.

Students with dyslexia often have trouble with writing and spelling as well as reading. *Will and Deni McIntyre/Science Source, Photo Researchers, Inc.*

words: "dys," which means trouble, and "lexia," which means words. "Trouble with words" in any language translates into difficulty with reading. Most people with dyslexia also have trouble with writing and spelling. In addition, some have difficulty with numbers. Dyslexia is sometimes referred to as specific reading disability.

Dyslexia affects about 10 to 15 percent of school-age children. About four out of every five children with dyslexia are boys. The disorder affects all races equally and is the most common type of learning disability.

What Causes Dyslexia?

No one knows for sure what causes dyslexia. However, scientists believe that it may be caused by a malfunction in part of the brain that recognizes and interprets words. Some scientists think that it is rooted in the development of the right side of the brain, which deals with processing words. When people with dyslexia look at or hear words, their eyes and ears work properly. However, a part of their brain misinterprets the words and delivers a faulty message back to them. In many cases, dyslexia may be genetic*, since people with the disorder often have a family history of learning disabilities.

One thing that is not related to having dyslexia is being unintelligent or lazy. People who have difficulty reading sometimes are told that they are "stupid." This is not true. In fact, most people with dyslexia have normal or above-normal intelligence. They simply have a part of their brain that does not translate messages about written words correctly.

How Do People Know They Have Dyslexia?

Dyslexia usually is not diagnosed very early in a child's life, because children are not expected to learn to read until about age six. However, once children with dyslexia start school, they may have a very hard time keeping up with their classmates. Words and letters appear much differently

to a person with dyslexia than to a person without it. Sometimes words look all jammed together, while other times there seem to be spaces between words where they do not belong.

Some people with dyslexia see words backwards, as if they were viewing the words in a mirror. They may see p's where there should be b's; for example, "pall" instead of "ball." They also may see words reversed; for example, "was" instead of "saw." More often, people with dyslexia do not recognize that words are made up of small units of sound, known as phonemes*.

Because reading goes hand in hand with writing, children with dyslexia often have a difficult time learning to write correctly. They may flip letters or write letters upside down. Letters that look similar may confuse such children when they try to write; for example, "doll" may become "boll." Since the letters are shaped incorrectly, the children's handwriting may be very hard to read. The ability to spell properly also is affected by dyslexia. Letters may not appear in the right order; for example, "purple" may become "pruple." Some letters may be left out entirely, making the word "puple."

When children have this kind of difficulty with reading, writing, and spelling, it is easy for them to fall behind in school and feel frustrated, even though they may be very intelligent. Not surprisingly, many adults with dyslexia say that they hated reading when they were young. Fortunately, most teachers today are trained to recognize dyslexia and take action to help the child.

How Is Dyslexia Diagnosed?

The first step in diagnosing dyslexia is often a thorough physical exam. The physician can run various tests, including vision and hearing tests, to rule out other problems. The physician also can do a neurologic exam* to measure how well the different parts of the nervous system are working.

If dyslexia is suspected, the physician may enlist the help of a specialist in learning disabilities. The specialist can administer tests to figure out how the child's brain processes information. The child may take an intelligence test* as well as academic achievement tests that assess reading and writing skills. Sometimes the child also may take tests that assess abilities in other areas, such as math, logic, and creative thinking.

Once testing is completed, the specialist can determine whether the child has dyslexia by comparing the child's intelligence test against the reading and writing tests. Average or high scores on an intelligence test and low scores on reading and writing tests are typical of people with dyslexia.

What Can Be Done about Dyslexia?

The earlier a child is diagnosed with dyslexia, and the earlier the child's family and teachers are made aware of the diagnosis, the better. Children with dyslexia must learn to read in a different way from those who do not have the disorder. Many children who do not have their dyslexia diagnosed until later do poorly in school year after year, as they try to learn to read the same way everyone else does. Eventually, after their dyslexia is diagnosed, they must go back and relearn how to read.

Reading Disability

When Tommy opened his history book, this is the story he saw:

Wenthe Pil grims la n bed ta Plymoutthey wer ein a mostbre cariouss itua tion.T heye ar saw lateandther e wasmuc h sickness s a mon g the sett l ers.

When Jason opened his book to the same page, this is what he saw:

When the Pilgrims landed at Plymouth they were in a most precarious situation. The year was late, and there was much sickness among the settlers.

For most people, reading about the first American settlers is easy and interesting. For some people, though, this passage is very difficult and frustrating to read, because it looks more like the first example, not the second. People who see or hear words this way have the disorder called dyslexia.

* **phonemes** (FO-neemz) are the smallest units of spoken language, such as the "puh" sound at the start of the word "pat."

* **neurologic exam** refers to systematic tests of how well various parts of the nervous system are functioning.

* **intelligence test,** also known as an IQ test, refers to a test designed to estimate a person's intellectual potential.

Dyslexia Hall of Fame

Many people with dyslexia go far beyond merely living up to their potential. Following is a list of just some of the famous people of today and times past who achieved their career dreams despite dyslexia or other learning disabilities:

- Hans Christian Andersen
- Cher
- Winston Churchill
- Tom Cruise
- Leonardo da Vinci
- Thomas Edison
- Danny Glover
- Whoopi Goldberg
- Bruce Jenner
- Greg Louganis
- Michelangelo
- Auguste Rodin
- Woodrow Wilson
- William Butler Yeats

Whether it is a younger child with dyslexia who is first learning to read or an older child who is relearning, a special approach must be taken. In many cases, an individualized reading program is the first step. This means that a reading specialist creates a plan that is designed just for that child. The plan is based on many factors, such as how severe the child's dyslexia is and what the child's strengths are in other areas in school.

Many times, the reading plan for a student with dyslexia will include a multisensory approach. This means that instead of just using the sense of sight, the student also will use other senses, such as touch or hearing. In some cases, a student might feel clay or wooden models of letters while saying the letters aloud. In other cases, the student might learn letter sounds while looking at pictures, or listen to letter sounds on a tape while looking at the letters. The student also can work with the reading specialist on phonemes. Eventually, the student learns to create combinations of phonemes to form words, and from there to recognize and read words.

Students with dyslexia can be taught in different settings. Some are placed in special classrooms with other students who have reading disabilities, while others work one-on-one with a reading specialist at certain points during the school day.

Various other types of therapy have been suggested for people with dyslexia, such as vision therapy (eye exercises) and colored glasses. However, none of these therapies have proved to be widely successful in treating the disorder.

Living with Dyslexia

Children with dyslexia face a special challenge: not only must they learn to read, but they also must learn to read in a special way. People with dyslexia usually learn to read very slowly, and it can take lots of practice. Emotional support is very important. Many children with dyslexia complain of feeling "stupid" because they cannot read as easily as most of their classmates. With enough help and support, however, children with dyslexia can learn to read and write well. The reading and writing level that a person with dyslexia can achieve depends a lot on the severity of the disorder. For example, someone with a mild form of dyslexia may learn to read and write very well, while another person with severe dyslexia may always find reading and writing more difficult.

Children with dyslexia usually grow up the same way that other children do: into healthy adults with normal lives. Many people with dyslexia go to college and excel in their classes, sometimes by using special methods such as tape recording their lectures or taking oral exams instead of written ones. Adults with dyslexia can do well in many different kinds of jobs.

Can Dyslexia Be Cured?

At present, there is no cure for dyslexia. There is no drug that people with dyslexia can take to correct the problem. Scientists constantly are studying the various parts of the brain to learn why information is interpreted incorrectly in some people. However, the brain is very complex, and there are still many mysteries about what causes dyslexia and other learning disabilities.

Resources

Books

Goldish, Meish. *Everything You Need to Know About Dyslexia*. New York: Rosen Publishing Group, 1998. An informational book for young people about dyslexia.

Moragne, Wendy. *Dyslexia*. Brookfield, CT: Millbrook Press, 1997. A book about dyslexia told through the true stories of teenagers with the disorder.

Organizations

LD Online. A website that offers information about learning disabilities for children, parents, and teachers.
http://www.ldonline.org

Learning Disabilities Association of America, 4156 Library Road, Pittsburgh, PA 15234-1349. A national organization for people with learning disabilities and their families.
http://www.ldanatl.org

National Information Center for Children and Youth with Disabilities, P.O. Box 1492, Washington, DC 20013-1492. A national information center that provides information to the public about learning disabilities and special education.
Telephone 800-695-0285
http://www.nichcy.org

The U.S. National Institutes of Health (NIH) and its member institutes have a *Consumer Health Information* website, with links to fact sheets about *Learning Disabilities* and about *Why Children Succeed or Fail at Reading*.
http://www.nih.gov/health/consumer/conkey.htm

▶ *See also*
Attention Deficit Hyperactivity Disorder

Dysrhythmia

Dysrhythmia (dis-RITH-mee-a), or arrhythmia (a-RITH-mee-a), is a change in the regular beat of the heart. The heart may seem to skip a beat, beat irregularly, or beat very rapidly or very slowly.

KEYWORDS
for searching the Internet and other reference sources

Cardiac system

Coronary disease

Annie's Story

Annie, who had just turned 15, was running for student council treasurer. On the morning of her campaign speech before the entire student assembly, her heart began to race in her chest. Stepping behind the podium in the auditorium, she felt a little dizzy and out of breath. During the first few minutes of her speech, she worried that she might faint, but as she kept speaking and gained confidence, the sensations vanished and her heartbeat slowed down. By the time she reached her last sentence, everything was back to normal.

What Is Dysrhythmia?

Dysrhythmia is any variation in the regular beat of the heart. Some of these changes are normal—like Annie's palpitations*—while others are more serious. People's hearts naturally speed up with emotion or exercise and slow down during sleep. Other dysrhythmias are associated with heart disease and can be life threatening.

The human heart is a muscular pump divided into four chambers— two atria located on the top, and two ventricles located on the bottom. But it is more than a pump; it is also an amazing piece of electrical machinery that, when healthy, keeps these chambers beating in an organized manner.

Normally, the heartbeat begins in the right atrium when the sinoatrial (SA) node, a special group of cells, transmits an electrical signal across the heart. This signal spreads throughout the atria and to the atrioventricular (AV) node. The AV node connects to a group of fibers in

* **palpitation** is the sensation of a rapid or irregular heartbeat.

The sinoatrial node is the heart's pacemaker.

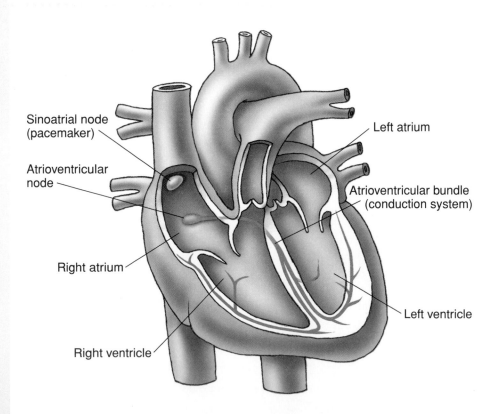

Sinoatrial node (pacemaker)

Atrioventricular node

Right atrium

Right ventricle

Left atrium

Atrioventricular bundle (conduction system)

Left ventricle

the ventricles that conducts the electrical signal and sends the impulse to all parts of the ventricles. This exact route must be followed to ensure that the heart pumps properly.

As the electrical impulse crosses through the heart, the heart contracts. This normally occurs about 60 to 100 times per minute, with each contraction equaling a single heartbeat. The atria contract about one-fifth of a second before the ventricles, allowing them to empty their blood into the ventricles before the ventricles contract.

Under some conditions, almost all heart tissue is capable of starting a heartbeat, or becoming the pacemaker. A dysrhythmia occurs when:

- the heart's natural pacemaker (the SA node) becomes defective;

- the normal conduction pathway to the AV node and the ventricles is interrupted;

- another part of the heart takes over as pacemaker.

What Causes Dysrhythmia?

External and internal forces can cause dysrhythmia. External factors include exhaustion, overexertion, emotional stress (such as Annie's campaign speech), cigarette smoking, drinking alcohol, and ingesting stimulants such as caffeine, decongestants, and cocaine. Internal factors include heart defects present at birth, thyroid problems, inflammatory diseases, and problems in the autonomic nervous system, which carries nerve impulses from the brain and spinal cord to the heart. The most important factor that contributes to serious dysrhythmias, however, is heart disease, including coronary artery disease, abnormal heart valves, and congenital heart disease.

Different Types of Dysrhythmia

Among the more common dysrhythmias are:

- **Bradycardia** (bray-dee-KAR-dee-a), a heart rate of fewer than 60 beats per minute in an adult.

- **Tachycardia** (tak-i-KAR-dee-a), a heart rate of more than 100 beats a minute in an adult.

- **Sick sinus syndrome**, in which the heart rate slows down or varies between slow and fast rates.

- **Atrial flutter**, a very fast (250 to 350 beats per minute) but steady heartbeat.

- **Atrial fibrillation** (AY-tree-al fib-ri-LAY-shun), in which the atria quiver instead of beating effectively. This is a major cause of stroke.

- **Ventricular tachycardia**, rapid heartbeat (>150 beats per minute) that can lead to ventricular fibrillation.

■ **Ventricular fibrillation** (ven-TRIK-yoo-lar fib-ri-LAY-shun), in which the ventricles quiver instead of beating, and the heart cannot pump any blood. Without emergency treatment, the person will die within minutes.

■ **Premature ventricular contractions**, extra heartbeats that are often felt as "missed beats" or "flipflops" in the chest.

Diagnosing Dysrhythmias

Symptoms of dysrhythmias can vary from none to fatigue, lightheadedness, dizziness, palpitations, fainting, or shortness of breath, to sudden collapse and death. Although many dysrhythmias are harmless, a doctor should check them because they can signal heart disease or other conditions that need treatment.

Like fingerprints found at a crime scene, electrocardiogram* (ECG or EKG) tracings are important pieces of physical evidence that track irregularities in the heartbeat. Sometimes, however, an abnormal heartbeat does not show up during a visit to the doctor. In that case, a 24-hour Holter ECG monitor can be worn to track the heartbeat. A stress test, in which the patient walks on a treadmill while being monitored, can help a physician see the effect of exercise on the heart.

Treating Dysrhythmias

Normally, people's heart rates vary a bit—even from one beat to the next. Many dysrhythmias—such as Annie's—require no treatment at all.

Some abnormal rhythms may need to be controlled with medication or, on occasion, electric shock. Dysrhythmia can also be treated with the implantation of a battery-powered pacemaker that sends small electrical charges through an electrode placed next to the wall of the heart. A cardioverter/defibrillator, a sophisticated device that actually senses an abnormal rhythm and delivers one or more lifesaving jolts of energy to shock the heart back to normal rhythm, can replace a defective natural pacemaker or a blocked pathway. Catheter ablation is a surgical technique that uses a tiny device at the end of a catheter (a flexible tube) inserted into the heart to burn away the part of the heart causing the abnormal rhythm.

If heart disease is not the culprit, the doctor may suggest that the patient not drink coffee, tea, colas (which contain the stimulant caffeine), or alcoholic beverages. Over the long term, it is important to eat a balanced, low-fat diet and get regular exercise to keep the heart healthy.

* **electrocardiogram** Electrodes attached to the skin detect the electrical impulses as they travel over various parts of the heart. An abnormal ECG can alert the doctor to trouble in a particular area or function of the heart.

▶ *See also*
Heart Disease
Heart Murmur
Stroke